W.B. YEATS
POETRY AND PLAYS

Sunil Kumar Sarker

ATLANTIC
PUBLISHERS & DISTRIBUTORS (P) LTD

Published by
ATLANTIC
PUBLISHERS & DISTRIBUTORS (P) LTD
7/22, Ansari Road, Darya Ganj, New Delhi-110002
Phones : +91-11-40775252, 40775214, 23273880, 23275880
Fax : +91-11-23285873
Web : www.atlanticbooks.com
E-mail : orders@atlanticbooks.com

Printed & bound in India by Atlantic Print Services

DEDICATED TO

the memory of

my grandfather

ATUL CHANDRA SARKER

PREFACE

Yeats, Pound and Eliot are the three germinative figures of modern poetry that announced its advent around the beginning of the First World War. The social, political, scientific, industrial, economic and philosophical back-drop of that period shook to the foundation the comfortable 19th century *zeitgeist*. The Victorian eye saw beyond the window-sill, but now, the canvass outside being torn to pieces, it was turned inwards. For, outside it now saw only the "Unreal City" of "broken images"; but the irony is that when it was turned inside, it saw only the "complexities" of the "bestial floor". The modern man could realise that "We are the hollow men/ We are the stuffed men/Leaning together/Headpiece filled with straw." Contrapped in a bleak maze in a black night, the modern man began soul-searching. In a desperate bid to paint such an abject condition of man, poets took recourse to dadaism, surrealism, expressionism, imagism, vorticism, ultraism, etc. In the case of language, the poets preferred that of the street; in the case of form, they preferred formlessness; and in the case of thought, they preferred angry vituperation or sighs of despair. All these were done, and yet there was no sign of the poetry, the modern poetry, through which the modern man could express his mind and sensitivity. And then came Yeats, Pound and Eliot, the three germinative figures, and showed what modern poetry must look like. Can Yeats's importance be overemphasised?

Like in poetry, Yeats played a major part in the modern play also. In consonance with modern play-goers' urge for intellectual, straight, but brief dramas, Yeats boosted up the new One-Act plays, bare in outline but full of suggestiveness. He brought back the verse drama from the limbo and added myth and mask to it with extreme courage and skill. As psychoanalysts would like to say, myths are man's unconscious heritage that prove the subsistence of the universal among the multitude of particular human beings. Yeats, therefore, as Eliot did later on, deliberately introduced myths in his plays. Yeats believed in the transcendent sphere, beside the immanent; the former seeming to be more real than the latter to the Platonic Yeats. His masks help his audience distance itself from the immanent world and thus enjoy the transcendent. To attire the new play with a new garb, he stole, being advised by Pound, the thunder of the Japanese Noh plays that so long remained in oblivion. Yeats's contributions to modern dramaturgy, therefore, cannot be ignored.

As our age is, our poets are 'doomed' to be difficult, and so Yeats is not an easy poet. Excellent critics and explicators of Yeats, such as, Finneran, Melchiori, Jeffares, Ellmann, Bloom, Robson, Rudd, Albright *et al.* have tried to explain Yeats,' but, perhaps, they are not easily approachable without an easy introduction to the poet. This book may serve like that — an easy introduction to Yeats's poetry and plays — to the Yeatsian world.

I am obliged to my friend, Dr. K.R. Gupta, M. A., Ph. D., Managing Director of the Atlantic Publishers and Distributors, for kindly publishing this book. My two sons, Suman and Sutanu, in their childlike curiosity, monitored from time to time, the progress of the manuscript and thus expedited its completion. In return, I extend my love to them.

Sunil Kumar Sarker

Contents

Chapter 1
Life and Works

William Butler Yeats is perhaps the greatest poet in the English language of his period and is the connecting link between the nineteenth and the twentieth centuries in the field of literature. He is a poet of distinction on more counts than one: he is a lyric poet, a mystic, a mythologist, a romantic — all at the same time; he is a poet with a political ideology (though for only some time), like few poets are; he is a poet with a prophetic vision and an occult philosophy; and he is a poet with experience in experiments in dramaturgy. He was the national poet of the Republic of Ireland (Ire). Like his slightly older contemporaries, such as Jonathan Swift, Oscar Wilde and Bernard Shaw, Yeats was born in Dublin. He was born on 13th June, 1865, at George's Ville, Sandymount Avenue, Dublin in South Ireland. But for the longer part of his life, he lived in England, and therefore he is both an Irish poet and an English poet. In this regard, Yeats may be compared with T. S. Eliot (1888-1965) who was born in America but spent the greater part of his life in England, and so is both an American poet and an English poet.

The Comparison between Yeats and Eliot may be taken a little bit further. Both of them were interested in and influenced by Indian philosophy. Eliot was so much influenced by Buddhism that once he even decided to be converted to Buddhism. Again, many of his poems (for instances, 'Dry Salvages', 'What the Thunder Said' etc.) show his inclination towards the philosophy to the *Bhagvadgita* and his attempts at justifying the ways of Lord Krishna. Likewise, Yeats was attracted to the occult sciences of India by Mohini Chatterjee and the Indian monk Purohit Swami. But, while Eliot moved from philosophy to poetry, Yeats was sliding away from poetry towards philosophy; and while Eliot started his life with pessimism but achieved a sort of salvation, Yeats began as an optimist but gradually became disillusioned and pessimistic.

Though, Yeats lived the longer part of his life in England, yet he could never forget his associations with Ireland and he never ceased to be an Irish poet. In fact, the lush green, the lively hills and dales, the sparkling streams as well as the profuse myths, the audacious nationalism and the Gaelic fancy of Ireland were his constant companions. All these national characteristics of Ireland, perhaps originated in the geographical situation of this dreamy island washed in the east by the Irish sea and in all other directions by the fierce Atlantic Ocean. Ireland had been a British colony island which is now divided into two parts: the Northern Ireland, which covers about one sixth of the whole island and is still under British control; and the southern Ireland, which covers about five sixth of the whole island and is now the Republic of Ireland. The central part of Ireland is a rolling plain, but along her coast there are mountains and up-lands. The island is studded with lakes, locally called *loughs*, and is washed by a net-work of rivers. In the western part of the country, there are peat bogs, that is swamps consisting of decayed plants. The common people cut out and take home slices of this peat for using as fuel.

The economy of Ireland depends mainly on raising cattle and sheep, because the country exports meat in large quantity. The Irish is mostly Celtic or Norman in origin and speak mostly in English, though the first official language in the Republic of Ireland is Gaelic or the oldest language of Ireland. The people are very much religious. The majority of the people of the Republic are Roman Catholics as the majority of the people of Northern Ireland are protestant. This sectarian difference among the people of Ireland has been the cause of constant conflicts. In Northern Ireland, until 1972, internal affairs were administered by the government of Britain, which was said to favour the Protestants there. The origin of the ancient Irish people was pagan and during A.D. 400's St Patrick converted them to Christianity.

The present inhabitants of Ireland probably went there from neighbouring territories about 8,000 years ago. The Celts went there much lately — probably around 350 B.C. The Vikings from Scandinavia frequently raided Ireland since A.D. 700, but most of them ultimately settled in Ireland. The Normans invaded Ireland during 1100's and occupied a large portion of the country and ruled the occupied territory for long 350 years. Some of these Normans also settled in Ireland.

Thus the population of Ireland gradually became cosmopolitan. The Tudor Kings of England exercised great influence in Ireland and ultimately Henry VIII assumed the title of 'King of Ireland' in 1542. Since then England was trying to take the whole of Ireland under her direct control, and eventually in 1801 the whole of Ireland came under the direct control of England. The people of Ireland did not take the colonial policy of England lying supine but started movements to overthrow the British imperialism in Ireland. They demanded Home Rule and immediate withdrawal of all British control from Ireland. The Home Rule movement intensified, day by day, and gave birth to other such movements and organisations. As we shall see later on, Maud Gonne and W.B. Yeats once took active parts in such national movements of Ireland. In the early 1900's the demand of the Irish people for independence assumed such a proportion that ultimately it culminated in the famous Easter Rising of 1916. England tried to suppress the Irish national movement with an iron hand, but at the end had to concede Home Rule to Ireland in 1921. Yeats lost a few of his friends in the Easter Rising and he immortalised them in his poem 'Easter-1916'. The concession of Home Rule to Ireland did not satisfy the Irish Republican Army (I.R.B.), and so it continued to agitate against the British colonialism. However, in 1937, the Southern Ireland was renamed Eire which was the ancient name of the country and in 1949 Eire became independent and severed all connections with Great Britain.

So we can understand that Yeats spent most of his life in a period of extreme national movements for independence, and, naturally, this made him extremely nationalist and independent-minded, though he was never a politician in the true sense of the term. The mystic twilight of Ireland, in the dreamy surrounding of greenery and medieval relics, enraptured the poetic genius of Yeats quite early. But Yeats was particularly enamoured of the romantic tinge of Sligo on the western coast of Ireland, where he spent most of his boyhood. Yeats received his early education in England, but while there he spent his summer holidays in his mother's family of the Pollexfens in Sligo, about 110 miles from Dublin. Yeats's father, John Butler Yeats, a Protestant and a lawyer turned painter, moved to London in 1867, when Yeats was only nine years old. Daniel Albright writes about Yeats's father and his household: "Yeats's father, John Butler Yeats — a valuable, energetic, unself-confident man — was a well-known painter, and his household attracted the leading cultural figures of the day; Edward

Dowden, the Professor of English at Trinity College, Dublin, whose Shakespearean criticism is still studied, was a regular guest of the Yeats's. Yeats's father was also involved with the British artistic world — he corresponded with D. G. Rossetti (the Pre-Raphaelite painter and poet), and he was commissioned to illustrate Robert Browning's *Pippa Passes*' (Albright, xviii). However, two years later, the Yeats family changed residence and moved to Bedford Park estate in Chiswick, but, in 1881 the family returned to Dublin, where Yeats was admitted in the Metropolitan School of Art. Yeats in his boyhood wanted to be an artist — a painter — like his father. But he could not get admitted in his father's *alma mater*, Trinity College, because his grade was too poor, and so he went to the Metropolitan School of Art. It was here in this art school that he made friendship with George Russell (A.E.) and they both became interested in mysticism. From then on Yeats remained so much interested in mysticism that in 1886 he founded the Dublin Lodge of the Hermetic Society. His father, John Butler Yeats, did not stay long in Ireland but returned to Bedford Park in England in 1887, where W. B. Yeats soon joined the Rhymers' Club and had a tryst with Madame Blavatsky, the renowned occultist. His meeting with Blavatsky doubled his enthusiasm for mysticism and occultism, and he soon joined MacGregor Mather's Rosicrucian Society or the Hermetic Order of the Golden Dawn.

A born poet, Yeats began writing poetry and plays at an early age. He was inspired in his poetic *debut* by the abundance of Irish folklore and legends. Yeats was born in an island of supernatural's, in an island that Drennan called 'The Emerald Island'. The mythological names of Fergus, Cuchulain, Conor, Maev, Deirdre, etc. are now well-known throughout the world, thanks to the writing of Yeats, Lady Gregory and such other nationalistic mythologists. The mythology of Ireland, the plaintive green of Sligo and the whistling of the Irish curlew always remained in Yeats's mind and inspired his poetry. Yeats was also inspired by his artist father who was a painter of moderate eminence. Actually, the Yeats family had a penchant for art. Yeats's brother, Jack Butler Yeats, was also an artist. On the other hand, Yeats's mother came from a merchant family of Sligo, the Pollexfen family.

Back in 1867, when Yeats was only two years old, his father took the family to 23 Fritzroy Road, Regent's Park, London. There Susan Yeats (nee Pollexfen), Yeats's mother gave birth to Robert (d. 1873). John Butler (Jack) and Elizabeth Corbet (Lolly). Earlier than all these, Susan Mary (Lily) was born at Enniscrone. The Yeats family was truly bohemian in nature. In 1874, the family moved to 14 Edith Villas, West Kensington and with the family Yeats also moved there. So from 1865 to 1874, Yeats remained either in Dublin, or at Sligo, and when he was nine years old, he went to London with the family and had been living at 14 Edith Villa, Kensington. In 1876, the Yeats family again moved, this time to 8 Woodstock Road, Bedford Park. Next year, Yeats was admitted in the Godolphin School in Hammersmith. The boy Yeats with his memories of Sligo was ill at ease at the school. "As a young man he seemed to others vague and dreamy. Yeats disliked the London life around him. He longed for the countryside of Sligo, in the west of Ireland, where he had grown up. A moment of nostalgia for it inspired his most famous poem 'The Isle of Innisfree': (Robson, 51):

will arise and go now, and go to Innisfree,
And a small cabin builds there, of clay and wattles made:
Nine beam-rows will I have there, and a hive for the honey-bee;
And live alone in the bee-loud glade.

By now, Yeats's father's income declined due to Land War, and he was forced to return to Ireland in 1881, and occupy a rented house, Balscadden Cottage, at Howth, Dublin. Here Yeats was admitted in a high school at Harcourt Street and he remained there till 1883. But before that, that is in 1882, the family once again moved to a small house, Island View, overlooking Howth Harbour. Yeats was then 17 and had the experience of first love with his cousin Laura Armstrong. In 1884, Yeats left the general school and entered the School of Arts in Dublin, when he was 19. But he did not find a vocation of choice even in the School of Art, for he felt an attraction to creative writing, and he actually began working on creative writing. The bohemian Yeats family, now in 1885, moved to 10 Ashfield Terrace, off Harold's Cross Road, Dublin, and consequently, Yeats's apprenticeship in art was suspended; but in the same year he published his first ever poem in the *Dublin University Review.* It was during this time that Yeats founded the Dublin Hermetic Society, and it was in 1885 that he met and grew friendship with Katharine Tynan and John O' Leary. Yeats's interest in occultism continued and in 1886 he had, for the first time, had the experience of a stance. The same year he published also his first book *Mosada,* when he was 21. During this time he was drawn to the works of Irish poets who wrote in English and to the English translations of the Gaelic sagas. Yeats was much imbued by these native sagas which continued to influence his poetic compositions.

In 1886, the itinerant Yeats family moved to 58 Eardley Crescent, Earls Court, London, where Yeats's Mother, Susan Yeats, experienced two consecutive heart-strokes. In the same year, Yeats met at Kelmscott House the poet, painter and utopian socialist William Morris. Morris's propensity towards Pre-Raphaelitism and love of medievalism left an indelible mark on Yeats's consciousness, but the aristocratic Yeats could never reconcile himself with Morris's hatred for capitalism. Goaded by his almost instinctive interest in religion and occultism, Yeats joined the London Lodge of Theosophists, the esoteric section of the theosophists. The Yeats family once more sought the pleasure of moving to another place: this time to 3 Blenheim Road, Bedford Park. It was during this time that Yeats began contributing poems to American journals.

Yeats's health was never strong, and due to hard work, that his health could hardly bear, he once experienced a mild collapse in 1889. And yet he was very active that year, for, this year he prepared a selection of poems for Walter Scott and published his *The Wandering of Oisin and Other Poems. The Wandering of Oisin* is a composition about the exploits of the third century legendary Gaelic bard Oissin (or Oisin). This poem shows Yeats's deep interest in the Gaelic legends and his boyhood memories of Sligo. In the same year he met the Dubliner dramatist, poet and wit Oscar Wilde (1854-1900) and Edwin Ellis with whom he decided to publish William Blake's poems. Also in the same year he edited *Faery and Folk Tales of the Irish Peasantry*. In 1889 itself began one of the most traumatic experiences in Yeats's life, when Maud Gonne, the paragon of beautiful women and an active nationalist, visited Bedford Park where the Yeats family had been putting up . Yeats was then 23 or 24. He met her, fell headlong in love of her, and as a token of his heart-burning offered to write *The Countess Cathleen* for her. Unfortunately, or may be fortunately for us, this love never found consummation, and yet Yeats bore this love in his heart throughout his life. It is interesting to read Yeats's own account, in his *Autobiographies,* of his first meeting with Maud: "How important it all seemed to me. How much would I have given so that she might think exactly right on all these great questions. And today all is faint to me besides a moment when she passed before a window dressed white and rearranged a spray of lowers in a vase. Twelve years after I put this impression into verse ('She pulled down the pale blossoms') I felt in the presence of a great generosity and courage and a mind without rest, and when she and all the singing birds had gone, my melancholy was not the mere melancholy of love. I had what I had thought was clairvoyant perception (of some immediate disaster) but I was I can see now but an obvious deduction of an immediate waiting disaster. ... I was in love but had not spoken of love and never meant to speak of love as the months passed, I gained a mastery of myself again. What wife would she make, I thought, what share could she have in the life of a student? Her complexion was luminous, like that of apple-blossom through which the light falls, and I remember her standing first day by a great heap of such blossoms in the window." (Jeffares, 53-54). Truly, Yeats had great fascination for Maud Gonne. Margaret Rudd writes about Yeats's fascination for her: "He loved her as the troubadours loved their ladies, and she seemed as unattainable. He was twenty-three when he first met this beautiful, vibrant woman, violent in her political fanaticism and breath-taking in her heroic loveliness. Yeats fell desperately in love." (Rudd, 45). During this time Yeats was very shy and somewhat awkward in the company of women, despite having two sisters of his own. In his early years, for some times he lived the life of celibacy, almost the life of an ascetic. In his *Autobiographies*, he wrote: "I thought that having conquered bodily desire and inclination of mind towards women and love, I should live as Thoreau lived, seeking wisdom." (Rudd, 45). The Yeats of this time may be compared with the existentialist philosopher Soren Kierkegaard who loved Regina Olson, but suddenly turned his back on her for fear that love might stand on his way of being a writer. However, before meeting Maud Gonne, Yeats experienced yet another brief pain of love when he was in his teens. Besides Laura, he fell in love with one Emilia (Shelley also fell in love with one Emilia Viviani, and one of Milton's wives was Emilia).

The first shock of unrequited love sharpened his propensity towards esoterism and Eastern wisdom, and he became a disciple of the great occultist Madame Blavatsky (Helena Petrovna Blavatsky: 1831-1891). Blavatsky, along with H.S. Olcott, founded the Theosophical Society in 1875. Blavatsky was born in Russia but originally, she came of a German stock. Her clairvoyant faculty was so high that even when she was a child she would be consulted by police for detection of crimes. At 17 she married General Blavatsky, a very elderly man; but soon separated herself and went to Egypt, Lebanon and Tibet for studying magic. Her *Isis Unveiled* and *The Secret Doctrine* have received wide acclaims. Yeats was drawn to Blavatsky by his school-mate Charles Johnston who became a confirmed believer in occultism by reading

A.P. Sinnett's *The Occult World* and *Esoteric Buddhism*. When Blavatsky was denounced as a charlatan by the Society for Psychical Research in 1885, Johnston protested and founded the Dublin Lodge for researches in occultism, in 1886. At first Yeats and George Russell (A.E.) refused to join Johnston's Dublin Lodge, but within a year, when Yeats met Blavatsky, he was so much impressed by Blavatsky that he soon joined the Dublin Lodge (December, 1888). In 1892, the magazine *The Irish Theosophist* began to be published, giving a boost to the nascent theosophical movement. The theosophical movement was searching after some mysterious power, and the coeval national movement was searching for some secret power to overthrow the British suzerainty, and therefore the two separate movements somehow had a confluence. The interest in occultism and theosophy led Yeats to an intense study of the works of William Blake (1757-1827) and to Blake's symbolism. His attraction for Maud Gonne still vibrant, Yeats plunged himself in the cultural movement of Ireland, perhaps as a means of vicarious gratification of his love for Gonne, because Gonne was also engaged in the cultural and national movements of Ireland, called the Celtic Revival. During the 1890's he published a mass of prose works and poems written under the influence of the symbolistic movement in France and England. All these works relate to the mythology and folklore of Ireland. For example, he published *Representative Irish Tales* (1891), *The Countess Kathleen and Various Legends and Lyrics* (1892), *Irish Fairy Tales* (1892), *The Celtic Twilight* (1893), *The Land of Heart's Desire* (1894) which was performed first in London in the same year, *Poems* (1895), *The Secret Rose* (1897), etc.

In 1894, Yeats went to Paris and there proposed to Maud Gonne for the second time, the first time he proposed was in 1889, but Gonne again declined. Yeats was so much fascinated by Maud's beauty that though each time his proposal was rejected by her, and he got depressed, he nevertheless constantly pursued her and proposed to her several times more. Albright writes about Maud Gonne: "She was nearly six feet tall, imperial in demeanor, and by many accounts the most best beautiful woman in Ireland. He (Yeats) met her in 1889, when she called at his house, ostensibly to meet his father; it was the season of apple-blossoms; she walked (Yeats wrote) like a goddess. He never quite recovered ...... Maud Gonne was attracted to radical politics; she was, for example, part of a scheme to blow up British troops on boats bound for south Africa during the Boar War .... In the mid-

1890's, Maud Gonne became a lover of a French anarchist editor, Lucien Millevoye; she bore him a child, who died in infancy; and she decided to assist the baby's reincarnation by sleeping with Millevoye in the vault under the dead child's grave .... In this fashion was Iseult Gonne (1894-1954) conceived." (Albright, xxxi-xxxii). That like Yeats, Gonne also had a proclivity towards believing in supernatural phenomena is evident here. It may be mentioned that though the marriage between Yeats and Gonne did not materialise, yet both of them once saw in 'vision' that they were spiritually married. Alas, Maud Gonne, *la belle dame sans marci*!

In 1889, Yeats came back to London from Paris and met Lady Gregory with whom he made friendship that lasted till his death. Lady Gregory or Isabella Augusta Gregory (1852-1932) was an aristocrat and dramatist (she wrote some comedies, including *The Workhouse Ward).* After the death of her husband, Sir W.H. Gregory, she came under the influence of Yeats who encouraged her to do researches in the Irish folklore. Lady Gregory was a constant guide to Yeats on almost all affairs. On 4th February, 1909, Yeats wrote in his *Diary*: "She (Lady Gregory) had been to me mother, friend, sister and brother. I cannot realise the world without her — she brought to my wavering thoughts steadfast nobility." (Jeffares, 96). Yeats first met her in 1896 when she "got him to help her in collecting folklore and became his ally in the movement to create an Irish theatre. She also helped him to put his 'house in order' and created conditions in which he could work regularly: '...I (Yeats) doubt if I should have done much with my life but for her firmness and her care." (Jeffares, 123). Lady Gregory was not a politician like her husband who served as Governor of Ceylon. In 1899, the Irish Literary Theatre was founded, thanks to the efforts of Lady Gregory, Yeats and Edward Martyn. She along with Yeats and J.M. Synge also founded the famous Abbey Theatre in Dublin. Gregory translated a number of Irish sagas. It was at Lady Gregory's house, Coole Park, that Yeats stayed for a time and got his aristocratic attitude and life-style reinforced. Lady Gregory's son, Major Robert Gregory, died in active service against England and this was the occasion of some of Yeats's best poems. However, in the same year Yeats founded the Rhymers' Club in London and became a member of the *Yellow Book* group that published the quarterly journal of the same name from 1894 to 1897. Such famous writers as Max Beerbohm, Henry James, Aubrey Beardsley and Walter Sickert contributed to the journal. Yeats and Lady Gregory, during this time worked relentlessly for the cultural revival of Ireland. It was actually with this in mind, that the Abbey Theatre was founded. The Abbey Theatre was to "present Irish plays on Irish subjects, performed by Irish actors."

On the other hand, though Maud rejected Yeats's proposal, she was still in friendly relation with him. In 1898, Yeats went on a tour to England and Scotland with Gonne. It was during this tour that they both experienced a "spiritual marriage" with each other. Again, it was during this tour that Yeats dreamed of founding an Irish theatre that materialised the next year as the Irish Literary Theatre or the Abbey Theatre. But before that, in 1896, Yeats went to Paris and there met J. M. Synge who founded the order of Celtic Mysteries. Yeats urged upon Synge to join the Irish League and in 1898 suggested him to visit the Aran Island, about 20 miles off the western coast of Ireland, from where Synge collected the material for his *The Aran Island.* Yeats also became a member of the Irish Republican Brotherhood (IRB) and "formed the idea of uniting Irishing political parties." But for some reasons Yeats cut off his relations with the IRB in 1900. In the same year, Yeats proposed to Maud for the third time and again, as expected, was disappointed, because Maud's affection was with Lucien Millevoye, the French anarchist editor, or, may be, with Major MacBride whom she later on married. The painful relation between Yeats and Maud Gonne, and the cause of the latter's rejection of the love of Yeats was beautifully recorded by Maud Gonne MacBride (after her marriage with Major MacBride) herself in her autobiography which was published in 1938 under the title *A Servant of the Queen.* Maud Gonne wrote: "Next day when he (Yeats) called to take me out to pay my customary visit to the Lia Fail, he said: 'You don't take care of yourself as Kathleen does, so she looks younger than you; your face is worn and thin; but you will always be beautiful, more beautiful than anyone I have known. You can't help that. Oh Maud, why don't you marry me and give up this tragic struggle and live a peaceful life? I could make such a beautiful life for you among artists and writers who would understand you.'

'Willie, are you not tired of asking that question? How often have I told you to thank the gods that I will not marry you. You would not be happy with me.'

'I am not happy without you.'

'Oh yes, you are because you make beautiful poetry out of what you call your unhappiness and you are happy in that. Marriage would be such a dull affair. Poets should never marry. The world should thank me for not marrying you. I will tell you one thing, our friendship has meant a great deal to me; it has helped me often when I needed help, needed it perhaps more than you or anybody knew, for I never talk or even think of these things.'

'Are you happy or unhappy?' he asked.

'I have been happier and unhappier than most, but I don't think about it. You and I are so different in this. It is a great thing to know one can never suffer again as much as one has suffered; it gives one great calm and great strength and makes one afraid of nothing. I am interested in the work I have undertaken; that is my life and I live, — while so many people only exist. Those are the people to be pitied; those who lead dull, uneventful lives; they might as well be dead in the ground. And now, Willie, let us talk of the Lia Fail. You know I hate talking of myself; I am not going to let you make me." (Jeffares, 78).

The love-sick and love-disappointed Yeats did not sit idle with vacant looks and a long face but continued his literary works and nationalistic and cultural movements. He continued to be actively engaged in the Abbey Theatre and to be so active till his death in 1939. After disengaging himself from the IRB and after his troubles with Mathers and Aleister Cowley, Yeats formed the New Order of Golden Dawn in 1900. In the same year he helped George Moore rewrite Martyn's *The Tale of a Town* which became *The Bending of a Bough.* The next year Yeats proposed to Maud Gonne for the fourth time and painfully learnt that love, however much genuine it may be, is not always requited on supplication. He broke down for a while but soon collected himself to be active again.

In 1902, Yeats co-authored *Diarmuid and Grania* with George Moore (1852-1933), the English novelist and playwright. The same year he became the President of the Irish National Dramatic Society. Also in the same year his *Cathleen ni Houlihan* was performed in Dublin and Maud Gonne acted in the title role. Gonne ultimately married Major John MacBride in 1903, the year in which three plays of Yeats were performed in London: *The Countess Cathleen, The Pot of Broth* and *The Hourglass*. The same year Yeats went on a lecture tour to USA, arranged by John Quinn. The next year Yeats became the producer-manager to Abbey Theatre. In 1906, he published his *Poems*

1895-1905 and in the next year to went to Italy along with Lady Gregory and her son.

The year 1908 is very important in Yeats's life, because in this year, in Paris, he met Ezra Pound (b. 1885) who, it is said "came to learn how to write poetry from Yeats." (Brown, 488). This year Yeats's *Collected Works* was published in eight volumes. Yeats was then living in Paris with lady Gregory. In 1911, Yeats again went to USA with players of Abbey Theatre and there met with his future wife, Georgie Hyde-Lees, whom he married in 1917, when he was well in his early fifties. Hyde-Lees, therefore, was much younger than Yeats and yet the marriage was a happy one. But even alter deciding to marry Hyde-Lees, Yeats could not forget Maud Gonne. He lived with her in Normandy for a part of 1912, and again in 1916, also in Normandy, when he proposed to Maud for the fifth and last time, after the death of Maud's husband, Major MacBride, in the Easter Rising of 1916. The Easter Rising was a rebellion in Dublin from 24 to 29 April, 1916, to secure immediate independence of Ireland. P.H. Pearse of the Irish Republican Brotherhood and James Connally of the Sinn Fein led the uprising. There was a heavy street fighting leading to great loss of lives. The Germans were expected to help the rebellion but ultimately no help came from them. The uprising was suppressed with an iron hand and fourteen leaders were subsequently executed. Yeats wrote the poem 'Easter 1916' to commemorate some of these leaders.

In the 1910's Yeats became worldly mature, which before he had not been, and consequently his poetry changed in theme and in form. He was now also mature in his love affairs, as is evident from his poem of just four lines that he wrote in 1909: 'The Coming of Wisdom with Time':

> Though leaves are many, the root is one:
> Through all the lying days of my youth
> I swayed my leaves and flowers in the sun;
> Now I may wither into the truth.

In 1912, the poet Rabindranath Tagore, while in England, paid a visit to Yeats and "was surprised by the enthusiasm of Yeats and others over some half-serious translation of his own poems." (Daiches, 513). In 1913, Yeats was granted Civil List pension of £ 150 per annum. He spent the autumn of this year with Ezra Pound and the next year went to USA only to return soon to England for Ezra Pound's marriage with Mrs. Shakespeare's daughter. Yeats was very close to Pound who always wrote W.B.Y. for Yeats's foil name. However, in 1915, Yeats was awarded knighthood but declined to accept the honour allegedly for the cause of Irish freedom. In 1916, Yeats was reading the works of French poets with Iseult Gonne, the only daughter of Maud Gonne. Love-thirsty as he was, Yeats desperately proposed to Iseult who promptly agreed. She was then 15. But when she attained the age of 22, she declined to marry Yeats who was then 52. Then, perhaps in utter despair and in great need of an understanding wife, Yeats turned to Georgie Hyde-Lees — this time very definitely — in whom there was not the infatuous beauty of Maud or Iseult, but there was abundance of love and understanding. Yeat's proposal was gladly and immediately accepted by Hyde-Lees. Meanwhile Yeats bought a Castle at Ballylee (the Tower) in early 1917, which was a derelict Norman stone tower. On 20th October, 1917, Yeats married Hyde-Lees to live happily with her in the Castle. The same year he published his collection of romantic poems: *The Wild Swans at Coole.*

Within a few months of their marriage, Yeats discovered that Hyde-Lees was a good mediumistic subject and an adept in automatic writing. From then on Yeats for a long time researched into the phenomena of planchet, eschatology and supernatural visions. The findings of these researches are the material of his *A Vision.* It may be mentioned here that Yeats had a great interest in occultism and parapsychological phenomena, and himself could sometimes attain parapsychological states, as is evident from his very correct description of 'peak experience', a parapsychological phenomenon, in one of his poems (Watson, 238):

> Something drops from eyes long blind,
> He completes the partial mind,
> For an instant stands at ease,
> Laughs loud, his heart at peace.

Yeats was also a superstitious person and this he admitted in his essay 'Ideas of Good and Evil': "I believe in the practice and philosophy of what we have agreed to call magic, in what I must call the evocation of spirits, though I do not know what they are." His poem 'A Prayer for my Son' was actually inspired by a premonition that his son would soon be ill that he received through the mediumship of his wife, and surprisingly the premonition proved true.

Hyde-Lees wrote thousands of pages in her mediumistic trance which were, as we have told, the foundation of Yeats's *A Vision* where

Yeats explains the general system for "explaining history, personality, and the progress of the soul after death." Yeats frequently enquired in Hyde-Lees's trance about his relation with the three women — Maud Gonne, Iseult Gonne and Hyde-Lees — and the revelation is very interesting: "According to one of Mrs. Yeats's favourite Controls, Thomas of Dorlowicz, Yeats and his 'three birds' (the three women) formed a kind of tetrad: Yeats was Heroic, Iseult Good, Maud Beautiful, George True; Yeats represented the Fall (the loss of unity of being), Iseult the Heart, Maud the Head, George the Loins; Yeats was Instinct, Iseult Desire, Maud Intellect, George Emotion; Yeats's element was Earth, Iseult Water, Maud's Air, George's Fire — and so on. William Blake — an edition of whose poetry Yeats published in 1893 — conceived the Fall of Man as the division of a single giant, Albion (the whole of human race), into four zoos, representing the various faculties of the soul, bickering, impending one another, working factitiously towards reunion ...... Thus, Yeats's poems about Iseult and Maud Gonne and his wife are simply a form of extended self-inquiry. The women are not autonomous beings, but portions of that fourfold being in which Yeats himself is comprised." (Albright, xxxiv). Daniel Albright further writes: "In addition to these three, Yeats celebrated other living women in his verse. In 18%, Olivia Shakespeare, a gentle and attractive married woman, had become Yeats's first lover; in 1914 her daughter Dorothy married Ezra Pound. Yeats's liaison with her lasted only a year, but they were to remain lifelong friends. Olivia Shakespeare was Yeats's like, but he (Yeats) craved for his opposite, a more devastating relation." (Albright, xxxv). However, despite the fire of love once in his heart for the regular beauty, Maud Gonne, Yeats was absolutely happy after his marriage with Hyde-Lees. Shortly, after his marriage with her, he wrote to Lady Gregory: "My wife is perfect wife, kind wise and unselfish. I think you were such another young girl once. She had made my life serene and full of order." (Jeffares, 207).

In 1918, the newly married couple lived at Oxford for some time and then at Coole to supervise the restoration of the Tower. Yeats loved this tower-house very much, and even wrote the poem of six lines 'To be Carved on a Stone at Thoor Ballylee' for this tower-house, which house was, perhaps dedicated to Hyde-Lees:

> I, the poet William Yeats,
> With old mill boards and sea-green slates,
> And smithy work from the Gort forge,

> Restored this tower for my wife George;
> And may these characters remain
> When all is ruin once again.

In the later part of that year the couple stayed in the house of Maud Gonne at 73 Stephen's Green. During this time Yeats frequently moved among Dublin, Thoor Ballylee and Oxford. On 26th January, 1919, Anne Butler Yeats was born to the couple. Next year Yeats again went to USA on a lecture tour. On 22nd August, 1921, a male child was born to the Yeats family: Michael Butler Yeats. In 1922, Yeats bought another house, the Georgian house, at 82 Merrion Square, Dublin. The same year Yeats's father, John Butler Yeats died in New York. From this time on various honours began to come thickly to Yeats. Dublin University conferred on him D. Litt. degree *(honoris causa)*. His nation also conferred honour on him; he was elected a Senator of Irish Free State in 1922. Next year Yeats was awarded the coveted Noble Prize for literature.

From 1923 to 1932, Yeats's life was not so eventful, except that he turned out an immense amount of literary works of different forms. Almost the whole of 1924 he spent completing his book on mysticism, *A Vision,* which was published in 1925, and reading history and philosophy. During this time, he had been suffering from high blood pressure, and to ameliorate his health he visited Sicily in November, 1924, and Rome and Milan in February, 1925, all the while reading Burke and Berkeley. Bade home in Dublin, he gave a speech on divorce in the Senate which, next year, appointed him the Chairman of Coinage Committee. His unrequited love for Maud Gonne still lingered in his heart as it is evident from his poem 'Among School Children' which is composed in 1926 during a visit to St. Otteran's School in Waterford:

> I dream of a Ledaean body, bent
> Above a sinking fire, a tale that she
> Told of a harsh reproof, or trivial event
> That changed some childish day to tragedy .....

In 1927, Yeats perhaps heard the warning of death, for he had extreme lung congestion bleeding. Henceforth, he gradually cut off his connections with the external world. In July, 1928, he gave his last speech in the Senate. Though much late, now the Oxford honour came to Yeats; in 1931, the Oxford University awarded him the degree of Doctor of Literature *(honoris causa)*. During the period from 1931 to

1932, Yeats moved between Coole and Ballylee like a shuttle-cork, but all the while kept him engaged in writing a lot of verses. In 1931, he also broadcasted on BBC Belfast and in 1932 he went on his last lecture tour to America.

In 1931, Yeats was around 66, when his spiritual quest that got a phillip, some years back, from his discussion about the matter with Mohini Chatterjee, now returned to him with a Violence. Mohini Chatterjee was a Bengali Brahmin learned in spiritual wisdom, whom Yeats met in England, probably in 1928 or 1929. Chatterjee stimulated him both spiritually and aesthetically and initiated him into mysticism. Later on Yeats's spiritual quest was intensified by his meeting with the Indian monk Purohit Swami and the Indian poet Rabindranath Tagore. Yeats was so much impressed by Mohini Chatterjee that he even registered his impression of Chatterjee in his poem 'Mohini Chatterjee':

> That he might set at rest
> A boy's turbulent days
> Mohin Chatterjee
> Spoke these, or words like these.

The poem was written between 23 January and 9th February, 1929, and it first appeared in *A Packet for Ezra Pound* (1929). Within two years of his meeting with Chatterjee, Yeats had a tryst with the Indian monk Purohit Swami. The Swami, born in 1882, was a Marathi Brahmin. He was younger than Yeats by 17 years. Rev. Dr. Robert Scott, who was a relative of Walter Scott, the novelist, was impressed by the spiritual excellence of the Swami, while Rev. Scott had been to India. Rev. Scott urged the Swami to go to England to preach his spiritual philosophy there. There in England the Swami acquainted himself with Sturge Moore and Masefield, the poet-laureate. The Swami had been explaining the spiritual philosophy of the *Bhagvadgita* at different places in England and Yeats knew about all these from Sturge Moore and requested Moore to arrange for a meeting with the Swami. This meeting took place on 6th June, 1931. Yeats was so much impressed also by the spiritual teaching of the Swami that he immediately became interested in the *Upanisads* and even started translating some of the *Upanisads* jointly with the Swami, in 1935. Yeats was acquainted with and interested in the *Upanisads* even before that. His predilection for the spiritual philosophy of the *Upanisads* can seen in his poem 'A Prayer for my Son' where he says that his son is but an incarnation of God. Yeats's poems in *Supernatural Songs* and his poem 'Meru' and also his play *The Herne' Egg* are heavily influenced by the spiritual teachings of the Swami. In fact, Yeats himself wrote about *The Herne's Egg* that it is suffused with Hindu philosophy: "Shri Purohit Swami is with me, and the play is his philosophy in a fable, or mine confirmed by him." Yeats found in the presence of the Swami a peace that he pined for but did never find anywhere else. He wrote: "The very fact that I am going with a man whose mind I touch on only one point, means peace." But it is true that Yeats was never spiritually converted to Hindu philosophy, as T.S. Eliot in his later life was once on the verge of being converted to Buddhism, for Yeats had his own peculiar spiritual philosophy. And yet in the niche of his heart, there was some love for Indian philosophy or spiritualism, as is evident also from some other poems of his, such as 'Anashuya and Vijoya', 'The Indian Upon God', 'The Indian to His Love', 'Mohini Chatterjee', etc. Yeats also wrote an Introduction to Shri Purohit Swami's *The Holy Mountain* (1934) and wrote to Olivia Shakespeare about this book that it was "one of those rare books that are fundamental." (Jeffares, 338). Yeats was also interested in the mythology of India, as is evident from his poem 'Meru' which he wrote about mount Kailash in Tibet. The poet was very much drawn to the difficult mysteries of Yoga. In fact, he had a natural fascination for everything mysterious and difficult. In his poem 'The Fascination of What's Difficult' he wrote:

> The fascination of what's difficult
> Has dried the sap out of my veins, and rent
> Spontaneous joy and natural content
> Out of my heart.

But in spite of his old age and his penchant for philosophy and occultism, Yeats could never overcome his cravings for love and sex. Darnel Albright writes: "Imaginative life returned to the elderly Yeats, partly in the form of a number of young women, some of whom were his lovers. In 1934, Yeats underwent the Steinach rejuvenation operation, a kind of vasectomy supposed to restore sexual potency; and he began a period of sexual swagger and passionate poetical effusions." (Albright, xxxv). The poem 'The Three Bushes' certainly contains allusions to carnal love, and surprisingly Yeats wrote the poem in 1937, just two years before his death:

> Said lady once to lover,
> 'None can rely upon
> A love that lacks its proper food;

And if your love were gone
How could you sing those songs of love?
I should be blamed, young man.

And in his poem 'Politics' written in just the year in which he died; Yeats wrote:

How can I, that girl standing there,
My attention fix
On Roman or on Russian
Or on Spanish politics,
....
But O that I was young again
And held her in my arms.

Yeats was not so much as interested in religious rituals but was certainly a religious person; of course his brand of religion, like that of Rabindranath Tagore, Wordsworth and such others, was that of a poet. "'I am very religious,' says Mr. Yeats in his *Autobiographies*, 'and deprived by Huxley and Tyndall, whom I detested, of the simple minded religion of my childhood, I had made a new religion, almost an infallible church of poetic tradition, of a fardel of stories, and of personages, and of emotions, inseparable from their first expression, passed on from generation to generation by poets and painters with some help from philosophers and theologians. I wished for a world where I could discover this tradition perpetually .... I had even created a dogma: Because those imaginary people are created out of the deepest instinct of man, to be his measure and his norm, whatever I can imagine those mouths speaking may be the nearest I can go to truth." (Leavis, 31).

In 1936, Yeats became seriously ill. For long he had been suffering from heart disease and nephritis. But even with his ill health, he broadcasted on modern poetry in the summer of 1936. In 1937, he was elected a member of Atheneum and continued to broadcast from BBC, London, during April, July and September of that year, and revised and published *A Vision*. In January, 1938, he wrote his last play *The Herne's Egg*. His last public appearance occurred in August, 1938, at Abbey Theatre where his play *Purgatory* was being performed. He is being extremely indisposed in the late summer of 1938, was visited by Maud Gonne for the last time .... the two warm and cold hearts had had the last glimpse of each other. Yeats died on 28th January, 1939, and was buried at Roquebrune, but nine years thereafter his 'mortal coil' was exhumed and reinterned at Drumcliffe, Sligo, in 1948, to let him lie in his dream-hunted mysterious Sligo. Yeats was perhaps aware of his end, as it appears from the titles and themes of his last two works: *The Death of Cuchulain* and *Purgatory*. Yeats himself wrote the following three lines for his epitaph which is still there today in Sligo for thousands of literary pilgrims to view, and which reminds one of T.S. Eliot's "Fare forward" .... and both, again, reminding one of Lord Krishna's advice to Arjuna in the *Bhagvadgita*:

> Cast a cold eye
> On life and death.
> Horseman, pass by!

Yeats always treaded on the transcendental track and kept himself at a remove from almost everything worldly, like the transcendental Shelley. True, he once engaged himself in the cultural causes of Ireland and actively participated in the national uprisings, but his soul all the while abided elsewhere. He had a deep philosophic bent of mind and had within himself a rare fusion of romanticism, realism and spirituality. Katharine Tynan (1861-1931), the Irish novelist, beautifully illustrates one aspect of Yeats's personality: "Yeats never had the remotest idea of taking care of himself. He would go all day without food unless someone remembered it for him, and in the same way would go on eating unless someone checked him. That first winter, a hard one, he would come to see me, five miles from Dublin, striding along over the snow-bound roads, a gaunt young figure, mouthing poetry, swinging his arms and gesticulating as he went. George Russell complained to me the other day that Willie Yeats had said somewhere of him, and printed it, that he used to walk about the streets of Dublin swinging his arms like a flail, unconscious of the alarm and bewilderment of the passers-by. It was Willie's own case. I remember how the big Dublin policemen used to eye him in those days, as though uncertain whether to 'run him in' or not. But, by and by, they used to say, 'Shure, 'tisn't mad he is, nor yet drink taken. 'Tis the poetry that's disturbing his head', and leave him alone." (Sutherland, 401). Yeats was so unmindful and absent-minded that once he broke his hand or was seriously wounded in the hand from a fall on the street.

Of Yeats's whimsical turn of mind and of his personality we may guess a little bit more if we read the following reminiscence of one Bertie Smyllie: "I never believed that W. B. (William Butler Yeats) knew anything much about philosophy, though he talked a great deal about it, but he invented a philosophy of his own, which was rather amusing. One very interesting and amusing thing occurred when he was expounding this highly esoteric theory of his one night up in the Arts Club. And among those present was a little man called Cruise O'Brien, a very brilliant journalist, and one of the very few people who could be rude with impunity to WB. WB gave him, as he very often gave me, a fool's pardon. This night, at any rate, he was expounding this philosophy of his which was connected in some queer way with the phases of the moon (vide Yeats's poem 'The Phases of the Moon' ...SKS); he was telling us all about the twenty phases of the moon and he had equated every phase against some historical figure. He said, 'Number one... the highest phase ... is perfect beauty.' With a respectful silence for a few seconds we all listened, and then he said, 'Number two was Helen of Troy... the nearest approximation to perfect beauty.' And he went right round the twenty-eight, or rather twenty-seven, phases and finally he came to the last and then he said that the lowest form of all is Thomas Carlyle and all Scotsmen. This shook us all a little bit and Cruise O'Brien spoke up at once. 'WB,' he said ... he'd a very mincing voice, Cruise ... 'have you ever read a word of Carlyle? You say Carlyle is the lowest form. Oh come! Have you ever read a word of Carlyle?' ... 'Carlyle, Cruise, was a dolt,' said WB ..... 'But I insist, ... WB, did you ever read one single word of Carlyle?'.... 'Carlyle, I tell, was a dolt.' .... 'Yes, but you haven't read him.' .... 'No, I have not read him; my wife, Georgie, has read him and she tells me he's a dolt.' That was the end of the philosophical treatise for the night." (Sutherland, 404).

Yeats was never a true political man, neither had he any clear-cut political philosophy. But, then, he hated democracy as something ignominious. This is evident at least from his poems in *The Green Helmet and Other Poems.* In 'Upon a House Shaken by the Land Agitation' in the same collection of poems, for instance, the poet laments for the reduction of rent of the Big houses or the houses of the aristocrats. he never liked any democratic uprising of the masses against the interests of the Big Houses, for the thought that those houses were the centres of tradition, art and culture, that he valued most. he thought that the uprising might destroy "the sweet-laughing eagle", the aristocrats, but that would not clear the way of the "Mean roof-trees", the poor, to reach the status of the aristocrats:

> Mean roof-trees were the sturdier for its fall,

How should their luck run high enough to reach?
The gifts of the governing men, ... ?

Yeats himself had the perfect aristocratic bearing as is evident also from his love "to go about his house brandishing a Japanese ceremonial sword". Further, perhaps, his temperament was a little bit fascistic, for he wrote marching songs for the Irish Fascistic brigades. Nevertheless, he was sometimes very queer too as it appears from his "eccentric essays about eugenics". (Hollander, 503).

Yeats was, perhaps, clear about another question of politics: he did not like the Marxian revolution of his day. In a letter to George Russell (AE) written in April, 1919, he wrote: "What I want is that Ireland be kept from giving itself (under the influence of its lunatic faculty of going against everything which it believes England to affirm) to Marxian revolution or Marxian definition of value in any form. I consider the Marxian criterion of values as in this age the spear-head of materialism and leading to inevitable murder. From that criterion follows the well-known phrase 'Can the bourgeois be innocent?'" (Jeffares, 204). And yet "he had no liking for parliamentary politicians. Violent activists were more attractive to him. Yeats was to be glowingly fascinated by violence." (Robson, 52).

Apropos of his own theory of personality, that we will see in chapter 4, we can say that Yeats himself had a dual personality, or, rather, his personality comprised of two antithetical elements — the Will and the Mask, in his own terminology, or the self and the antiself, in Jungian terminology. Yeats described himself as a man (Will) of Phase 17 and so he had the Mask of Phase 3. In his *Autobiographies* he wrote that he is "'a gregarious man, going hither and thither looking for conversation, and ready to deny from fear or favor (his) dearest conviction.' Frequently he chides himself for his interest in politics. Yet the Mask, the antiself of man of phase 17, hates 'parties, crowds, propaganda' and delights in 'the solitary life of hunters and of fishers and 'the groves pale passion loves.'" (Brooks, 186). Yeats was really a queer person: he was an aristocrat, and yet loved peasants and beggars; he had a passion for what was difficult, and yet had no respect for wisdom; and though he was basically a mystic, he was active in worldly matters. His antithetical self is also present here. W.W. Robson writes: "He hates the middle class, the 'merchants and clerks', the 'hucksters'. His great good place is an imaginary eighteenth-century Ireland: landed gentry, fine horsemen, gracious ladies at the top; peasants, beggars, and priests at the bottom. There is no middle class. Yeats's philosophy is as exotic as his social attitude. He exalts ignorance and folly, even madness, above wisdom. He equates sexual union with mystical experience." (Robson, 58). Such was William Butler Yeats — an odd mixture of generality and speciality and even peculiarity.

And finally, to know about the most important thing about Yeats, to know him as only a poet, let us read what T.S. Eliot writes about him: "When he visited London he liked to meet and talk to younger poets. People have sometimes spoken of him as arrogant and overbearing. I never found him so; in his conversations with a younger writer I always felts that he offered terms of equality, as to a fellow worker, a practitioner of the same mastery. It was, I think, that, unlike many writers, he cared more for poetry than for his own reputation as a poet or his picture of himself as a poet. Art was greater than the artist: and this feeling he communicated to others; which was why younger men were never ill at ease in his company." (Eliot, 253). Yeats was always full of life and always wanted life in its fulness, as it may partly be seen in his poem 'A Dialogue of Self and Soul'. "Yeats rejected Nirvana. In the 'Dialogue' he chooses rebirth, rather deliverance from birth. Despite all the suffering and ignominy and frustration which human life entails, still he chooses to be born again, to go on with the unending cycle." (Robson, 56-57).

Unlike his contemporary poet, T.S. Eliot, Yeats was a voluminous writer. He wrote verses, plays, fictions, philosophical essays and essays on criticism. He also edited a number of collections of poems, of some of which he wrote the introductions. Perhaps his most famous edition of collection of poems is *The Oxford Book of Modern Verse 1892-1935* whose introduction also he himself wrote. Besides, Yeats wrote his biography: *Autobiographies.* To cap all these, he also wrote numerous long correspondences. A list of his works is being given below, following Stan Smith's *20th Century Poetry* (Great Writers Library, Macmillan Press, 1983):

1. Collections

i. *Letters*, edited by Allan Wade, 1954.

ii. *Poems, Prose, Plays,* and *Criticism* (selections), edited by A. Norman Jeffares, 4 vols., 1963-64.

iii. Variorum Edition of the Plays, edited by Russell and C.C. Alspach, 1966.
iv. Variorum Edition of the Poems, edited by Peter Allt and Russell Alspach, 1967.

2. Verse

i. *Mosada: A Dramatic Poem*, 1886.
ii. *The Wandering of Oisin and Other Poems*, 1889.
iii. *The Countess Kathleen and Various Legends and Lyrics*, 1892.
iv. *Poems*, 1895; revised edition, 1899, 1901, 1904, 1908, 1912, 1913, 1927, 1929.
v. *The Wind among the Reeds*, 1899.
vi. *In the Seven Woods, Being Poems Chiefly of the Irish Heroic Age*, 1903.
vii. *Poems* 1899-1905, 1906.
viii. *Poetical Workers: Lyrical Poems, Dramatic Poems*, 2 vols., 1906-07.
ix. *Poems, Second Series*, 1909.
x. *The Green Helmet and Other Poems*, 1910; revised edition, 1912.
xi. *A Selection from the Poetry*, 1913.
xii. *A Selection from the Love Poetry*, 1913.
xiii. *Poems Written in Discouragement*, 1912-13, 1913.
xiv. *Nine Poems*, 1914.
xv. *Responsibilities: Poems and a Play*, 1914.
xvi. *Responsibilities and Other Poems*, 1916.
xvii. *The Wild Swans at Coole, Other Verses and a Play in Verse*, 1917, revised edition, 1919.
xviii. *Nine Poems*, 1918.
xix. *Michael Robertes and the Dancer*, 1921.
xx. *Selected Poems*, 1921.
xxi. *Later Poems (Collected Works I)*, 1922.
xxii. *Seven Poems and a Fragment*, 1922.

xxiii. *The Cat and the Moon and Certain Poems*, 1924.

xxiv. *October Blast*, 1927.

xxv. *The Tower*, 1928.

xxvi. *Selected Poems, Lyrical and Narrative*, 1919.

xxvii. *The Winding Stair*, 1929.

xxviii. *Words for Music Perhaps and Others Poems, 1932.*

xxix. *The Winding Stair and Other Poems*, 1933.

xxx. *Collected Poems*, 1933; revised edition, 1950.

xxxi. *Wheels and Butterflies*, 1934.

xxxii. *The King of the Great Clock Tower: Commentaries and Poems*, 1934.

xxxiii. *A Full Moon in March*, 1935.

xxxiv. *New Poems*, 1935.

xxxv. *New Poems*, 1938.

xxxvi. *Last Poems and Two Plays*, 1939.

xxxvii. *Selected Poems*, edited by A. Holst, 1939.

xxxviii. *Last Poems and Plays*, 1940.

xxxix. *The Poems*, 2 *vols*. 1949.

3. Plays

i. *The Countess Kathleen* (produced 1899). In *The Countess Kathleen and Various Legends and Lyrics*, 1892; revised version as *The Countess Cathleen*, 1912.

ii. *The Land of Heart's Desire* (produced 1894).

iii. *The Shadowy Waters* (produced 1904), 1900; revised version in *Poems*, 1906.

iv. *Diarmuid and Grania*, with George Moore (produced 1901), 1951.

v. *Cathleen ni Hoolihan* (produced 1902), 1902.

vi. *The Pot of Broth* (produced 1902). In *The Hourglass and Other Plays*, 1904.

vii. *Where There Is Nothing* (produced 1904). 1902; revised version, with Lady Gregory.

viii. *The Hourglass: A Morality* (produced 1903), 1903; revised version (produced 1913), in The Mask, 1913.

ix. *The King's Threshold* (produced 1903), 1904; revised version, 1913.

x. *The Hourglass and Other Plays, Being Volume 2 of Plays for an Irish Theatre* includes *Cathleen ni Houlihan* and *The Pot of Broth*, 1904.

xi. *On Bailees Strand* (produced 1904). In *Plays for an Irish Theatre* 3, 1904; revised version, in *Poems*, 1906.

xii. *Deirdre* (produced 1906). In *Plays for an Irish Theatre* 5, 1907.

xiii. *The Golden Helmet* (produced 1908); revised version, as *The Green Helmet* (produced 1910), 1910.

xiv. *At the Hawk's Well, or Waters of Immortality* (produced 1916). *In The Wild Swans at Coole*, 1917.

xv. *The Dreaming of the Bones* (produced 1931). In *Two Plays for Dancers*, 1919.

xvi. *Two Plays for Dancers* (includes *The Dreaming of the Bones* and *The Only Jealousy of Emer*) 1919.

xvii. *The Player Queen* (produced 1919), 1922.

xviii. *Four Plays for Dancers* (includes *At the Hawk's Well, The Only Jealousy of Emer, The Dreaming of the Bones, Calvary*), 1921.

xix. *Plays in Prose and Verse* (Collected Works 2), 1922.

xx. *Plays and Controversies* (Collected Works 3), 1923.

xxi. *King Oedipus*, from the play by Sophocles (produced 1926), 1928.

xxii. *The Resurrection* (produced 1934), 1927.

xxiii. *Oedipus at Colonus*, from the play by Sophocles (produced 1927, In *Collected Plays*, 1934.

xxiv. *Fighting the Waves* (produced 1929). In *Wheels and Butterflies*, 1934.

xxv. *The Words upon the Windowpane*, 1934.

xxvi. *Collected Plays*, 1934; revised edition, 1952.

xxvii. *Nine One-Act Plays*, 1937.

xxviii. *The Herne's Egg*, 1938.

xxix. *The Herne's Egg and Other Plays* (includes *A Full Moon in March* and *The King of the Great Clock Tower*), 1938.

xxx. *Purgatory and The Death of Cuchulain*, in *Last Poems and Two Plays*, 1939.

4. Fiction

i. *John Sherman and Dhoya*, 1891.

ii. *The Secret Rose* (stories), 1897.

iii. *The Tables of the Law: The Adoration of the Magi*, 1897.

iv. *Stories of Red Hanrahan*, 1905.

5. Others

i. *The Celtic Twilight: Man and Women, Dhouls and Fairies*, 1893; revised edition, 1902.

ii. *Literary Ideals in Ireland*, with AE and John Eglinton, 1899.

iii. *Is the Order of R. R. and A. C. to Remain a Magical Order?*, 1901.

iv. *Ideas of Good and Evil*, 1903.

v. *Discoveries: A Volume of Essays*, 1907.

vi. *Collected Works*, 8 vols. 1908.

vii. *Poetry and Ireland: Essays*, with Lionel Johnson, 1908.

viii. *Synge and the Ireland of His Time*, 1911.

ix. *The cutting of an Agate*, 1912; revised edition, 1919.

x. *Reveries over Childhood and Youth*, 1915.

xi. *Per Arnica Silentia Lunae*, 1918.

xii. *Four Years*, 1912.

xiii. *The Trembling of the Veil*, 1922.

xiv. *Essays (Collected Works 4)*. 1924.

xv. *A Vision*, 1925; revised edition, 1937; edited by George Mills Harper and W. K. Hood, 1978.

xvi. *Early Poems and Stories* (Collected Works 5), 1925.

xvii. *Estrangement, Being Some Fifty Thoughts from a Diary Kept in 1909*, 1926.

xviii. *Autobiographies (Collected Works 6)*, 1926

xix. *The Death of Synge and Other Passages from an Old Diary*, 1928.

xx. *A Packet for Ezra Pound*, 1929.

xxi. *Stories of Michael Robertes and His Friends*, 1932.

xxii. *Letters to the New Islands*, edited by Horace Reynolds, 1934.

xxiii. *Dramatis Personae*, 1935.

xxiv. *Dramatis Personae* 1896-1902, 1936.

xxv. *Essays 1931 to 1936*, 1937.

xxvi. *The Autobiography*, 1938; revised edition, as *Autobiographies*, 1955.

xxvii. *On the Boiler* (essays, includes verse), 1939.

xxviii. *If I Were Four-and-Twenty*, 1940.

xxix. *Pages from a Diary Written in 1930*, 1940.

xxx. *The Senate Speeches*, edited by Donald Pearce, 1960.

xxxi. *Reflections, edited by Curtis Bradford*, 1970.

xxxii. *Ah, Sweet Dancer: Yeats and Margaret Ruddock: A Correspondence*, edited by Roger McHugh, 1970.

xxxiii. *Uncollected Prose*, edited by John F. Frayne and Colton Johnson, 2 Vols., 1970-74.

xxxvi. *Interviews and Recollections*, edited by E.H. Mikhail, 1977.

xxxvii. *The Correspondence of Robert Bridges and Yeats*, edited by J. Finneran, 1977.

6. Editor

i. Editor, *Fairy and Folk Tales of the Irish Peasantry*, 1888; as *Irish Fairy and Folk Tales*, 1893.

ii. Editor, *Stories from Carleton*, 1889.

iii. Editor, *Representative Irish Tales*, 1891.

iv. Editor, *Irish Fairy Tales*, 1892.

v. Editor, with E. Ellis, *The Works of Blake*, 3 vols., 1893.

vi. Editor, *The Poems of Blake*, 1893.
vii. Editor, *A Book of Irish Verse*, 1895; revised edition, 1900.
viii. Editor, *A Book of Images Drawn by W. Horton*, 1898.
ix. Editor, *Twenty-One Poems* by Lionel Johnson, 1905.
x. Editor, *Some Essays and Passages*, by John Eglinton, 1905.
xi. Editor, *Sixteen Poems*, by William Allingham, 1905.
xii. Editor, *Poems of Spenser*, 1906.
xiii. Editor, *Twenty-One Poems*, by Katharine Tynan, 1907.
xiv. Editor, *Poems and Translations*, by J. M. Synge, 1909.
xv. Editor, *Selections from the Writings of Lord Dunsany*, 1912.
xvi. Editor, with F. Higgins, Broadsides: *A Collection of Old and New Synge*, 2 vols., 1935-37.
xvii. Editor, *The Oxford Book of Modern Verse 1892-1935*, 1936.
xviii. Editor, *The Ten Principal Upanisads*, translated by Shri Purohit Swami and Yeats, 1937.

Chapter 2
The Age of Yeats

Yeats's age is an age of transition — between Morris and Pound, and between Swinburne and Eliot. It was an age of rapid social change, for the nations in Europe were passing through intense industrial and political changes, and consequently structural changes occurred in almost all the components of the society. The growth spurt in population, the immigration of the rural population to the urban centres, the flush of factories newly established, etc. complicated the social scenario. Further, all these changes, in their turn, brought about changes in the moral perception. These two changes were complementary and cooperative in changing the *Weltanschauung* of the people. Yeats's age was transitional because he lived between the Victorian age (1837-1890) and the modern age that began in or around 1890, according to general consensus.

In the nineteenth century, England achieved her greatest colonial expansion, when she dictated terms over about one quarter of the surface of the globe. But since the conquest of Ireland by King Henry VIII, the Irish people were seething under the foreign yoke of the British people. The Catholic Emancipation Act partially removed some of the discontents of Ireland, but the chronic discontent did not die down. The Irish people are mostly Catholics, and the English are mostly Protestants, and so the Irish Catholics had to pay titles for the support of the Irish Protestants. The Catholic Emancipation Act, by which the tithe was abolished, alone could not dissuade the Irish people from resorting to violent movements. O'Connell started agitation for the abolition of the union of Ireland with England and for the independence of Ireland. Thinking that the fundamental cause of the agitations was economic, England passed the Poor-Law to fetch the starving Irish people some relief, but the agitations continued as before.

Then, according to Peel's Irish policy, Reel dealt firmly with O'Connell and a Commission was appointed to enquire into the grievances of the Irish people.

Nevertheless, the national movements rather snow-balled. The Young Ireland, the extremist political party, advocated force for national liberation. Encouraged by the 1848 European revolutions, the Young Ireland, led by Smith O'Brien, made a revolt, but the revolution fell through. The next effort for the independence of Ireland was made by a secret society started by its members called Fenians, in 1859. It was helped by a similar society in America. Thus reinforced, the Fenians revolted in 1867, when W.B. Yeats was only two years old, but this uprising also failed, and since then major uprisings were not to be seen in Ireland. Next, Gladstone, the Prime Minister of England, undertook further remedial measures in Ireland. In 1873, the Home Rule League was founded in Ireland, with Isaac Butt as its leader. Thus pressurised, Gladstone introduced the Home Rule Bill in the English Parliament, but it was rejected by the Commons. In 1892, Gladstone again introduced the Bill and this time the Commons passed the Bill, but this time the Lords rejected it. Thus, politically, Yeats's age was one of troubles both in Ireland and in England, and so Yeats lived through a period in which Ireland had been striving for transition from colonialism to independence.

In the literary scenario also there was a transition. William Morris and Algarnon Swinburne, the last Victorians, died in 1896 and 1909, respectively; and Ezra Pound and T.S. Eliot, the two harbingers of modernism, were born in 1885 and 1888, respectively. Yeats stands between the two groups of poets: he is both Victorian and modern. In his book *The Last Romantics*, Graham Hugh rightly called Ruskin, Rossetti, Morris, Pater and Yeats the last romantics. Further, Yeats himself said that he was one of the last romantics:

> We were the last romantics — chose for theme
> Traditional sanctity and loveliness;
> Whatever's written in what poet's name
> The book of the people; whatever most can bless
> The mind of man or elevate a rhyme.

The Victorian period cannot be sharply demarked, and yet we can say that it coincides more or less with the reign of Queen Victoria, from 1837 to 1901, and that Victorianism came to a close in 1901 with the death of Queen Victoria. Sometimes the Victorian period is divided into two halves: the early Victorian period, from 1837 to 1870; and the late Victorian period, from 1870 to 1901. The Victorian period is marked by social and political upheavals, intense class tensions and poverty. On the philosophical and aesthetic plane, the period is marked by moral priggishness, narrow-mindedness, respectability and complacency; and on the literary plane, the period showed an attitude of self-criticism. The romantic period, on the contrary, has a longer time span: it extends from 1789, the year in which the French Revolution began, or from 1798, the year in which Wordsworth and Coleridge published their *Lyrical Ballads*, to 1832, the year in which Sir Walter Scott died. Romanticism broke away from the immediately preceding neo-classical age (17th and 18th centuries) in which there was a strong tendency of submerging the individual. "The Romantic Movement is at its greatest in lyric poetry, for romanticism is basically an emphasis on individuality, and the lyric is the ultimate in direct personal expression." (Brown, 392). Though the fire of romanticism extinguished with the death of Scott, its fervour was carried on scatteredly by some poets. Thus Ruskin, Rossetti, Morris and Pater followed the romantic aestheticism. The early Yeats was also very much romantic in temperament.

However, to go back to the Victorian period, it was an age of realism. It was devoid of dramatic genius, but this lack was immensely compensated by the huge quantum of poetic and prose works that the Victorian writer turned out each year. It was not an age of romanticism but an age of realism where moral excellence was an ideal. All the same, it was a very complex age, an age of neurosis, and an age of imbalance — so much so that at one time, the appellation 'Victorian' was used in a pejorative sense. In his essay 'Victorianism', Jerome Hamilton Buckley writes about Victorianism: "All in all, the Victorian period achieved little of the stability we have learned to associate with a semi-mythical neoclassic culture. It moved from form to form, and nothing stood. Almost every Victorian thesis produced its own antithesis, as a ceaseless dialectic worked out its designs. Throughout the period there were vast difference between rural and urban society; the field of the agrarian south were, as Mrs. Gaskell suggested, a far cry from the smoking cities of the industrial North. ... The Victorian age as a whole was forced to adopt itself to new values as old traditions crumbled; and the term 'Victorian' is, therefore, egregiously abused when invoked to describe attitudes that the Victorians inherited or discarded," (Wright, 7-8). And yet, it must be admitted that, as Symonds writes, "the

English Renaissance of the sixteenth century became renascent in the nineteenth." (Wright, 12).

In Queen Victoria's reign there was the influence of Darwinism and the religion of the Bible on every aspect of art and literature. Further, the people did not forget their past art and literature. G.M. Trevelyan writes: "For one day in the week, novels and magazines were laid aside, and great classical literature like the Bible, *Pilgrim's Progress*, and *Paradise Lost*, besides more secular poetry and history, had a chance of perusal which they no longer enjoy." (Trevelyan, 577). The early Victorian England witnessed a constant conflict between the newfangled science and the traditional religion, and also a credo for industrialization that somehow disrupted the social cohesion. All these, consequently, made the lives of the people mechanical. "The later Victorians, though incapable of coping with their own distress, were beginning to be aware of it. Ruskin had inspired the rising generation of writers and thinkers with disgust at the industrial civilisation that had filled their fathers with such pride. Looking back through history, they thought they saw a fairer world than modern Lancashire; as early as 1868 William Morrison, in the Prologue to *The Earthly Paradise*, had written:

> For six countries overhung with smoke,
> Forget the snorting steam and piston stroke,
> Forget the spreading of the hideous town;
> Think rather of the pack-horse on the down,
> And dream of London, small, and white, and clean,
> the clear Thames bordered by its garden green....

But there was no going back, except in imagination." (Trevelyan, 592).

The end of Victorianism coincides with the beginning of *fin-de-siecle* or *la generacion del'98* ('the generation of 1998') which began immediately after the break-up of the vast Spanish empire. After the break-up, the Spanish intellectuals started a movement of which "One of the main precepts was that there should be a rebirth of energy, ideas and achievement in the 20th c., to replace those losses, both material and cultural, which were blamed firmly specifically on the 19th c. — by then already held in scorn." (Cuddon, 284). The *fin- de-siecle* broke the bond between art and society and proclaimed the superiority of art above all other things. About Whistler, one of the exponents of the *fin-de-siecle*, Graham Hugh writes: "It was left to Whistler to develop an attitude, the germ of which had always been implicit in pre-Raphaelitism, but which had never actually developed among the pre-Raphaelites themselves—a belief in the superiority of the artist, merely because he is an artist, to anything that the non- creative critic could say about him, and his utter independence of all moral and social considerations." (Hugh, 176). The influence of the *fin-de-siecle* was certainly felt in England, but, nevertheless, the spirit of Victorianism continued through the reign of Edward VII (1901- 1910) and the first half of the reign of George V (1910-1936).

In the last decade of the nineteenth century, besides the influence of the *fin-de-siecle,* there was also the influence of the Rhymers' Club on English literature. The Rhymers' Club was established in 1890 or 1891 with such members as Yeats, Arthur Symons, Lionel Johnson, Dowson, John Davidson, Victor Plarr, Selwyn Image and Richard le Gallienne. The Club was founded in imitation of the pre-Raphaelite Brotherhood (P.R.B.) which was founded in 1848 by D.G. Rossetti, William Holman Hunt and John Millais. The members of the Rhymers' Club were professedly traditionalists and were influenced by the symbolists of France. Yeats did not feel at home in the Club as the Club-members thought him *de trop.* Yeats was "accused of talking like a man of letters and not a poet. It seems to us to-day that he was the only member of the group with sufficient intellectual and spiritual vigour to form a philosophy of poetry for himself. ... the others were strictly content with the pure impression, the isolated aesthetic emotion, and forbade all system-building." (Hugh, 205). For this reason, the Rhymers's Club failed to leave a Marie on Yeats's poetry. However, the young poets soon wanted to come out of the last vestiges of Victorianism that bred only bewilderment.

The Victorian bewilderment found a reaction in the succeeding Georgian spirit that was expressed in the Georgian poetry, The term 'Georgian poetry' originated in the five volumes of poems edited by Edward Marsh and published between 1912 and 1922, during the reign of George V. The major Georgian poets were: A.E. Housman, W.H. Davis, John Masefield, Edward Thomas, Walter de la Mare, Ralph Hodgson, James Stephens, Flecker, J.C. Squire, Andrew Young, Robert Graves, D.H. Lawrence, Siegfried Sassoon, Rupert Brooke, Wildffed Owen, Edmund Blunden and others. The Georgian poets extolled rural English society, using slack conventional form. But the Georgian poetry soon disappeared as the young poets and the reading public were waiting for an appropriate genre of poetry that could reflect the modern spirit that by then settled over England.

The early Yeats breathed in an atmosphere conjured up by John Ruskin (1819-1900), Walter Horatio Pater (1839-1894), Dante Gabriel Rossetti (1828-1882), and William Morris (1834-1896)—all of whom Graham Hugh calls the last romantics. John Ruskin, son of a prosperous wine merchant, studied drawing, and took lessons of the Bible from his mother. His wide travels gave him an opportunity to acquaint himself with the painting and architecture of Europe. He had a keen interest in visual art and had a "prophetic" prose style. With these he began his career of an artist and of a moral and social critic. He was fascinated by the Gothic art and architecture and hated the Renaissance art and architecture. He said that "the pestilent art of the Renaissance" arose from "an immoral society" (Daiches, 454). He was also averse to industrialism and business ethics of the Victorian era. Ruskin did not like "'reckless luxury, the deforming mechanism, and the squalid misery of modern cities' against his own vision of city beautiful, and in doing so expressed more eloquently than any other English writer has done the aesthetic and moral case against uncontrolled industrial development." (Daiches, 454). In his *Unto the Last* and *The Crown of Wild Olive* and in other works, Ruskin vehemently attacked Victorianism. In 1871, he founded the Guild of St. George to preach his philosophy of simplicity and honesty: 'food can only be got out of the ground and happiness out of honesty.' Walter Pater, while still at college, was attracted by Platonism, and when afterwards he went to Germany on a visit was influenced by German transcendentalism, particularly by the transcendentalism of Hegel. Again, when he went to Italy, he was drawn to the Renaissance art there. Against the background of all these influences, Pater formed his concept of humanist art. He was influenced by Renaissance humanism so much that it became almost a substitute for religion for him. Like Gautier, Swindburne and others, he believed in the theory of art-for-art's-sake. In literature, he was influenced by Greek, French and German literature. He believed in the good, moral and ordered life with a sense of obligation. His collections of essays, such as *Imaginary Portraits* (1887), *Appreciations* (1889) and *Plato and Platonism* (1893) very much influenced a group of young writers and intellectuals.

Like Pater, Dante Gabriel Rossetti was a believer in the theory that art is only for art's sake, and that the artist is an 'outsider', that is the view that the artist is not concerned either with the problems of society or its ideology. He too hated the Victorian *éclat* for science which, according to him, debased the society. Trained as an artist, he founded the pre-Raphaelite Brotherhood (PRB) along with his students William Holman Hunt and John Everett Millais. "The name [of the Brotherhood] came partly from Keats's claim that the earlier Italian painters were greater than Raphael (whose technique was the model of the academicians), and partly from the study at that very time of certain medieval frescoes which were thought to show greater intellectuality and nobler accuracy." (Daiches, 451). Rossetti's poetry was influenced by his poetry, and vice versa: "There is an obvious connection between Rossetti's poetry and painting; his painting is often allegorical mythological and 'literary'; his poems are highly visual and use words in a way that suggests an original colourist." (Daiches, 452). The PRB movement began with a fanfare in 1848. It "insisted that a painter should paint whatever he sees, regardless of the formal rules of painting. Nature was to be portrayed just as it was experienced, without being altered because of the traditional methods of previous painters." (Brown, 361). The PRB insisted on the freedom of art and painting from all sorts of constraints and set rules laid down by Raphael, "in their efforts at fidelity to nature and experience, they achieved sharply realised details; but their conception of nature and experience was exceedingly limited. They took not the least account of the ugliness or the vitality of contemporary England and its problems, turning instead to a heroic and decorative world of the Middle Ages, and to a poetry which by symbolism, imagery, and music created a pictorial impression or a vague mood from which all ideas sometimes disappeared. For the sensual elements ('fleshy mysticism') of such poems as Rossetti's *The Blessed Damozel* they were condemned as the 'fleshy school'. "The Pre-Raphaelites rendered a distinct service to art by insisting that it is *not* the business of the artist to instruct or to solve social problems. But their complete withdrawal from contemporary life into mere sensuous and decorative beauty left their experiences and their poetry thin and bodiless. Their aesthetic goals influenced the symbolist poets." (Brown, 361). Yeats in his early life was influenced by the PRB movement and particularly by its member D.G. Rossetti, directly or indirectly.

D.G Rossetti was the most imposing figure among the Pre-Raphaelites. "Rossetti was an unusual a figure in England as Baudlaire was in France. Just as Baudlaire set his cult of Ideal Beauty against such eminent figures as Victor Hugo, who too often treated poetry as an instrument of propaganda, so Rossetti concentrated on the beautiful and gave himself to its service. In this he was undoubtedly strengthened by the example of Keats, for whom he had an almost unqualified admiration. He accepted Keats not with reservations as Tennyson and Swinburne did, but with his whole heart as a man who sought beauty and nothing else.... His literary art might owe something to Keats, but its roots were in medieval Italy...... He assumed the existence of an ideal world and sought to find it through beautiful things. He was a kind of Platonist both by nature and by education." (Wright, 250-32). Rossetti was a romantic and he expressed his romanticism particularly in the hundred and three sonnets of his *The House of Life.* Like Keats he believed that poetry must be 'intense' and 'amusing'.

William Morris was a poet, a designer and a social thinker who hated capitalism. He began composing poems in Tennysonian style and with medieval subject-matter, and his association with the PRB movement "encouraged his love of medievalism. Morris was interested in the Gothic art and architecture and this interest influenced his poetry to a great extent. Morris was a votary of the philosophy of simplicity, be it in the day-to-day life or in art. "The demand for simplicity was meant in the first place to bring about an art that the people as a whole might be expected to consume; but perhaps even more important, that the people might be expected to produce an art that 'will be the gift of the people to the people.'" (Hugh, 96).

The Pre-Raphaelites were romantics but in a circumscribed sense. Because, firstly, though like the romantics they raised the standard of revolt, they did not revolt against any identifiable element of the society in the hope of replacing it by anything better. They rather escaped into a "happy day-dream and exalted fancy." (Wright, 249). Secondly, as C. M. Bowra in his article 'The House of Life' writes, "the different imaginary worlds which they fashioned for their consolation were on the whole built less from an immediate experience of life than from art and literature. They thus lacked the vigour which comes from direct contact with the living scene. They gave their attention to the master-pieces of the past, and this made their work in some degree derivative." (Wright, 250). Thirdly, Bowra says that "whereas the Romantics, in their belief in a world beyond the senses, made little attempt to define it exactly or to know precisely its nature, the Pre-Raphaelites tried to find out what it was, to see within what limits its manifestations appeared, and to relate it to some coherent plan. The result was a lack of that cloudy magnificence which permeates the work of the Romantics, and its replacement by something which is perhaps magical and less alluring. Though, the Pre-Raphaelites revolted against realism, they were touched by it to the extent that they wished even their wildest longings to be directed to some definable goal." (Wright, 250).

In his younger days, Yeats was writing poems under the spell of the Pre-Raphaelite movement that enshrined medievalism in art, urged for pictorial realism with symbolic overtones, and professed the need for the union of the flesh and the spirit. When the Pre-Raphaelite movement died down, we cannot say for certain (of course we know that it began in 1848), but we can say that in the last decade of the nineteenth century it spent most of its energy. It now gave way to a new kind of poetry, and the reason of this change is not far to seek. The new scientific credo, the growth spurt in industries, the speedy urbanisation, the social and societal movements, etc. destroyed the Victorian sham of morality and orthogonal thought processes. The advent of Darwinism and particularly of psychoanalysis complicated the concept of man. Sigmund Freud, the founder of psychoanalysis, was born in Austria nine years before Yeats and died with Yeats in 1939. His emphasis on the unconscious motives changed the perception of writers and readers. Like Freud, his followers as well as detractors, such as C. G. Jung (1875-1961), Alfred Adler (1870-1937) and other psychoanalysts, denigrated the presence of rationality in humans. On the other hand, philosophers, like Henri Bergson (1859-1941), William James (1842-1910) and others emphasised the theory of "stream of consciousness". All this made *homo sapiens* question the authenticity of rationality. And the last quarter of the nineteenth century and the first decade of the twentieth century gave rise to the spirit of questioning which, in turn, brought in the collapse of the faith in traditional mode of thinking. Man confronted an era of uncertainty. But uncertain man can never remain; he built up a new *Weltanschuung* and a new belief system. Previously, Karl Marx (1818-1883) broke down the phenomenological capitalistic world-perception, and consequently, the prevalent social perception tended to be changed. But as there was no sign of a new social order and social perception, people were confused and bewildered, and were dancing attendance of a new social existence and corresponding new literary forms, techniques and contents.

This baffling social environ spawned a few new-fangled literary movements: the symbolic and surrealist movements of France, the expressionist movement of Germany, and the impressionist and imagist movements of, again, France. When the litterateurs of England found themselves at the end of a road and felt a sense of *ne plus ultra* in the sphere of literature, they, particularly the younger group of them, looked towards France — the country that has the capability of producing varied movements in literature, and towards Germany. Thus from France, England learnt the philosophy of symbolist literary expression. The word 'symbolism' is derived from the Greek verb 'symballein' which means "to throw together" and from the Greek noun 'symbolon' which means 'mark', 'emblem', 'token' or 'sign'. The symbolists believed, almost like Plato, that behind the manifestations of the world, there was an invisible spiritual world, or a world of beauty. They believed that this material and objective world was in a flux, but the screened invisible world was eternal, immutable and fixed. To the symbolists that invisible world was the ultimate reality of which this world was but a reflection. With such a Platonic and Parmenidean view of the world, they hated realism as much as naturalism. This was why they could not see eye to eye with Emile Zola. The symbolists believed that the invisible reality could not be expressed directly but only indirectly through appropriate symbols. It is very difficult to say what actually symbolises what and what is the limit of symbols. Examples of symbols are: scales for justice, the rose for beauty, the lion for strength, the lily for purity, etc. Actions and movements of human beings can also be used as symbols. For instances, clenching of fists or rolling of the sleeve means the intent of aggression. In literature, we use words as symbols and in literary symbols we combine images with concepts. A symbol is not to be confused with an allegory, for while the former has real existence, the latter has none. The symbolists began their new genre of poetry in September, 1886, in France. Their manifesto was published in an article in *Le Figaro.* But the poets of the symbolist movement were not the first persons to use symbols so seriously. Literature has always had symbols: Dante's *Divina Commedia* is structurally symbolic; Hamlet's weeds and diseases are symbols of corruption and decay; Melville's *Moby- Dick* is the symbol of a mysterious superpower; etc.

According to the symbolists, the literary symbols somehow *exist.* It was Baudlaire who especially so emphasised this aspect of a symbol that it has some a sort of existence. "Baudlaire and his followers created the image of the poet as a kind of seer or *voyant,* who could see through and beyond the real world to the world of ideal forms and essences. Thus the task of the poet was to create this 'other world' by suggestion and symbolism; by transforming reality into a greater and more permanent reality." (Cuddon, 673). The symbolists believed that the artist was an "outsider" to the society, and so he had no social commitments — his sole preoccupation was to clarify the beauty behind the misty screen of the visible. "The symbolists rejected sociological and ethical themes, insisting that art pursues the 'sensation of beauty' apart from moral and social responsibility .... Contemptuous of their environment and of middle class morality, some of them flaunted their perversions and despair, a 'new shudder' (the phrase was first applied to Baudlaire) deliberately induced through drugs, alcohol, and sadism." (Brown, 432-33). In his early years, Yeats was also influenced by the French symbolist movement, and though he did not believe in the philosophy of the symbolist movement, never did he put off his symbolist clout. "Yeats did say 'I have no speech but ssymbols', but he also said some years later (Rajan, 13):

> Players and painted stage took all my love
> And not those things that they were emblems of."

We find Yeats frequently using such symbols as the moon, a tower, a winding stair, a hawk, etc. In fact, perhaps, no poet can deny being partially a symbolist. Blake rightly said that "it is in particulars that wisdom consists" — the particulars being used as symbols.

The symbolists, due to their insouciance to the responsibility to the society and due to their anarchist literary eccentricity, were soon referred to as decadents. The word 'decadence' (Latin: *de-cadere)* means 'falling away', presumably from former recognised standard. "In modern poetry decadence has been identified most persistently in works related to the French symbolist decadent movement of the late 19th century whose influence in the British Isles encouraged native tendencies already nurtured by the ideas of Walter Pater, the poetry of Rossetti and Swinburne, and the general ambience of the Pre-Raphaelite Movement." (Preminger, 185). Alex Preminger writes about the features of the decadent literature: "A basic characteristic of decadence has been a failure to recognise objective or timeless values that transcend and give form and direction to individual experience and effort. In these terms the decadent poet is seen living in a state of Heraclitic or Bergsonian flux, with his values confined within narrowly egocentric limits and unlikely to satisfy his desires. Here the poet tends to be concerned not with 'the fruit of experience' but with 'experience itself and with private sensations; and his poems are likely to reveal a number of the following 'decadent' characteristics: search for novelty with attendant artificiality and interest in the unnatural; excessive self-analysis; feverish hedonism, with poetic interest in corruption and morbidity; abulia, neurosis, and exaggerated erotic sensibility; aestheticism, with stress on 'Art for Art's Sake' in the evocation of exquisite sensations and emotions; scorn of contemporary society and mores; restless curiosity, perversity, or eccentricity in subject matter; overemphasis on form, with resultant loss of balance between form and content—or interest in jewel-like ornamentation, resulting at times in disintegration of artistic unity; bookishness; erudite or exotic vocabulary; frequent employment of anaesthesia or *transpositions d'art;* complex or difficult syntax; attempt to make poetry primarily a means of enchantment, with emphasis on its musical and irrational elements; experiments in the use of new rhythms, rich in evocative and sensuous effects, alien to those of tradition and often departing from the mathematical principal of control in established prosody; anti-intellectualism and stress of the subconscious; abandonment of punctuation, and use of typography for visual and psychological effects; substitution of coherence in mood for coherence and synthesis in thought; 'postromantic' irony in the manner of Coitoiere, Laforgue, and the early Eliot; obscurity, arising from remote, private, or complicated imagery or from a predominantly connotative and evocative use of language, with obvious reluctance to *name* an object'; an overall aura of something lost—a nostalgic, semi-mysticism without clear direction or spiritual commitment, but with frequent reference to exotic religions and ritual, or to such mysterious substitutes as Tarot cards magic, alchemy, Rosicrucianism, Theosophy, the Kabbala, Satanism, and the like." (Preminger, 185). Along with Whitman, Baudlaire, Verlanie, Mallarmé, Rimbaud, Rilke, Eliot and Pound, the early Yeats was a symbolist as well as a 'decadent'.

Another literary movement came into being in France in 1924. The prevalent emphasis on rationality and the discovery of psychoanalysis by Freud in 1901, and also the revival of an interest in the works of Nietzsche and Schopenhauer who emphasised the importance of the unconscious mind, led André Breton and his followers to launch the surrealist movement through the publication of their *Manifesto* in 1924. The surrealists believed that rationality disintegrates the reality and that we can experience the reality only through irrational means, such as analysing dreams, hallucinations and through automatic writings. They believed that rationality only categorises and thus distorts the reality. In his *Second Manifeste du Surréaliste* which was published in *La Revolution Surréaliste* in 1929, Andre Breton wrote: "The idea of surrealism tends simply to the total recuperation of our psychic forces by a means which is not other than a vertiginous descent within ourselves, the systematic illumination of hidden places and the progressive darkening of all other places, the perpetual rambling in the depth of the forbidden zone... . Everything leads one to believe that there exists a certain point in the mind from which life and death, the real and the imaginary, the past and the future, what is communicable and what is incommunicable, the high and the low, cease to be perceived as contradictory. Vainly would one assign to surrealist activity another ambition that the hope of determining this point." (Preminger, 821). About the nature of the surrealist poetry, Preminger writes: "Surrealist poetry is primarily an instrument of knowledge which brings the poet to clearer awareness of the world perceived by the senses. In turn the poet becomes a revolutionary in that he seeks, by solving the principal problems of life, to change the human condition. There is no attempt, in this poetry, to adhere to established rules of versification, nor even to create new ones. ..... By considering words as images having an autonomous life of their own and by bringing together word-images of widely removed species (...), the surrealist poet creates new images of a remarkable ignescent quality. This, rather than the use of metaphors, or other figures of rhetoric, is the basis of surrealist poetry. "The main themes of surrealist poetry are love, revolt, the marvellous, freedom, the exaltation of desire, 'black humor' and the universe of subconscious thought. The love of woman, of a frankly erotic character, is considered as a form of liberation. Revolt, for the surrealists, is directed principally against logic, social morality, and conventional norms. These they would replace by an unconditional pursuit of the marvellous in everyday life, especially as it manifests itself in urban civilisation. 'Black humor' is also an expression of revolt in that it is characterised by an explosive and liberating effect. The exaltation of desire is upheld because of a belief in the ultimate worth of all passions." (Preminger, 821). The principal surrealist writers were Andre Breton (b. 1896), Louis Aragon (b. 1897), Tristan Tzara (b. 1896) and others.

A little bit older than the surrealist movement was the Dadaist movement which originated in Zurich in 1916, and which probably contributed to the launching of the surrealist movement. The founders of dadaism were Tristan Tzara of Rumania, Hans Arp of Alsace, and

Hugo Ball and Richard Huelsenbeck, both of Germany. The word 'dada' does not bear any connotation in itself; yet it was deliberately chosen for the movement to signify "everything and nothing at the same time"; but, generally, it means 'nothing'. The Dadaists were averse to "reason, morality, and religion, which they believed to have led the world into a senseless war, they undertook to sweep clean all the ideals and rules prevalent among the successful poets and artists of their time...... . They waged war against cliché imagery and standard syntax, and they invested the metaphor with elements of absurdity and irony." (Preminger, 180). The Dadaist movement was short-lived and it died down around 1821.

Still another movement that left a mark on the literary scenario of the first quarter of the twentieth century was the expressionist movement that originated in Germany in 1905. The expressionists "sought to avoid the representation of external reality and, instead, to project themselves and a highly personal vision of the world. Briefly, the main principle involved in the movement was that expression determined form, and therefore imagery, punctuation, syntax, and so forth. "Indeed, any of the formal rules and elements of writing can be bent or disjointed to suit the purpose." (Cuddon, 253). In this regard, it had some affinity with symbolism, for like symbolism, it also denigrated realism and wanted to show the psychological reality underlying the concrete surface. Though, expressionism had its influence principally on the theatre, yet it had also dominated, at least partially, the minds of such poets as W. H. Auden and T. S. Eliot, for some time.

Yet another literary movement of that period was the impressionist movement. Actually, impressionism was a genre of rather an earlier time. It probably originated in Claude Monet's painting *Impression: Soleil Levant*, first exhibited in Paris in 1874. "The impressionists were a school of painters who were particularly concerned with the transitory effects of light, and they wished to depict the fleeting impression from a subjective point of view. They were not interested in a precise representation; the resulting impression depended on the perception of the spectator." (Cuddon, 325-26). In this regard, they were in a sense close to the expressionists.

The youngest movement of the period was the imagist movement, touched off by a group of poets, immediately before the First World War, the most prominent among them being Ezra Pound, T. E. Hulme, Richard Aldington, Amy Lowell and Hilda Doolittle (H.D.). Ezra Pound edited the first anthology of imagist poems, *Des Imagists*, in 1914, and so the imagist movement may be understood to have started in that year. While the surrealist, expressionist and impressionist movements originated in painting, the imagist and the symbolist movements were launched principally by poets, and, naturally, their influence on poets was more enduring and profounder. The imagists believed that "a hard, clear image was essential to verse. They also believed that poetry should use the language of everyday speech and have complete freedom in subject matter." (Cuddon, 324) An example of the imagist poem can be found in the following four lines of T.E. Hulme's poem 'Above the Dock':

> Above the quiet dock in midnight,
> Tangled in the tall mast's corded height,
> Hangs the moon. What seemed so far away
> Is but a child's balloon, forgotten after play.

Besides the influences of these movements on Yeats's age, there was the influence on it coming from such writers as Walter de la Mare (1873-1956), John Masefield (1878-1967), Edward Thomas (1878- 1917), Ezra Pound (b. 1885), T.S. Eliot (1888-1965) and others. De la Mare had the "gift for suggesting eeriness, ghostliness, mystery, *A Vision*ary or uncanny quality in actual experience." (Daiches, 141). Masefield "made a serious attempt at the realistic long narrative poem." *(ibid).* Though, like Yeats, he always had a longing for the romantic, Edward Thomas combined a fine feeling for details with a power for generalisation. Ezra Pound brought with him not only his imagism, but also a new technique of modern poetry which called for the use of everyday words in poetry, like the Russian ego-futurist and cubo-futurist poets of the early twentieth century who abandoned conventional words and used common and neologistic words in poem. All these literary forces were instrumental in changing Yeats's earlier style to his mature style in poetry. Here Pound exerted the most formidable influence on Yeats, though Pound himself once came to Yeats to learn how to write poetry. Besides, there was a revival of interest in John Donne's poetry, in the last quarter of the nineteenth century, by which also Yeats was influenced. The intellectual quality of Donne's poems attracted Yeats, and so we find in his poetry the same bringing together of far-fetched and incongruous imageries.

The scientific credo of the Victorian and Edwardian England brought with it the new invention of cinematography which also exerted some influence on literature. In the modern age, there were also innovations in the field of music, sculpture, painting and other fine arts, which were also instrumental in directing the course of the literary style. The literary style of the modern age is marked by a cleavage from the traditional literary language. In the modern age, colloquialism and even slang language began to be used in prose as well as in poetry. Again, the freed verse (*vers libérés),* mostly employed by the French *Symbolistes* and free verse (*vers libres*), commonly employed in the seventeenth century France, exerted some influence in the new technique of modern poetry. The difference between freed verse and free verse is that whereas in free verse "there were subtle variations of line and stanza length and alterations of masculine and feminine rhymes in order to achieve special effects", in the freed verse the "intention was to free French versification from classical conventions. But this 'liberated' verse was still syllabic and still rhymed." (Cuddon, 741- 42). However, the influences of all these literary currents gave rise to the development of a new modern technique of poems that Yeats in his later poems was very much influenced by.

Chapter 3

The Growth and Development of the Poet

It is fashionable to categorise Yeats's poems, into four phases of development, or, at least, into two periods of writing. The four phases, generally accepted, are the Celtic twilight phase, the middle phase, the transitional phase, and the last phase. And the two periods of his writing are: the early period and the later period (or the mature period), the water-shade between the two periods being roughly the year 1914. But such categorisation of Yeats's poems, or dividing his creative period into two halves, is quite prejudicial and arbitrary. Graham Hugh rightly says: "The chronology of his [Yeats's] works and the split between his early and his later writing have perhaps been overemphasised, as his leading ideas are pretty constantly active throughout his career. Underlying them all is the realisation that poetry had lost its contact with religion: its images no longer expressed man's deepest thoughts about his own nature and own destiny." (Hugh, 226). This contention of Graham Hugh is reiterated by Balachandra Rajan: "The sharp division of the earlier and later Yeats, with its assumption that we are really dealing with two poets connected by little more than the same name, is now decidedly out of fashion. Indeed, we have the proposition that the later Yeats is inherent in the earlier and critics have been busy hammering his thoughts into unity with even more assiduity than the poet himself." (Rajan, 13). The truth lies, perhaps, somewhere between fixity or oneness and change, or perhaps on the different emphases the poet laid on the different dimensions of his life-philosophy and on the different elements of his poetic technique, at different stages of his life.

Nevertheless, for the sake of convenience of discussion, we too may follow the generally accepted four phases of poet's development, and the two categories of his poems: the earlier poems and the late poems. Yeats had perhaps the longest possible poetic life of over fifty years, in the history of English literature. He began his poetic career as a romantic and Spenserian bard. His natural attraction to dreaminess and mythology was predominant at the early stage. Yeats "wrote his early poetry out of a love of a particular place, Sligo, in the west of Ireland, with its folklore, its belief in the supernatural, and its legends. He found material for his own mythology in translations of the Gaelic tales into English. These tales of the Red Branch cycle and the Fenian cycle become tinged in his handling with *fin de siècle* melancholy, with what was called the Celtic twilight." (Ward, 509). Perhaps every country has its own special genius: the Germans are rational, the French are emotional and artistic, the British people are a matter-of-fact people, the Indians are religious and philosophic, and so on, and in the same way, the Irish people are fond of mythologies and legends. When in the early part of the 19th century, there was a spat of emigrations from Ireland and the emigrating people settled in England, there was a fusion of the Irish culture and the English spirit. As a result, English literature was greatly enriched by the mythology of Ireland. But even before that, the Irish mythology had constantly been influencing English literature. For instance, "Matthew Arnold, in the lectures collected as *The Study of Celtic Literature*, considers Shakespeare full of Celtic magic in his handling of nature." (Sampson, 716).

On the part of England, she has always been much interested in the mythology of Ireland. One instance of English welcome of Irish and Scottish mythologies is the warm reception accorded to James Macpherson's (1736-96) *Ossian Poems* "purporting to be translations from the legendary 3rd century Gaelic bard Ossian (or Oisin). Macpherson's *Fragments of Ancient Poetry, collected in the Highland of Scotland, and Translated from the Gaelic or Erse Language* (1760) aroused so much interest that money was collected to finance the author on further trips to collect similar material. The results were *Fingal, an Ancient Epic Poem, in six Books* (1762), and *Temora, an Epic Poem in Eight Books* (1763). These were followed by a collected edition of *The Works of Ossian* (1765)." (Brown, 327). Further, the legends of Deidre and other mythical figures were known to the English people since long. Deidre of the old Irish legend fled with her lover Noise and his brothers to Scotland to escape her marriage arranged by her guardian king Conchobar. The king promised forgiveness after her return to Ireland with all her train, but when they returned, all except Deidre were put to death, after which Deidre killed herself.

Yeats had been a dreamy and romantic boy. "Yeats in the eighties, in his father's studio and among his painter friends, grew up in the pre-Raphaelite afternoon, and it is sufficiently evident that the gathering Celtic twilight owed something of its colour to the somber glow from Rossetti's painting room. Even as late as 1913 Yeats finds the old influence still capable of revival." (Hugh, 216). As he grew up to his thirties, the romanticism and dreaminess of Yeats receded, and realism, though he had never a firm conviction about it, took their place of prominence. About a decade later after that, Yeats became a mature man and a mature poet. Realism continued to prevail upon him, but in addition, complexity over casted it. Yeats's last phase is very short: from 1936 to his death in 1939. It should be pointed out here that the transition from one phase to the next was almost imperceptible. In the alluvian and dilluvian processes in the transition from one phase to the next, certain elements of thought and style accrued and certain others were shaded off, but the innermost poetic self-remained almost the same. For instance, even though in his mature phase he was realistic, he did never cease to be romantic.

1. The Celtic Twilight Phase

Critics have borrowed the term 'Celtic Twilight' from Yeats's prose romance *The Celtic Twilight* (published in 1893). At a very early stage of his life, Yeats went to London only to be back home in Ireland soon. But while in London, he was attracted by the Georgian and pre-Raphaelite poets. He was also attracted by the sonorous versification of Spenser, Shelley and Keats. Being naturally interested in mythology, magic and mysteries, he was drawn to Blake and Rossetti, as well. His romanticism at this period was almost absolutely uncritical. Back home from London, he engrossed himself in the mythology and fairy tales of Ireland: the myths of Chchulain, Oisin, Red Hanrahan, etc. and the fairy tales of ancient Ireland. Yeats himself compiled and edited many of the folk-tales of Ireland. However, during this phase, Yeats was an escapist, for with his romantic imagination, he could not take this world as a habitable place. Yeats's poetic genius was inspired by the mythology and folklore of Ireland, and the poet could find a shelter in the world of the fairies.

In his young years, Yeats admired those folktales and also thought to write an epic on some theme of one of the ancient Irish heroes' exploits. "Yeats also benefited from the depth of focus of Irish culture. Not long before Yeats's birth, scholarly English translations of the ancient Irish mythological texts started to appear;... Yeats often insisted that only Greece rivalled Ireland in the exuberance and power of its mythology. ... But it is clear that Yeats himself thought of being Ireland's epic poet — and not only its Homer, but its Sophocles and its Sappho as well." (Albright, xiv). Some idea about some of the mythological and legendary characters of ancient Ireland may be given here. Dagda was the 'father of all' and the greatest god of the Celts, but not in the sense that he was the progenitor of all other gods. He was the father-figure as Danu was the mother-figure of the Celts. Dagda, the omnicompetent, was gross, ugly, pot-bellied and coarse. He wore "short tunic and hood of the peasant with raw hide as sandals." He was the god of life and death and also of nourishment, which was symbolised by his cauldron which never got emptied and could satisfy everyone hungry. The god Lug, like Dagda, was also omnicompetent. He was a carpenter, a smith, a warrior, a poet, a historian, a hero, a sorcerer — everything. But, unlike Dagda, he was handsome and young. Therefore, he was "more in keeping with the Celtic ideal of an all-efficient deity." Similar to Dagda and Lug was another god: Nuada. He was a sort of chieftain god with a shadowy figure and an all-conquering sword. In ancient Ireland, it was believed that all the gods and goddesses were the 'People of the Goddess Danu', but actually all of them were not her progenies; only Brian, Iuchar and Iucharba were her descendants. Danu was not different from Anu of Christianity. Another goddess of Irish mythology was Brigit who was the tutelary deity of learning, culture and skill. Brigit had widely been worshipped in ancient Ireland. The goddess Macha was the deity of fertility and she was also much venerated.

The greatest of the legendary heroes was Cuchulain or Cú Chulainn, details of whom is to be found in the Ulster Cycle. Cú Chulainn was human with superhuman powers and was the defender of his tribe. Son of at least one divine being, Cú Chulainn's original name was sétanta and this name was somehow connected with the British tribe Setanti. The name Cú Chulainn, 'the Hound of Culann' was given to him after he was forced to kill the watch-dog of Culann, the smith. In recompense he undertook to guard the kingdom of Ulster and thus became the champion of his people. He was taught wisdom, warfare and magic by Sencha, Fergus and Cathbad. Cú Chulainn was also taught magic by Scathach. He was the idol of the Celtic nobility. Cú Chulainn was proud, brave and skilled in magic. He was also the idol to the Celtic warriors who could converse on equal terms with poets and Druids.

"In his normal state Cú Chulainn is pictured as a young man with well-defined physical attributes. He had seven pupils in each eye, seven fingers on each hand and seven toes on each foot. His cheek was multi-coloured, yellow, blue, green and red. His long dark hair was of three tints, dark close to the roots, red in the middle and lighter in colour towards the tips, suggestive of the practice of the Celts of smearing their hair with a thick wash of lime. Rich and gorgeous jewellery adorned him, a hundred strings of jewels on his head, a hundred golden breast ornaments. Far different was Cú Chulainn in his battle-frenzy when his body was seized by contortions. He turned round in his skin so that his feet and knees were to the rear and his calves and buttocks to the front. His long hair stood on end and on the tip of each hair a spot of blood or a spark of fire. From his open mouth spurted fire and from the tip of his head a jet of black blood rose mast high. One eye receded far back into his skull while the other protruded onto his cheek. Finally, on his forehead appeared the 'hero's moon', a strange inexplicable sign. When in this state, Cú Chulainn's fury was uncontrollable and he needed to be plunged into three vats of cold water before he could be pacified." (Hamlyn, 233). Queen Medb was the Irish legendary heroine, who was Cú Chulainn's number one enemy. She plotted to kill him and with this end in view arranged to compell Cú Chulainn to violate some of the *geasa* or taboos. A *geis* (pl. *geasa*) was an injunction to avoid certain action in certain circumstance and to perform certain action in certain circumstance. Being thus tricked by Medb to violate some of the *geasa,* Cú Chulainn fell in a battle with Queen Medb in the Plain of Muir theme.

What Yeats found in those fairy tales and myths was, perhaps, the eternal beauty that this concrete matter-of-fact earth could hardly proffer. Never for a moment throughout his life could Yeats reconcile himself with this pale and ugly earth. In later years Yeats certainly changed his themes and styles of poetry, but his early longing for eternal beauty, that these myths and legends offered him, lingered throughout his long life. Daniel Albright writes: "If, as Yeats said of Shelley, 'there is for every man someone scene, some one adventure, some one picture that is the image of his secret life, for wisdom first speaks in images'—what is Yeats's one scene, one adventure? Perhaps it is this: a frustrated man seeks escape from an inadequate world—escape from nature, escape from society, escape from history, escape from himself; in pursuit of the Eternal Beauty that lies beyond, he immerses himself in dreams of supernatural splendor; he dwells in an austere and symbolical tower and tries to transmute himself to metal or stone, in order to assume a permanence equal to that of the beauty he seeks; but in the end (as in the circus Animals' Desertion') he finds that what he has painfully sought, what he has painstakingly constructed, is nothing but an image of his own simple perishing face." (Albright, xliv-xlv).

As we have seen, in his youth, Yeats was drawn to the lyricism of Spenser and, in fact, he first tried his hand in versification in the Spenserian strain. "Yeats's first poetry was an attempt at a Spenserian epic on the story of Roland, which was abandoned for the Spenserian and Shelleyan blend that was to develop into Yeats's first published poetry, not to be found in his *Collected Poems*, but printed in the *Dublin University Review* when Yeats was twenty". (Hollander, 505). During this time Yeats also wrote the long poem *The Island of Statues,* subtitled *An Archadian Faery Tale.* Yeats's romantic mind pervaded all the composition of this phase. MacNeice writes about the early Yeats and the influence on him of the romantic tradition: "Yeats's early poems are in the Victorian tradition which itself was a development from the Romantic Revival. Tennyson would not have come into being without Keats. Rossetti would not have come into being without Tennyson. Yeats would not have come into being without Rossetti. One of the chief characteristics of this line of poets — in their poems — is an autumnal almost morbid, languor .... Rossetti is a decadent poet but the seeds of his decadence are to be found in Tennyson, and before that, in Keats."' (Bloom, 108).

Yeats's urge to write poetry, in his early years was whetted by his feeling of nationalism, which was again inspired by John O'Leary. O' Leary urged and inspired Yeats to write poems of high quality. A. Norman Jeffares writes about O' Leary and his influence on Yeats: "John O'Leary (1830-1907) when a medical student in Trinity College, Dublin, was influenced by the Young Ireland Movement, and became one of the Triumvirate in the Fenian movement which succeeded it... He had a large collection of books and greatly influenced Yeats. (He was also friendly with Yeats's father, John Butler Yeats.) It was through O' Leary's influence that Yeats moved from his father's Home Rule views to a more strongly nationalist point of view. O'Leary, 'the handsomest old man' Yeats had ever seen, was romantic figure... He despised inferior writing and told Yeats, 'Neither Ireland nor England knows the good from the bad in any art, but Ireland unlike England does not hate the good when it is pointed to her. (...) From debates in a Young Ireland Society, from O'Leary's conversation and the Irish books he lent Yeats came 'all I have set my hand to since' (...). O'Leary belonged to Yeats's romantic conception of Irish nationality: he — like his disciple the barrister J.F. Taylor — seemed to Yeats to be the last to speak an understanding of life and Nationality, built up by the generation of Grattan, which read Homer and Virgil, and by the generation of Davis, which had been pierced through by the idealism of Mazzini, and of the European revolutions of the mid-century." (Jeffares, 110).

In the early phase Yeats published the following works:

Poetry

i. *The Juvenalia* (1885): it includes immature boyish poems and poetic plays (most of these were not later on included in his collected works).
ii. *The Wandering of Oisin and Other Poems (1889).*
iii. *The Crossways* (1889): this collection of poems also included the poems earlier published *in The Wandering of Oisin and Other Poems.*
iv. *The Rose* (1893): including the poems first published in *The Countess Cathleen and Other Poems.*
v. *The Wind Among the Reeds (1899).*

Drama

i. *Mosada* (1886): it is a dramatic poem.
ii. *The Wandering of Oisin* (1889).
iii. *The Countess Cathleen* (1891).
iv. *The Land of Heart's Desire* (1894).
v. *The Shadowy Waters* (1900).

Prose Works

The Celtic Twilight (1893).

Fictions

i. *John Sherman and Dhoya* (1891).
ii. *The Secret Rose* (stories) (1897).

iii. *The Tables of the Law: The Adoration of the Magi* (1897).

Editions and Selection

i. *The Poems of William Blake* (1893) (ed. Yeats).
ii. *Irish Fairy and Folk Tales* (1893). (ed. Yeats).
iii. *A Book of Irish Verse* (selected by Yeats) (1895).

In the Celtic Twilight period, Yeats was influenced by almost all the literary movements of France and Germany, then prevalent in England and Ireland — such as symbolism, surrealism, expressionism, imagism, impressionism and Gerogianism. As we have seen, he was also infused with Irish mythology and the childhood memories of Sligo. "For Yeats the countryside was not only a memory of peaceful beauty. It was a source for the myths and legends which he craved. He read books of Celtic folklore. He sought eagerly among the Irish peasantry for supernatural tales. Like other members of his family, he was 'psychic', and a man of many superstitions. He believed in omens and ghosts. He liked to imagine himself a sage or magician." (Robson, 51)

All these personal idiosyncrasies and experiences of Yeats found expression in his early poems. During this period, Yeats was also very much influenced by William Blake. Perhaps his interest in magic and mysteries and his attractions to supernatural powers led him towards the philosophy and art of Blake. The Irish national movement also touched his heart, as we have seen before. "'There should', he wrote, 'be a pride in that national heritage that should lead to a new flowering of art and national life.'" (Albright,v). Yeats's national feeling was honed by his passionate love of the nationalist leader and the paragon of beauty, Maud Gonne, the love that was never requited.

Yeats's early poems were written in the late romantic tradition. As we have seen, he was influenced by the pre-Raphaelites and their successors, particularly by William Morris who was a friend of Yeats. Dreamy as he was, Yeats liked the dreamy poems of Morris. Yeats's poems of this phase were written mostly about things past. W.W. Robson writes about these poems: "Sorrow and heartbreak do not break the spell but are blended into the dreamy beauty. There is no moralising, nothing didactic; no vigour, intellectual or emotional; little sense of the poet himself or his circumstances. All is reverie." (Robson, 52). Most of these qualities of Yeats's early poems can be found in a single poem of his which he wrote in 1892: 'Who goes with Fergus?':

Who will go drive with Fergus now,
And pierce the deep wood's woven shade,
And dance upon the level shore?
Young man, lift up your russet brow,
And lift your tender eyelids, maid,
And brood on hopes and fears no more.

And no more turn aside and brood
Upon love's bitter mystery;
For Fergus rules the brazen cars,
And rules the shadows of the wood,
And the white breast of the dim sea
And all disheveled wandering stars.

It should be noted here that the quintessence of the poetic spell of this period or phase — that is the spell of dreaminess — did never leave Yeats throughout his life, and therefore he rightly said, at least about himself, that "our intellect at twenty contain all the ideas we shall ever really grasp." (Robson, 52). The early poems of Yeats contain in abundance Irish mythology, folklore and fairy-tales, especially the exploits of the Irish mythical heroes, like Cuchulain and Hanrahan. Some of the poems deal also with the myths of Druids or the priests among the ancient Celts of Britain, Gaul or Germany. The word 'druid' means 'oak-tree' or 'wizard'. The Druids were priests, soothsayers and healers, all at once. The Druids had woven many tales of mysterious beings and their uncanny exploits. The early poems of Yeats were written while the poet wafted himself above into a dreamy sphere where there were peace and repose and listlessness; in short, it was an airy Arcadia. The Yeats of this phase escaped into the dream-land of fairies and called others to follow him:

Come away, O human child!
To the waters and the wild
With a faery, hand in hand,
For the world's more full of weeping than you can understand.

The poet was very much indignant of the earthly world of drab reality. He was disgusted with the Victorian credo for scientism and industrialism. The Victorian world was one of vulgarism and indifference; it was a tinsel world without any human qualities and sympathies. To escape this familiar world of indifference, he wished himself wafted away into the Celtic Twilight (hat his early poems depicted.

As the themes of the early poems were dreamy, mysterious, fairy and legendary, so, consonantly, his style was Spenserian, Shelleyan, Keatsian and Tennysonian. The poems were infused with pale colour, dark shadows, opaque mists and musicality, In these poems there is profusion of romantic imagery worked out under the inspiration of the pre-Raphaelites—imagery that is not internally essential but is only decorative. Another peculiarity of the poems of this phase is also noteworthy. The poet is preoccupied with the spell of words, as if he is engaged more with words than with beauty of a poem. The words he chooses are mellifluous and sonorous, as if the poem is to be sung with a feminine voice. In fact, this lyricism had always remained with the poet throughout his life, but, nevertheless, we can say that his early poems had a pre-eminence in it. The early poems are vague, disillusioned and escapist, and yet we must say that in them there is an undercurrent of realism as well as of patriotism. Perhaps a good amount of the features of Yeats's early poems can be found also in the following few lines of his poem 'The Song of the Happy Shaperd' that he wrote for his philosopher friend George Russell (A.E.):

The woods of Arcady are dead,
And over is their antique joy;
Of old the world on dreaming fed;
Grey Truth is now her painted toy;
Yet still she turns her restless head:
But O, sick children of the world,
Of all the many changing things
In dreary dancing past us whirled,
To the cracked tune that chronos sings.
Words alone are certain good.

2. The Transitional or Middle Phase

The early romanticism of Yeats continued to remain with him till the poet reached the age of around thirty-five, or till the turn of the nineteenth century. He left his last testament of romanticism in his *The Wind Among the Reeds* which was published in 1899. Yeats now felt the myriad buffets of reality: his second proposal to Maud Gonne in 1899 was declined by the *la belle dame sans merci*, and his third in 1900, too; Maud Gonne's marriage with Major MacBride in 1903 was a great blow to him; and he was unwittingly involved in some public controversy that broke into pieces his romantic nationalist sentiment. He could now realise the hypocrisy of some of the nationalist leaders, and so turned his back to politics, forever. Before that, in 1898, Yeats, as the President of the Wolf Tone memorial Association, tried to unite the different nationalist political parties under one banner. But the parties behaved wildly and quarreled among themselves. This made Yeats disgusted with the political parties, and ultimately, he said goodbye to politics. Further, in 1907, when J.M. Synge's *The Playboy of the Western World* was being performed in Dublin, the performance raised an indecent hue and cry among the Dubliners against the way Synge dealt with the Irish peasantry. Yeats was much disturbed by the wild mentality and behaviour of his compatriots. He could not bear with the idea of trampling down of art by the common and ignorant folk. All this made him climb down from the tower of his nationalistic dreams and walk on the concrete pavements. So far he had been viewing the Irish cause in his mind's romantic eye, and now he began to see it out there, at a distance. He could now realise that romanticism could no longer hold one once he turned his gaze to the real world of mobs. His romanticism was now broken to pieces, and he began to accost the reality face to face. With the changes occurring in the personality and view of the poet, a new genre of poetry began to issue forth from his pen, as he entered into his Middle or Realistic phase. This new poetic debut continued to engage the poet till around the breaking out of the First World War. The romanticism gone, Yeats began to write realistic poems, dramas and fictions. His writings during this period include:

Verse

i. *In the Seven Woods* (1904).
ii. *The Green Helmet and Other Poems* (1910).
iii. *Poems Written in Discouragement* (1912-13).
iv. *Nine Poems* (1914).
v. *Responsibilities: Poems and Plays* (1914).

Plays

i. *Diarmuid and Grania* (written with George Moore and produced in 1901).
ii. *The King's Threshold* (produced in 1903).
iii. *The Hourglass: A Morality* (produced in 1903).
iv. *The Shadowy Waters* (produced in 1904).

v. *The Pot of Broth* (produced in 1904).

vi. *Where There Is Nothing* (produced in 1904).

vii. *The Golden Helmet* (produced in 1908).

Fiction

Stories of Red Hanrahan (1905).

Prose

i. *Ideas of Good and Evil* (1903).

ii. *Discoveries: A Volume of Essays* (1907).

iii. *Poetry and Ireland: Essays* (with Lionel Johnson, 1908).

iv. *Synge and the Ireland of His Time* (1911).

Editions

i. *Twenty-one Poems* by Lionel Johnson (1905).

ii. *Some Essays and Passages* by John Elginton (1905).

iii. *Sixteen Poems* by William Allingham (1905).

iv. *Poems of Spenser* (1906).

v. *Twenty-One Poems* by Katharine Tynan (1907).

vi. *Poems and Translations* by J.M. Synge (1909).

vii. *Selections from the Writings of Lord Dunsany* (1912).

Yeats's poetry in this transitional or middle phase changed considerably, as we said, from that of the preceding phase both in theme and in style. The romanticism of the earlier phase was replaced by the realism of this transitional phase. In this phase, he was away from the mythology and romantic escapism of the earlier phase, as his balloon of romanticism burst under the impact of concrete realism. But, yet, the early romanticism was not set aside completely, rather, perhaps we may say, the romanticism took a new form and showed subdued expression. Yeats is basically a mythopoeic poet, and so though the accepted mythology was no more to be found in his poetry of the transitional period, he created a new mythology. Nevertheless, the old mythical heroes, like Oisin, Cuchulain, King Goll and Fergus, and their mythical exploits continued to influence the imagination of the poet even in this transitional phase.

On the contrary, while in London in the last decade of the nineteenth century, Yeats was influenced by the current of realistic literature prevalent there, and consequently, he was gradually coming away from his fairy land. Yeats was now going to be a mature person, after he had realised the true meaning of life. This change in Yeats's *Weltanschaung* was first observable in *In the Seven Woods.* His maturity was further enhanced by his repeated frustrations in his love for Maud Gonne. The poet's frustrations can be clearly realised in his poem 'O Do Not Love Too Long':

> Sweetheart, do not love too long:
> loved long and long,
> And grew to be out of fashion
> Like an old song.

During this phase, Yeats was also being more and more influenced by all the prevalent diverse literary movements of the time: symbolism, surrealism, imagism, expressionism and impressionism. Yeats was always full of symbols and myths, because he was always after symbols and myths. In the Introduction to his play *The Resurrection,* which was produced in 1934, he wrote: "I have been preoccupied with certain myth that was itself a reply to a myth." Richard Ellman in his *Yeats: The Man and the Mask* says that Yeats "read mystical writers because they saw symbols in everything, and with the same general purpose he sought out those who said they could manipulate external nature by magic." (Rudd, 57). Again, in his *Essays* (1924) Yeats wrote: "'I cannot now think symbols less than the greatest of all powers when they are used consciously by masters of magic, or half-consciously, by their successors, the poet, the musician, and the artist..., Whatever the passions of great men have gathered about becomes a symbol in the great memory, and in the hands of his who has the secret, it is a worker of wonders, a caller up of angels or of devils." (Rudd, 20-21). Yeats took lessons in symbolism from French masters, like Mallarmé and others. But "Though as early as 1894 Yeats took with him on a visit to Paris a letter of introduction to Mallarmé, he seems to have learned about symbolist ideas largely from his friend Arthur Symons, who dedicated to Yeats his *Symbolist Movement in Literature* (1899). A letter that he wrote many years later in 1937 indicates how slight the direct influence of Mallarme had been." (Wimsatt, 596). On the contrary, W.W. Robson does not agree with William K. Wimsatt and Cleanth Brook on this point. Robson says that regarding symbolism Yeats was much influenced by French masters, and further he says that Yeats was also influenced by the Rhymers' Club and Walter Pater: "Meanwhile a new literary influence had entered Yeats's poetry. Through his friend Arthur Symons he learned of the French symbolist poets, Baudlaire, Verlaine and Mallarmé. They reinforced his hieratic and cabbalistic view of art. But English influences may have been more important. The Rhymers' Club, the circle of writers to which Yeats belonged, looked to Walter Pater for their philosophy." (Robson, 53). Yeats now left the lyrical and ornate style and adopted common words and idioms. His diction slowly became harsh and choppy, and his rhythm became conversational. The colourful images were no more there in his poems. The languid rhythm of the earlier phase gradually became sharp and jerky. The listless music stopped and conversational style appeared in his poems. The images came more into relief with more and more resolutions. The verse grew severe, vigorous and intense. The Spenserian and Keatsian rhythms gave way to the simpler Wordsworthian rhythm. His verses became rather Dantesque: intense, sublime, exalted and enigmatic. Some of all these changes in style may be comprehended from the following lines of his poem 'A Coat' that was published in *Responsibilities* (1914):

> I made my song a coat
> Covered with embroideries
> Out of old mythologies
> From heel to throat;
> But the fools caught it,
> Wore it in the world's eyes
> As though they'd wrought it.
> Song, let them take it,
> For there's more enterprise
> In walking naked.

3. The Phase of Complexity and Maturity

The preceding phase completely dispersed Yeats's romanticism and prepared him for confronting life face to face — for a tryst with reality. In the phase of complexity and maturity, the poet did not look at life askance, but looked at life in the face. By now he had a rich variety of experiences, sweet and sour. His love and political aspirations having been frustrated, he became quite disillusioned. But now he was not to escape reality but to choose to live a foil life with all its seamy sides. He could never forget his love of beauty, but life was not at all beautiful; he could never forget his love of love, but life had everything else but love. In the earlier phases, he decided to seek happiness by escaping from the rude life, but now he understood that the happiness to be found in a dream-world was itself a dream. Therefore, he decided to say goodbye to his natural romanticism and accept the hard life with a sense of irony.

Further, his various knowledge and experiences of eastern philosophy, Rosicrucianism, Platonism, etc. on the one hand and the prevailing credo for progress in science on the other, complicated his vision of life. The poet became intensely aware of the exteriority of life. Around the poet, the world was preparing for the devastating First World War. Humanity was being dashed to the ground, morality overthrown from its traditional height of sanctity, and peace torn to pieces. In addition to this, Ireland was passing through her internal turmoils due to Easter Rebellion, civil wars, etc. The poet could not bear with the consequent carnal blood-spilling, and so he was pining for peace, after some purgation, somewhere in an imaginary Byzantium. He felt the urge of life, but life seemed to be obnoxious, and so he was ambivalent towards it. Now he did not love life but loved to satirise it. He became almost cynic. Being naturally a romantic poet, Yeats therefore now found in himself very little of poetic genius to write verses. "In the twentieth century Yeats was coming to seem a mere survival from a past age. John Middleton Murry, reviewing his poetry in 1919, concluded that Yeats's inspiration was exhausted: he had nothing more to say. And there are signs that Yeats himself agreed with him (Robson, 54). Yeats could find neither new themes nor new techniques for versification, apropos of the modern sensibility. He also could not find any model of modern versification in English, for it was only in France that the poets there found new themes and accordingly devised new techniques of versification. This same *ne plus ultra* situation occurred also to T.S. Eliot who wrote in his Essays: "The kind of poetry that I needed, to teach me the use of my own voice, did not exist in English at all; it Was only to be found in French." (Eliot, 252).

But soon Yeats found what he was searching for: new themes and new techniques. In the ambivalent approach to life, Yeats's mood became too complex, more complex than it was in his immediately preceding phase, and accordingly he devised a new technique that is simpler but more intractable. Keeping pace with the changes in his mood, the poet resorted to still newer technique for poetic communication. In the second phase, the poems were simple, but now these became even simpler in structure. The verse was now without any decoration; it was almost starkly naked. The diction became more conversational, more colloquial. The words in the verses were glittering and drab, alternately. The colour of the first phase and the symbolism of the second were now mixed together to make the verse even more complex. Further, new images were added and even ugliness was introduced in poetry. But it should be noted that the beauty of the first phase and the newly introduced ugliness somehow reconciled in this third phase. In thought and mood also the poet attempted to reconcile diverse elements. For all these, perhaps, this phase may be called the phase of reconciliation.

Astonishingly, in spite of his mental turbulations, Yeats could turn out, during this phase, an enormous amount of literary productions. Yeats's writings during this phase include:

Verse

i. *Responsibilities and Other Poems* (1926)
ii. *The Wild Swan at Coole* (1917)
iii. *Nine Poems* (1918)
iv. *Michael Robertes and the Dancer* (1921)
v. *Seven Poems and a Fragment* (1922)
vi. *The Cat and the Moon and Certain Poems* (1924)
vii. *October Blast* (1927)
viii. *The Tower* (1928)
xi. *The Winding Stair* (1929)
x. *Words for Music Perhaps and Other Poems* (1932)
xi. *Wheels and Butterflies* (1934)

Plays

i. *At the Hawk's Well* (produced in 1916)
ii. *The Dreaming of the Bones* (1919)
iii. *Two Plays for Dancers* (1919)
iv. *The Player Queen* (produced in 1919)
v. *Four Plays for Dancers* (1921)
vi. *The Resurrection* (1927)

vii. *Oedipus at Colonus* (produced in 1927)
viii. *King Oedipus* (1928)
ix. *Fighting the Waves* (produced in 1929)
x. *The Words upon the Window-pane* (1934)
xi. *The King of the Great Clock Tower* (1934)
xii. *A Full Moon in March* (1935)

Fiction

Nil

Prose Writings

i. *Reveries Over Childhood and Youth* (1915)
ii. *Per Arnica Silentia Lunae* (1918)
iii. *Four Years* (1921)
iv. *The Trembling of the Veil* (1922)
v. *A Vision* (1925)
vi. *Estrangement* (1926)
vii. *The Death of Synge and Other Passages from an Old Diary* (1928)
viii. *A Packet for Ezra Pound* (1929)
ix. *Stories of Michael Robertes and His Friends* (1932)
x. *Dramatis Personae* (1935)

Editing

Oxford Book of Modern Verse 1892-1935 (1935)

It should be mentioned here that the complexity of Yeats's mood during this phase did not mar his poetry, rather it enriched his poetry so much so that his poetry of this phase stands out distinct in richness, profundity and finesse.

4. The Last Phase

This is the shortest of Yeats's poetic life, extending from 1936 to his death in 1939. In the third phase, though the poet was experiencing all sorts of frustrations under the impact of hard realities, he was craving the buoyancy of life. Though he was being swept away by fierce current, yet he was trying to swim against that current. But in the fourth phase, he was gradually becoming mellowed, as he became aware of the impending catastrophe — death. He realised that life was but a soap-bubble, sure to burst after glancing a while. He painfully realised life as a meaningless tragedy: "... it is a tale/Told by an idiot, full of sound and fury, Signifying nothing." Yeats looked back and took stock of what he had achieved, and again became frustrated and disillusioned. He tried to laugh at the futility of life and actually laughed and that too boisterously. But he did not leave his poetry behind, rather with its help he tried to bury his sorrow. At the fag end of his life he was self-reflecting and thus was drawn to the philosophy of the Upanishads, once again. He wanted a sort of purgation and liberation. All this had been amply reflected in his writings of this phase. Yes, he was an active poet till the moment of leaving his 'mortal coil.'

This phase being the shortest, Yeats naturally could write very little, and yet he produced the following:

Verse

i. *New Poems* (1938)
ii. *Last Poems and Two Plays* (1939)

Plays

i. *Nine One-Act Plays* (1937)
ii. *The Herne's Egg* (1938)
iii. *Purgatory* (1939)
iv. *The Death of Cuchulainn* (1939)

Fiction

Nil

Prose Writings

i. *Autobiography* (1938)
ii. *On the Boiler* (1939)
iii. *If I were Four-and-Twenty* (1939)

Translation

The Ten Principal Upanisads (with Purohit Swami, 1937).

Some critics are of the opinion that Yeats's poetic genius declined in the last phase, but this is not true. The poems of the last phase are as lively and fine as those of the earlier phases. This is so because Yeats was full of life and art till the last minute of his life. Yeats is an exceptional poet on at least two counts: that his poetic life was the longest and that it lasted till his end. In the last phase, he was not only disillusioned but also felt some sort of total isolation from the world outside. He became frustrated with Maud Gonne, felt disgusted under the stark reality all around, and became apprehensive of the end of his life. Consequently, he turned towards his own self, and this was reflected in the works of his last phase. He always wanted youthful vigour, but was crippled by old age, and he ironically resented this. He was forced to realise that life was no romance, no poetry:

> But I grow old among dreams,
> A weather-worn, marble Triton,
> Among the streams.

However, like Shakespeare's, Yeats's poetic development was also slow, but Shakespeare's creative period was much shorter than Yeats's. Nevertheless, and in spite of the fact that we generally divide Yeats's creative life into four phases, we must not think, at least regarding Yeats's technique, that there were as if four poets of the same name in Yeats, or even two — the earlier Yeats and the later Yeats, unlike, may be, in the case of Shakespeare. T.S. Eliot is very explicit here: "But in the case of Yeats the kind of development seems to be different. I do not want to give the impression that I regard his earlier and his later work almost as if they had been written by two different men. Returning to his earlier poems after making a close acquaintance with the later, one sees, to begin with, that in technique there was a slow and continuous development of what is always the same medium and idiom." (Eliot, 254).

Chapter 4

Yeats's Philosophy and Psychology

When we speak of Yeats's philosophy and psychology, we do not mean he was a philosopher and a psychologist in the academic sense of those words. In a sense, Yeats must be a philosopher and a psychologist, for every man is a born philosopher and a born psychologist. But Yeats was a greater philosopher and a greater psychologist than the common man. He really had a philosophy and a peculiar one at that — peculiar and obscure too, like that of William Blake. The obscurity of Yeats's philosophy was much due to that of Blake by whom Yeats was very much influenced. Margaret Rudd rightly opines that perhaps 'Yeats' extraordinary hero-worship of his 'master' Blake can shed much light on what is obscure in Yeats' own philosophy." (Rudd, xi). Poetry may not encroach upon the boundary of philosophy, but philosophy always encroaches upon that of poetry, for poetry is nothing but the expression of a philosophy through the perfectest employment of words. In his *The Last Romantics,* Graham Hugh very aptly says that great poetry cannot be written without any philosophy. Examples are: Dante's poetry explained the medieval philosophy of the scholastics; Keats had his own philosophy of truth and beauty; etc. Yeats himself said that he wrote poems "as texts for exposition', 'to explain my philosophy of life and death' to express 'convictions about this world and the next.'" (Hugh, 258).

Yeats's philosophical stand-points are to be found mostly in his *A Vision* which was the result of his wife's voluminous automatic writings and his experiments with her *métier* in the fields of the supernaturals. In the Introduction *to A Vision,* Yeats wrote that he was surprised by Mrs. Yeats's automatic writing, especially on 24th October, 1917. He wrote: "What came in disjointed sentences, in almost illegible writing, was so exciting, sometimes so profound, that I persuaded her to give an hour or two days after day to the unknown writer, and after some half-dozen such hours offered to spend what remained of life explaining and piecing together those scattered sentences. 'No' was the answer, 'we have come to give you metaphors or poetry.'" (Jeffares, 306). Such a commanding voice from beyond the visible world stunned Yeats. *A Vision* is a justification of the supernatural region and forces. Yeats was here influenced by his "teaching spirits", as he admitted, and by his reading of the philosophy of history developed by Vico and Hegel; his reading of Plato, Plotinus and Berkeley whom he called the "God-appointed" philosopher; and also by his reading of Kant, Croce and Gentile, in *A Vision* he wrote: "I read for months everyday Plato and Plotinus. Then I started on Berkeley and Croce and Gentile." This study of philosophy was then reinforced by his reading of Vico, Kant, Hegel, Schopenhauer, Hartman, Bergson, James, Bradley and other philosophers. Yeats was much haunted by the problem of fantasy and reality, and he concluded that the two are not different. In a correspondence to Moore, he wrote: "points most of my fantasies and extravagancies were meant to suggest are .... that images of the mind and images of sense must have a common root... and that whatever their cause or substratum that substratum is not fixed at one spot in space.'" (Wimsatt, 601). He advanced a solution of the problem of the real and the imaginary, or of the sense and the images, from the view-point of the philosopher Immanuel Kant. In fact William K. Wimsatt and Cleanth Brooks call Yeats a Kantian of some sort: "In general Yeats was a good—if somewhat unconventional—Kantian. He termed 'the vast Kantian argument' the "most powerful in philosophy." (Wimsatt, 601)

Yeats had a natural tendency to philosophy. He was born in the heyday of Victorian science, but, nonetheless, he could not accept without indignation the thoughtless materialistic world-view of science which he repudiated with "monkish hatred". He could intuit some unseen reality behind the concrete expression of the world, and so being buoyed by the exuberance of life, he searched for the unseen reality. This was why he was interested in the Irish mythology, magic, religion and other cognate subjects in his early phase. In all these he could ensconce himself from the hue and cry of science. But this does not mean that he was anti-science; it only means that he was against science when it overleapt its boundary. He could never deny the concrete world, but at the same time, he felt a pull of the abstract reality behind the concrete reality. Consequently, he had been suffering from some sort of tension between science and religion, or, better, between science, on the one hand, and art, mythology, folklore, magic, imagination, religion, etc., on the other. This same tension was there in Blake as well, but Blake could find a release from the tension in the sphere of religion, in the concept of Christ who is the substantiation (science) of the trans-substance (imagination); whereas Yeats, because he soon negated religion, ever suffered this tension. Blake could find a union of matter and spirit, or of science and supernature, in the concept of Christ, but Yeats failed to do this. Margaret Rudd, in her *Divided Image*, beautifully portrays the tension between matter and spirit and the possible release from such tension with the help of the following diagram:

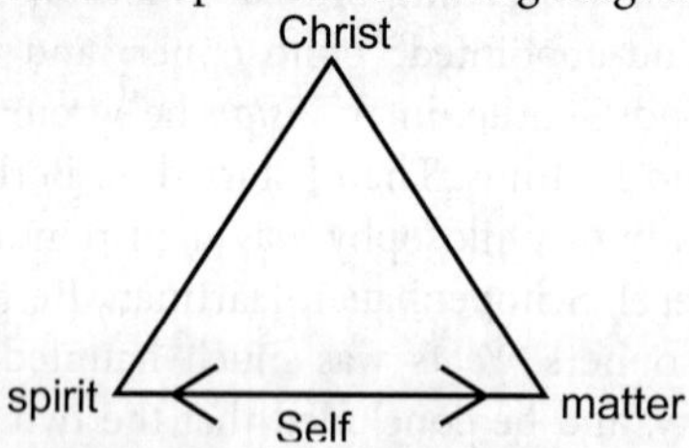

There is always a tension between the spirit and matter, but Christ represents both of them, in his human form. So if one can identify oneself with Christ, one can reconcile the two opposing forces of the spirit and matter. By failing to reconcile the two opposing forces, Yeats suffered a sort of psychosis. Denis Donoghue writes: "Reading Yeats, we would posit a poet who suffered from a psychosis characteristic of our time and familiar to other times: namely, an intense and painful preoccupation with the seemingly irreconcilable claims of Soul and Body. Intense and painful, because being a poet he was driven, as by an entelechical motive typical of the artist, toward images of wholeness, unity, and perfection. There seemed no possibility, however, of realizing or enacting 'Unity of Being'... Thus Yeats as *sufferer* (sic). As *agent* he sought to heal himself: first by the sheer act of lamenting the lost harmony, working within (he optative mood, describing great-rooted chest-nut trees that suffered from none of man's antinomies. Second, and more characteristic: with a dramatist's instinct he broke down the psychosis into its two great conflicting part, thereafter interpreting experience, as his mood or 'condition' prodded, now in terms of Soul (or Spirit or Essence), now in terms of Body (or Nature or Circumstance). The psychosis was a complex and unmanageable simultaneity: Yeats replaced it, imperatively, by a more tolerable scheme of successiveness. He resolved a contradictory 'yes-no' by setting up a plot that developed from 'yes' to 'no' and *vice versa*." (Cowell, 69). Thus Yeats found a sort of release from the tension only in the sphere of art. Consequently, though there is a difference between Blake and Yeats regarding the ways in which they got release, there is also some similarity between them. Margaret Rudd writes about the similarity between the two poets: "The important likeness between Blake and Yeats is that both are concerned with the drama of the inner life. To an extant this is true of all poets not limiting their subject-matter to externalities of description and narrative. But it is particularly true of those poets who consciously sort out their actors into those two main camps dealt with throughout the ages by theologians more than poets." (Rudd, 189). Further, Yeats always wanted to mould himself into a surrogate Blake, even till the end of his life. In his *Last Poems and Plays*, Yeats writes:

> Grant me an old man's frenzy.
> Myself must I remake
> Till I am... William Blake
> Who beat upon the wall
> Till Truth obeyed his call.

Yeats's metaphysics was pantheistic, like that of Spinoza, or, better, like that of Plato whose works he read avidly. He believed like Plato in a spiritual world, curtained off by the visible manifold, and believed, by inference, in the Unity of Being. He believed that the phenomenal world is the mode of the spiritual world, as Plato said that the world of the manifold particulars or of the senses is the world of instances of the spiritual world of universal. True, according to Plato, there are innumerable universal or concepts, but then these are arranged like a pyramid, so that on the apex of it is the highest universal or concept — the concept of the Good. The Good expresses itself through the manifold of the mundane world. This idea is beautifully expressed by Shelley, who, too, like Yeats, believed in Platonism: "Life, like a dome of many-coloured glass/Stains the white radiance of eternity." The Good is, according to Plato, the soul of the world: it is the World-Soul. So Plato believed the world to be 'living' and, likewise, Yeats believed that the world is' living'—it is an Anima Mundi.

According to Yeats, the world consists of souls and bodies, each soul having a body. This is in near agreement with theological doctrines; but Yeats finds the explanation of religion of the dichotomy of soul and body inadequate, because it lays stress only on the soul. He believes that there is as much beauty, for example, in the body as in the soul. "In other words, Yeats finds the solution of the Church too abstract, turning too much away from the world whose natural beauty the poet must love as much as spiritual beauty." (Rudd, 22). Yeats found the solution of the dichotomy of mind or spirit and body not in religion but in magic. In his *Essays*, first published in 1924, he justified his belief in magic thus:

"I believe in the practice and philosophy of what we have agreed upon to call magic, in what I must call the evocation of spirits, though I do not know what they are, in the power of creating magical illusions.... and I believe in the doctrines, which have, as I think, been handed down from early times, and been the foundation of nearly all magical practices. These doctrines are —

1. That the borders of our mind are ever shifting, and that many minds can flow into one another, as it were, and create or reveal a single mind, a single energy.
2. That the border so four memories are as shifting, and that our memories are a part of one great memory, the memory of Nature herself.
3. That this great mind and great memory can be evoked by symbols."

(Rudd, 20 and Wimsatt, 599).

Of human beings, Yeats did not believe in a unitary soul, but in twin souls: the primary soul and the anti-soul, or the self and the anti-self. During the first decade of the twentieth century, he remained engrossed in the problem of the duality of the self. He calls the anti-self the Mask that covers the self and thus obfuscates the perception of it. His preoccupation with the problem of the duality of the self-resulted in his *A Vision.* He was haunted by the problem and was torn to pieces on the debate of the two souls, as is evident from his poem 'A dialogue of Self and Soul' (1928). Richard Ellman, in his *Yeats: The Man and the Mask,* writes about Yeats's fretful condition during this period: "'Of all periods of Yeats's life the years from 1889 to 1903 are the most difficult to follow. He has so many interests and activities during this time, with so little relation between them, that a strictly chronological account would give the impression of a man in a frenzy, beating on every door in the hotel in an attempt to find out his own room. But while he was somewhat confused, the maze was not without plan, a clue to which can be found in his increasing self-consciousness. His inclination, which had begun much earlier, to pose before the world as something different from what he was, to hide his secret self, had come to a point where he saw himself divided into two parts." (Rudd, 21).

The opposition between the self and anti-self, as exposed by Yeats, refers us to the psychology of the Austrian psychoanalyst Carl Gustav Jung (1875-1961), though Yeats's psychology is to some extent different from Jung's. Jung found many parameters of the soul or self: the anima-animus, the persona-shadow, the old wise man and the earth mother, the conscious-unconscious, and the personal consciousness and the collective unconscious. According to him, as according to Hindu philosophy, the self has two dimensions or orientations—the higher and the lower. In ancient Chinese philosophy also the self was divided into two parts: *yang*, representing the light forces, and *yin*, representing the black or dark forces. According to Jung, in the multi-dimensional self, the anima, is opposed to the animus, the persona is opposed to shadow, and so on. He says that the individual is a syzygy of the self and the anti-self, of positivity and negativity. Jung said that the anti-self always tries to intrude into the functions of the self. Yeats also agreed upon this with Jung. Yeats confesses that in his poetic writings, he was somehow helped by his anti self. In his poem 'Ego dominus Tuus' he therefore invokes the help of his anti-self, hi*s döppelgánger, the daimon:*

> I call to the mysterious one who yet
> Shall walk the wet sands by the edge of the stream
> And look most like me, being indeed by double,
> And prove of all imaginable things
> The most unlike, being my anti-self,
> And standing by these characters disclose
> All that I seek.

Therefore, in Yeats also we find that the individual consists of the primary self and the anti-self or the Mask—i.e. the other half of the self. Again, like Jung, Yeats says that the Mask controls or disciplines the primary self and *vice versa*. This process Yeats termed enantiodromia. Further, Jung's concept of the persona is not very different from Yeats's concept of the Mask.

We may perhaps surmise that Yeats was somehow influenced, in this regard, by his contemporary psychoanalyst Jung, or, may be, Jung was influenced by Yeats, or may be, the two great minds thought in similar lines. It may be mentioned that Jung was also interested, like Yeats, in such things as magic, mysticism, mythology, symbolism, oriental philosophy, etc. However, W. W. Robson opines that actually it was Jung who rather got his ideas about mind or soul or self and its workings from Yeats. Robson says: "In his intuitive way Yeats had grasped the conception of the mind that psychoanalysis was to arrive at later. He was convinced that the conscious thought makes up only a small part of mind's activities. In his essay 'Magic' (1901) he anticipated Jung's theory of the collective unconscious of mankind, which Yeats calls the Great Memory. He explained the sudden leaps in the history of human thought by the intervention of 'unknown instructors'. No better explanation has been found." (Robson, 53). Again, Yeats distinguished between the notions of Soul and self. His notion of the Soul may be compared with the notion of the One and Infinite Supreme Self, as in the philosophy of the Indian philosopher Samkara, and his conception of the finite soul or self of the individual may be compared with Samkara's conception of the finite self. Yeats said that when the self, i.e., the finite self will loosen itself from the clutches of the material world and immerge itself with the One Supreme and Infinite Soul or Self, only then will it get liberated. This again reminds one of the philosophies of Samkara.

The tension between the self and the anti-self that tormented Yeats, was a concern also to T.S. Eliot (1888-1965). However, Yeats could hardly meet the conflicting demands of the body and those of the soul: the antithesis was insoluble. Even the poems of Yeats's last phase indicate this antithesis. Similarly, Eliot could hardly solve the duality or the bidimensionality of the soul, till he accepted the philosophy of the *Bhagvadgita:* "And do not think of the Suit of action./Fare forward." ('The Dry Salvages'). Though Yeats believed in the existence of both matter and spirit, yet he believed that spirit is superior to matter, and so he demanded that the spirit should dominate over the matter. It was with the aim of reinforcing his spirit for dominating over his body that Yeats joined the Rosicrucian Society. Rosicrucianism is a mystery edit and a blend of alchemism, esoterism and Christianity. It grew out of Protestantism while, in the 16th century, Protestantism with its mysticism and symbolism was about to be wiped out. Rosicrucianism believes in Pan Sophia or the World Soul or the White Queen and identifies Christ with the philosopher's stone. It believes that only Christ can lead man to the path of spirituality. Yeats got many of his symbols from his association with Rosicrucian Brothers. The Rosicrucian's believe that the conscious mind arises out of the unconscious mind, and that with the help of some mysterious means, such as incantation and use of symbols; the materials of the unconscious mind can be evoked to appear in the conscious mind. In this regard Yeats was thoroughly superstitious. He admitted in his *Ideas of Good and Evil* that he believed in "pre-ordained energies" and disembodied powers". Further, Yeats believed that Ireland had her buried memory of her past glory, richness of imageries, heroic ideals, and Christian culture. He wanted to revive the memory of Ireland's heritage and unify the memory of the past and the science of the present. He wanted to unify the spiritual and the material, and wanted the former to dominate the latter. His belief in the supremacy of the spiritual over the material world was confirmed by Indian philosophy that he learned from Mohini Chatterjee and, later on, from Purohit Swami. But though the two Indian philosophers taught him the meaninglessness of the material world, Yeats was firm in his conviction that the two worlds were complementary.

The Platonic influence on Yeats led the poet to see the world as a congeries of symbols and, at the most, to see the world itself as big symbol. A symbol denotes something else than itself for which it stands. Symbols are freely used in mysticism, magic, religion and psychoanalysis. When Plato said that this mundane world is but a shadow of the Real World, he used the world as a symbol. In poetry, symbols play a dominant role. Symbols are of two kinds: universal symbols, arising out of the collective unconscious, and personal symbols, invented by individuals. Yeats believed that we could control objects, that symbols refer to, by using appropriate symbols. His contention was in consonance with the theory of magic, for magicians used to use symbols to control nature. In the same way, poets use symbols to create beauty or arouse emotion. Like the mystic poet Blake, Yeats believed in the mysterious and important function of a symbol. Thus Yeats gave ontological status to both spirit and matter.

Yeats did not believe that the world is scattered into particular things; rather he maintained that the manifold of the world constitutes but one unity. Again, he said that there were no different worlds: no scientific world, no philosophical world and no poetic world; but there was only one world, variously interpreted by different persons of diverse persuasions. In the same way, each nation or nationality has its own unity that manifests through its literature, philosophy, mores, etc. Even the legends, folklores, art, magic, mysticism, etc. of a nation weave into a single texture. To this end of evolving a unity, Yeats tried to bring to gether poetry and nationalism, on the one hand, and magic, mysticism and philosophy, on the other.

Yeats quixotically believed that there was a correspondence between the changes of the moon and the changes in human personality. The life of a man corresponds with the life of the moon, i.e. like the 29 phases of the moon in which it waxes and wanes, man's personality also has changes. But each man's personality is primarily dominated by certain phase of the moon. For instance, Yeats was dominated by Phase 17 of the moon. The full-moon represents complete subjectivity and unity of being while the complete darkness of the moon represents absolute objectivity and disintegration of being. Complete objectivity or complete darkness of the moon is Phase 1 and complete subjectivity, or the full-moon is marked by Phase 15. In Phases 8 and 22, there are equilibria between subjectivity and objectivity. The dark sides of the moon represent the primary soul, and the bright sides the antithetical soul or self. The 29 Phases make a hill wheel that Yeats calls the Great Wheel of the Lunar Phases. Yeats drew the Great Wheel thus (Jeffares, 521):

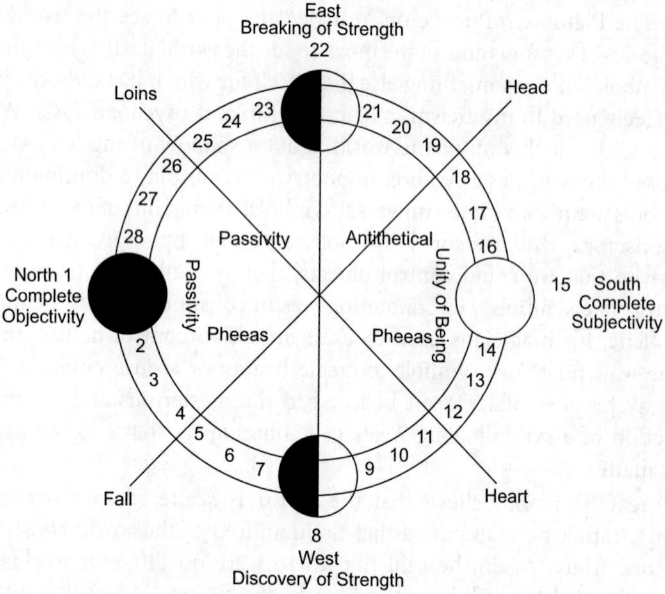

The Great Wheel of the Lunar Phases

It may be mentioned here in passing that Yeats's contemporary William Flies, an Austrian doctor and friend of Sigmund Freud, who died very young, also thought that he discovered that there was a sort of periodicity in the life of a man, though not related to the phases of the moon. (Jones, 252).

According to Yeats, not only human personality but also history is subject to changes. Like Oswald Spengler (1880-1936), the German philosopher, Yeats believed that civilizations are born, grow up into efflorescence and then experience decay and death; and, again, like the mythological phoenix it arises out of its ashes or ruins. This is Yeats's cyclical theory of history: history is like an ever-revolving wheel or gyre. His conception of the periodicity of man's life is in consonance with this cyclical theory of history. Apropos of this theory of history, Yeats believed that his contemporary European and Irish civilization reached their zenith, and so had begun to disintegrate and die. Here Spengler agrees with him. Spengler's *Decline of the West* assumes that each civilisation has a life of roughly 1,000 years, within which period it grows, matures and then declines and dies. Spengler saw Faustian features in the contemporary Western civilisation that desired to reach the apogee of every field of knowledge. Having reached the zenith of its development, the civilisation of the West had only its immediate precipitous fall ahead. Spengler's theory was partially foreshadowed by the German economist and social theorist Werner Sombart (1863-1941). But Sombart did not actually put forward the cyclical theory of history; he only said that each age had its particular kind of spirit that guide and dominate the civilisation of that age. We do not know if Yeats was influenced by Spengler and/or Sombart, but this much we can say that Yeats's cyclical theory of history was nothing very whimsical or wayward. In his poem 'The Second Coming', Yeats talks about the coming of a new civilisation after the fall of the present one, according to the biblical prophecy of Matthew xxiv and St. John's prediction in Apocalypse. Yeats himself annotated the poem and in course of his annotation, explained his cyclical theory of history or civilisation.

He wrote: "'The mind, whether expressed in history or in the individual life, has a precise movement, which can be quickened or slackened but cannot be expressed by a mathematical form. A plant or an animal has an order of development peculiar to it, a bamboo will not develop evenly like a willow, nor a willow from joint to joint, and both have branches, that lessen and grow more lighter as they rise, and no characteristic of the soil can alter these things.... To the Judwalis, as interpreted by Michael Robertes, all living mind has likewise a fundamental mathematical movement, however adopted in plant, or animal, or man to a particular circumstance; and when you have found this movement and calculated its relations, you can foretell the entire future of that mind. A supreme religious act of their faith is to fix the attention on the mathematical form of this movement; until the whole past and future of humanity, or of an individual man, shall be present to the intellect as if it were accomplished in a single moment. The intensity of the Beatific Vision when it comes depends upon the intensity of this realisation. It is possible in this way, seeing that death is itself marked upon the mathematical figure, which passes beyond it, to follow the soul in the highest heaven and the deepest hell. This doctrine is, they [the Judwalis] contend, not fatalistic because the mathematical figure is an expression of the mind's desire, and the more rapid the development of the figure the greater the freedom of the soul. The figure while the soul is in the body, or suffering from the consequences of that life, is frequently drawn as a double cone, the narrow end of each cone being in the centre of the broad end of the other.

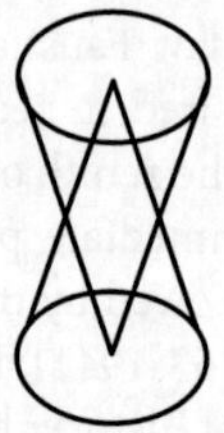

It had its origin from a straight line which represents, now time, now emotion, now subjective life, and plane at right angles to this line which represents, now space, now intellect, now objective life; while it is marked out by two gyres which represent the conflict, as it were, of plane and line, by two movements, which circle about a centre because a movement outward on the plane is checked by and in turn checks a movement onward upon the line; and the circling is always narrowing or spreading, because one movement or other is always the stronger. In other words, the human soul is always moving outward into the objective world or inward into itself; and this movement is double because the human soul would not be conscious were it not suspended between contraries, the greater the contrast the more intense the consciousness. The man who sees all reflected within himself, the subjective man, reaches the narrow end of a gyre at death, for death is always, they contend, even when it seems the result of an accident, preceded by an intensification of the subjective life; and has a moment of revelation immediately after death, a revelation which they describe as his being carried into the presence of all his dead kindred, a moment whose objectivity is exactly equal to the subjectivity of death. The objective man, on the other hand, whose gyre moves outward, receives at this moment the revelation, not of himself seen from within, for that is impossible to objective man, but of himself as if he were somebody else. This figure is true also of history, for the end of an age, which always revives the revelation of the character of the next age, is represented by the coming of one gyre to its place of greater expansion and of the other to that of its greatest contraction. At the present moment the life of gyre is sweeping outward, unlike that before the birth of Christ which was narrowing, and has almost reached its greatest expansion. The revelation which approaches will however take its character from the contrary movement of the interior gyre. All our scientific, democratic, fact-accumulating, heterogenous civilisation belongs to the outward gyre and prepares not the continuance of itself but the revelation as in a lightning flash, though in a flash that will not strike only in one place, and will for a time be constantly repeated, of the civilisation that must slowly take its place." (Jefiares, 201-03).

Daniel Albright very aptly explains Yeast's concept of gyre and his theory of human personality and history, which may be quoted here at some length. Albright writes: "Yeats's fullest participation in the world of images — the occult world, full of such outrageous entities as walking mummies, metal birds that scorn flesh, flames begotten of flame, the whole supernatural apparatus of such poems as 'Byzantium'— came through his wife's trances, her bouts of automatic writing and speech. The wisdom, the ſund of images bestowed by the spiritual Controls, were systematized in *A Vision* (1925, revised 1937). ..... The fundamental principle is that of the double gyre (a word Yeats pronounced with a hard g). Imagine two interlocked springing cones, the point of each screwing into the centre-point of the base of the other. Now imagine a cross-section of this contraption oscillating slowly from one base to the other and back. A cinematic image of this cross-section would show two concentric circles (let one be black, the ether white) expanding and contracting reciprocally. As the white circle grows larger, the black circle grows smaller, until the white circle reaches its maximum size, and the black circle dwindles to a point. Then the white circle starts to shrink, and the black circle starts to widen. As Yeats said of one of his diagrams, there 'two pulsations, one expanding, one contracting. I can see them like jelly fish in clear water'. (AV, p. 200).

"The double gyre was handy model for defining different relationships. Yeats had long conceived of the spiritual reality as something 180 degrees out of phase from normal reality: the lambs of faeryland were born in November while ours were born in spring (according to *The Hour Glass);* the boughs withered when we told them our dreams. The gyre of the spirit (faeryland, fantasy, art) expands as the gyre of commonplace life contracts. Throughout *A Vision* their chimes Yeats's favourite sentence of Heraclitus': gods and men are always 'Dying each other's life, living each other's death' (*A. V.*, pp. 68,197, 275).

"The double gyre could also be used to specify the dynamic of the human personality. In western philosophy, most models of the psyche are dualistic—based on the conflict of two principles. In Freudian psychology, for example, the id (un-differentiated lust and greed) is hampered or channelled by the superego (conscience, internalized restriction of conduct). In Plato's *Phaedurs*—a text that was an inspiration for the whole of *A Vision* —the Soul's chariot is pulled by two horses, a black horse hankering for earthly pleasure, snorting, difficult to control, and a white horse driving upwards towards divine ideals. Yeats's model is equally dualistic; and the two opposing principles that tug at us, vex us, almost tear us in two, he called the subjective (or *antithetical,* and the objective (or *primary).* Yeats's simplest formulation of the opposition is as follows: *The primary* is that which serves, the *antithetical* is that which creates' *(AV,* p. 85). Therefore the two basic drives of mankind are the urge to fantasize, to wish, to gratify wishes, and the urge to rest content in received reality. The balance between these competing urges describes the identify of each of us.

"Yeats discovered 26 basic personality types, which he plotted on the calendar of the lunar month, 28 days long. Two days were missing because an absolutely subjective personality (symbolically, the full of the moon, the 15th night—Phase 15, in his technical term was impossible to find on earth; we are all of us mixed, imperfect creatures. Similarly, an absolutely objective personality (the dark of the moon, Phase 1) was only a supernatural abstraction, never actually born. As the soul progressed from one incarnation to the next, it was usually reborn in the next Phase; so after 28 deaths and rebirths the soul returned to its starting-point on the Great Wheel of human personality. Each of us, therefore, has been everyone; I have been a farmer, a politician, a hero, a poet, a preacher, a pedant, as I have worked my way around the wheel.

"The objective gyre is at its maximum at Phase 1; the subjective gyre at Phase 15. Highly subjective people (such as Keats at Phase 14, Blake at Phase 16, Yeats at Phase 17) live in a state of creative fury; while highly objective people (Queen Victoria at Phase 24, John Calvin at Phase 25, cloddish farmers at Phase 2) submit themselves to external codes of behaviour, or to nature itself.....

"In another part of *A Vision,* Yeats described how history is governed by a similar scheme. Subjective and objective eras alternate; and on the largest scale (periods of 2000 years) each era is inaugurated by the birth of a god. The Christian era has provided mankind with 2000 years in which the objective virtues were taught: obedience, pity, chastity, self-abnegation before the abstract and rigid God. But before the birth of Christ came a subjective age, Greek antiquity, which prized the opposing virtues: beauty, aristocracy, sexual prowess, heroic splendour of conduct. The Christian era was beginning by a virgin birth; but the classical era was beginning by Aswan's rape of a girl (according to 'Leda and the Swan'); and the subjective age that will annihilate Christian virtue will come in AD 2000, when a rough beast slouches towards Bethlehem to be born (according to 'The Second Coming')....

"But the mathematics of Yeats's historical system is much complicated by the existence of gyres within gyres, wheels within wheels — some periods of 1000 years, other periods of some 500 years. Just as Ptolemy could describe any planetary motion by his unwieldly system of epicycles, so Yeats could account for any inconvenient deviations in history from circular perfection by appealing to some subsidiary system. He would have liked to name Charlemagne as the demigod initiating a subjective era beginning in AD 1000, but such finagling was difficult even for Yeats, since Charlemagne was crowned emperor on Christmas day, AD 800." (Albright, xxxix-xli). Yeats believed that his system of philosophy, psychology and history was scientific, and yet he called his system a 'magical' system. Cleanth Brooks writes: "Yeats has called his system 'magical' and the term may mislead us. Yeats even claims for the system a capacity for prediction. In 1917, in his 'Anima Hominis', he wrote: 'I do not doubt those heaving circles, those winding arcs, whether in one man's life or in that of an age, are mathematical, and that some in the world, or beyond the world, have foreknown the event and pricked upon the calendar the life-span of a Christ, a Buddha, a Napoleon'; and in the earlier edition of *A Vision*, there actually occurs a prophecy of the next two hundred years. But the system does not serve the ends of 'vulgar magic'. Yeats obviously does not propose to use his system to forecast the movements of the stock market, or to pick the winner of the Grand National."(Brooks, 177).

Yeats's philosophy and psychology are a curious mixture of mythology, mysticism, magic, Platonism, Neo-Platonism, etc. The congeries of all these contrived by him was to him a sort of religion. Unlike T.S. Eliot, he did not believe in the established religions, but himself created one which did not reject science, like those religions, but accommodated it within itself. About his own 'religion', he wrote in *his Autobiographies* (1955) that it was "almost an infallible Church of tradition, of a fardel of stories, and of personages, and of emotions, inseparable from their first expressions, passed on from generation to generation by poets and painters with some help from philosophers and theologians .... I had even created a Dogma: 'Because those imaginary people are out of the deepest instinct of man, to be his measure and his norm, whatever I can imagine those mouths speaking may be the nearest I can go to truth." (Jeffares, 4).

It is true that Yeats believed in superstitions, but this does not mean that he was an escapist in the sense in which the romantic poets were escapists. The romantic poets escaped from their scientific age and escaped into the sphere of the super naturals, while Yeats did not escape from science or anything else. He rather believed that science was as good a part of reality as the super naturals are, and that both science and the super naturals make up the whole reality. Only scientific and logical explanations are inadequate, and therefore he "wished for an account of experience which would surmount such defects: as he once put it, a philosophy which was at once 'logical and boundless." (Brooks, 175).

Chapter 5

Yeats's Theory of Poetry

It is very difficult to say anything definitely about Yeats's theory of poetry, for he had no constant theory, but his view about poetry underwent several changes, throughout his poetic life of nearly fifty years. As we have seen, his poetic life can be divided into four phases. In almost each phase, he had a different theory of poetry, and in each phase, he not only changed his style and technique, but also wrote about those styles and techniques, and it is good for us that he wrote much about poetic technique, like very few poets, like T.S. Eliot and Ezra Pound. Yeats's ideas and views about poetic techniques are strewn throughout his correspondences, Introductions to edited works, and in the Introductions to his own works. Besides, in *his Autobiographies, Ideas of Good and Evil* and *The Cutting of an Agate* also, he expressed his opinions about poetry.

In the first phase, Yeats enshrined lyricism and romanticism in poetry. In this phase, he was very much influenced by his father's attitude to poetry. His father, J.B. Yeats thought that poetry must be dramatic, well-defined, sharp with high resolution, and clear; and hated vagueness in poetry. He then highly prized lyricism in poetry, as a consequence of his taking Shelley as his ideal poet. In *Reveries Over Childhood and Youth,* Yeats "tells us that he made Shelley's *Prometheus Unbound* the first of his sacred books of poetic scripts. In *Four Years,* the next of his *Autobiographies,* the influence of Shelley is cited as having given him his two prime images. "'In later years,' he twites, 'my mind gave itself to gregarious Shelley's dream of a young man, his hair blanched with sorrow, studying philosophy in some long tower, or of his old man, master of all human knowledge, hidden from human sight in some shell-strewn cavern on the Mediterranean shore.'" (Hollander, 509). Here Yeats's hero-worshipping of Shelley is explicit. Besides Shelley, Yeats was also influenced by Blake and Spenser. During the first phase, Yeats's poetry was romantic in inspiration as well as technique. The romantic poets were Yeats's ideal and so he imitated their technique. The romantic poets were antipathetic to poetic rhetoric and to intrusion of rationality in the sphere of emotion. They believed that "True poetry had to eschew rhetoric and all its artificialities. It ought to be simple and spontaneous, and to seem 'natural' in something of the sense that a tree or a flower is natural. It could not be mechanically contrived but had to be organic; not derived from the top of the poet's head, but somehow an upsurge from the depths of his whole being.... At its best, a poetry so conceived attains to an art that conceals art." (Brooks, x). The romantic poetry is sensuous: multifarious sensuous images are here interwoven in an unified texture. There is a kind of symbolism in romantic poetry, for the romantic poets also built up pictures to communicate their feelings. Yeats started writing poetry on this romantic tradition with all its themes and techniques. Cleanth Brooks writes: "Today I should want to lay more stress on the extent to which Eliot, Yeats, and the other modern poets built upon the Romantic tradition and incorporated structural devices that are a part of the general Romantic inheritance." (Brooks, xiv).

In the first phase, Yeats believed that the themes of poetry were not confined within the bounds of beautiful objects of nature and human passions grown out of human relations, but might include mythology, folklore, nationalism, etc. He also believed that poetry should be a means of escape from the hard realities of life. With this belief he engaged himself in writing poetry of escape. He sought for themes in the Irish mythology and folklores. Yeats's father believed that poetry should be dramatic, a belief that later on we find in Eliot. Being persuaded by his father, Yeats wrote dramatic poetry. In the poems of Yeats's first phase, one also promptly finds colourfulness and personalistic approach. The poems of this phase are also dreamy and sonorous. However, in spite of all these, perhaps we cannot say that he had any established theory of poetry, during the first phase. Whatever he wrote he wrote only in imitation of others, like Shelley, Blake and Spenser. He wrote about the beauty of nature, its abandon, its colours, its communicativeness and its sympathy with one who suffers. He thought that poetry must be personal: it must give expression to the intense tragedy of the poet and must evoke like feeling in the reader. Of course he, even in his later life, did not move away from this conviction completely. In 1937, only two years before his death, he wrote in the General Introduction to his works: "A poet writes always of his personal life, in his finest work out of his tragedy, whatever it be, lost love, or mere loneliness." (Rajan, 16). Yet we must say that he wrote about more personal things in his earlier phases, like Sappho, than in his later phases. He might, then, have said, like Symons, that "'the poet has no more part in society than a monk in domestic life.'. (MacLeish, 111). At that time Yeats's motto was that art is for life's sake, for it is a sort of escapade. Thought later on he changed his stance to say that art is for art's sake, he always maintained the independence of art. For instance, in his poem 'Lapis Lazuli', written iii 1938, he "maintains stubbornly the independence of art and the priority of its concerns to those of the State." (Rosenthal, 33)

Roughly around 1903, Yeats began to reformulate his poetic theory and technique, and almost immediately this change in his conception of poetry influenced Ezra Pound to write modern poetry. Yeats himself wrote about this change in his conception of poetry: "'My work has got more masculine. It has more salt in it'.... 'the error of late periods like this is to believe that some things are inherently poetical'.... 'I believe more strongly every day that the element of strength in poetic language is common idiom.'" (Ford, 170). This change was not confined within the sphere of diction only, but was effective in his total view of poetry. Yeats now began to believe that art was not for life's sake, but for simply art's sake. He thought that poetry could have no other vocation than expressing different forms of beauty or expressing beauty in different forms. He was now no more interested in the ancient folklore and mythology of Ireland, and turned to the concrete modern reality around him. The experience of the concrete reality did not stand in his way of *writing pure poetry,* i.e. poetry whose sole concern is simply beauty. He was now no more interested in painting the beauty of landscapes and the exploits of his early years' mythological heroes. He began to give expression to the pure flow of sensation that was evoked by everything around—beautiful, wholesome, or no. In his early poetry, he wanted to give expression to romantic feelings and agonies, but now in his later verses, he wanted to seek the *truth* behind the reality. He also shaded off all his earlier decorations and embroideries from his poems, as is evident from his poem 'A Coat'. He did no longer write his 'vision' into poetry, but looked into the inner regard of his self to seek the fountain of poetic inspiration. About this time, he wrote in a letter to his father about the change in his attitude to poetry: "'All our art is but the putting our faith... into words or forms and our faith is in ecstasy. Of recent years instead of 'vision', meaning by vision the intense realization of a state of ecstatic emotion symbolized in a definite imagined region, I have tried for more self-portraiture.'" (Albright, xxxi).

But though he began to introduce self-portraiture in his poetry, the self-portraiture was never autobiography. It was rather the expression of the universal feeling localised in his self. In his later poetry, Yeats thought that poetry should be liberated from the age in which it occurs and also from the life of the poet, to wit from the personal equations of the poet. He said that poetry must be non-personal; it must be universal; and it must be shorn of all sorts of external decorations. Though he changed his view of poetry, yet his early poetic technique continued to remain with him till his publication *of Responsibilities* 1914, and he began to write poems in the new technique since *The Wild Swans at Coole* that he published in 1919. The water-shade between his early style and his later style can be seen in the poems written between these two collections of poems. This changeover in his attitude to poetry and its technique was due to several factors that influenced Yeats. There was, for one thing, the symbolist movement in poetry that originated in France, principally at the hands of such masters as Laforgue and Baudlaire. Yeats was so much influenced by this movement that he said that he could not think but in symbols. The expressionist, impressionist and other sorts of movement in poetry of the early part of 20th century also influenced Yeats. As a result of all these, his poetry became more and more complex, and he was gradually moving away from his early lyric poetry of simple thought and simple technique. His diction also changed phenomenally: he began to use colloquial diction, *a la* Ezra Pound and Eliot.

In his later poetry or mature poetry, Yeats was of the opinion that poetry is the expression of the soul and not of the mind, as according to Pound and Eliot. He now held the highest value for poetry, and said that the quintessence of all poetry is its sincerity and that this sincerity can be achieved only when the poet, without sitting on the rational plane, submits himself at the command of his subconscious, or, may beat the command of his unconscious. Therefore, poetry should be personal, and that the universal in poetry must be expressed through the particulars of the poet. He believed that literature is always personal, because it is the expression of the artist's or the poet's personal view of the life and world around him. Actually both the early and the late poems of Yeats are personal to some extent, and in this regard, he is quite different from both Pound and Eliot who believed in the objectivity of poetry. W.W. Robson writes: "Yeats's poetry is the record of a personal drama which must be understood as a whole. It is not that he is a confessional poet. He omits much that the curious might like to know about his life and circumstances; and what he leaves in, he often alters. He selects, he arranges, he dramatizes. This is a matter of deliberate literary theory for Yeats." (Robson, 51). Yes, Yeats reveals his partial biography in his poetry and, nevertheless, we must not forget that he always wore a mask. But there are not only personal elements in Yeats's poetry, for had it been so, it would have been buried with his coffin. There is also universal appeal in his poems. In addition to this, there is some philosophy—universal philosophy—in his poems. Graham Hugh in his '*Epilogue*': 'Conversation in Limbo' (between W.B. Yeats and H.G. Wells) in his book *The Last Romantics*, rightly puts into the mouth of Yeats the following speech, because Yeats really believed in it: "... whatever philosophy has been made poetry is alone permanent." (Hugh, 265).

It is generally held that the opposite of poetry is science, because while the province of the former is emotion, the province of the latter is logic and intellect. Therefore, the further away one is from the other the better. I.A. Richards, among others, subscribes to this view. "Yeats, on the contrary, instead of breaking science and poetry completely apart, has preferred to reunite these elements in something of the manner in which they are fused in a religion. His system has for him, consequently, the authority and meaning of a religion, combining intellect and emotion as they were combined before the great analytic and abstracting process of modern science broke them apart. In short, Yeats has created for himself a myth." (Brooks, 176). Yeats, likewise, tried to combine poetry and dream. He said that the poet should appeal to his subconscious and, may be, also to his unconscious. Poetry must not be the effect of conscious exercises, but it must come out from the inner niché of the poet's mind, like the dream, spontaneously. Again, poetry may be compared, Yeats said, with music, for like music, poetry should be supra-rational. In fact, it was Edgar Allan Poe (1809-49) who first saw the analogy between poetry and dream, and between poetry and music. Nearly a century later, Yeats found the analogy very appropriate. William K. Wimsatt, Jr. and Cleanth Brooks write: "dream and music were used by Poe to suggest the special kinds of purity that he demanded of poetry, and this analogizing of poetry to dream and to music was to run all the way through the speculations of the French symbolists. Poe refers to *Marginalia* to 'points of time where the confines of the waking world blend with those of the world of dreams. Nearly a century later, Poe's very phrasing returns to us in a passage of one of W.B. Yeats's last poems, referring to

... "forms that are or seem
When sleepers wake and yet still dream,
And when it's vanished still declare,
With only bed and bedstead there,
That heavens had opened" (Wimsatt, 589).

Regarding use of words, Yeats was very careful: he was never sloppy, vague or absent-minded. He used words after carefully weighing them; he always, particularly in his mature poems, wanted to be absolutely perfect in using words. Daniel Albright writes: .... Yeats hated vagueness. He spent years in editing an edition of William Blake's poetry (published in 1893), and he quoted with approval Blake's expostulation against chiaroscuro—his hatred of 'blot and blur' and his preference for 'firm and determinate outline'. Blake learned this from his master, the engraver James Brasire; and Yeats might have learned a similar lesson from his father, who partly followed the pre-Raphaelite style, a style in which shallow fields were often constructed from profuse fine detail." (Albright, xx). We may remember that Yeats in his youth wanted to be a painter, like his father, and whatever he painted he did with sharp resolution, and this fascination for sharp outlines he retained to his last. But he did not delineate in his poetry with precision the concrete things of nature, but rather the objects of his imagination, for he was naturally a subjective poet. Daniel Albright again writes: "But Yeats wanted precision and security of outline, not in order to specify what his physical eye saw, but to specify what his imagination saw. Yeats hated dualism. For Yeats, as for the Romantic poets he loved, there were two chief species of art: one mimetic and factual, the other subjective, luminous; one the mirror, the other the lamp." (Albright, xxi).

Was Yeats more in favour of the form than in favour of the content of a poem, or the other way round? Daniel Albright answers this question thus: "The young Yeats thought that modern art has triumphed by a steady emptying of its contents. He believed that Wordsworth, Tennyson, Browning had all erred by overinclusion—by trying to absorb into their work science, politics, philosophy, ethics, until their poems became hopelessly heavy, distended. "But after the turn of the century, a counter movement begins to be felt in Yeats's work. Instead of cultivating disembodiment, Yeats argued in favour of a new physicalness, a new solidity of gesture. In a letter of 1903, he wrote: 'I am no longer in much sympathy with an essay like 'The Autumn of the Body'.... The close of the last century was full of a strange desire to get out of form, to get to some kind of disembodied beauty, and now it seems to me the contrary impulse has come. I feel about me and in me an impulse to create form, to carry the realization of beauty as far as possible.' And next day, he restated this: 'I have always felt that the soul has two movements primarily: one to transcend form, and the other to create forms.... I think I to some extent got weary of that God Dionysus, and I am hoping that the Far-Darter (Appollo, the God of forms will come in his place."' (Albright, xxviii-xxix). From this it is clear that Yeats was ambivalent to the problem of form and content in poetry. Nevertheless, we can say that in the mature poetry of his later phases, Yeats was more inclined towards the form rather than towards the content. But, at the same time, we must not forget that he could never reconcile himself with the idea of lessening the proper importance of the content of the poem; and in this sense, he was never a perfect aesthete. Daniel Albright writes: "And yet, despite Yeats's unworldliness, his concentration on art, it is a mistake to think of Yeats as an aesthete. No poet believed less in art-for-art's-sake; far from exalting style, he exalted the subject matter of art: 'I was so angry with the indifference to subject, which was the commonplace of all (recent) art criticism... that I could at times see nothing else but subject'. In his essay on Cavalcanti, Pound stated an opinion about art, an opinion with which Yeats agreed: 'The best Egyptian sculpture is magnificent plastic; but its force comes from a non-plastic idea, i.e. the god is inside the statue.'" (Albright, xxv).

Regarding the content, in his mature poetry, Yeats was interested in the portrayal of corporeality in terms of symbols. He was interested in the human body, in its details. Daniel Albright writes: "Yeats was not the only modern writer who tried to heighten the corporeality of his work. Indeed certain poets in the later nineteenth century had already laboured to make art more vibrant, more physically stimulating. Many of Yeats's later contemporaries also contributed to the literature of the body — D.H. Lawrence and James Joyce, with the exact descriptions of engorged tissue and intestinal upheavals. Even T.S. Eliot, often fastidious about bodily functions, commended poets whose 'words have often a network of tentacular roots reaching down to the deepest terrors and desires' (Selected Essays, p. 135); and further wrote that a poet is not looking deep enough if he obeys the old advice 'to look into our hearts and write': "Racine or Donne looked into a good deal more than the heart. One must look into the cerebral cortex, the nervous system, and the digestive tracts' (p. 250). And yet Yeats's interest in the body differs from Joyce's and Eliot's, and perhaps from Lawrence's, in that everybody is an embodiment of something—vehicle chosen by a spirit for external expression." (Albright, xxx).

It needs a great effort, a great skill, to evoke the supra-physical in the physical—to bring in the extra-terrestrial in the terrestrial. Yeats performed this oeuvre with the help of manipulating the common language and with the help of specialised symbols. It also needed a great skill to express the universal in the particular, to express the formless in the form; and Yeats did this feat masterfully, again with the help of images, brought from the universal storehouse of images he called the Anima Munch or the Soul of the World. He believed that each man has this store house of images, and that when one is able to tune himself with this storehouse of images, he is able to experience poetic vision, revelation or miracle. But what sort of images did Yeats seek? "In general he favoured images of extravagance. He assumed the world of experience comprises punny, deformed, incomplete, perishing things; whereas the world of imagination comprises things that are excessive, immeasurable, autonomous, triumphant. What he especially esteemed in the Old Irish literature was a quality of superhuman abundance: he wrote of some translations of Galelic love songs 'they seem to be continually straining to express a something which lies beyond the possibility of expression.'" (Albright, xxii).

Yeats was very serious and careful about his verses, and always wanted appropriate images to express his ideas. He was frequently conscious about his mask or anti-self, while writing poetry, for he thought that poetry is much influenced by the anti-self. "Yeats, as man and as poet, was unusually afraid of incoherence, the sensation of being soft wax". (Albright, xxxvi). Yeats writes about the evolution of his poetry: "'I had set out on life with the thought of putting my very self into poetry... I thought of myself as something unmoving and silent living in the middle of my own mind and body... Then one day I understood quite suddenly, as the way is, that I was seeking something unchanging and unmixed and always outside myself, a Stone or an Elixir that was always out of reach, and that I myself was the fleeting thing that held out its hand. The more I tried to make my art deliberately beautiful, the more did I follow the opposite of myself...'" (Albright, xxxvi). From this, perhaps, we may presume that Yeats believed that poetic creations are at least partially unconscious creations.

Lastly, a few words about Yeats's punctuation and rhetoric. And again let us quote Daniel Albright at some length: "He (Finnetan) supposes (as did Curtis Bradford) that Yeats's punctuation was rhetorical rather than grammatical, an imaginative attempt to notate breath-pauses, stresses, and so forth; and that the bizarre punctuation in some of Yeats's later poems is due to the influence of experimental modernists such as T.S. Eliot and Laura Riding. I suppose that Yeats was too ignorant of punctuation to make his deviations from standard practice significant. Although Yeats surely wished to make his canon a text worthy of reference, he conceived poetry as an experience of the ear, not of the eye. He could not spell even simple English words; he went to his grave using such forms as *intreage* and *professorship.* Finally, Yeats himself admitted, 'I do not understand stops. I write my work so completely for the ear that I feel helpless when I have to measure pauses by stops and commas.' "Among Yeats's punctuational quirks were these: he rarely used hyphens; he did not like to enclose vocatives in commas; and he often neglected to put commas before quotations, or to capitalize the first word in a quotation." (Albright, xiviii). Yeats was a transcendental poet; he was more concerned with the intensity of feelings and passions; and this was, perhaps, why he committed so many common grammatical errors like neglectful schoolboys.

Chapter 6

Forty-one Selected Poems

CROSSWAYS —1889

Yeats's early poems are replete with romantic mood, Irish mythology and dreaminess. They are the products of his romantic striving for an escapade into an imaginary Arcadia far more perfect than the real and ancient Arcadia in Peloponnesus that was a pastoral paradise on earth. Yeats himself said: ....“When I first wrote went here and there for my subjects as my reading led me, preferred to all other countries Arcadia and the India of Romance.’” (Jeffares, 3-4). *Crossways,* a collection of poems, mostly taken from an earlier volume, *The Wanderings of Oisin and Other Poems* (1889), was published in 1889. The title *Crossways* was chosen “because in these poems he ‘tried many pathways.’” Yeats himself wrote about *Crossways* in 1925: “‘Many of the poems in *Crossways,* certainly those upon Indian subjects or upon shepherds and fauns, must have been written before I was twenty, for from the moment I began *The Wandering of Oisin,* which I did at that age, I believe, my subject matter became Irish.’” (Jeffares, 3). This collection of poems was dedicated to the poet's boyhood friend George William Russell (1867-1935)—a mystic, a poet, a painter and the editor of *Irish Statesman* — whose pen-name was Aeon, or simply AE (shortened from Aeon). The epitaph of this collection is: ‘*The stars are threshed, and the souls are threshed from their husks.*’—William Blake. It was taken from Blake's poem ‘Night the Ninth being the Last Judgement’ occurring in his *Vala, or the Four Zoas.* MacNeice says that during the early phase, Yeats wrote in the romantic tradition, which was represented by Keats, Tennyson, Rossetti and such others. MacNeice writes that “One of the chief characteristics of this line of poets — in their better poems — is an autumnal, almost a morbid, languor. The Isle of the Lotus Eaters. Keats, Tennyson, Rossetti, each of them has a remarkable eye and an ear for verbal music, but they looked at the world through glasses coloured with self-pity and their music is sultry, overcharged with emotions accumulated during the summer and waiting for some thunderstorm to freshen them or clear them away." (Bloom, 108). The poems of *Crossways* betray this romantic mood and the techniques of the romantic poets.

1. The Song of the Happy Shepherd

This poem was written in 1885 and was first published in *Dublin University Review* (Oct., 1885) where it was entitled 'An Epilogue'. Later on, when it was published in *The Wanderings of Oisin and Other Poems* (1889), it was re-entitled 'Song of the Last Arcadian' and when finally it was printed in *Crossways,* it got this present title.

THE SONG OF THE HAPPY SHEPHERD

The woods of Arcady are dead,
And over is their antique joy;
Of old the world on dreaming fed;
Grey truth is now her painted toy;
Yet still she turns her restless head:
But O, sick children of the world,
Of all the many changing things
In dreary dancing past us whirled,
To the cracked tune that Chronos sings,
Words alone are certain good.
Where are now the warring kings,
Word be-mockers? — By the Rood,
Where are now the warring kings?
An idle word is now their glory,
By the stammering schoolboy said,
Reading some entangled story:
The kings of the old time are dead;
The wandering earth herself may be
Only a sudden flaming word,
In clanging space a moment heard,
Troubling the endless reverie.

Then nowise worship dusty deeds,
Nor seek, for this is also sooth,
To hunger fiercely after truth,
Lest all thy toiling only breeds

New dreams, new dreams; there is no truth
Saving in thine own heart. Seek, then,
No learning from the starry men,
Who follow with the optic glass?
The whirling ways of stars that pass —
Seek, then, for this is also sooth,
No word of theirs—the cold star-bane
Has cloven and rent their hearts in twain,
And dead is all their human truth.
Go gather by the humming sea
Some twisted, echo-harbouring shell,
And to its lips thy story tells,
And they thy comforters will be,
Rewarding in melodious guile
Thy fretful words a little while,
Till they shall singing fade in ruth
And die a pearly brotherhood;
For words alone are certain good:
Sing, then, for this is also sooth.

I must be gone: there is a grave
Where daffodil and lily wave,
And I would please the hapless faun,
Buried under the sleepy ground,
With mirthful songs before the dawn.
His shouting days with mirth were crowned.
And still I dream he treads the lawn,
Walking ghostly in the dew,
Pierced by my glad singing through,
My songs of old earth's dreamy youth:
But ah! she dreams not now; dream thou!
For fair are poppies on the brow:
Dream, dream, for this is also sooth.

As we have seen, Yeats's early poems are poems of escapade. In this poem also, the youthful poet escapes from the world of science, from the materialistic world, and escapes into the world of dreams, into Arcady, a district of ancient Greece, whose simple-minded people were given to pastoral life with music and dancing. Being primitives, they were not vitiated by science or artificial civilisation. The poet is frustrated, and he bewails the loss of the Arcadian life: "The woods of Arcady are dead,/ And over is their antique joy". He calls the ancient wisdom of these people grey truths. He believes that "one should believe whatever had been believed in all countries and periods, and only reject any part of it after much evidence, instead of starting all over afresh and only believing what one could prove." (Jeffares, 4). But now this ancient wisdom has been rejected by the scientific world. As a consequence of this, the people of the scientific world are suffering, and so the poet invites the "sick children of the world"—the joyless materialistic-minded people—to seek joy in poetry, because "Words alone are certain good." The poet urges upon us to look at the dancing past tuned to the songs of Chronos, one of the Titans. He says that science, civilisations and even the powers of kings are transitory, and that these ultimately live only in words or in some stories. The poet calls the past Kings "Word be-mockers", because they mocked at words, as they believed not in words but in actions. He vows on the "Rood" or the Cross on which Jesus Christ was crucified that these kings are no more present now, but only in words, i.e. in the songs of the poet about them.

Therefore, in the second stanza of the poem, the poet urges upon the inhabitants of the modern materialistic world to renounce the worship of science: "Then nowise worship dusty deeds". He also advises them not to run after truth: 'To hunger fiercely after truth". Because, the discovery of one truth will only incite one to run after another truth—to "New dreams, new dreams". The poet says that truth lies only within the heart, and so it is vain to go to wise men with powerful glasses, with "optic glass", for gathering knowledge about science ("The whirling ways of stars that pass —"). The "optic glass" refers to Galilio's use of telescope with which scientists scan the sky and discover new planets. The discoveries of science have only rent into shrades the human heart. So the poet advises the science-sick modern man to go to the sea and collect conch-shell and blow it to create sound (or word) to freshen his heart. Of course after some time the sound will die away, but before that the sound will bind people's hearts together, so that they will "die a pearly brotherhood". The poet again says that words, including singing, alone are really good: "For words alone are certain good."

In the last stanza, the poet says that he must go to where there are daffodils and lilies, fauns and "mirthful songs" of youth. While the whole world remains forgetful of fantasies, the poet urges upon everyone to go and get the influence of the narcotic poppies, to forget the caustic cares of the material world, and be wafted away in a dream-land, because the dreamland is as real as the material world, and is more soothing and wholesome.

In this poem, the poet contrasts the olden days with the modern age.

The ancient life, he says, was like the life in paradise, full of mirth and merriment. In that age, people were innocent, bereft of the pretenses of science, but were full of love and songs and dreams. Comparing the one with the other, the poet questions which of the two is better, and himself answers that the olden time was better than the modern age, because in the modern age of science, there is no life—life that was full-blown in the pre- scientific age. Therefore, he bemoans the lost life of the past, for he cannot bear with the inanity of the scientific age. He thinks that he is not alone in this regard, but all other people are also suffering the same inanity in the scientific-materialistic age, and are leading joyless lives. This is why he is calling the "sick children of the world" to leave behind the pursuits of science and go back to the dreamy world of yore. For, to him, the dream world is no less real and true than the world of science; and, moreover, because the dream-world has much mirth to proffer, while the scientific world can offer us only *schmerz* or pain.

The poem contains many of the qualities of Yeats's early poetry: an urge for an idyllic life — a life of dreams and songs and listlessness; his "monkish hatred" for science; his Keatsian epithets; etc. Some of Yeats's Keatsian epithets and images in this poem are: "painted toy", "endless reverie", "starry men", "humming sea", "pearly brotherhood", etc. The poem is very lyrical; at places his lyricism wafts him away and he moves on the crest of music. The descriptions of the scenes and images are generally pre-Raphaelite. Daniel Albright comments on *Crossways:* "Though its verbal textures show a refined metrical sense, and its images and figures are carefully crafted, *Crossway* has little of the thematic concentration of the other volumes, to read it is to stroll through a Palace of Art decorated with panels of remote and exotic landscapes." (Albright, 413). This comment of Albright is very much appropriate in the case of this poem. The poem suffers from prolixity; the message could well be communicated with greater precision and compactness.

2. Anashuya and Vijaya

The poem, written in 1887, first appeared in *The Wanderings of Oisin and Other Poems* (1889), with the title 'Jealousy'. The character Anashuya ('Anashuya' in Sanskrit means 'charity') has been taken from *Ramayana.* She is the wife of *Rishi* Atri, and lives with her husband in the forest of Chitrakuta. She is a friend of Sakuntala. Yeats, perhaps, took the story of Anashuya and Vijaya from Kalidas's (3rd century A.D.) play *Sakuntala* translated by Monier Williams. In a note, dated 1925, Yeats wrote that the "little Indian dramatic scene was meant to be the first scene of a play about a man loved by two women, who had the one soul between them, the one woman walking when the other slept, and knowing but daylight as the other only night. It came to my head when I saw at Rosses Point (in Sligo) carrying two salmons. 'One man with two souls,' I said, and added, 'O no, two people with one soul.' I am now once more in *A Vision* busy with the thought, the antithesis of day and night and of moon and sun." (Jeffares, 6).

ANASHUYA AND VIJAYA

A little Indian temple in the Golden Age. Around it a garden; around that the forest. Anashuya, the young priestess, kneeling within the temple.

Anashuya. Send peace on all the lands and flickering com.—
O, may tranquillity walk by his elbow
When wandering in the forest, if he loves
No other. — Hear, and may the indolent flocks
Be plentiful. — And if he loves another,
May panthers end him. — Hear, and load our king
With wisdom hour by hour. — May we two stand,
When we are dead, beyond the setting suns,
A little from the other shades apart,
With mingling hair and play upon one lute.

Vijaya *[entering and throwing a lily at her]*. Hail! hail, my Anashuya.

Anashuya. No: be still.
I, priestess of this temple, offer up
Prayers for the land.

Vijaya. I will wait here, Amrita.

Anashuya. By mighty Brahma's ever-rustling robe,
Who is Amrita? Sorrow of all sorrows!
Another fills your mind.

Vijaya. My mother's name.

Anashuya. [*sings, coming out of the temple*].
A sad, sad thought went by me slowly:
Sigh, O you little stars! O sigh and shake your blue apparel!
The sad, sad thought has gone from me now wholly:
Sing, O you little stars! O sing and raise your rapturous carol
To mighty Brahma, he who made you many as the sands,
And laid you on the gates of evening with his quiet hands
[*sits down on the steps of the temple*].

Vijaya, I have brought my evening rice;
The sun has laid his chin on the grey wood,
Weary, with all his poppies gathered round him.,

Vijaya. The hour when Kama, full of sleepy laughter,
Rises, and showers abroad his fragrant arrows,
Piercing the twilight with their murmuring barbs.

Anashuya. See how the sacred old flamingoes come,
Painting with shadow all the marble steps:
Aged and wise, they seek their wonted perches
Within the temple, devious walking, made
To wander by their melancholy minds.
Yon tall one eyes my supper; chase him away,
Far, far away. I named him after you.
He is a famous fisher; hour by hour
He ruffles with his bill the minnowed streams.
Ah! there he snaps my rice. I told you so.
Now cuff him off. He's off! A kiss for you,
Because you saved my rice. Have you no thanks?

Vijaya. [*sings*]. *Sing you of her, O first few stars,*
Whom Brahma, touching with his finger, praises, for you hold
The van of wandering quiet; are you be too calm and old,
Sing, turning in your cars,
Sing, till you raise your hands and sign, and from your car-heads peer,
With all your whirling hair, and drop many an azure tear.

Anashuya. What know the pilots of the stars of tears?

Vijaya. Their faces are all worn, and in their eyes
Flashes the fire of sadness, for they see
The icicles that famish all the North,
Where men lie frozen in the glimmering snow;
And in the flaming forests cower the lion
And lioness, with all their whimpering cubs;
And, ever pacing on the verge of things,
The phantom, Beauty, in a mist of tears;
While we alone have round us woven woods,
And feel the softness of each other's hand,
Amrita, while—

Anashuya [*going away from him*]

Ah me ! you love another,

[*Bursting into tears.*]

And may some sudden dreadful ill befall her!

Vijaya. I loved another, now I love no other.
Among the mouldering of ancient woods
You live, and on the village border she,
With her old father the blind wood-cutter;
I saw her standing in her door but now.

Anashuya. Vijaya, swear to love her never more.

Vijaya. Ay, ay.

Anashuya. Swear by the parents of the gods.
Dread oath, who dwell on sacred Himalaya,
On the far Golden Peak; enormous shapes,
Who still were old when the great sea was young;
On their vast faces mystery and dreams;
Their hair along the mountains rolled and filled
From year to year by the unnumbered nests
Of aweless birds, and round their stirless feet
The joyous flocks of deer and antelope,
Who never hear the unforgiving hound?
Swear!

Vijaya. By the parents of the gods, I swear.

Anashuya. [*sings*]. *I have forgiven, O new star!*
Maybe you have not heard of us, you have come forth so newly,
You hunter, of the fields afar!
Ah ! you will know my loved one by his hunter's arrows truly, shoot on him shafts of quietness, that he may ever keep A lonely laughter, and may kiss his hands to me in sleep.
Farewell, Vijaya. Nay, no word, no ward;
I priestess of this temple, offer up
Prayer for the land

O Brahma, guard in sleep
The merry lambs and the complacent kine,
The flies below the leaves, and the young mice
In the tree roots, and all the sacred flocks
Of red flamingoes; and my love, Vijaya;

And may no restless fay with fidget finger
Trouble his sleeping: give him dreams of me.

This is a dramatic and lyric poem with a romantic theme. Anashuya, a young priest, is jealous, or imagines being jealous, of her lover Vijaya who, she imagines, loves another woman. Anashuya prays to Brahma in the temple for Vijaya's peace and tranquillity on condition that he will love no other woman. But if he does, prays she, "May panthers end him." Meanwhile, Vijaya arrives there and calls her by the name of Amrita. At this, Anashuya is afraid that Vijaya really loves another woman of that name. But her fear vanishes when Vijaya says that Amrita is the name of his mother. Anashuya then sings that her "sad thought has gone from me now wholly". She tells Vijaya that she has brought her "evening rice" when it is evening and the sun is inclining towards the west being influenced by poppies. Vijaya adds that just at this time Kama, the god of love, wields his sway over love among human beings. Anashuya says that the old bright red-coloured birds, flamingoes, came to eat away her rice but Vijaya drove them away. She thanks Vijaya for that. Then Vijaya sings to the stars and asks them to sing for Anashuya and "*drop many an azure tears.*" Anashuya asks why the stars are mournful and Vijaya replies that they are mournful because the icicles are famishing in the North (Himalaya) and the phantom, Beauty, is "in a mist of tears". But, Vijaya adds, they (himself and Anashuya) are in love-lock: "While we alone have round us woven woods./ And feel the softness of each other's hand".

But Anashuya is still apprehensive and blatantly tells Vijaya: "Ah me! you love another", and bursts into tears and curses that unknown woman. Moved, Vijaya consoles her by saying that once he really loved another woman, but "now I love no other." Anashuya urges upon Vijaya to swear upon this: "Swear by the parents of gods". Richard Ellmann says that by the parents of gods Yeats probably meant "the Tibetan adepts Koot-Hoomi and Morya, the masters of Madame Blavatsky whom Yeats saw on her door in poorly drawn pictures supposed to have been tele pathetically projected." (Jeffares, 6). However, Vijaya complies with her supplication: "By the parents of gods, I swear." Reassured of Vijaya's love for her, Anashuya now sings again. In her song she appeals to the stars to shoot on Vijaya "shafts of quietness, that he may ever keep. A lonely laughter, and may kiss his hands to me in sleep." Anashuya then bids farewell to Vijaya and prays to Brahma for the prosperity of the land and urges upon Brahma to guard every creature of the world, and, particularly, "my love, Vijaya". She prays, further, so that Brahma may give Vijaya quiet sleep and dreams of her: "give him dreams of me."

Like the previous one, this is also a romantic poem, and is as immature. It suffers from prolixity and flaws in syntax. But it nicely treats with an Indian theme in an Irish setting. The lyrical and dramatic qualities of the poem are really very enjoyable.

3. The Stolen Child

The poem was first printed *in Irish Monthly* in December, 1886, and later on it appeared in *Crossways* (1889). It has a speciality in that it was in this poem that Yeats for the first time painted the Irish scenario, instead of the Arcadian or Indian. The poem is lyrical and romantic, and it bears the evidence of Yeats's mythopoeia and escaping tendency. The poet can hardly bear with the grey science and the bustle of the modern technological age, and so pines for verdure, shade, serenity, and the dream-land of the faeries. It also betrays Yeats's belief in supernatural phenomena. In fact, he believed that the faeries are the necessary causal link between supernatural beings like the gods, and the things of the concrete world. When the poem first appeared in *Irish Monthly,* the poet added a note to it. He wrote: "The places mentioned are round about Sligo. Further, Rosses is a very noted fairy locality. There is here a little point of rocks where, if anyone falls asleep, there is danger of their waking silly, the fairies having carried off their souls." (Jeffares, 11). Daniel Albright in his edition of Yeats's poems writes: "This is a poem about the seduction of a child by faeries, in the tradition of Goethe's Der Erlkonig'. Yeats later wrote a play on this theme, *The Land of Heart's Desire* (1894), in which the child's surrender to the faery enticement is equivalent (as in Goethe's poem) to death, The Indian lovers of 'The Indian to his Love' seek an erotic refuge from the world's sadness; the Stolen Child seeks a refuge of pure play. The faeries are like immortal children, hiding berries, chasing bubbles, mischievously distorting the dreams of fish." (p. 423).

THE STOLEN CHILD

Where dips the rocky highland
Of sleuth Wood in the lake,
There lies a leafy island
Where flapping herons wake
The drowsy water-rats;
There we've hid our faery vats,
Full of berries
And of reddest stolen cherries.

Come away, O human child!
To the waters and the wild
With a faery, hand in hand,
For the world's more full of weeping than you can understand.
Where the wave of moonlight glosses
The dim grey sands with light,
Far off by farthest Rosses
We foot it all the night,
Weaving olden dances,
Mingling hands and mingling glances
Till the moon has taken flight;
To and fro we leap
And chase the frothy bubbles,
While the world is frill of troubles
And is anxious in its sleep.
Come away, O human child!
To the waters and the wild
With a faery, hand in hand,
For the world's more full of weeping than you can understand.
Where the wandering water gushes
From the hills above Glen-Car,
In pools among the rushes
That scarce could bathe a star,
We seek for slumbering trout
And whispering in their ears
Give them unquiet dreams;
Leaning softly out
From ferns that drop their tears
Over the young streams.
Come away, O human child!
To the waters and the wild
With a faery, hand in hand,
For the world's more fall of weeping than you can understand.
Away with us he's going,
The-solemn-eyed:
He'll hear no more the lowing
Of the calves on the warm hillside
Or the kettle on the hob
Sing peace into his breast,

Or see the brown mice bob
Round and round the oatmeal-chest.
For he comes, the human child.
To the waters and the wild
With a faery, hand in hand,
From a world more full of weeping than he can understand.

The poem consists of four stanzas, in the first of which the poet says that he, along with others, possesses hidden "faery vats" or containers of fairies, which are full of "stolen berries", at the place where "rocky highland" meets the lake. The highland is of Sleuth Wood which lies between Lough Gill and Dromahair. The word 'Sleuth' is derived from Irish 'sliv' which means 'a slpoe'. The poet is inviting, or rather enticing, men who are weary of the world, to the "leafy island" in the lake in which "flapping herons wake. The drowsy water-rats". In the refrain (*Come away, O human child!... you can understand.),* the poet says that human beings do not know the extent to which the world is full of woes, and so he urges upon them to come with a fairy, hand in hand, "To the waters and the wild". About the refrain of the poem, Yeats wrote to Katharine Tynan in 1888: "almost all a flight into fairyland from the real world... The Chorus to the 'Stolen Child' sums it up — that it is not the poetry of insight and knowledge but of longing and complaint — the cry of the heart against necessity. hope someday to alter that and write poetry of insight and knowledge."(Jeffares, 12).

In the second and third stanzas, Yeats is further describing the "leafy island". He says that there moonlight brightens the colourless sand far off Rosses or Rosses Point, a sea-side village to the north-west of Sligo. In his *Mythologies* (1959), also Yeats describes the places around Rosses Point thus: "At the northern corner of Rosses is a little promontory of sand and rocks and grass: a mournful, haunted place. Few countrymen would fall asleep under its low cliff, for he who sleeps here may wake 'silly', the Sidhe having carried off his soul." (Jeffares, 12). However, the poet says that men like him dance and love in the moonlight, when "the world is full of troubles". There are rivulets there that originate in the hills above Glen-Car, a lake in the north-east of Sligo. There are pools too — shallow pools — where they will find "slumbering trouts" and whisper "unquiet dreams" in the ears of the fishes. There dew from fern leaves drop on those pools and streams.

In the last stanza, the poet sees the *"human child"* coming up, in response to his call, to the fairyland from the real world of lowing calves, boiling kettles and "brown mice". In the foregoing three refrains, the poet repeatedly urged the "*human child*" to come to this land of wonders and fairies, and now, in the last refrain, he sees him gladly coming to the waters of the lakes and pools in the wilderness. And now the human child is coming "*With a faery, hand in hand from a world more full of weeping than he can understand,*"

Like the two foregoing poems, this one is also very romantic. Here the poet shows his longing to escape from the reality and to escape into the land of the fairies. When Yeats wrote this poem, he was in his blooming youth. By then he had already experienced the pangs of unrequited love, and may be, this had intensified his feeling of disenchantment with the real world. He, therefore, wants to find love and peace in the land of the fairies, and longs to dance with one of them, hand in hand. The poem is full of romantic imageries: 'leafy island', 'flapping heron', 'berries', 'moonlight', 'olden dances', 'wandering water', 'unquiet dreams', 'young streams', etc. Here the poet is, as if, carried away by his emotion, forgetful of the reality around, forgetful of the world of necessities. The romantic agony of the poet is almost palpable. The verses are as sonorous as the diction. The rhyme scheme is not regular. The refrain that occurs four times, once with some variation, adds an extra beauty to this lyrical poem.

4. The Indian Upon God

This little poem of only twenty lines is so lyrical that it can, perhaps, be sung. It was written in 1886 and was first published in *Dublin University Review*, the same year. It was again published in *Crossways* in (1889) with the present title, but, like some other poems of Yeats, this one also had some other titles, previously, the original title was a very long one: 'From the Book of Kauri the Indian—Section V. On the Nature of God'. The next title it received was: 'Kanva, the Indian, on God'. It may be mentioned here that *The Wandering of Oisin and Other Poems* (1889) also included a poem of similar title: 'Kanva on Himself. A. Norman Jeffares writes about this poem: "It is possible that this poem and the poem 'The Indian to his Love' were inspired by the Brahmin Theosophist Mohini Chatterjee, who visited Dublin in 1885 and gave a lecture to the Hermetic Society, a group of young men who had taken a room in York Street, Dublin, as their headquarters." (Jeffares, 7). Daniel Albright in *W. B. Yeats: The Poems,* edited by him, writes: "The premise of this poem — that every being constructs an image of God on its own likeness—is related to passage from Browning's dramatic monologue 'Caliban upon Setebos' (1867), where Caliban invents a Caliban-shaped image of God. Yeats's interest in this premise can be seen in a letter to Katharine Tynan, where Yeats remarked 'When I was a child... I used often to say, "what religion do the ants have?" They must have one you know."

The theme of this poem is reincarnation which is also the theme of Yeats's two other poems: 'Mohini Chatterjee' and 'Fergus and the Druid'. Mohini Chatterjee once said in reply to the question if one should pray or not: "No, one should say before sleeping: 'I have lived many lives, I have been a slave and a prince. Many a beloved has sat upon my knee, and I have sat upon the knees of many a beloved. Everything that has been shall be again." (Jeffares, 7). Jeffares says: "This poem's theme is recaptured in 'Mohini Chatterjee', written in February 1929, where it is far better handled. F.F. Farag points out that Mohini meant that one 'should realise the permanence of the soul in the eternal essence amidst all the transient forms through which it has passed." (Jeffares, 7-8).

In this poem, the poet imagines that some Indian is passing through a wilderness and confronting four creatures, one after another, on his way: a moorfowl, a lotus, a roebuck and a peacock. Each one of the creatures is, as if, in a prayer or is engrossed in the thought of God. Thus each creature is creating its own idea of God. In this poem, the poet wants to say that the idea of each creature about God is quite different from the ideas of other creatures.

THE INDIAN UPON GOD

I passed along the water's edge below the humid trees,
My spirit rocked in evening light, the rushes round my knees, My
spirit rocked in sleep and sighs; and saw the moorfowl pace
All dripping on a grassy slope, and saw them cease to chase Each
other round in circles, and heard the eldest speak:
Who holds the world between His bill and made us strong or weak?
Is an undying moorfowl and He lives beyond the sky.
The rains are from His dripping wing, the moonbeams from His eye.

I passed a little further on and heard a lotus talk:
Who made the world and ruleth it, He hanged on a stalk,
For I am in His image made, and all this tinkling tide
Is but a sliding drop of rain between His petals wide.
A little way within the gloom a roebuck raised his eyes
Brimful of starlight, and he said: *The Stamper of the Skies,*
He is a gentle roebuck; for how else, I pray, could He
Conceive a thing so sad and soft, a gentle thing like me?

I passed a little further on and heard a peacock say:
Who made the grass and made the worms and made my feathers gay,
He is a monstrous peacock, and He waveth all the night
His languid tail above us, lit with myriad spots of light.

The Indian passed through a wet forest while it was evening, and while he was walking through the forest and by "water's edge", his spirit was bobbing in the evening light, rushes were entwining round his knees, and his spirit was bouncing "in sleep and sighs". There the Indian found a moorfowl—a kind of red or black grouses—which were dipping in the grass on a slope. Suddenly they ceased to chase each other in round circles in merriment, and the eldest of the moorfowls said that God, who created them all, was like themselves a moorfowl, and that he lives somewhere beyond the sky. The eldest moorfowl also said that rain was but water-drops falling from the moorfowl-God's wings, and also that moon-beams came from the moorfowl-God's eyes. The Indian walked further and saw a lotus which said that God looked like itself and hanged from a stalk like itself, and that rain-drops came from the water on its petals. Then the Indian saw in the shade a gentle roebuck, or a male deer, with glittering eyes. The roebuck said that God must be like him a roebuck, otherwise how "*could He/Conceive a thing so sad and soft, a gentle thing like me?*" The Indian advanced further and heard a peacock say that the creator of the world was like itself—was "a monstrous peacock". The peacock said that the peacock-God made their feathers and worms and that the peacock-God distended His tail "with myriad spots of light", that looked like the starry sky at night.

Yeats believed in the ancient philosophy of Empedocles that the world is made of four elements: earth, water, fire and air. In this poem, earth is represented by the moorfowl; water by the lotus; fire by the glittering eyes of the roebuck; and air by the peacock. Yeats also believed in the Neoplatonic mythology, according to which images are created, probably by reflection, by water. Daniel Albright, in his edition of Yeats's poems, writes: Water is conspicuous in much of this poem, as if to suggest that each animal sees his water-reflection as God. In the Neoplatonic mythology important to Yeats, water is the medium for the generation of images: 'Did not the wise Porphyry think that all souls come to be born because of water, and that "even the generation of images in the minds is from water?" (p. 418).

5. The Ballad of Moll Magee

The poem was first printed in *The Wandering of Oisin and Other Poems* (1889) and then in *Crossways* (1889). But according to Katharine

Tynan, it was first published in *The Gael* (1887). The poem was written on the basis of a sermon that was given in the Chapel at Howth, a fishing village, near Dublin Bay. Yeats's nationalistic sentiment is obvious in this poem. Here he uses certain words which belong to the Irish language, exclusively. For instances: 'say' (meaning 'sea'), 'boreen' (meaning 'lane'), 'keenin' (meaning "professional mourners who utter the keen (the lamentation over the dead) for the dead awakes (trails behind a moving body; here the dead body) at funerals in Ireland." (Jeffares, 16). Some English words, pronounced as Irish, are also used in this poem. For instances: 'saltin' (meaning 'salting'), 'Blowin' (meaning 'blowing'), 'momin' (meaning 'morning'), 'pityin' (meaning 'pitying'), etc.

THE BALLAD OF MOLL MAGEE

Come round me, little childer;
There, don't fling stones at me
Because I mutter as I go;
But pity Moll Magee.

My man was a poor fisher
With shorelines in the say;
My work was saltin' herrings
The whole of the long day.

And sometimes from the 'salt in' shed
I scarce could drag my feet,
Under the blessed moonlight,
Along the pebbly street.

I'd always been but weakly,
And my baby was just born;
A neighbour minded her by day,
I minded her till mom.

I lay upon my baby;
Ye little childer dear,
I looked on my cold baby
When the mom grew frosty and clear.

A weary woman sleeps so hard!
My man grew red and pale,

And gave me money, and bade me go
To my own place, Kinsale.

He drove me out and shut the door,
And gave his curse to me;
I went away in silence,
No neighbour could I see.

The windows and the doors were shut,
One star shone faint and green,
The little straws were turnin' round
Across the bare boreen.

I went away in silence:
Beyond old Martin's byre
I saw a kindly neighbour
Blowin' hermornin' lire.

She drew from my story—
My money's all used up,
And still, with pityin', scornin' eye,
She gives me bite and sup.

She says my man will surely come,
And fetch me home agin;
But always, as I'm movin' round,
Without doors or within.

Pilin' the wood or pilin' the turf,
Or goin' to the well,
I' mthinkin' of my baby
And keen in' to mysel'.

And sometimes I am sure she knows
When, openin' wide His door,
god lights the stars, His candles,
And looks upon the poor.

So now, ye little childer,
Ye won't fling stones at me;

But gather with your shinin' looks
And pity Moll Magee.

Moll Magee, a poor fisherman's wife, has been forced out of house by her husband. The charge against her was that their little female baby died due to Moll Magee's negligence — she, in her deep sleep, turned on the little baby which died under her weight. She is now moving here and there in search of food and shelter, muttering words of her woe. Little children ('childer' in colloquial Irish means 'children') taking her to be a mad woman or a witch for her shabby clothes and disheveled hair, are stoning at her. Moll Magee asks them not to pelt at her, but to show pity for her. She is now narrating her sorrowful life's story to them. She says that her husband was a poor fisherman who would catch fishes in the sea ('say' in Irish means 'sea') and that she would be salting ('saltin'') herrings all day long. After day's hard work, she would become so tired that she could hardly walk back to their home from the salting shed, through the path full of pebbles, in the moonlight night. She tells them that her constitution has always been weak, particularly after the birth of the child. A neighbour would look after the baby in the day, while she would go to work in the salting shed. Bark home at night, she would look after the child throughout the night. One night she unwittingly turned on the child and in the frosty morning came to see that the child died due to her negligence: "I lay upon my baby;/Ye little childer, I looked on my cold baby/When the mom grew frosty and clear."

Moll Magee was repentant and cursed herself for her so deep a sleep: "Aweary woman sleeps so hard!" Her husband became extremely angry at her, gave her some money, and ordered her to go back to her father's house at Kinsale. He shut the door on her face and cursed her, and she went away without uttering a word. No neighbour came to help her anyway. As her husband shut the doors as well as the windows, she went away through the dark night, only one "faint and green" star shining in the lonely sky. As she went away, there was a whirlwind in the lonely lane ('boreen') and the whirlwind was wafting the straws strewn in the street: "The little straws were turnin' round/Across the bare boreen."

She says that she went away silently beyond old Martin's byre or cowhouse, where she met a kindly neighbour who had been blowing the fire of her hearth. The neighbour patiently heard the sad story of Moll Magee and understood that this wretched woman had no money to go by. The neighbour felt pity for Moll Magee, scorned her husband and gave her food ("She gave me bite and sup" Moll Magee is still hopeful that her husband will surely come to take her back again (agin'). This kindly neighbour did not give her lodge and so Moll Magee is again moving from place to place in search of some shelter: "But always, as I'm movin' round,/Without doors or within." Now she is serving as a char-woman, piling ('Pilin') wood and turfs and drawing water from well. While thus working hard, she always remembers her dead child and wails for her dead child ('Keenin'). Moll Magee says that she feels that the soul of her dead child which is in heaven knows when God opens His door of heaven and lights His candles, to wit the stars, in the sky, and looks downwards sympathetically at the poor folk. Thus narrating her life's story, Moll Magee entreats the little children not to throw stones at her, perhaps taking her to be a mad woman or a witch, but to gather themselves round herself and have pity for her.

This poem of 56 lines is a beautiful 'folk' or 'popular' ballad. Perhaps Yeats took the story of Moll Magee from some thesaurus of folk-tales. The poem is a ballad because it focuses "on a single crucial episode or situation" of Moll Magee. Secondly, like the ballad, it is dramatic, for Moll Magee is narrating her life's story to a group of urchins. And lastly, like the ballad, it is impersonal, for her the poet is describing the situation and expressing the emotion not of himself but of Moll Magee. Yeats himself also has called the poem a ballad as is evident from the title of the poem. The ballad has been done in very simple and perspicuous words and it has striking local colour. It is very touching and can well arouse genuine pity and sympathy.

THE ROSE — 1893

The Rose, that was published in 1893, contained some shorter poems taken from. *The Countess Kathleen and Various Legends and Lyrics* (1892). Daniel Albright writes: "*The Rose* is not the title of a published volume, but the title of a section of Yeats's collected poems... Yeats explained the titles of *Crossways* and *The Rose* by saying that, in the first volume, the poet has 'tried many pathways'; and in the latter volume, 'he has found, he believes, the only pathway whereon he can hope to see with his own eyes the Eternal Rose of Beauty and of Peace'. *The Rose* is perhaps the most carefully organized of all Yeats's organized book of poetry, and its great sophistication of design reflects Yeats's desire for synthesis — synthesis of his love for Maud Gonne and his occult researches and his patriotic desire to isolate and liberate the Irish national spirit.... "In his poetry [the poems of the volume entitled *The Rose*], Yeats developed a vocabulary based on a single prime symbol, the Rose, which could stand for any desirable thing, and therefore could subsume a multitude of disparate objects. The Rose varies between two poles: the historical and particular Maud Gonne, and a state so simple and all-inclusive that it is almost a symbol of symbolism itself, an allegation of the oneness of all beautiful objects, a hypothetical apex where all upward-striving things converge. Such immense predicates are found in Romantic poetry, as in Shelley's 'Hymn to Intellectual Beauty' (1818), addressed to an abstract Beauty in which all finite beautiful things are gathered; but as Yeats said in a 1925 note, 'the quality symbolized as The Rose differs from the Intellectual Beauty of Shelley... in that I have imagined it as suffering with man and not as something pursued and seen from afar.'" (Albright, 427). Yeats's concept of beauty is also different from Edmund Spenser's (1552-99) concept of beauty as is evident from Spenser's 'Foure Hymnes'.

The Rose contains some 23 poems, including such poems as 'To the Rose upon the Rood of Time', 'Fergus and the Druid', 'Cuchulain's Fight with the Sea', 'The Lake Isle of Innisfree', 'Who Goes with Fergus?' 'To Ireland in the Coming Times', etc. Daniel Albright writes: "In these poems, there is complex and unsettled relationship between the natural world—full of worms, mice, and the sadness of unrequited love—and the supernatural world, where all is ecstasy. In the Rosicrucian philosophy that Yeats was studying at this time, the sensible world is only the lowest in a series of graded emanations from spiritual reality; there is a ladder connecting the low and the high. But in the Indian philosophy that Yeats studied under Mohini Chatterjee, the sensible world was nothing but a distraction from and impediment to the contemplation of higher truths; .... These two opposing models—one suggesting the spiritual truth is hidden everywhere in the objects around us, the other suggesting that (in Shelley's phrase) the deep truth is imageless—complete in Yeats's poetry. The former model rendered symbolism possible; but the latter justified the urgency of escape. "The adjustment of focus, then, between the physical world and the spiritual world continually shifts. In some poems, such as 'The Rose of the World', the physical world is transparent, easily penetrated, unable to sustain itself in front of the spiritual truth of things. But in other poems the physical world can organize itself into a fairly satisfactory expression of the spiritual world. Indeed in one poem, 'The Lake Isle of Innisfree', it even appears that the seeker can find a good approximation of the kingdom of the spirit right here on earth. Yeats was fond of quoting the occult motto attributed to Hermes Trismegistus, 'The things below are as the things above'. Yeats sought out those holy places—Castle Rock, Innisfree —which best seemed to mirror the shape of heaven." (Albright, 427-28).

Yeats dedicated *The Rose* to Lionel Johnson (1867-1902), the English poet and critic, who was Yeats's friend and a fellow member of the

Rhymers' Club. The epitaph, in Latin, is from St. Augustine's *Confessions* X 27. In translation, it reads: 'Too late have I loved you, Beauty so old and so new! Too late I have loved you.' "Augustine was addressing God as an indwelling Beauty that vivifies the senses with the desire to approach Him. In 1901 Yeats quoted these same Latin lines, to illustrate that the artistic life and the religious life have the same goal." (Albright, 428).

6. Cuchulain's Fight with the Sea

Cuchulain is an Irish mythical character, perhaps the most revered of all the mythical characters in Ireland. Yeats dwelt with the theme of Cuchulain in several of his poems, such as 'To the Rose upon the Rood of Time', 'The Secret Rose', etc., and in one of his plays, *On Baile's Strand* (1904). This poem of 86 lines was first published in *United Ireland* on 11th June, 1892, with the title 'The Death of Cuchulain'. Later on it was extensively revised and published in *The Rose* (1893).

The theme of this poem is based on the legend of Cuchulain that Yeats came across perhaps in J. Curtuis's *Myths and Folklore of Ireland (1890).* The legend came down to Curtuis through oral tradition. Yeats probably knew about the legend of Cuchulain also from a 9th century tale in *The Yellow Book of Lecan.* The legend is like this. King Cuchulain, the legendary Irish hero, has come back to his castle after winning a battle and sent the news to his wife Emerthathe has brought with him a beautiful and sweet-throated woman. At this news, Emer flies into a rage out of jealousy and asks her step-son Conleach (son of Cuchulain's former beloved wife Aoife. But Yeats confused Aoife with Emer) to go and fight with his father Cuchulain and kill him. The son, moved by the crest-fallen plight of his step-mother, goes out to fight with his father, King Cuchulain, The king, knowing not who it is that throws the gauntlet before him, sends army to kill the enemy. Battle ensues and eventually Cuchulain's son, Conleach, is slain. Later on, as the king comes to know of the death of his son in the battle, he breaks down in agony. Cuchulain then determines to destroy all the wrongful men of his army, in revenge. To save the army from proximate extinction, Conchubar sends some of his Druids or medicine-men (Celtic or Gaelic 'draoi' means 'magician') to throw spell on Cuchulain so that he may forget to kill the men of his own army, and instead, fight the imaginary horses of the sea, to wit, the waves of the sea. The spell of the Druids works well, and Cuchulain begins to fight with the imaginary horses of the sea.

Daniel Albright believes that there might be some similarity between Conleach's relation with his father Cuchulain and W.B. Yeats's relation with his father J.B. Yeats. Albright writes: "Yeats's difficulties with his own father may be related to this fascination [of Yeats for the Cuchulain theme] —John Butler Yeats once smashed a glass-fronted picture with his son's head in a dispute over John Stuart Mill's philosophy. It is clear that Yeats feared that his father's dominant personality would overthrow him: the Yeats-like boy [of] the so-called 'Island' version of the unfinished novel *The Speckled Bird* feels that disobeying his father is like disobeying God; and further, that every thought of his, every feeling, is merely a shadow of some thought or feeling of his father." (Albright, 432). Daniel Albright further writes: "The image of a hero struggling with the ocean came to represent to Yeats the highest pitch of tragic intensity. As Yeats wrote in 1917, 'The poet finds and makes his mask in disappointment, the hero in defeat. The desire that is satisfied is not a great desire, nor has the shoulder used all its might that an unbreakable gate has never strained." (Albright, 432-33).

CUCHULAIN'S FIGHT WITH THE SEA

A man came slowly from the setting sun,
To Emer, raddling raiment in her dun,
And said, 'I am that swineherd whom you bid
Go watch the road between the wood and tide,
But now I have no need to watch it more.'

Then Emer cast the web upon the floor,
And raising arms all raddled with the dye,
Parted her lips with a loud sudden cry.

That swineherd stared upon her face and said,
'No man alive, no man among the dead,
Has won the gold his cars of battle bring.'
'But if your master comes home triumphing
Why must you blench and shake from foot to crown?'

Thereon he shook the more and cast him down
Upon the web-heaped floor, and cried his word:
'With him is one sweet-throated like a bird.'

'You dare me to my face,' and thereupon
She smote with raddled fist, and where her son
Herded the cattle came with stumbling feet,
And cried with angry voice, 'It is not meet
To idle life away, a common herd.'

'I have long waited, mother, for that word:
But wherefore now?
'There is a man to die;
You have the heaviest arm under the sky.'

'Whether under its daylight or its stars
My father stands amid his battle-cars.'

'But you have grown to be taller man.'

'Yet somewhere under starlight or the sun
My father stands.'
'Aged, worn out with wars
On foot, on horseback or in battle-cars.'

'I only ask what way my journey lies,
For He who made you bitter made you wise.'

'The Red Branch camp in a great company
Between wood's rim and the horses of the sea.
Go there, and light a camp-fire at wood's rim;
But tell your name and lineage to him
Whose blade compels, and wait till they have found
Some feasting man that the same oath has bound.'

Among these feasting men Cuchulain dwelt,
And his young sweetheart close beside him knelt,
Stared on the mournful wonder of his eyes,
Even as Spring upon the ancient skies,
And pondered on the glory of his days;
And all around the harp-string told his praise,
And Conchubar, the Red Branch king of kings,
With his own fingers touched the brazen strings.

At last Cuchulain spake, 'Some man has made
His evening fire amid the leafy shade.
I have often heard him singing to and fro,
I have often heard the sweet sound of his bow.
Seek out what man he is.'

One went and came.
'He bade me let all know he gives his name
At the sword-point, and waits till we have found
Some feasting man that the same oath has bound.'

Cuchulain cried, 'I am the only man
Of all this host so bound from childhood on.'
After short fighting in the leafy shade,
He spake to the young man, 'Is there no maid
Who loves you, no white arms to wrap you round,
Or do you long for the dim sleepy ground,
That you have come and dared me to my face?'

'The dooms of men are in God's hidden place.'

'Your head a while seemed like a woman's head
That I loved once.'
Again the fighting sped,

But now the war-rage in Cuchulain woke,
And through that new blade's guard the old blade broke,
And pierced him.
'Speak before your breath is done.'

'Cuchulain I, mighty Cuchulain's son.'

'I put you from your pain, I can no more.'

While day its burden on to evening bore,
With head bowed on his knees Cuchulain stayed;
Then Conchubar sent that sweet-throated maid,
And she, to win him, his grey hair caressed;
In vain her arms, in vain her soft white breast,
Then Conchubar, the subtlest of all men,
Ranking his Druids round him ten by ten,
Spake thus: 'Cuchulain will dwell there and brood
For three days more in dreadful quietude,
And then arise, and raving slay us all.
Chaunt in his ear delusions magical,
That he may fight the horses of the sea.
The Druids took them to their mystery,

And chaunted for three days.
Cuchulain stirred,
Stared on the horses of the sea, and heard
The cars of battle and his own name cried;
And fought with the invulnerable tide.

An errand came slowly at dusk, accosted Emer, the wife of Cuchulain, who was in her redorochre ('raddling' in Irish means 'red' or'ochre') clothes (raiment), and reminded her that she had bidden him to watch "the road between the wood and tide" through which Cuchulain went away to fight and through which he would return. The errand told Emer that now he had "no need to watch it more." Hearing this Emer, in apprehension of Cuchulain's death in the battle cast her clothes or woven stuff ('web') down 'on the floor and raising her red-coloured hand cried aloud. The errand, a swineherd, informed Emer that no man could bring from battle-field as precious a thing as Cuchulain did. Assured that Cuchulain was not slain, she asked the errand why then he was shaking in fear if his master came triumphantly back: 'But if your master comes home triumphing. Why must you blench and shake from foot to crown?' At this, this swineherd was shaking rather more. He fell down on the floor strewn with Emer's clothes and cried out to tell her that Cuchulain had brought with him a beautiful and sweet-voiced woman: 'With him is one sweet-throated like a bird.'

Hearing this, Emer became furious and instantly killed the errand with her "raddled fist" and went to where her step-son (Conleach) had been grazing cattle, and told him that it was no good idling away life by grazing cattle. The step-son said that he was waiting for just that advice. He asked her what he was to do then. Emer asked him to kill a man (meaning Cuchulain) with his "heaviest arm under the sky." After this, a dialogue followed between Emer and her step-son. The son said that his father fought throughout his life in the day and at night and was victorious everywhere. But Emer told her son that he was born to be greater even than his father: "But you have grown to be the taller man." The son repeated that his father stood the most glorious man in the world; but contrarily, Emer said that his father was now an worn out man. At last the son asked his mother to tell him straight what he was to do for her. He understood that her mother was very bitter and so certainly she wants to do something commendable: "For he who made you bitter made you wise." Emer told him that the Red Branch army of Cuchulain was celebrating its victory at a place between the wood and the sea: "Between wood's rim and the horses of the sea." She asked him to go there with his men, light a camp-fire, disclose his identity to them, and find out his father Cuchulain who had been feasting there—Cuchulain who was bound by oath to her. (The 'Red Branch' means Conchubar or Cuchulain and his army).

Cuchulain was then feasting in the border of the forest ("wood's rim") while his newly brought sweetheart (Eithne Inguba) knelt beside him and stared at the "mornful wonder" of Cuchulain's eyes, like spring stared at the wonderful sky in ancient times. The young beauty was recounting the glorious exploits of king Cuchulain, and someone was playing songs on a harp in praise of the king. Even Cuchulain (or Conchobar, the king of the Red Branch) himself was playing on a harp brazenly (because its notes would arouse indignation to Emer). Now Cuchulain saw the camp-fire made by his son (Emer's step-son) and also heard his voice and the sound of his bow, and thus faintly recognised him. Cuchulain then asked his men to find out that man (his son *incognito*) that matte the camp-fire: "Seek out what man he is." One of Cuchulain' s men went out in search of the man *incognito,* came back, and reported that the man *incognito* would disclose his identity only at the point of sword and that he would be waiting till he found out the "feasting man" (Cuchulain who was bound by oath (to his mother). At this Cuchulain got angry and said that it was only he who was "so bound from childhood on."

Then fighting ensued between Cuchulain and the young man (his son *incognito*), in the "leafy shade". Cuchulain asked the young man contemptuously to flee away if he had any sweet-heart or else fight to die. The young man replied that what was lotted could not be blotted out: "The dooms of men are in God's hidden place." In the short respite during the battle, Cuchulain told the young man that his face resembled that of a woman (Cuchulain's former wife) that he once loved. However, soon the soft touch vanished from Cuchulain's breast and the fighting was resumed. Cuchulain now fought fiercely, and ultimately the young man had to yield to Cuchulain's blade. He was mortally wounded, and Cuchulain asked the young man to disclose his identity before he breathed his last. The young man told him: "Cuchulain I, mighty Cuchulain's son." and then died.

The sun set in the west and Cuchulain became extremely dejected and kept his "head on his knees". Then Conchubar of the Red Branch sent the newly brought young maid to console Cuchulain, and she began to caress his grey hair, but in vain. After that Conchubar, "the subtlest of all men", called iris Druids and told them that Cuchulain would remain in "dreadful quietude" for three days, and afler that he would arise and in revenge "slay us all". Therefore Conchubar asked them to throw over Cuchulain magic spell and thus create delusions, so that, instead of killing his own men,

Cuchulain might fight "the horses of the sea", to wit, the waves of the sea. Accordingly, the Druids sang (chaunted) their magical verses for three days and Cuchulain broke silence. He then "Stared on the horses of the sea" and also heard battle-cry in his name, and began to fight against the redoubtable waves of the sea: "And fought with the invulnerable tide."

The mythology of Cuchulain is very deftly handled by Yeats in this poem. The romanticism of king Cuchulain pervades the whole poem. The setting is rustic, dreamy and tell-tale. The emotion of Emer at the news of the king bringing in another woman, and the emotion of the king when his son was killed by his men *incognito,* are very intense and proper, and we can easily associate ourselves with Emer and Cuchulain. The diction is simple, the form is dramatic or conversational, and the note is musical. The poem betrays Yeats's fascination for legends, particularly for those of Ireland. As a narrative poem also this poem stands out unique for its brevity, imagery and immediacy.

7. The Lake Isle of Innisfree

Yeats wrote this poem in 1890, when he was in Bedford Park, London, and it first appeared in *National Observer,* on 13th December, 1890. The title' of the poem refers to an island in Innisfree, not far from Sligo where Yeats spent his boyhood days. On 30th November, 1922, some schoolgirl asked the poet, in a letter, if the Innisfree of the poem was real or imaginary. In reply Yeats wrote: "I had still the ambition, formed in Sligo in my teens, of living in imitation of Thoreau on Innisfree, a little island in Lough Gill, and when walking through the Fleet Street very homesick I heard a little tinkle of water and saw a fountain in a shop-window which balanced a little ball upon its jet, and began to remember lake water. From the sudden remembrance came my poem Innisfree my first lyric with anything in its rhythm of my own music.

I had begun to loosen rhythm as an escape from rhetoric and from that emotion of the crowd rhetoric brings, but I only understood vaguely and occasionally that I must for my special purpose use nothing but common syntax. A couple of years I would not have written that first line with its conventional archaism — 'Arise and go' — nor the inversion in the last stanza." (Jeffares, 30). Here by way of replying to the query of the schoolgirl, Yeats explained the occasion of the poem. The splendid sight of the ball on the jet of water and the music of the fountain aroused poetic inspiration in Yeats. We may remember that Rabindranath Tagore's first poem was also inspired by water drops falling from leaves of trees. When Yeats was young, he was very much influenced by the life-style and philosophy of Thoreau, the American essayist and nature writer and naturalist. From 1845 to 1847, for 26 months, Thoreau lived at Walden. Pond, in a hut built by himself, growing and cooking edibles by himself "to front only the essential facts of life", as another American, novelist and short-story writer, Nathaniel Hawthorne, experimented in communist living in Brook Farm, doing everything himself. Thoreau's experiences at Walden Pond was expressed in his *Walden* which perhaps influenced Yeats. Yeats wrote in *A utobiographies*: "My father had read to me some passage out of *Walden,* and I planned to live some day in a cottage on a little island called Innisfree, and Innisfree was opposite Slish Wood." (Jaffares, 30).

How much Yeats longed for the solitude and natural beauty of Innisfree can be understood from yet another fact that he also utilised the scenario of Innisfree in his story *John Sherman* where whenever the central character is in troubled mind, longs to go away and live in Innisfree. There is a pictorial description of Innisfree and an expression of Yeats's longing for the place in *John Sherman*: "[Innisfree's] rocky centre, covered with many bushes, rose some forty feet above the lake. Often... it had seemed good to dream of going away to that islet and building wooden hut there and burning a few years out, rowing to and fro, fishing, or lying on the island slopes by day, and listening at night to the ripple of the water and the quivering of the bushes." (Albright, 437). Innisfree again appears in Yeats's poem 'The Danaan Quicken Tree' where "the poet sails to Innisfree to eat berries of an enchanted tree 'according to one legend, poisonous to mortals, and according to another, able to endow them with more than mortal powers." (Albright, 437).

The poem became instantly popular. In 1916, Ezra Pound wrote a parody of this poem, 'The Lake Isle' which ends as follows:

O God, O Venus, O Mercury, patron of thieves,
Lend me a little tobacco-shop,
  or install me in any profession
Save this damn'd profession of writing,
  where one needs one's brains all the time.

The word 'Innisfree' means 'heather island'. In 1920, James Joyce wrote in a letter to Ezra Pound about this poem: "This is avery poetical epistle.... It should be read in the evening when the lake water is lapping." (Albright, 438).

THE LAKE ISLE OF INNISFREE

I will arise and go now, and go to Innisfree,

And a small cabin builds there, of clay and wattles made:
Nine bean-rows will I have there, a hive for the honey-bee,
And live alone in the bee-loud glade.

And shall have some peace there, for peace comes dropping slow,
Dropping from the veils of the morning to where the cricket sings;
There midnight's all a glimmer, and noona purple glow,
And evening full of the linnet's wings.

I will arise and go now, for always night and day
I hear lake water lapping with low sounds by the shore;
While I stand on the roadway, or on the pavements grey,
I hear it in the deep heart's core.

The poem consists of three stanzas, each stanza consisting of four lines. In the first stanza, the poet expresses his wish and determination to go to the island of Innisfree, to live there in a cabin made of clay and wattles or flexible twigs. He wishes to plant beans and "a hive for honeybee". It would be a romantic and idyllic place where bees will hum in the glade or open space inside the wood. But the poet will not allow anyone else there besides himself — he will be there alone. The poet's dissatisfaction with the busy industrial world is obvious here. He cannot bear with the lifelessness of the city life, and so says in imitation of the prodigal son of the Bible (Luke xv. 18): "I will arise..." In the next stanza, he expects that he will "have some peace" in Innisfree — peace which no one can get in the city of London. He says that peace can be found only there where there are mists (veils) in the morning, and where crickets sing in the evening, like in Innisfree. There peace will drip from the "veils of the morning". There in the island of Innisfree, the night is moonlight (glimmer) and the noon too is beautiful for its "purple glow". "Yeats explained in a radio broadcast that this referred to the reflection of heather in the water." (Albright, 437). However, there in the evening, beautiful linnets or finches fly to and fro. In the last stanza, the poet once again expresses his determination to go to the island of Innisfree, because he is enamoured of the sound of the "lake water lapping" "by the shore". He says that he hears the sound of the lapping water "always night and day". This refers us again to the Bible (Mark, v.5) where unclean spirits work cleansing themselves: "And always, night and day, he was in the mountains." (Jeffares, 31). The poet means to say that going to Innisfree will be tantamount to cleansing his soul. Yeats might have thought his soul unclean, for in his *Autobiographies* he wrote of the time in which he composed this poem: "I thought that having conquered bodily desire and the inclination of my mind toward women and love, I should live, as Thoreau did, seeking wisdom." (Jeffares, 30). The poet compares the "roadway" and the "pavements grey" of Bedford Park, London, where he then lived with the scenario at Innisfree and feels a compulsion to go to Innisfree.

This is a very sweet poem, and is almost autobiographical. The romantic strain of the poet is obvious here: his world-weariness and longing for an escapade. Therefore, it may be called an escape poem. The imagery is pleasing and the versification sonorous and musical. The two allusions to the Bible have added to its meaning and depth. Though the poet speaks, in this poem, only of himself, only of his own longing for an escapade, yet it is not a personal poem, because we all share his emotion. What the poet is actually desiring is release from the world of hard facts, and the immediacy of undisturbed peace, and this we all desire.

8. When You are Old

In this short poem of only twelve lines Yeats, when he was only 26, thought about Time and its ravaging power. It was written on 21st October, 1891, and was addressed to his object of love, the paragon of beauty, Maud Gonne. By that date, Yeats had already proposed at least twice to her and was refused the same number of times, she is being then on the crest of her pride, obstinacy and the spirit of nationalistic movement. Though the poem was written in imitation of the 16th century French poet Pierre Ronsard's famous sonnet 'Quand Vous Serez Bien Vieille' in his *Sonnets pour Héléne,,* part II (1578), it reminds one of the sonnets nos. 64 and 65, of Shakespeare, where Shakespeare is also concerned with the pillage of time. In these two sonnets, Shakespeare also, like Yeats after him, addressed his beloved. In sonnet no. 63 Shakespeare speaks of "Time's injurious hand" Again, in sonnet no. 64, Shakespeare speaks of "Time's fell hand". In these sonnets, Shakespeare is concerned with the decay of beauty due the tide of time. In sonnet no. 65, he mourns over the thought of the decaying beauty of his beloved:

> O, how shall summer's honey breath hold out
> Against the wreckful siege of battering days,
> When rocks impregnable are not so stout,
> Nor gates of steel so strong, but Time decays?
> O fearful meditation! where, alack,
> Shall Time's best jewel from Time's chest lie hid?

In 'When You are Old' also Yeats is concerned with Time and beauty.

But whereas Shakespeare is mournful for the decay of the beauty of his beloved, Yeats feels a sort of pride because when Time will snatch away beauty from her (Maud Gonne), beauty for which she is boasting and rejecting him, she will find that only the poet loved her with a religious zeal: "But one man loved the pilgrim soul in you." Yeats feels some satisfaction that, even if belatedly, she will realise his love for her, and perhaps will repent so.

Daniel Albright adds that though this poem was written in imitation of the sonnet of Ronsard, yet "after the first lines Yeats' s poem diverges from its original" whereas Ronsard predicts that, when he becomes a boneless phantom hovering by his grave, his beloved — an old hunched woman— will regret her proud disdain of the poet's love, the gentler Yeats ascribed the failure of love, not to the woman's haughtiness, but to Love himself, who abandons the orbit of human concerns." (Albright, 439-40.)

WHEN YOU ARE OLD

When you are old and grey and foil of sleep,
And nodding by the fire, take down this book,
And slowly read, and dream of the soft look
Your eyes had once, and of their shadows deep;

How many loved your moments of glad grace,
And loved your beauty with love false or true,
But one man loved the pilgrim soul in you,
And loved the sorrows of your changing face;

And bending down beside the glowing bars,
Murmur, a little sadly, how Love fled
And paced upon the mountains overhead
And hid his face amid a crowd of stars.

In the first stanza of the poem, the poet tells his beloved (Maud Gonne) that when she will grow old, her hair will turn grey, and she will always feel drowsy and sit by the fire to warm her cool body. The poet asks her to take up then his book of verses and read it slowly, and remember her young days when she wore a soft look in her eyes and dark shadows under her eyes. In the second stanza, the poet asks her to remember also the persons who once loved her physical beauty ("glad grace") truly and who loved it falsely. But, he tells her that only one man (the poet) loved her soul that transmigrates from one body to another (therefore hers is a pilgrim soul). The influence of the philosophy of Plato, particularly his theory of transmigration of the soul is obvious here. The poet says that it is only he who loved not only her dazzling beauty of youth but also her sorrows and her waning beauty: And loved the sorrows of your changing face.' In the third stanza, the poet further says that when his beloved will grow old, she will brood, with drooping head "beside the glowing bars" of the fireplace, and mourn for him (the poet) who by then will have fled to mountain tops and thence to the stars, after he will have left his 'mortal coil.'

This little poem is full of intense feeling of love of the poet for his beloved. The poet has been rejected by her at least twice by now, but he warns her that one day when she will become old and shed all her physical beauty, she will have to repent for his love for her, which is not physical like that of many others, but spiritual. The intense feeling of love of the poet certainly touches us all. Here lies the universal appeal of the poem. The rhyme scheme in all the three stanzas is abba. The words 'love' and 'loved' to occur six times in the matter of only twelve lines, and this testifies to the intensity of the poet's feeling of love for his beloved. Further, the imagery used in the poem is very attractive.

9. To Ireland in the Coming Times

In his young days, Yeats was extremely nationalist. He loved Ireland, loved its mythological heroes and its folklores and admired its urge for freedom. In this poem, he expresses all this his sentiment as well as his belief that literature can well play a part in politics. The poem was first printed in the collection of poems entitled *The Countess Kathleen and Various Legends and Lyrics,* published in 1892, when Yeats was only 27. The original title of the poem was 'Apologia addressed to Ireland in the Coming days', but later on it was changed to 'To Ireland in the Coming Times'. A. Norman Jeffares writes about the poem: "This is in part a defence of the obscurity caused by 'a passion for the symbolism of the mystical rose which has saddened my friends', in part an explanation of Yeats's attitude to the role of literature in the struggle for Irish independence, in part a love poem to Maud Gonne. He argued that his patriotism was to be considered as being no less than that of the Younger Icelanders and patriotic writers of the past." (Jeffares, 40).

As we have seen, from his early youth to his maturity, Yeats was agog with national feeling which inspired him to look back to the legendary' past of Ireland. He wanted to revive in his poetry the exploits of the ancient Irish legendary heroes with a view to infuse vitalism in the ongoing nationalist movement. But there were some who thought that Yeats's poetry had no part to play in the Irish politics. Daniel Albright writes that in this poem "Yeats refutes the charge that his symbolic and artful method of composition is irrelevant to Irish political realities. He claims that politics is properly an effect of art, not a cause of it; that poetry instigates action, instead of responding to external events. This poem strives to make a convergence between patriot and poet, between Maud Gonne and the Rose, between time and eternity — between those contraries that seemed so difficult to resolve in the prefatory poem, 'To the Rose upon the Rood of Time'. Yeats insisted that the Rose had sufficient breadth of reference to include nationals as well as private concerns: 'The Rose is a favourite symbol with the Irish poets. It... is used, not merely in love poems, but in addresses to Ireland." (Albright, pp. 448-49). Albright further comments: "This poem is an elaborate meditation on the relation between the measured and the unmeasured. Measurement is temporal and rhythmic, imagistic; the beat of the dancer's footsteps, of the emphatic tetrameter of the poem itself, produces a measured design. Measurement, proportion, is the basis of all art. But eternity is unmeasured; and the measured stresses of art spring from and return to a condition of elemental simplicity, a fruitful void. Yeats contrasted the mystic with the visionary: the mystic received such immediate intuitions of eternity that he could not be an artist; whereas the visionary perceived eternity through finite images—a less direct but more communicable experience: 'The systematic mystic is not the greatest of artist, because his imagination is too great to be bounded by a picture or a song'. In this sense 'To Ireland in the Coming Times' describes how apprehensions of eternity incarnate themselves in symbols." (Albright, 449).

TO IRELAND IN THE COMING TIMES

Know, that I would accounted be
True brother of a company
That sang, to sweeten Ireland's wrong,
Ballad and story, rann and song;
Nor be I any less of them,
Because the red-rose-bordered hem
Of her, whose history began
Before God made the angelic clan,
Trails all about the written page.
When Time began to rant and rage
The measure of her flying feet
Made Ireland's heart begin to beat;

And Time bade all his candles flare
To light a measure here and there;
And may the thoughts of Ireland brood
Upon a measured quietude.

Nor may I less be counted one
With Davis, Mangan, Ferguson,
Because, to him who ponders well
My rhymes more than their rhyming tell
Of things discovered in the deep,
Where only body's laid asleep.
For the elemental creatures go
About my table to and fro,
That hurry from unmeasured mind
To rant and rage in flood and wind;
Yet he who treads in measured ways
May surely barter gaze for gaze.
Man ever journeys on with them
After the red-rose-bordered hem.
Ah, faeries, dancing under the moon,
A druid land, a Druid tune!

While still I may, I write for you
The love I lived, the dream I knew.
From our birthday, until we die,
Is but the winking of an eye;
And we, our singing and our love,
What measure time has lit above,
And all benighted things that go
About my table to and fro,
Are passing on to where may be,
In truth's consuming ecstasy,
No place for love and dream at all;
For God goes by with white footfall.
I cast my heart into my rhymes,
That you, in the dim coming times,
May know how my heart went with them
After the red-rose-bordered hem.

In the first stanza, the poet prophesies that in the future he will be counted along with the past great poets of Ireland, and he will be a "True brother" of their company. These poets are Davis, Magnan, Ferguson and others, of whom he speaks in the second stanza. These poets sang to alleviate the sorrows of the Irish people. They wrote ballads, stories, ranns (verses in Irish) and songs. Yeats says that he will not be a lesser poet than they, because he will write verses in praises of Ireland with her "red-rose-bordered hem"—Ireland whose history began before God created the angelic Irish people ("clan"). The history of Ireland is preserved in the pages of books, and will preserved in the verses of the poet. Yeats says that since Time began to "rant and rage", Ireland began to dance (a reference to Maud Gonne), that is, since pre-historic times, Ireland is enamoured of rhymed versification. He says that the nationalist movements and political thoughts of Ireland will be preserved in his quiet verses. According to Daniel Albright, the poet means to say that Ireland's "political troubles were only a pretext to engage Maud Gonne's energy, a stage on which she could dance." (Albright, 449-50). The dance of Maud Gonne("measures of her flying feet") enlivened Ireland, but the political thoughts of Ireland will be preserved in the mute and rhymed verses ("measured quietude") of the poet.

In the second stanza, the poet again says that he will not be counted as lesser than Davis, Mangan and Ferguson. "Thomas Obsome Davis (1814-45) founded N *[The Nation]* in 1842, and was leader of the Young Ireland party. He wrote poems and prose of a popular, patriotic kind. James Clarence Magnan (1803-49), was a romantic Irish poet and essayist, who wrote prolifically for the magazines and journals of his period, sometimes translating, sometimes adapting Irish metrical and German. Sir Samuel Ferguson (1810-86) was an Irish lawyer, poet and antiquary who translated the Gaelic legends in a masculine manner truer to the originals that Yeats's twilight style." (Jeffares, 41). Daniel Albright here adds more about the three past poets of Ireland: "Davis, Mangan, Ferguson: Irish poets. Thomas Davis (1814-45) was the guiding spirit behind the passionate 'Young Ireland' movement, urging the creation of an Irish national literature; Yeats thought him a sincere man who wrote slightly insincere verse in dull, mechanical rhythms *(A Book of Irish Verse);* but Yeats also conceded that Davis 'has influenced generations of young men's by means of his 'moral radiance', despite the defectiveness of his talent. "Clarence Mangan (1803- 49) was a gloomier, more introverted poet; Yeats spoke of his 'immoral and unpractical but solitary and individual life' and considered that, even if he had 'drunk less whisky and smoke less opium... he would have been no more than a good rhetorician' despite his ample gifts. "Sir Samuel Ferguson (1810-86), 'the greatest Irish poet' wrote fluent poems on Irish mythological themes, and was an important influence on Yeats's early poetry, particularly on *The Wandering of Oisin.* Yeats liked the 'lyrical strength and pantherlike speed' of Ferguson's narrative poems, and thought that he was, in breadth and golden severity... like the ancients.... his spirit had sat with the old heroes of the country'; Yeats praised Ferguson for bring us 'a clear glass once more' after city-oriented poets and hidden nature behind 'the sad soliloquies of a nineteenth century egoism'. In 1907 Yeats ranked the three as follows: 'It was our criticism... that set Clarence Mangan at the head of the Young Ireland poets in the place of Davis, and put Sir Samuel Ferguson... next in the succession'. (Albright, 450).

According to Yeats, these three poets will certainly hold places of prominence in the history of Ireland, but, says Yeats, he will not be a less prominent poet than those, because his verses will tell more about Ireland than the verses of those three poets. Yeats says that his verses will discover more of the spirit of Ireland than about her material facts: "*Because, to him who ponders well,/My rhymes more than their rhyming tell/Of things discovered in deep,/Where only body's laid asleep.*" "Some early reviewers reproached Yeats for immodesty in this comparison of himself to his distinguished predecessors; Yeats replied, 'I did not in the least intend the lines to claim equality of eminence... but only community in the treatment of Irish subjects after an Irish fashion." (Albright, 450).

In the third stanza, the poet says that he will continue to write about his love (perhaps for Maud Gonne) and his romantic dreams about Ireland, throughout his life which is very short: "*From our birthday, until we die,/Is but the winking of an eye*". The poet says that everything—"our singing and our love" and all other things — are passing towards some void: nothing is permanent. Everything is existing ephemerally in the delightful ecstasy of some great truth, because everything will ultimately pass into "the white radiance of eternity" (Shelley): "For God goes by with white footfall." The poet is despairing for he finds no love and no dream in this life: "No place for love and dream at all". But he is not all despair, rather he hopes to remain in the memory of the people of Ireland who will read his verses and thus he will be remembered by them. He says that he has poured his heart into his verses so that in the frosty future Ireland may know how much his heart went with Ireland and her "*red-rose-bordered hem*".

This is also a lyric poem in rhymed couplets, that expresses Yeats's concern for his country and his love for the ancient heroes and legends and folk-tales of Ireland. Yeats's fascination for mythology and symbolism (the rose) is apparent in this poem.

THE WIND AMONG THE REEDS — 1899

In 1897, Yeats thought of a change in the form and matter of his poetry. That year, in his essay 'The Autumn of the Flesh' (the title was later changed to 'The Autumn of the Body') Yeats "claimed that poetry, having tried to embrace science, politics, and all human affairs in the generation of Tennyson and Browning, was now working towards relinquishment and intensification; the new poetry would be keener, more disembodied, than the old." (Albright, 451). Only two years later, in 1899, Yeats published *The Wind Among the Reeds,* a volume of poems, that proved true to his recent manifesto. The poems of this volume are very intricate, full of symbols, transcendental in mood and suggestive of meaning. Daniel Albright writes about this volume: "Here is the flesh's autumn, the spirit's November, all prosaic life is vanishing into ominous wisps of meaning. In his earlier poem, 'To the Rose upon the Rood of Time', Yeats felt anxious that he might 'learn to chaunt a tongue men do not know'; and in this volume he has almost attained that condition of frustration. The poems are not unintelligible, but they do not terminate in full expression. Again and again the poet speaks of the end of the world, of unimaginable things; he seems to writhe in limbo, unable to speak the unspeakable. It is noteworthy that Yeats published this book with an extremely long set of explanatory notes, as if he were conscious of the reader's difficulties and trying to make amends. But the notes do not define Yeats's discourse any more fully than the poems themselves; Yeats was working at the outermost fringes of human experience." (Albright, 452).

This volume of poems bears some striking features: it is written in the mood and technique of French *symbolisme;* some of the poems in it have very long titles; it shows three modes of the poetic imagination; the speaker of the poems is not simply the poet but also the lover, and the poems are poems of suggestiveness. In 1899, Arthur Symons published his *The Symbolist Movement in Literature,* in which he discussed elaborately the symbolistic approach to poetry notably by Verlaine, Rimbaud, and Mallarme. Symons dedicated the book to Yeats who was very much influenced by the persuasive argument of the book. "Yeats, in a sense, fulfilled Symons's wish, and in the very year it was uttered; for *The Wind among the Reeds* is perhaps the closest approximation (in major English poetry) to the mood and technique of French *symbollisme.* Yeats's grasp of French (and of every language other than English) was imperfect, and he relied considerably on Symons's ideas and citations; but Yeats did grasp something of the *symbolistes'* ingenuity in constructing faintly suggested half-objects, their technique of creating an evacuated lyric space populated only by ghosts, and their mood of transcendental eeriness." (Albright, 451).

Some of the poems in volume with very long titles are: 'He mourns for the Change that has come upon him and his Beloved, and longs for the End of the World'; 'The Lover asks Forgiveness because of his Many Moods'; 'He thinks of those who have Spoken Evil of his Beloved'; 'He thinks of his Past Greatness when a Part of the constellations of Heaven'; etc. But in some other volumes of poems also there are one or two poems with very long titles. For examples, the poem 'To a Wealthy Man who promised a Second Subscription to the Dublin Municipal Gallery if it were proved the People wanted Pictures' occurs in *Responsibilities,* 'I see Phantoms of Hatred and of the Heart's Fullness and of the Coming Emptiness' in *The Tower*,; etc. In this volume Yeats uses predominantly three characters — Michael Robertes, Hanrahan, and Aedh. In his notes, Yeats wrote about these three characters: "I have used them in this book more as principles of the mind than as actual personages... Hanrahan is the simplicity of an imagination too changeable to gather permanent possessions, or the adoration of the shepherds; and Michael Robertes is the pride of the imagination brooding upon the greatness of its possessions, or the adoration of the Magi; while Aedh is the myrrh and frankincense that the imagination offers continually before all that it loves. (Albright, 452).

The speaker of the poems in this volume is both a poet and a lover. Daniel Albright writes: "the speaker of these poems is not just 'The Poet': he is 'The Lover' as well. The later 1890s was a period of crisis in Yeats's personal life: his relation with Maud Gonne had become increasingly tangled and hopeless; and, in 1896, he had taken his first lover, a kindly woman named Olivia Shakespeare (Yeats refers to her under the pseudonym 'Diana Vernon' in *Memoirs),* Yeats carefully mixed the poems written to Maud Gonne with those written to Olivia Shakespeare\, in order to disguise the autobiographical element; but often the poems written to Olivia Shakespeare are those which discuss the hair of the beloved. The three figments Hanrahan, Michael Robertes, and Aedh denote attitudes towards the beloved as well as attitudes towards poetry — voluble and careless, proud, or self-abasing. In some of the poems given to Aedh the self-abasement is carried to suicidal extremes; and indeed, according to *The Wanderings of Oisin* 1187, Aedh was the name of a god of death." (Albright, 453). Lastly, regarding the features of the poems of this volume, these are very disengaging and suggestive. The notes adduced to this volume, by Yeats, remind one of the notes by Eliot at the end of his *The Waste Land*, and also vouchsafe the intricacy of the poems.

The poems are mystical and revelatory, and they express a truth that is not consciously begotten, but comes of its own to the poet in his semiconscious state of mind. Therefore the ideas are strange even to the poet himself, and the poet cannot but express the ideas with the help of symbols. Jeffares writes: "Yeats introduces this volume (first published in 1899) in CW1 (*Collected Works* 1) in 1906 with the comment that he had so meditated on the images that had come to him in writing 'Ballads and Lyrics', 'The Rose' and 'The Wanderings of Oisin' and other images from Irish folklore that they had become true symbols. He had when awake, but more often in sleep, moments in vision; 'a state very unlike dreaming, when these images took upon themselves what seemed an independent life and became a part of a mystic language, which seemed always as if it would bring me some strange revelation.' Being troubled by what was thought to be reckless obscurity he tried to explain himself in lengthy notes into which he put 'all the little learning I had, and more willful phantasy than I now think admirable, though what is most mystical still seems to me the most true." (Jeffares, 42). W.W. Robson thinks that Yeats turned to mysticism, spiritualism and esoterism at the time of writing these poems, because he felt weary of the material life and became frustrated in his efforts to get love. He says that these are sort of love poems where the poet transmutes the physical into something spiritual. Robson writes: "There can be little doubt that Yeats's esoterism was in part an attempt to escape from painful suffering; or at least to transmute it into something that could be contemplated. And this suffering was due to frustrated love. In *The Wind Among the Reeds (*1899) Yeats writes a new kind of love-poetry. The theme is the spiritualizing of a carnal love that has been renounced. But still the note of longing and regret predominates; the poems are essentially equivocal." (Robson, 54).

Regarding the title of the poem Daniel Albright writes: "this phrase appears in a prose sketch for an unwritten poem about Maud Gonne, circa 1897: 'I/ hear the cry of the birds/ & the cry of the deer/ & I hear the wind among the/reeds, but I put my hands/ over my ears for were not/ they my beloved whispering to/me'" (Albright, 453).

10. The Lover Tells of the Rose in his Heart

This is a short poem of only eight lines. It first appeared in *National Observer* on 12th November, 1892, with the title 'The rose in my Heart'. Later on it was given the title 'Aedh tell of the Rose in his Heart'. But when it appeared in the 1908 edition of *The Wind Among the Reeds,* in the Collected Works, it was entitled 'The Lover Tells of the Rose in his Heart'. The poem is addressed to Maud Gonne for whose love the poet pines and who is like a rose in his heart. When Yeats composed this poem, he was steeped in the magical tradition to which the words "greenknoll" refer. A. Norman Jeffares writes about these two words that they "may refer to his [the poet's] dream of creating a Celtic order of mysteries, centering on the island in Lough Key." (Jeffares, 48). Aedh referred to above "was the self-sacrificing gift-giver among Yeats's poetical personae." (Albright, 455). In this poem the poet tries to metamorphose the universe, or reduce the universe, into a congeries of imageries, and mould it into the shape of Maud Gonne's mode.

THE LOVER TELLS OF THE ROSE IN HIS HEART

All things uncomely and broken, all things worn out and old,
The cry of a child by the roadway, the creak of a lumbering chart,
The heavy steps of the ploughman, splashing the wintry mould,
Are wronging your image that blossoms a rose in the deeps of my heart.
The wrong of unshapely things is a wrong too great to be told;
I hunger to build them anew and sit on a green knoll apart,
With the earth and the sky and the water, re-made, like a casket of gold
For my dreams of your image that blossoms a rose in the deeps of my heart.

In the first stanza, the poet says that the image of his beloved (Maud Gonne) "blossoms a rose in the deep of my heart." But the blossoming of that rose is being hindered by everything ugly, such as "things uncomely", things broken and worn out and old. The shining of the rose of beauty of the beloved is also marred by the cry of a forlorn child and the creak of a hackneyed cart, and by the sight of the toiling ploughman who is struggling in the cold mud in the winter. Here the poet means to say that the building of a lovely image needs the perception of only beautiful things and happy moments. He intends to build up the image of his beloved in his mind, and to love it with all his heart. But the ugly and painful things all around would not let him do so.

In the second stanza, the poet says that the view of ugly and wrongful things gives us pain. Therefore, he determines to be a revolutionary. He aspires to remake the ugly things into beautiful things and remake the wrongful things into rightful things. He wants to "build them anew". Not only that, but he will also remake the whole universe—the earth, the sky and the watery expanse—and transform it into a "casket of gold". He will do all these to dream of the image of his beloved, so that the image may blossom into "a rose in the deep of my heart." And he will do the transmogrification by sitting "on a green knoll apart" (a round hillock at a distance), that is by using his mysterious and magical powers.

The romantic bent of the poet is plainly evident in this poem: he wants to change the whole universe wholesale into a golden casket and to dream of the features of his lady-love. He is also averse to ugly things and is disturbed at the wanton wrongs done. Yeats's humanitarian feeling is also evident here: he sympathises with the toiling peasant and feels compunction for the forlorn child.

11. The Song of Wandering Aengus

This is again a romantic poem full of legends and imageries and mysteries. It was written on 31 January, perhaps in 1893, and first appeared in *The Sketch* with the title 'A Mad Song', on 4th August, 1897. After this, it was again published in March, 1905, *in McClure's Magazine* without any title on its head. The title of the poem refers to Aengus, the Celtic god of music, love and repose. Yeats himself wrote a long note to this poem which may profitably be quoted here: 'The Tribes of the goddess Danu [...] can take all shapes, and those that are in the waters take often the shape of fish. A woman of Burren, in Galway, says, 'There are more of them in the sea than on the land, and they sometimes try to come over the side of the boat in the form of fishes, for they can take their choice shape.' At other times they are beautiful women: and another Galway says, 'surely those things are in the sea as well as on land. My father was out fishing one night off Tyrone. And something came beside the boat that had eyes shining like candles. And then a wave came in, and a storm rose all in a minute, and whatever was in the wave, the weight of it has like to sink the boat. And then they saw that it was a woman in the sea that had the shining eyes. So my father went to the priest and he bid him always to take a drop of holy water and a pinch of salt out in the boat with him, and nothing could harm him.' 'the poem was suggested to me by a Greek folk song; but the folk belief of Greece is very like that of Ireland, and I certainly thought, when I wrote it, of Ireland, and of the spirits that are in Ireland. An old man who was cutting a quickset hedge near Gort, in Galway, said, only the other day, 'One time I was cutting timber over in Inchy, and about eight o'clock one morning, when I got there, I saw a girl picking nuts, with her hair hanging down over her shoulders; brown hair; and she had a good clean face, and she was tall, and nothing on her head, and her dress no way gaudy, but simple. And when she felt me coming she gathered herself up, and was gone, as if the earth and swallowed her up. And I followed her, and looked for her, but I never could see her again from that day to this, never again.' 'The country Galway people use the word 'clean' in its old sense of fresh and comely." (Jeffares, 52).

THE SONG OF WANDERING AENGUS

I went out to the hazel wood,
Because a fire was in my head,
And cut and peeled a hazel wand,
And hooked a berry to a thread;
And when white moths were on the wing,
And moth-like stars were flickering out,
I dropped the berry in a stream
And caught a little silver trout.

When I had laid it on the floor
I went to blow the fire aflame,
But something rustled on the floor,
And some one called me by my name:
It had become a glimmering girl
With apple blossom in her hair
Who called me by my name and ran
And faded through the brightening air.

Though I am old with wandering
Through hollow lands and hilly lands,
I will find out where she has gone,
And kiss her lips and take her hands;
And walk among long dappled grass,
And pluck till time and times are done
The silver apples of the moon,
The golden apples of the sun.

As we have seen, the poem originated in a mysterious tale and therefore everything in it seems to be unnatural. The speaker of this poem is Aengus or Angus, the Master of Love or the God of Youth, beauty and poetry, as Yeats tells us, who reigned in Tirnan-Oge or the country of the young. In this poem, Aengus says that one night he went to the hazel wood. Sheila O'Sullivan suggests that the "hazel wood" may refer to a similar hazel wood in the story of Diarmuid and Grainne in *Transactions of the Ossianic Society*, vol. Ill, published in 1857. Aengus went to the hazel wood

"Because a fire was in my head". This phrase may mean that Aengus was distraught or full of imagination or passion or was under a queer mental compulsion. O' Sullivan again suggests that this phrase and even the whole story of this poem might have been inspired by 'The Story of the Fisherman' in *The Arabian Nights' Entertainment translated* by E.W. Lane. However, going to the wood, Aengus cut a hazel twig, peeled off its bark and made it into a wand. It may be mentioned here that the hazel tree symbolises life or knowledge or the heavens. With the help of that wand Aengus brought down a berry. At that time white moths were flying to and fro and stars were twinkling in the sky. Aengus "dropped the berry in a stream" and caught a little white trout or a freshwater fish of the salmon genus.

In the second stanza, we hear that Aengus laid the trout on the ground (floor) and was lighting fire to cook the fish. But suddenly he heard rustling on the ground, and then heard that some human being was calling him by his name. Aengus looked back at the place where he kept the trout, and to his utter astonishment he found that there was no trout but a beautiful damsel with "apple blossom in her hair". Aengus understood that the trout itself metamorphosed into that "glimmering girl". A. Norman Jeffares suggests that the "glimmering girl" is the image of Maud Gonne with whom Yeats associated apple blossom. In *The Arabian Nights Entertainment*, the story is a whit different. There some fishermen catch four fishes, queerly coloured, and send these to the Sultan. The servants of the Sultan proceed to fry the fishes when the walls of the kitchen crumble down and an exquisitely beautiful girl appears on the spot. However, after appearing on the spot where the trout was laid, the damsel of this poem called Aengus by his name and ran away, and after a while, when it was almost day-break, she disappeared.

Since then Aengus has been wandering for long in search of that beautiful damsel and now has become old. He has wandered through "hollow lands and hilly lands" but has not been able to find her out. Nevertheless he is determined to find out that beautiful damsel someday, and when he finds her out, he will "kiss her lips and take her hands" and walk with her through the lush, long and spotted grass. He will unendingly pluck "The silver apples of the moon/The golden apples of the sun." These two lines have a reference to a folk tale in Mr Larmine' s *West Irish Folk Tales*. The story runs thus. "A young man 'saw a light before him on the high road, when he came as far, there was an open box on the road, and a light coming up out of it. He took up the box. There was a lode of hair in it. Presently he had to go to become the servant of a king for his living. There were eleven boys. When they were going out into the stable at ten o'clock, each of them took a light but he. He took no candle at all with him. Each of them went into his own stable. When he went into his stable, he opened the box. He left it in a hole in the wall. The light was great. It was twice as much as in the other stables.' The king hears of it, and makes him show him the box. The king says, 'You must go and bring the woman to whom the hair belongs.' In the end, the young man, and not the king, marries the woman." (Jaffares, 67). Therefore, plucking "silver apples" and "golden apples" mean plucking the silver hair and golden hair, that is marrying the beautiful mysterious damsel that have fled away from Aengus and into the beyond.

IN THE SEVEN WOODS — 1904

This volume of poem belongs to Yeats's transitional or middle period, the period being the first decade of the twentieth century. In this volume we find that the poet is gradually coming out of his mythological world and entering into the practical world. During this period, he engaged himself in growing a literary spirit in Ireland, with which end in view he, along with Lady Gregory, was striving to found the great Abbey Theatre; Consequently his literary production of this period was relatively less. By then, his mental vagaries being over, Yeats became a settled man; and the torturous ambivalence towards Maud Gonne was no more with him, for she married Major MacBride in 1903. *In the Seven Woods* was first published by Elizabeth Corbet Yeats's DunEmer Press (renamed Cuala Press) in 1903. In that edition of this volume, Yeats added a note about the poems included in this volume. He wrote that the ideas of some of these poems came to his head when he had been "walking about among the Seven Woods, before the wind of nineteen hundred and three blew down so many trees, & troubled the wild creatures, & changed the look of things; and I thought out there a good part of the play which follows [*On Baile's Strand*]. The first shape of it came to me in a dream, but it changed much in the making, foreshadowing, it may be, a change that may bring a less dream-burdened will into my verses. I never re-wrote anything so many times; for at first I could not make these wills that stream into mere life poetical. But now I hope to do easily much more of the kind, and that our new Irish players will find the buskin and the sock." (Jeffares, 73).

And about the quality of the poems of this volume, Daniel Albright writes: "The poems of *In the Seven Woods* are mostly less intense but clearer in focus than those of the previous volume. Yeats does not manipulate a tangle of strangled mythological personae, but instead tends to speak (particularly in 'Adam's Curse') in an agreeably humane and contemporary voice. Faery land is still a constant theme, but the world to which it is an alternative makes its presence felt more strongly. Also, the aristocratic ideal represented by Lady Gregory, Yeats's fellow researcher into folklore—an ideal of high manners and of selfless devotion to a code of service—beings to embody itself in his poetry. His metres begin to evolve during this period from the slow, congested subtleties of his earlier style to sparer, more determined and rapid rhythms, with high contrast between stressed and unstressed syllables." (Albright, 482).

The Seven Woods of the title of this volume is at Coole Park, that was an estate of Lady Gregory, in Co. Galway. Yeats very beautifully describes the Seven Woods in his poem 'Introduction to a Dramatic Poem' that first appeared in *The Speaker* (1st December, 1900) and later was printed in *The Shadowy Waters* (1900) with the title 'I walked among the Seven Woods of Coole':

I walked among the seven woods of Coole;
Shan-walla, where a willow-bordered pond
Gathers the wild duck from the dawn;
Shady Kyle-dortha: sunnier Kyle-na-no
Where many hundred squirrels are as happy
As though they had been hidden by green boughs
Where old age cannot find them; pairc-na-lee,
Where hazel and ash and privet blind the paths;
Dim Pairc-na-carraig, where the wild bees fling
Their sudden fragrance on the green air;
Dim Pairc-na-tarav, where enchanted eyes
Have seen immortal, mild, proud shadows walk;
Dim Inchy wood, that hides badger and fox
And marten-cat, and borders that old wood
Wise Biddy Early called the wicked wood:
Seven odours, seven murmurs, seven woods.

In the Seven Woods (1904) includes such important poems as 'In the Seven Woods' (the title poem), 'the Folly of Being Comforted', 'Adam's Curse', 'O Do Not Love Too Long', etc. All the poems of this volume are lyrical, like the earlier poems.

12. The Folly of Being Comforted

This lyric first appeared in *The Speaker* on 11th January, 1902. In it the poet tells that his love for Maud Gonne is not for her physical beauty, but for her soul. Though Yeats has been rejected by her several times, yet he cannot forget her, cannot think that he will not love her anymore. Even if she grows old abruptly, nevertheless his love for her will not diminish even an iota. About the time of writing this poem, Yeats had been undulating between hope and despair. He made the two following drafts of poems about 1897, in which Ellmann discovered Yeats's hope and despair in his love for Maud Gonne (Jeffares, 75):

I

O my beloved you only are not moved by
my songs
Which you only understand
You only know that it is
of you I sing when I tell
of the swan on the water
or the eagle in the heavens
or the faun in the wood.
Others weep but your eyes are dry.

II

O my beloved. How happy
I wish that day when you
came here from the
railway, and set your hair
aright in my looking glass
and then sat with me at
my table, and lay resting
in my big chair. I am
like the children O my
beloved and I play at
marriage—I play
with images of the life
you will not give to me O
my cruel one.

About five years after, we see Yeats with his same sense of despair as is evident in this present poem. His despair was being punctuated by occasional rays of hopes, but his intense love for Maud Gonne never flagged. Daniel Albright adds: "In this poem Yeats seems to be cultivating his obsession with Maud Gonne, as if his poetic inspiration were dependent on his hopeless affection." (Albright, 484).

THE FOLLY OF BEING COMFORTED

One that is ever kind said yesterday:
'Your well-beloved's hair has threads of grey,
And little shadows come about her eyes;
Time can but make it easier to be wise
Though now it seems impossible, and so
All that you need is patience.
Heart cries, 'No,
I have not a crumb of comfort, not a grain.
Time can but make her beauty over again:
Because of that great nobleness of hers
The fire that stirs about her, when she stirs,
Bums but more clearly. O she had not these ways
When all the wild summer was in her gaze.'

O heart! O heart! if she'd but turn her head,
You'd know the folly of being comforted.

This is sonnet with rhyming couplets, divided into three parts: two sextets and a concluding couplet. Yeats is despairing for his unrequited love for Maud Gonne. His friend, perhaps Lady Gregory, who is "ever kind", tries to comfort him by saying that the beauty of Maud, by which Yeats is so much attracted is no more on her person. The friend tells him that now there are "threads of grey" in the hair of his beloved, and there are "little shadows come about her eyes". The poet's friend says that after a lapse of some time, the poet will be able to forget her, and then it will be "easier to be wise". But this is not possible just now, for Yeats is still full of amorous emotion for her. The friend therefore advises the poet to have patience and wait for his emotion being diffused.

But the poet will not take the advice of his friend. He says that the advice of keeping patient will not comfort him. Contrary to the suggestion of his friend that with the lapse of time Gonne will grow old and lose beauty, and then it will diminish the intensity of his love for her, Yeats says that Maud Gonne will rather grow in beauty with the passage of time: "Time can but make her beauty over again". The poet says that though time may diminish her physical beauty, her "nobleness" will only be enhanced by the passage of time. He calls this nobleness of hers "fire that stirs about her, when she stirs". Further, the poet says that this fire, this nobleness, was not so clear in her younger days. Therefore, he concludes that if she now shows her head with grey hair, it will rather increase the intensity of his love for her, and will expose the folly of the suggestion of his friend of being comforted.

This is a simple love poem and a very sonorous song in simple words, but full of intense emotion. The alliteration in the tenth line is very pleasing: "The fire that stirs about her, when she stirs". The poem has no imagery, no allegory, and no legend. Such poems during the early phase of the poet are very rare. Yeats shows strands of realism from about this time on.

13. Adam's Curse

This is a rather long poem of 38 lines. It was written perhaps sometime before 20th November, 1902, and was first published in *Monthly Review*, in December, 1902. Like the foregoing poem, this one was also composed keeping in view the matinee idol of the poet, Maud Gonne, and is addressed to her. It records the personal reminiscence of the poet; and by the way, expresses the poet's opinion about artistic creation and the common folk. It also contains the poet's frustration and disillusionment at the rejection of his love by Maud Gonne. The occasion of the poem was recorded by Maud Gonne (now Madame MacBride) in her autobiography, *A Servant of the Queen*: "While we were still at dinner Willie Yeats arrived to see me and we all went into the drawing-room for coffee. Kathleen [her sister, Mrs Pilcher] and I sat together on a big sofa amid piles of soft cushions. I was still in my dark clothes with the black veil I always wore when travelling instead of a hat, and we must have made a strange contrast. I saw Willie Yeats looking critically at me and he told Kathleen he liked her dress and that she was looking younger than ever. It was on that occasion Kathleen remarked that it was hard work being beautiful which Willie turned into his poem 'Adam's Curse.'" (Jeffares, 78).

The title of the poem bears a reference to the biblical story of Adam and Eve, the first couple in the heaven that disobeyed the forewarning of God and therefore underwent the curse of Him and had to toil endlessly for sustenance of life. In Genesis 3:16-19, of the Bible, we read: "Unto the woman [God] said, I will greatly multiply the sorrow and thy conception; in sorrow thou shalt bring forth children... and unto Adam he said ... In the sweat of thy face shalt thou eat bread, till thou return unto the ground." Kathleen Pilcher told Yeats during that conversation that as Adam needed to labour for survival, so women needed to labour for her beauty. Daniel Albright adds: "Like 'Easter, 1916' and certain other poems, its theme is the process whereby random casual life attains, at a great cost, dignity and permanent form. Yeats's first assumption seems that expressed in his poem 'He tells of the Perfect Beauty': the poet labours endlessly while beauty is unlabouring, effortless. But Kathleen Pilcher corrects this: a woman's beauty requires equal labour—to be the model for the artist is as expensive as to be an artist." (Albright, 487).

ADAM'S CURSE

We sat together at one summer's end,
That beautiful mild woman, your close friend,
And you and I, and talked of poetry.
I said: 'A line will take us hours maybe;
Yet if it does not seem a moment's thought,
Our stiching and unstiching has been naught.
Better go down upon your marrow-bones
And scrub a kitchen pavement, or break stones
Like an old pauper, in all kinds of weather;
For to articulate sweet sound together
Is to work harder than all these, and yet
Be thought an idler by the noisy set
Of bankers, schoolmasters, and clergymen
The martyrs call the world.'

And thereupon
That beautiful mild woman for whose sake
There's many a one shall find out all heartache
On finding that her voice is sweet and low
Replied: 'To be born woman is to know—
Although they do not talk of it at school —
That we must labour to be beautiful.'
I said: 'It's certain there is no fine thing
Since Adam's fall but needs much labouring.
There have been lovers who thought love should be
So much compounded of high courtesy
That they would sigh and quote with learned looks
Precedents out of beautiful old books;
Yet now it seems an idle trade enough.'

We sat grown quiet at the name of love;
We saw the last embers of daylight die,

And in the trembling blue-green of the sky
A moon, worn as if it had been a shell
Washed by time's waters as they rose and fell
About the stars and broke in days and years.

I had a thought for no one's but your ears:
That you were beautiful, and that I storve
To love you in the old high way of love;
That it had all seemed happy, and yet we'd grown
As weary-hearted as that hollow moon.

The poet remembers that at the end of a summer, he along with his beloved Maud Gonne and her sister ("That beautiful mild woman, your close friend") sat together, and talked about poetry. He says that the composition of even a single line of a poem may take hours together, and sometimes even after that long time, it does not produce beauty or provoke any thought that a good poem should evoke ("does not seem a moment's thought"), and the toil in the composition becomes futile: the "stitching and unstitching has been naught." Corinna Salvadori comments that "stitching and unstitching" "are an exact definition of *sprezzatura*, and draws attention to Yeats's comment on a group of dancers whose toil must have been long and difficult but whose movements were full of joy". (Jeffares, 78-79). Daniel Albright adds here that during the time of composing the poem, "Yeats was learning about the Renaissance ideals of noble courtesy described in Castglione's *The Courtier.* This book recommended *sprezzatura* or elegant disdain—the mastery that dismisses its own effort." (Albright, 487). Yeats says that it is better to work hard scrubbing kitchen utensils or breaking stones as old and poor people do "in all kinds of weather", than writing uninspiring lines of a poem. He further says that "to articulate sweet sounds" in a poem is harder than washing utensils or breaking stones. Nevertheless, the "noisy set" or the people who like only meaningless noise,—like bankers, schoolmasters, clergymen and martyrs, —think that the poet is nothing but "an idler". Hearing this peroration of the poet, Maud Gonne's sister, the low-and-sweet-voiced Kathleen Gonne (afterwards Mrs Kathleen Pilcher), for whom there was no want of lovers, replied that women naturally know, or rather have the in nate knowledge of, the fact that if they want to be beautiful, they must toil for it: "we must labour to be beautiful", though they do not talk about it or admit it openly.

Yeats agrees with Kathleen and says that really "there is no fine thing" that does not require a great amount of labour, because there was, by implication, a curse upon Adam that he must toil endlessly for creating beautiful things. This applies squirely even to the sphere of the art of love-making. True, there are lovers who think that love-making needs only a combination of "high courtesy" in the shape of frequent sighs and quotations "out of beautiful old books" along with "learned looks' but Yeats comments that now such things are "idle trade".

After so much of conversation, all of them kept silent for a while looking at the last glow of the setting sun. "saw the last embers of daylight die". And after the sun set, they discovered a moon "in the trembling blue-green of the sky". The moon seemed to be worn out and looked like a shell that has been washed by the ebbs and tides of the sea of Time. The ebbs and tides of the sea of Time as if broke the stars into days and years.

At this time, a thought arose in the mind of the poet to be told only to his beloved Maud Gonne. It was that Maud Gonne was exquisitely beautiful and that the poet has striven to love her in the old and traditional fashion. He then felt happy, but somehow soon they had grown "weary-hearted" and their hearts became as hollow as the shell-like moon in the sky above. Daniel Albright comments on the two hyphenated words, "weary-hearted": "to maintain the discipline of love, or of beauty, or of poetry, exhausts the natural self—just as fantasy exhausts nature in 'The Withering of the Boughs'. According to the doctrine of the Mask, developed around 1909, every elaboration of a studied and disciplined self tends to impoverish one's natural being." (Albright, 487).

This is a lyric but realistic poem. Yeats here does not use any mythology or mysticism, but uses only his personal experiences and feelings. This is a poem of his transitional period when he turned his back to allegory, mythology and all that, and turned to realism, and yet his themes are not objective but personal. 'The Folly of Being Comforted' and 'Adam's Curse' may be taken as representative poems of his transitional period. One special feature of this present poem is that in it in course of giving poetic expression of his personal feelings, Yeats has here beautifully commented upon the necessity of labour in art creation: "we must labour to be beautiful". In the poem, the poet is disgruntled at the petty things of the world, for example with the "noisy set", for he is only after the beautiful. In this poem, his frustration and bitterness with the hard facts of life is also apparent.

THE GREEN HELMET AND OTHER POEMS — 1910

Yeats's collection of poems, *The Green Helmet*, was first published in 1910 by the Cuala Press. In 1912, Macmillan published another edition of the collection with six more poems, under the new title *The Green Helmet and Other Poems.* The poems of this volume also belong to the transitional period of the poet. The mythology, fairy tales, mysteries and the escapades of the earlier poems are absent here. Yeats has now accosted reality, and has left behind him the earlier "languor and resignation, nostalgia and deliberate restriction" of his previous poems. The poems in *The Green Helmet and Other Poems* reveal that the poet during the period of the composition of these poems had been going through diverse troubles. In 1903, after long hesitation, Maud Gonne married Major MacBride, shattering even the last rays of hope of Yeats for the love of Maud Gonne. At first Yeats despaired but as time passed and as he collected himself, he rather regretted the wastage of time and spirit that he devoted for the love of Maud. Therefore, we see that Maud's last rejection could not quite shatter the spirit of Yeats. After some time of the marriage of Maud with MacBride, Yeats thought that his supplications to Maud Gonne were not all amiss, because he thought that her beauty gave his poems "dignity and symbolic rhetoric" which could otherwise be "cold and simple in style". By now the "old ideal of romantic poetry had come to a stop, and there is an air of finality about the love poetry Yeats wrote after Maud's marriage: it is static, detached yet none the less poignant." (Jeffares, 85).

The additional poems that Macmillan included in their volume are: 'That the Night Came', 'Friends', 'The Cold Heaven', 'On hearing that the students of our New University have joined the Ancient Order of Hibernians and the Agitation against Immoral Literature', 'The Attack on the "Playboy", and 'At the Abbey Theatre'. All these poems reveal his realistic attitude and his interest in diverse public affairs: theatre, politics, etc. During this period "he had decided his Dionysiac phase was over and he must leave the modes of Mallarme or Symons for an Apollonian activity." (Jeffares, 85). As the themes and thoughts of his poems changed, he was after discovering new modes, new styles and new means of giving a fuller expression of his sensibilities. The poems of this volume do not betray the decor of his former poems. Yeats's technique here resembles that of the metaphysical poets. He also follows their use of prosaic diction: hard, matter-of-fact, colloquial, and rugged words.

Daniel Albright writes about this volume of poetry: "The themes *of In the Seven Woods*, such as the praise of the classic splendour of Maud Gonne and the scrutiny of the technique of verse-construction, continue here, but this volume is still more public and contemporary—the debonair poet appears at the university, the theatre, a fine old country house, the racetrack; he is so comfortably fomous that he can afford to ridicule his imitators in a witty epigram. Although some of the poems in this volume are intimate and soulful in the old manner, in other poems the poet is rather detached and aloof, a spectator rather than a participant." (Albright, 501). However, the title of this volume comes from Yeats's second play of the Cuchulain cycle, *The Green Helmet*, along with which these poems were published.

14. No Second Troy

The poem was written perhaps in December, 1908, and was first published in *The Green Helmet* in 1910. Yeats's poems of the *The Green Helmet* are short; but they possess "vast immensities" *a la* Donne's poems. The source of this poem is Maud Gonne's marriage with Major John MacBride in 1903 (the marriage was terminated in 1905). Yeats was utterly fascinated by Maud's regular features, her nobility and spriteliness, her commanding personality, and by her ineffable and charismatic superiority. The theme of the poem refers to the story of Helen or Helena, the daughter of Jupiter and Leda, and wife of Menelaus. She was the paragon of beauty in her day. She fell in love with Paris, the son of Prium, the king of Troy, and eloped with him. This caused the famous war of Troy. Yeats imagines himself in the plight of Menelaus when Maud marries MacBride, because he thinks that Maud was actually the rightful possession of himself. Yeats compares Maud with Helen in her power of destruction that culminated in the war of Troy. Like Helen, Maud, with her revolutionary zeal led the youths of Ireland through the nationalist movement. Before her marriage, Maud involved herself in the nationalist movement against the British domination. She linked herself with the I.R.B. (Irish Republican Brotherhood), a secret revolutionary society, and employed the French military intelligence against the British. She was also instrumental in the bombing of British battle-ships, through the agency of some Boers. Albright adds: "The theme of this poem is the contrast between the stress of Maud Gonne's splendor and the laxness and cowardice of the modern age — no easy relation between them is possible. Yeats may have been fond of this poem, for he copied it into his journal as the epitaph [of Memoirs, edited by Dennis Donoghue in 1972]." (Albright, 505). However, in this poem, the poet is apprehensive because Maud's too much of national feeling may have destroyed the future of the younger generation.

NO SECOND TROY

Why should I blame her that she filled my days
With misery, or that she would of late

Have taught to ignorant men most violent ways,
Or hurled the little streets upon the great,
Had they but courage equal to desire?
What could have made her peaceful with a mind
That nobleness made simple as a fire,
With beauty like, a tightened bow, a kind
That is not natural in an age like this,
Being high and solitary and most stem?
Why, what could she have done, being what she is?
Was there another Troy for her to burn?

The poet recounts his days of misery caused by Maud Gonne's rejection of his love, and yet he does not want to put the blame for this on her. Before withdrawing from public affairs, Gonne persuaded the ignorant youths of the nation to take arms against the British people—youths who did not know anything about the possible outcome of the nationalist movement: "taught to ignorant men most violent ways". And yet the poet would not blame her for this. True, it was Gonne for whose efforts it was possible for the little semi-literary and semi-political clubs of Ireland ("the little streets") to merge with the larger body of the Sinn Fein. But Yeats is doubtful if the youths of all these organisations had courage enough to accomplish what they wanted to accomplish ("Had they but courage equal to desire?"). However, after all these, Gonne has got married and, perhaps, the poet thinks, is in peace of mind. The volatile, high-spirited "nobility" of Gonne has now gone away, and she is now "simple as fire". But her beauty remains undiminished—beauty "That is not natural in an age like this". Yeats compares Gonne's beauty with "a tightened bow", strapping and inviting. The symbol of "tightened bow" is drawn from Blake and refers to the "archer who shoots an arrow beyond the earth". Yeats means to say that Gonne's beauty is not earthly, but ethereal. He says that Gonne is now aloof, withdrawn and solitary. He imagines what Gonne might have done in the national movement and also in the life of himself had she not withdrawn herself from everything by marrying MacBride. He insinuates that had she not withdrawn herself into her cocoon, she, with her Helen-like beauty, might have repeated the Trojan war in which the poet might have engaged himself, and might have died for her beauty: "Was there another Troy for her to burn?" Daniel Albright explains this line thus:" this question is answered by the title. In the so-called 'Leroy' version of the unfinished *The Speckled Bird,* the hero contrasts ancient times, when warriors died gladly for those whom poets praised, and a city was burned for Helen, with modern times, when beauty appeals only to a few, and the masses prefer a coarse prettiness." (Albright, 505-06).

In simple diction and short length, the poem expresses an intense emotion of poised grief. Though the emotion is intense, yet it is not romantic, but is realistic. Again, though the grief is personal, yet it has been elevated to the plane of the universal, because everyone in the same situation will be overcast with the same grief. Like most of the other poems of Yeats's transitional phase, this poem in its limited periphery, contains "vast immensities". It is one of the finest poems of this transitional period. The metaphysical poet's conceit is present here: Yeats compares Gonne's beauty with "a tightened bow" —two far flung things compared closely. Most of the lines of this poem show compactness of meaning, a sign of Yeats's other poems of the transitional period, and also of his mature poems.

15. The Coming of Wisdom with Time

This is a very short epigrammatic poem of only four lines. It was written either on 21st March or on 22nd March, 1909. Yeats first wrote it in his Diary. The original title of the poem was 'Youth and Age', when it was published in *McClure's Magazine* in December, 1910. But when it appeared in *The Green Helmet and Other Poems,* it was entitled 'The Coming of Wisdom with Time'. Daniel Albright adds: "This poem is one of many Yeats wrote on the bleak consolations of old age. It turns on the contrast between blatant self-expression, self-publicity, and reticent self-knowledge — a theme similar to that of 'All Things can Tempt Me'." (Albright, 510).

THE COMING OF WISDOM WITH TIME

Though leaves are many, the root is one;
Through all the lying days of my youth
I swayed my leaves and flowers in the sun;
Now I may wither into the truth.

The poet compares himself with a tree which has many leaves but only one root. In his youth, the poet wrote poems with multiple decorative elements which were like the leaves of a tree which has but one root; i.e. his poems had many leaves, but each of the poems had only one key idea or central truth. He now thinks that he then, as if, flaunted his decorations of his poetry before the reading public: "swayed my leaves and flowers in the sun". However, now he decides not to use those decorations in his poems. He will let the leaves of the tree of his poems wither, so that only the truth of a poem becomes obvious, without being shrouded by the decorations: "Now I may wither into the truth." Albright writes about the last line of the poem: 'the poet devolves from his leaves to his root, from the many to the one. Compare Yeats's statement, 'to die into the truth is still to die' (AV, p. 271). Pound commented, 'Yeats burbles when he talks of "withering into the truth". You *wither* into non-curiosity."' (Albright, 510).

In this poem Yeats plainly and clearly declares his adoption of a new technique of poetry, the technique of modern poetry. The poem was written in 1909 when Yeats had been passing through his transitional period of poetry—when he decided to change the theme and technique of his poetry. Before that, in his poetry, he used profusely the Irish folktales, mysteries, legends, etc. as well as pre-Raphaelite decorations in words and imageries. But since now, he decided to shed off all these and write, instead, stark, precise and brief poems, with the application of barren and every day or colloquial words. He decided to be austere and restrictive in the use of words, imageries, etc. This poem is therefore, as if, an announcement of the coming up of his new poetry in the future. Strangely, this poem itself is a good specimen of the kind of poems he was going to write in the future. For, within the compass of only four lines of simple and barren (non-decorative) words, he has superbly been able to express his central thought and message.

16. Upon a House Shaken by the Land Agitation

Though in the last decade of the 19th century Yeats gradually retracted himself from the on-going politics of Ireland, he did not close his eyes to the contemporary political events for all times. In 1910, the government of Ireland reduced the rent of big houses under pressure of popular movements, and the action of the government affected the house of Lady Gregory where Yeats had been putting up. This poem is a protest against the popular movements and against the action taken by the government. The poem was first published in *McClure's Magazine*, in December, 1910, under the title 'To a Certain Country House in Time of Change'. Next, when it appeared in *The Green Helmet*, it took the title 'Upon a Threatened House'. And lastly, when it was published in *The Green Helmet and Other Poems*, it was entitled 'Upon a House shaken by the Land Agitation'. Yeats wrote a draft of the poem and an explanation of it in his Diary on 7th August, 1910, which will enlighten us about the meaning of the poem. He wrote: "Subject. A Shaken House. How should the world gain if this house failed, even though a hundred houses were the better for it, for here power has gone forth, or lingered giving energy, precision: it gives to a far people beneficent rule; and still under its roof loving intellect is sweetened by old memories of its descents from far off; how should the world be better if the wren's nest flourish and the eagle's house is scattered." (Jeffares, 93). And in the explanation of the theme of the poem, he wrote in the same Diary: "I wrote this poem on hearing the result of reduction of rent by the courts. One feels that when all must make their living, they will live not for life's sake but for the work's and all be the poorer. My work is very near to life itself and my father's very near to life itself, but I am always feeling a lack of life's own values behind my thoughts. They should have been there before the stream began, before it became necessary to let the work create its values. This house has enriched my soul out of measure because her life moves within restraint through gracious forms. Here there has been no compelled labour, no poverty thwarted impulse." (Jeffares, 93). Yeats cannot bear with the idea that the poor should grow on the ruins of the rich. His aristocratic propensity is evident here. But this does not mean that he supports the divide between the propertied class and the proletariat. What he actually means to say is that culture, the love of the beautiful, resides only in the houses of the aristocrats, and therefore, should the houses of the aristocrats be destroyed, beauty will fly away, and this will pain him the most.

UPON A HOUSE SHAKEN BY THE LAND AGITATION

How should the world be luckier if this house,
Where passion and precision have been one
Time out of mind, became too ruinous
To breed the lidless eye that loves the sun?
And the sweet laughing eagle thoughts that grow
Where wings have memory of wings, and all
That comes of the best knit to the best? Although
Mean roof-trees were the sturdier for its fall,
How should their luck run high enough to reach
The gifts that govern men, and after these
To gradual Time's last gift, a written speech
Wrought of high laughter, loveliness and ease?

Yeats has been staying at the house of Lady Gregory, his friend, at Coole Park. The house is the centre of art and culture ("passion and precision"). Art and culture are the tradition of the house since when the poet does not know. According to the court orders, or to the decision of the government, the rent of the house has been reduced, which will not let the house continue its traditional art and culture, because of the consequent reduction in the income. The poet thinks that the judgement of the court is a serious blow to the "big-house tradition". Because of the court order, the house has somehow become "ruinous", and so the poet is aggrieved. He raises the question: will the world be better if this house is reduced? He compares the owner of the house with an eagle. The eagle is a Blakean image and "refers to the belief that only an eagle can stare into the sun without blinking. Yeats uses the eagle as a symbol for an active objective person." (Jeffares, 93). The eagle refers to Lady Gregory, and the sun may symbolise the higher up pursuits of art and culture and beauty. The poet means to say that only the aristocratic Lady Gregory can look upwards to the preservation and continuance of art and culture and beauty, like an eagle's staring at the sun. The eagle craves light—the light of art, culture, morality and heroic deeds.

The poet repeats the image of the eagle in the fifth and the sixth lines. He says that the big houses have a tradition and that the big houses are "sweet" and magnanimous ("eagle thoughts"), like the eagle. This has also a reference to Blake's line The Eagle, that doth gaze upon the sun' in his poem 'King Edward the Third' or to Blake's lines in his poem 'Visions of the Daughters of Albion':

> .... and the eagle returns
> From nightly prey and lifts his golden beak
> to the pure east,
> Shaking the dust from his immortal pinions
> to awake
> The sun that sleeps too long.

In fact, Yeats was to a great extent influenced by Blake's poetry. He even edited a collection of Blake's poems and published it in 1893 under the little *The Poems of Blake.* It is natural therefore that Blake's images will enter into his poetry.

However, the poet says that because of the fall of the big house of Lady Gregory, the poorer people ("Mean roof-trees") may become stronger and the poor people may think them equal to the owners of the big houses. But he says that thereby the poorer people shall not be able to reach the loftiness and magnanimity of the big houses, of the governing men: "How should their luck run high enough to reach/The gifts that govern men". He is sure that they will never be able to acquire the loveliness and the ideals of the higher stratum of the society. Yeats thinks that the government of Ireland, pressurised by the mob, have done something which will in reality not benefit the poor folk in any higher pursuits, in the end.

The poem bears the features of the poetry of Yeats's transitional period. Its theme is realistic, and almost paltry — a theme that perhaps cannot be the theme of a romantic poetry. However, Stephen Spender finds faults of Yeats in this poem. Spender accuses Yeats of upholding the ideal of aristocracy in an age of democracy, as Yeats elsewhere sighs for the rural verdure in an age of industry. And therefore to Spender, Yeats seems to be out of tune with the life around him.

RESPONSIBILITIES —1914

Responsibilities was published by the Cuala Press in 1914. It included some of Yeats's mature poems and his play *The Hour-Glass.* A few of the poems of this volume earlier appeared in *The Green Helmet and Other Poems.* During the period of writing these poems, Yeats got himself involved in public affairs and in the consequent controversies, particularly in the controversy regarding his relationship with Maud Gonne. He was irritated by the behaviour of his common compatriots. About *Responsibilities,* A. Norman Jeffares writes: "These particular poems reflect his delight in the patronage given by the rulers of Italian Renaissance courts, with which he compared his attitude of Ireland's new rich. He weighed the new politicians against the old heroes and found them sadly lacking: in 'The Fisherman' he contrasted his hopes for Ireland with the reality. His experience of secret societies, committees, public meetings emerged in bitter political rhetoric: there was a bitterly disillusioned note in the poetry too; the Celtic trappings were finally, decisively, renounced in 'A Coat' and his own ancestors were given mythological significance, while he continued to write love poems, still deeply moved by the beauty of Maud Gonne and, while angered by the way in which the Irish crowd had behaved to him and to her ('The People'), yet ready to accept her continuing regard for the people as selfless and impressive. These love poems have some gentleness and excitement; they are also compassionate in their evocation of old memories. There are also poems recording intense personal experiences, such as that superb and timeless poem 'The Cold Heaven.'" (Jeffares, 98).

The features of Yeats's earlier poems are hardly to be found in *Responsibilities.* He has by now said good-bye to the mythologies, the mellifluous words, the escapades, the faeries, etc. of his earlier poems. He has now experienced the buffets and slings of the world. Yeast's poetic technique is now plain and direct. The emotion is restrained, the poem is more compact and pregnant, and the language compressed. Regarding his shedding off of the decorations ("embroideries") of his earlier style, the poet himself beautifully writes in his poem 'A coat':

I made my song a coat
Covered with embroideries
Out of old mythologies
From heal to throat;
But the fools caught it,
Wore it in the world's eyes
As though they'd wrought it.
Song, let them take it,
For there's more enterprise
In walking naked.

During this period, the poet was suffering from disillusionment and frustration as well as from public acrimony against himself. He was full of remorse for his past frivolities as is evident in his poem 'The Cold Heaven'.

Yeats began writing poetry with dreams in his head and keeping aloof from the world around him: from politics and other public affairs. He then felt no responsibilities to anybody else, or to the society; and thought that art was for art's sake. But during the time when the First World War was breaking out, Yeats for the first time found that he had some responsibility towards the world. He then changed the nature of his themes and his technique. He thought that once Tennyson and Browning showed their responsibilities towards the world in their poetry, but after them, for about two generations, poets are writing only personal and lyric poems. He wanted to turn the tide and write responsible poems—poems such as are included in *Responsibilities.* Yeats says that his sense of responsibility originated in his dreams, that is, in his dreams of perfection and splendor. Daniel Albright writes: "*Responsibilities* offers ..., a new spirit of inclusiveness and historical interest. This volume comprises poems about the premiere of Synge's *The Playboy of the Western World,* about the ghost of the politician Charles Parnell, and about a legal dispute over the location of some Impressionist paintings. But Yeats might still properly claim that his responsibility began in his dreams, for, as he studies the social scene, he judges what he sees by the standards of perfection and felt splendor that he had been elaborating in his speech during his whole career. To some extent the form of the volume is dictated by the epigraph: at the beginning there are a number of poems about responsibility (such as the Introductory Rhymes and 'To a Wealthy Man ...'), and afterwards come a number of poems about sleep, wishes, and dreams (The Three Beggars; 'the Hour before Dawn'), about vision and inspiration ('The Magi', 'A Coat', the Closing Rhymes). Responsibility thus reveals its origin in dreams." (Albright, 517). But there are also some poems in this volume which show that the poet was also concerned with irresponsibility's. Daniel Albright writes: "*Responsibilities* shows a considerable preoccupation with the irresponsible—with incompetent politicians, venal rich men, bad poets, Philistines; and also with beggars, children, and others who are too simple and lowly to be responsible." (Albright, 517).

But what does Yeats mean by responsibility and irresponsibility? In his *A Vision,* Yeats gave an idea of the responsible man: "'... a code of personal conduct... being formed from social and historical tradition, remains always concrete in the mind. All is sacrificed to this code; moral strength reaches its climax.... There is great humility— 'she died every day she lived' — and pride as great, pride in the code's acceptance, an impersonal pride, as though one were to sign oneself 'servant of servants' ... The code... is obeyed in pain—can there be mercy in a rigid code?— the man is flooded with joy of self-surrender; and flooded with mercy — what self can there be in self-surrender?—for those over whom the code can have no rights, children and the nameless multitude. Unmerciful to those who serve and to himself, merciful in contemplating those who are served, he never wearies of forgiveness.'" (Albright, 518). Perhaps Lady Gregory was the model of a human being with a sense of responsibility, to Yeats, for we find her to be continually referred to in these poems.

Most of the poems of this volume are narrative. In some poems, Yeats is striving to establish "a strong relation between an ancient story and modern life." Some such poems are 'The Grey Rock' and 'The Hour before Dawn'. The volume contains two epigraphs; and, interestingly enough, the first epigraph, 'In *dreams begins responsibility*', was not actually taken from any 'Old Play', as Yeats tells us, but was written by Yeats himself. (Albright, 518).

17. September 1913

This poem of 32 lines was written in September (the 7th of September), 1913, from which date it derives its title. It first appeared on 8 September, 1913, in *Irish Times,* with the title 'Romance in Ireland'. Next, it was published in *Nine Poems* (1914) and there it was entitled 'Romantic Ireland (September 1913)'. Lastly, when it was published *in Responsibilities Poems and a Play (1914),* it took the present title. It is apolitical and national ballad in which the poet heaps up praises for those who have died for the cause of Ireland, particularly for John O' Leary (1830-1907), Lord Edward Fitzgerald (1763-98), Robert Emmet (1778-1803), and Theobald Wolfe Tone (1763-98). The poet also condoles the deaths of other innumerable

Irish men — the 'Wilde Geese', who suffered unbearably for the freedom of the nation and for retrieving the past glory of Ireland. At the same time, he inveighs the present leaders, in utter bitterness, for their meanness. He concludes with the remark that it is good that men like O' Leary are dead now, because they are past the mean countrymen's mean assessment of them.

SEPTEMBER 1913

What need you, being come to sense,
But fumble in a greasy till
And add the halfpence to the pence
And prayer to shivering prayer, until
You have dried the marrow from the bone?
For men were born to pray and save:
Romantic Ireland's dead and gone,
It's with O' Leary in the grave.

Yet they were of a different kind,
The names that stilled your childish play,
They have gone about the world like wind,
But little time had they to pray
For whom the hangman's rope was spun,
And what, God help us, could they save?
Romantic Ireland's dead and gone,
It's with O' Leary in the grave.

Was it for this the wild geese spread?
The grey wing upon every tide;
For this that all that blood was shed,
For this Edward Fitzgerald died,
And Robert Emmet and Wolfe Tone,
All that delirium of the brave?
Romantic Ireland's dead and gone,
It's with O' Leary in the grave.

Yet could we turn the years again,
And call those as they were
In all their loneliness and pain,
You'd cry, 'Some woman's yellow hair
Has maddened every mother's son':

They weighed so lightly what they gave.
But let them be, they're dead and gone,
They're with O'Leary in the grave.

The poem is divided into four stanzas, each stanza having eight lines. In the first stanza, the poet addresses his present compatriots and asks them to try to understand and not to misunderstand, as they are doing now, the contributions of the dead patriots — thousands of them. He says in an ironic note that his compatriots should rather put their attention to the greasy ("oily") drawer or chest for money ("till") and only accumulate money: "add halfpence to the pence." They are also praying in the Churches till they "have dried the marrow from the bone." Actually people are doing two things: accumulating money and praying to God. Consequently, they have forgotten their past glory of Ireland: "Romantic Ireland's dead and gone." After John O'Leary, who was a great hero and patriot, died, Ireland's glory has been forgotten. O'Leary, when he was a medical student in Trinity College, Dublin, joined the Young Ireland Movement. Next, he became one of the three great leaders of the Fenian movement that came into force after the Young Ireland Movement subsided. "He was arrested in 1865, condemned to twenty years' penal servitude, but set free after serving nine years of his sentence, on condition that he did not return to Ireland for fifteen years. He spent his exile in Paris and returned to Dublin in 1885." (Jeffares, 110).

In the second stanza, the poet says that the dead patriots were people quite different from the people of the present generation. They are dead now; but when they were alive and politically active, they could stop the people being engaged in paltry vocations like accumulating money and praying to God—vocations that are but children's plays. The dead heroes inflamed the spirit of nationality in all the nooks and comers of the country: "They have gone about the world like wind." But they could hardly find time to accumulate money and pray to God. Some of these heroes put the hangman's rope-noose round their necks and died — for them "the hangman's rope was spun." Yeats now regrets their deaths, because they died but in vain—they could not retrieve the past glory of Ireland and now Ireland has been immersed in meanness: "And what, God help us, could they save ?" And therefore the poet repeats the refrain: "Romantic Ireland's dead and gone,/ It's with O'Leary in the grave."

In the next stanza, the poet speaks more about the past heroes. He says that thousands of Irish men—the "wild geese" — suffered for the cause of the nation. The "wild geese" refer to the "Irishmen who served abroad in the armies of France, Spain, and Austria, largely as a result of the Penal Laws passed after 1691. [The Penal Laws were highly restrictive of the freedom of conduct of the Irish Catholics.] Sarsfield and 11,000 men left for the French service, out of loyalty to James II, after the Treaty of Limerick was signed in 1691; the Irish Brigade fought with the French until the Revolution. In all, it is said that 120,000 'Wild Geese' left Ireland between 1690 and 1730." (Jeffares, 110). These "wild Geese" crossed the oceans and fought in different foreign lands: "the wild geese spread/ The grey wing upon every tide." They shed their blood in foreign lands for the cause of Ireland herself. Prominent among them were Edward Fitzgerald, Robert Emmet and Wolfe Tone. These heroes and other brave men immolated themselves, so to say, to retrieve the romantic past of Ireland. "Lord Edward Fitzgerald (1703-98), a romantic figure who served in America, became M.P. for Athy and Kildare, and joined the United Irishmen in 1796. He was president of the military committee and died of wounds received while being arrested." (Jeffares, 111). "Robert Emmet (1778-1803), who was educated at Trinity College, Dublin, led an abortive revolt in 1803, was tried for high treason and hanged publicly in Dublin." (Jeffares, 111). "Theobald Wolfe Tone (1763-98), educated at Trinity College, Dublin, founded the United Irish Club, was appointed chef-de-brigade in France, and led a French force to Ireland. He was captured in Lough Swilly and condemned to death by a court martial. He committed suicide in prison." (Jeffares, 111). Yeats mourns doubly for all these persons because their dream of the future Ireland has not been materialised, and so he repeats the refrain: "Romantic Ireland's dead and gone,/ It's with O'Leary in the grave."

In the last stanza, the poet shows his pity for those dead heroes, because, he says, if we could turn the wheel of time backwards and get the time when these heroes were alive and active in the national movement, even then the present generation would not believe in the nationalistic spirit in the breasts of these heroes. The present generation would not understand their fire of nationalism even if they see their "loneliness and pain." Rather, the degenerated modern generation would imagine that these national heroes did what they did, not for the cause of the nation, but for some beautiful young woman with yellow hair: "You'd cry, 'Some woman's yellow hair/Has maddened every mother's son." The poet says that the heroes did not care for their lives that they sacrificed at the altar of the nation: "They weighed so lightly what they gave." And in the last two lines the poet persuades himself to believe that it is better for the heroes that they are dead now because this lowly generation of Ireland cannot understand the great deeds of the past heroes: "But let them be, they're dead and gone, They're with O'Leary in the grave."

Yeats's indignation at the selfishness of the present leadership is evident here. The poem bears evidences of Yeats's spirit of nationalism, and his desire for the return of the romantic age of Ireland. It is a short but beautiful ballad with a political theme. The diction is sometimes appropriately pungent and the mockery poignant. The refrain that occurs thrice sustains the complex emotion of remorse and irony throughout the poem. In the last two lines, the refrain changes slightly, and here the irony reaches its pick.

18. To a Shade

The poem was composed at Code on 29th September, 1913, and it was first published in *Poems Written in Discouragement* (1913). In it the poet expresses his bitterness at the meanness of his countrymen. The 'Shade' here refers to Charles Stewart Parnell (1846-91) who once had been an Irish Parliamentary leader. Ha was born in County Wicklow in an Anglo-Irish Protestant family. Parnell was a leader of the Home Rule movement also, and was a gifted orator. He supported Gladstone's Home Rule Bill and remained a great leader of Ireland till 1890, in which year he was implicated in an affair with Mrs. Kathleen O'Shea (1845-1921), wife of Captain O'Shea. For this Gladstone vehemently repudiated him and the public opinion about him also swung to the opposite pole. The public denounced him so much so that his health broke down and as a result he died in the next year. Parnell was entombed in Glasnevin Cemetery, Dublin, and a monument was erected in his memory in the northern end of O' Connel Street, Dublia Parnell was buried on 11th October, 1891. Yeats did not attend the funeral of his friend Parnell, but wrote a poem 'Mourn and then Onward!' on the occasion, and the poem was published in *United Ireland on* 10th October, 1891. The poem which was never reprinted is being given below:

> Ye on the broad high mountains of old Eri,
> Mourn all the night and day,
> The man is gone who guided ye, unweary,
> Through the long bitter way.
>
> Ye by the waves that close in our sad nation,
> Be full of sudden fears,
> The man is gone who from his lonely station
> Has moulded the hard years.

Mourn ye on grass-green plains of Eri fated,
For closed in darkness now
Is he who laboured on, derided, hated,
And made the tyrant bow.

Mourn — and then onward, there is no returning
He guides ye from the tomb;
His memory now is a tall pillar, burning
Before us in the gloom!

Besides this poem and the poem To a Shade', Yeats wrote some other poems also to commemorate the contribution of Parnell. However, here in this poem the poet says that Parnell did much for the people of Ireland, and moreover, once the people also were grateful to him; but now even they have all forgotten all about his contributions, only for the simple reason of Parnell's alleged affairs with Mrs. O'Shea. Without going into the tenability of the charges against Parnell, Yeats in this poem castigates his countrymen for their lack of magnanimity and for their ingratitude shown towards Parnell. The poet takes a cudgel to chastise his countrymen who are, he thinks, ignorant and uncultured.

TO A SHADE

If you have revisited the town, thin Shade,
Whether to look upon your monument
(I wonder if the builder has been paid)
Or happier-thoughted when the day is spent
To drink of that salt breath out of the sea
When grey gulls flit about instead of men,
And the gaunt houses put on majesty:
Let these content you and be gone again;
For they are at their old tricks yet.
A man
Of your own passionate serving kind who had brought
In his full hands what, had they only known,
Had given their children's children loftier thought,
Sweeter emotion, working in their veins
Like gentle blood, has been driven from the place,
And insult heaped upon him for his pains,
And for his open-handedness, disgrace;
Your enemy, an old foul mouth, had set
The pack upon him.

Go, unquiet wanderer,
And gather the Glasnevin coverlet
About your head till the dust stops your ear,
The time for you to taste of that salt breath
And listen at the comers has not come;
You had enough of sorrow before death —
Away, away! You are safer in the tomb.

The poet imagines that the soul of Charles Stewart Parnell (the "Shade") has come out of his grave at night and is visiting his own monument. The poet knows his countrymen to be so mean that he has doubt whether the builder of the monument had been paid for his labour . Here he exposes the utter meanness of his countrymen and their immense ingratitude to Parnell: "(I wonder if the builder has been paid)." Or, perhaps, says the poet, the soul or ghost of Pamell has come out of the grave to enjoy the salty air of the sea in a happy mood, when men do not loiter about, but only grey gulls fly to and fro. Perhaps the ghost has come out in the dark of the night when even the thin and gaunt houses of the poor put on images of majesty, because the darkness of night covers the various lacks and indecencies of the poor houses. The poet asks the ghost to remain content with only this much that he is enjoying the refreshing scenario of the surrounding, and not to expect anything more. He tells the ghost that his countrymen are no more grateful to him for all that he did for them, rather they are still now very much critical about himself — they are still now full of biting criticisms and raillery: "They are at their old trick yet." And therefore the poet asks the ghost to go back to his tomb.

Yeats, next, speaks about another great man of Ireland: Sir Hugh Lane who was similarly treated by the Irish people. Lane, like Parnell, did much for them, but they have shown only ingratitude to him. Like Parnell, Lane served the country passionately. He did so much for Ireland, says the poet, that if the people knew all that then they would surely tell their children and grandchildren about Lane's contributions: "had they only know,/Had given their children's children loftier thought." The people would then hold Lane as an ideal before their progeny. They would infuse appropriate and lofty emotion in the blood of their grandchildren *a la* Lane: "Sweeter emotion, working in their veins/Like gentle blood," That is, then the people would not teach their progeny to be ungrateful, arrogant and mean-minded, like themselves. But all that has not occurred. The Irish people have forgotten the contributions of both Parnell and Lane. They only know whatever doubtful and minor wrongs they allegedly had committed, and banking on these doubtful wrongs, the people of Ireland have forgotten both of them altogether. They have shown their ingratitude to both of them, insulted them, and ultimately driven them out of their memory, and consequently, both of them suffered much sorrow: "has been driven from the place,/And insult heaped upon him for his pains." Yeats tells the ghost of Parnell that Lane's enemy, probably William Martin Murphy who owned two news-papers and in them published biting criticisms against Lane ('had set/The pack upon him.") is a foul-mouthed rascal.

The poet thinks that the ghost of Parnell has, perhaps, been unquiet in its grave and so it has come out to wander around the monument. But the ghost will find nothing to be happy in the present meanness of Ireland, and so the poet exhorts the unhappy ghost to go back to the grave at Glasnevin and shroud itself in the coverlet of dust, so that it does not hear the raillery of the people again. The poet tells the ghost of Parnell that the time has not yet come when it may enjoy the fresh air of the sea and hear people praise him: "The time for you to taste of that salt breath/And listen at the comers has not come." The poet recalls that Parnell had had much sorrow before his death due to the ingratitude of his benefactors, and therefore says that he is better happy and safe in the tomb.

The poem betrays some of Yeats's political philosophy. He has all contempt for the underdogs that lack in gratitude and generosity and fail to appreciate the difference between the high and the low. For the same reason, Yeats hates democracy and hold up the spirit of aristocracy. He cannot bear with the injustice done to his friends by the people, and this is the theme of the poem. The occasion of the poem is certainly personal, but the poet raises it to the universal level, for we all can identify ourselves with the poet and feel his sentiment as ours as well. David Daiches rightly found elegance and ironic tone in the line "(I wonder if the builder has been paid)." But perhaps the same tone pervades the whole poem.

19. Friends

This poem was written in January, 1911, and was first published in *The Green and Other Poems* (1912). In it, the poet expresses his gratitude to his three most intimate friends—all women. Though the poet does not disclose the identity of the three friends in the poem, yet we can easily recognise them. These three women are Mrs. Olivia Shakespeare (1867-1938), Lady Gregory and Maud Gonne, about the last two of whom we have already known. About Mrs Shakespeare, A. Norman Jeffares writes that she was "a cousion of Lionel Johnson, whom Yeats first met in London in 1894. They corresponded until her death in 1938 when he wrote 'For more than forty years she has been the centre of my life in London, and during all that time we have never had a quarrel, sadness sometimes, but never a difference.' In 1895 Yeats and she exchanged many letters when he was in Sligo and she sent him the manuscript of her work *Beauty's Hour* while he wrote to her on his ideas of the coincidence of opposites." (Jeffares, 123).

It may be mentioned here that in Yeats' s poetry we find two categories of persons or characters: dead and living. Among the dead are: poets — Lionel Johnson and Ernest Dowson; relatives — George Pollexfen and Alfred Pollexfen; friends—Robert Gregory and MacGregor; warriors—those executed in the 1916 Easter Rebellion; and beautiful women — Florence Farr, Eva Gore-Booth, and Con Markiewicz. And among the living characters are: Maud Gonne, Iseult Gonne,Georgie Hyde-Lees, Mrs. Olivia Shakespeare, and Isabella Augusta Persse Gregory (1852-1932).

FRIENDS

Now must I these three praise —
Three women that have wrought
What joy is in my days:
One because no thought,
Nor those unpassing cares,
No, not in these fifteen
Many-times-troubled years,
Could ever come between
Mind and delighted mind;
And one because her hand
Had strength that could unbind
What none can understand,
What none can have and thrive,
Youth's dreamy load, till she
So changed me that I live
Labouring in ecstasy.
And what of her that took
All till my youth was gone
With scarce a pitying look?
How could I praise that one?
When day begins to break
I count my good and bad,
Being wakeful for her sake,
Remembering what she had,
What eagle look still shows,

What up from my heart's root
So great a sweetness flows
I shake from head to foot.

At the beginning of the volume of poems, *Responsibilities*, there are some poems in which Yeats celebrates some of his fellow poets of the Rhymers' Club, and at the end of the volume, he celebrates, in some of his poems, a few women who somehow or other moulded his life and thoughts. Thus in 'Friends', Yeats celebrates three women—Mrs. Olivia Shakespeare, Lady Gregory and Maud Gonne. The poet says that he must praise these three women who have given all the joy that he has had in his life. The first woman is Mrs. Olivia Shakespeare who looked after him for fifteen long years of many troubles. It was for her that he was never troubled by any unwanted thought and care, for she always delighted his mind. "Yeats spoke of himself, and Olivia as likes, and of himself and Maud Gonne as Complementary unlikes." (Albright, 542). The second woman is Lady Gregory who has always been a strong influence over him and who persuaded him to forget his pathos due to his unrequited love of Maud Gonne: "Youth's dreamy load." And it was she who consoled him in his heart-ache and helped him write poetry, that is, she helped him in his "Labouring in ecstasy." Daniel Albright adds: "Yeats attributed to her influence his change from morbid introspection to high purposefulness." (Albright, 542). The third or the last woman is Maud Gonne who has remained in his imagination throughout his life. Gonne took away, says the poet, everything from him throughout his youth, but did never show even a sign of pity to him. The poet, therefore, cannot decide how to praise her. Each day, from daybreak, the poet began to count his fortunes and adversities, keeping her image always in his mind. He has always remembered her attractive, hypnotising features. He would till now (in spite of being rejected by her several times) like to love her "eagle look" or elegant grace that took roots in his heart. According to A. Norman Jeffares, "eagle look" means "the detachment and objectivity Yeats associated with active rather than contemplative persons. Yeats was always struck by Maud Gonne's refusal to discuss herself: 'You know I hate talking of myself; I am not going to let you make me.'" (Jeffares, 124). The poet would love the sweetness that exuded from her psycho-physical being, and he says that the sweetness is so overpowering that he could not but tremble.

The poem is obviously lyrical and autobiographical. To Mrs. Shakespeare and Lady Gregory, the poet expresses his gratitude, but when he comes to the case of Maud Gonne, his emotion becomes complex, due to a mix up of bitterness and attraction, — due to his ambivalence to

Gonne. In many of his poems, Yeats expressed this sort of emotion, and in many of his poems he idolised Gonne *a la* Frnacesco Petrarch (Laura), Alighieri Dante (Beatrice) and William Shakespeare (Dark Lady).

20. The Cold Heaven

The poem first appeared in *The Green Helmet and Other Poems* in 1912. "Maud Gonne asked Yeats its meaning and was told that it was an attempt to describe the feelings aroused in him by the cold detached sky in winter. He felt he was alone, responsible in his loneliness for all the past mistakes that were torturing his peace of mind. This was a momentary intensity of perception, made more poignant for him by the memory of his love. It has the air of a dream clinging to it and Yeats wrote in 'The Trembling of the Veil' of his belief that after death men live their lives backwards. Henn sees in this poem the effect of Yeats's reading of Grierson's edition of Donne." (Jeffares, 124). Daniel Albright adds: "According to *A Vision,* the soul after death moves towards oblivion of its past life through a number of stages: one of these stages is called the *Dreaming Back*, in which 'the *Spirit* is compelled to live over and over again the events that had most moved it ... They occur in the order of their intensity or luminosity, the most intense first, and the painful are commonly the more intense' (*A V*, p. 226). When Yeats wrote this poem, he had not yet formulated this doctrine; but this poem seems to be a premonition during life of the dead soul's agony in reliving its memories. Another poem in which the poet seems to anticipate the feelings of his ghost is 'All Souls' Night.'" (Albright, 543).

This short poem of only twelve lines is generally regarded as the finest lyric among the poems included in *Responsibilities* (1914). But it is a lyric of a different kind by virtue of it having a cosmic dimension and a texture of diverse emotions. Though the poet was inspired by the sight of the detached sky in a winter, the theme of the poem is Maud Gonne's rejection of his love. He is bearing intense agony for that reason, but, yet, he does not blame Gonne herself but himself. And ultimately, he lays the whole blame upon the high heaven itself which punishes men after their deaths, but which is punishing him even in this life. Therefore the title of the poem is very appropriate.

THE COLD HEAVEN

Suddenly I saw the cold and rook-delighting heaven
That seemed as though ice burned and was but the more ice,
And thereupon imagination and heart were driven
So wild that every casual thought of that and this

Vanished, and left but memories, that should be out of season
With the hot blood of youth, of love crossed long ago;
And I took all the blame out of all sense and reason,
Until I cried and trembled and rocked to and fro,
Riddled with light. Ah! when the ghost begins to quicken,
Confusion of the death-bed over, is it sent
Out naked on the roads, as the books say, and stricken
By the injustice of the skies for punishment?

The poet was loitering about while suddenly he saw the sky to be "cold and rook-delighting." The sky seemed to be cold because it is indifferent to the sufferings of the poet, to wit, God is, as if, punishing him without rhyme and reason. And the sky seems to be delightful only to the rooks or the ominous species of crows, because, like the rooks, it feeds on, and enjoys, the pain of its victims. The word 'rook' may also mean a simpleton or one who is insensible to anything. In that case, the sky seems to be a simpleton insensible, for it is indifferent to the pains of the poet. The poet saw lightning in the sky that was like a moving line of fire, and yet the icy sky became rather more cold, more indifferent: "That seemed as though ice burned and was but the more ice." The sight of such an indifferent sky somehow fired the imagination of the poet and spurred his emotion: "And thereupon imagination and heart were driven." The poet's imagination and emotion were so much ignited that they became wild. Consequently, the poet lost all sense of rationality: "every casual thought of that and this/Vanished." And he was left only with his memories of what he did in his youth, in his hot blood, — the memories of love he had come across long ago. The poet recalls from his memories his intense love for Maud Gonne, his repeated proposals to her, her rejections of his proposals, his consequent frustrations, and all that, and he recalls all the pains and agonies he underwent, all of which were beyond any sense or reason, because he thinks that it was not just that he suffered.

However, suddenly he realised the Truth, the mystery which overpowered him so much that he "cried and trembled" and felt that he was being swayed "to and fro." The overpowering mystery or Truth came to him in the shape of a "light" which "Riddled" him or non-plussed him. The Truth or light was that it is the command of the Supreme Being that man must suffer. The poet believes that after death or after the "Confusion of the death-bed over", the soul or ghost is sent back to heaven, as the scriptures say. The soul then moves backwards, as Yeats believes and the scriptures say, that is from the stage of old age to the stage of young age and from that to the stage of childhood. Therefore, he says that when the soul reaches the heaven, then it is "naked". However, there in the heaven, the soul is unjustly punished, as he himself is being unjustly punished in this present life. This is, says the poet, the fate of man due to the divine commandment.

In this poem, the mood of the poet is very complex: he is full of bitterness, and, yet, he is also stoic enough not to let the bitterness overpower himself. The expression of the emotion is absolutely controlled. The poet suffers intense agony and pain — the heavenly punishment —, and accepts all these as *fiat accompliex Divina.* The poem is very lyrical, very compact with diverse images, and is full of intense emotion. The poet has also drawn upon the myth that after death the soul moves backwards toward the heaven. Taking all these into account, we can say that this is one of the finest lyrics of Yeats's middle phase.

21. The Magi

Yeats's mature poetry tends to concentrate on a single image and this feature is obvious in this poem. The other feature of his mature poem is that here Yeats either creates new myths or transforms old ones to serve his purpose. Yeats wrote this short poem of only eight lines on 20th September, 1913. It first appeared in *Poetry* (Chicago; in May, 1914. It is complementary to Yeats's poem The Dolls'. The word 'Magi' is the plural form of the Old Persian word 'magus' meaning 'magician'. In ancient Persia and Babylonia, the Magi were priests who sometimes acted as soothsayers and incantators. Hence, in course of time, the term 'Magi' became interchangeable with the terms 'soothsayers', 'magicians', 'exorcists' and 'astrologers'. For the same reason, they were also known as the 'Wise Men of the East'. According to the biblical tradition, after the birth of Christ, the Magi of the East went to Jerusalem with presents for Christ. While they were walking towards Jerusalem, they kept their eyes fixed on a star in the sky, and so ultimately they were transformed into stars. Since then, they are intently gazing at the "bestial floor", that is at the earth under. They are gazing at the earth in expectation of some horrible and gruesome thing to happen — the crucifixion of Christ at Calvary or Golgotha.

But Yeats transforms this biblical myth into a new myth. He says that history repeats itself: world-events move in a gyre (another image of Yeats). The crucifixion of Christ was not the final horrible thing to happen, but another terrible thing will again occur. And so the poet imagines that the Magi are looking down intently from the sky on the "bestial floor" or the earth. Yeats calls the earth the "bestial floor" because, he says, the earth is beastly and wicked, and not divine or at least humane.

As we have told, this poem is complementary to 'The Dolls'. After writing The Dolls', the poet wrote about the occasion of writing 'The Magi'. He wrote that he "looked up one day into the blue sky, and suddenly imagined, as if lost in the blue of the sky, stiff figures in procession. I remembered that they were the habitual image suggested by blue sky and looking for a second fable called them 'The Magi', complementary forms of those enraged dolls." (Jeffares, 126).

THE MAGI

Now as at all times I can see in the mind's eye,
In their stiff, painted clothes, the pale unsatisfied ones
Appear and disappear in the blue depth of the sky
With all their ancient faces like rain-beaten stones,
And all their helms of silver hovering side by side,
And all their eyes still fixed, hoping to find once more,
Being by Calvary's turbulence unsatisfied,
The uncontrollable mystery on the bestial floor.

Looking at the blue sky, the poet is perceiving some figures, like humans, but, yet, different from them. They are in their engrossed beings and in painted clothes, like the clothes of the ancient Magi. It transpires that they are unsatisfied, perhaps because they think that the crucifixion of Christ was not the last and final terrible things to occur on earth, but the terrible thing will recur, for "history occurs in alternate movements" or in gyres. The figures are intent upon that imminent danger on earth. The poet looks at the ancient Magi in the sky in their faces and sees that the faces are not as soft as those of the actual Magi, but are harder "like rain-beaten stones." The imaginary figures in the sky have "helms", or helmets, of silver and they are staring intently: "all their eyes still fixed." They are not satisfied with the terrible crucifixion of Christ at Calvary—with "Calvary's turbulence", and so they are expecting some similar things to occur on earth once more: "hoping to find once more,/Being by Calvary's turbulence unsatisfied." History moves in a gyre, in alternate movements, as the poet says, and this is a great mystery, "uncontrollable mystery", on which the imaginary Magi are intent. The poet compares the earth with "the bestial floor" because he finds nothing on earth divine or even humane.

The myth to the Magi is perhaps prehistoric, but Yeats transforms here the same myth to express his new idea. He says that the imaginary Magi of the sky, in line with the Magi of the actual myth, are expecting a terrible thing to happen shortly on earth. Such myth-making frequently occurs in

Yeats's mature poems. The technique of comparing two different images of the metaphysical poets, is to be seen in this poem. Here the poet compares between the earth and the sky, and also between the faces of the ancient Magi that are soft and gay with the imaginary Magi in the sky wearing hard and pinched faces — "faces like rain-beaten stones." One thing more is to be observed in this poem. As told earlier, Yeats in this poem lays the heaviest stress on the key-image of "the bestial floor." Until we come to this key-image, the meaning of the whole poem remains partly obscure and as soon as we come across this image, the meaning becomes crystal clear and complete. Not only in this poem, but in many of his mature poems, Yeats resorts to this unique and attractive technique.

22. A Coat

This short poem of only ten lines was written in 1912 and was first published in *Poetry* (Chicago) in May, 1914. In it the poet declares that he has abandoned altogether his earlier technique of using elaborate decorations with the help of sonorous diction, folk-tales, mythologies, etc. Such declaration of a poet's change in style is very rare. This change was deliberate and almost instantaneous in effect. In a manuscript revision of this poem, Yeats added two extra lines after the first line: "And gave it to my song/And my song wore it —/" (Jeffares, 127). But later on these two lines were omitted. Had these two lines been included, the meaning of the poem would be clearer. Daniel Albright adds: "This poem ends the short sequence that began with 'The Magi', and shows explicitly that Yeats rejects what is "other than human life"—this poem announces directly that Yeats prefers the raw to the cooked. This poem also ends the main part of the volume, and seems to announce that subsequent volumes will be different in style and theme. 'A Coat' may be compared with a passage in *Reveries over Childhood and Youth*, written not long after the poem: 'When I had finished *The Wandering of Oisin*, dissatisfied with its yellow and its dull green, with all that overcharged colour inherited from the romantic movement, I deliberately reshaped my style, deliberately sought out an impression as of cold light and tumbling clouds." (Albright, 546). Daniel Albright further writes: "But the reader should remember that Yeats, far from removing his embroidery of old mythologies once for all, made a career out of taking off his coat—in 'Reconciliation', in 'The Fascination of What's Difficult', in 'A Coat', in 'Ona Picture of a Black Centaur...', and in 'The Circus Animals' Desertion'." (Albright, 546).

A COAT

I made my song a coat
Covered with embroideries
Out of old mythologies
from heel to throat;
But the fools caught it,
Wore it in the world's eyes
As though they'd wrought it.
Song, let them take it,
for there's more enterprise
In walking naked.

The poet made for his song (here personified) a coat and beautifully embroidered it with old mythologies. He is speaking about his old or earlier style of writing poetry. Earlier in his poems he profusely used Celtic myths, folklores, different images from common stock, and legends. The coat with such embroideries covered his poetry almost completely: "From heel to throat." But soon some poetasters or minor poets came and followed in his foot-steps and thereby lowered the dignity of his poetry. These poetasters may include 'Seumas O'Sullivan' and others who were proteges of A E (George Russell). However, for this reason, he renounced his earlier style. The other reason of his changing style may be his dissatisfaction with the confusion, incoherence and inarticulateness of his earlier poems. In a letter to Katharine Tynan he expressed this dissatisfaction. In the poem, Yeats says that some poetasters imitated his style of using embroideries in poetry and flaunted their poetry before the readers: "But the fools caught it,/Wore it in the world's eyes." Yeats further says that these poets not only used this borrowed technique, but also told the people that this technique was invented by themselves—they said that the technique was "wrought" by them.

The poet' s earlier technique was pre-Raphaelite because the poet used to depict elaborately the details of his subject-matter. The earlier poems were the result of his self-introspection, for which reason he now thinks his earlier poems to be "womanish." Instead of carrying on with that technique, he is now going to use a masculine style: brief must be the poem, and hard in diction and also shorn of all decorations. In his earlier poems, he tended to be an escapist, but now he wants to accost the reality and write objective poems. Therefore, he does not sorrow for his style being stolen away by some minor imitating poets. Yeats asks his song not to mourn for the loss of its embroideries: "Song, let them take it." Because the poet says that it requires more power and skill to write poems of all worth without using those embroideries, and it is more glorious to write poems that are "naked": "For there's more enterprise/In walking naked."

THE WILD SWANS AT COOLE — 1919

This collection of poems was first published by the Cuala Press in 1917, along with Yeats's player *At the Hawk's Well.* But when next it was published by Macmillan in 1919, the play was dropped, and instead, seventeen more poems were included. One among these seventeen poems is 'The Phases of the Moon'. Harold Bloom writes: With the publication of the second version of *The Wild Swans at Coole,* in 1919, a deliberately 'Different' Yeats presented himself to his public." (Bloom, 190). The poems of this volume written between 1915 and 1918, when Yeats was around 55, clearly show the gradual development of the poet, and his emergence from the "slough of *Responsibilities.*" But he was still an unhappy soul as he continued to be so until his marriage in 1917. Only after his marriage, he became a happy family man engaged in writing poems and *A Vision*, his newly married wife, Georgie Hyde-Lees, helping him with her automatic writing. Consequently the later poems of this volume are influenced by the mystical experiences of *A Vision.* The emotional disturbance of Yeats was no more there. He now bought the Tower in 1917 and kept his family in it. A. Norman Jeffares writes about the poems of this volume: "The system of AV *[A Vision*] lurks behind many of the later poems even when these are not acting as direct mouthpieces for his thought. The results of his early reading of Theosophy, magic, occultism, Kabalism, astrology, Blake, Swedenborg, and Boehme all combined steadily with his increasing knowledge of history and philosophy ... Besides the innovations in subject matter, the poems in the WSC *[The Wild Swans at Coole]* reveal Yeats developing his use of ancestors and friends as subjects for poetry: he is now prepared to delineate details of personality just as he is to use personal names. His regret that his own youth, even if it has been replaced by wisdom, is vanishing is the substance of his personal cry—'O Heart we are old'. This awareness of approaching age, sharpened by contemplation of Iseult's beauty, echoes through the poems even if momentarily lulled by the symbolism of the Solomon and Sheba poems recording the early years of his marriage. These seemed to combine age and wisdom for a time until, indeed, to old complaint broke out once more in *The Tower* about: "Decrepit age that has been tied to me/As to a dog's tail." (Jeffares, 129-30).

W. W Robson writes about this volume of poems: "After 1916 Yeats was no longer satisfied to dwell in the imagined heroic past of Ireland. But his poetry is still nostalgic, backward-looking, full of longing and regret. The difference is that these emotions now take on a tone of mordant bitterness. This is the prevailing mood of *The Wild Swans at Coole* (1917). Some of the poems in that volume show a resentment of growing old. This is not a new theme for Yeats. He had always been preoccupied as a poet with age and time. But here the theme is stated more astringently. Yeats is beginning to speak out. Poems which deal directly with sexual feeling replace the dreamy, languid, shy poetry of his early period. Yeats has become increasingly aware of the confusion and incoherence of modern life. His search for what he called Unity of Being is more desperate." (Robson, 55). All these changes in the poet's mood and technique were due to several reasons. To begin with, Maud's marriage with MacBride in 1917 was a bolt from the blue to Yeats. It altogether shattered the lingering longing for romanticism and escapades. Yeats now became almost absolutely realistic. Secondly, he found in his newly wedded wife, Georgie Hyde-Lees, a new and mysterious world of another kind of super naturals, not the supernatural world of Ferguses and Hanrahans, but the world of spirits. "Yeats spent several years struggling with these communications [from the spirits through mediums], mostly derived from two helpful dead men, Dionertes and Thomas, who spoke through his wife, first in automatic writing, later orally in a trance. Yeats's wife had been thoroughly imbued with his ideas, and was perhaps better acquainted with classical philosophy than he; and so Yeats fought to make sense of a garbled, dreamlike synthesis of his own ideas with those of better thinkers, seemingly presented as objective truths from the world beyond the grave. It is fitting that, in *The Wild Swans at Coole*, Yeats sometimes uses the persona of Solomon, gifted with divine wisdom and clarity; and that he speaks of his wife as Sheba. But often the battle with the unintelligible, the dramatizing of ignorance, are more compelling in these poems than the sense of attained lucidity." (Albright, 549). All these brought in changes in his theme and style: "when Yeats was a young man, he devoted himself to the perfection of tight, closed lyrics.; but now, in his early fifties, he seems more flexible, more open — open to spiritual revelation from dubious sources, open to new themes, new personae, new verse techniques. Not only does he experiment with the mask of Solomon, but he even writes a kind of dramatic monologue spoken by a contemporary persona, wearing an aviator' shelmet ('An Irish Airman Foresees his Death'). And in 'Broken Dreams' he verges, for almost the only time in his career, on something like free verse; yet this modernity is counterpoised by other poems that resurrect the most archaic verse forms, such as the pastoral elegy in "Shepherd and Goatherd'. Not all of these experiments proved useful; but many features of his later volumes are extensions or consolidations of discoveries made in *The Wild Swans at Coole*." (Albright, 549-50).

And about the title of this volume, Daniel Albright Writes: "*The Wild Swans at Coole* derives its title from a poem about the presence and absence of swans—and commingled themes of absence and presence keep arising through the volume: absence of dead friends, presence of fulfilled love; absence of full comprehension, presence of hair-raising suggestions of truth. Yeats continually evokes images in which exaltation and depression combine into a kind of wonder." (Albright, 549).

23. To a Young Beauty

This poem was written in 1918, perhaps in the autumn, and was first published in *Nine Poems*, in October, 1918. It was written keeping Iseult Gonne (Maud Gonne's daughter, before her marriage) in view — Iseult whom Yeats here addresses as "Dear fellow-artist". During the time of which the poet speaks here, Iseult was keeping a Bohemian company in Dublin, and this Yeats disapproves of. A.E. Dyson writes about this poem: "A Song' and 'To a Young Beauty' are two of those slighter poems, often juxtaposed for deliberate effect, in which Yeats uses ballad or lyric for a momentary perception or mood. The complexities are less calculated than in the more substantial poems, but seldom absent. May be it is the sheer quantity of these small gems ——— which contributes to our sense of Yeats's *richness* as poet. They tend to stay in the mind, and often to reappear glancingly, as we wrestle with (say) 'Byzantium' or 'Lapis Lazuli' — not as elucidations exactly, but as reminders of the range of attitudes, and momentary clarities, throughout his work." (Dyson, 17).

TO A YOUNG BEAUTY

Dear fellow-artist, why so free
With every sort of company,
With every Jack and Jill?
Choose your companions from the best;
Who draws a bucket with the rest
Soon topples down the hill.

You may, that mirror for a school,
Be passionate, not bountiful

As common beauties may,
Who were not born to keep in trim?
With old Ezekiel's cherubim
But those of Beauvarlet.
I know what wages beauty gives,
How hard a life her servant lives,
Yet praise the winters gone:
There is not a fool can call me friend,
And I may dine at journey's end
With Landor and with Donne.

The poet addresses Iseult Gonne as a "fellow-artist" perhaps because keeping beautiful also requires great labour and skill and the beautiful Iseult must be an artist on that account. The poet mildly admonishes Iseult for being "so free" in the company of her Bohemian friends who are, to Yeats's eyes, mean and lowly. Yeats's aristocratic bent of mind is evident here. He says that artists should not be so flee as to mix with one without discrimination —to mix with "Jack and Jill." He advises her that as an artist she should choose companions from amongst the best persons, for those who labour, or keep company, with lowly ones, fall down from their stations: "Who draws a bucket with the rest/Soon topples down the hill." In the second stanza of the poem, Yeats further advises Iseult not to be bounteous and unreserved, though she may be moderately passionate, unlike common beautiful girls. He asks her to look into the mirror to see and well realise her own beauty and thus be wise, and foolish like common beautiful girls. Perhaps, Yeats means to say that Iseult can be a model for any school of art or painting: "that mirror for a school." He says that the common girls are not born to keep them trim like the cherubim's of Ezekiel. The cherubim's are many-eyed angels of which we hear in the book of Ezekiel in the Bible. Yeats says that the cherubim's mentioned in Ezekiel are more beautiful than those painted by the artist Beauvarlet. Jacques Firmin Beauvarlet (1731-97) was a mediocre French painter and engraver. Yeats, in the poem, tells Iseult that she should be as magnific as the cherubim's of Ezekiel and not like the cherubim's painted by Beauvariet.

In the last stanza, the poet changes his thought. The image of Iseult recalls in his mind the image of Maud Gonne and the sorrows he had to bear for her rejecting his love for her. It was all winter then for the poet, and yet he does not blame Maud Gonne for all that, perhaps because his experiments in love somehow made him the wiser: "I know what wages beauty gives,/ How hard a life her servant lives,/ Yet praise the winters gone." These lines may have yet another meaning. The poet understands the labour required in a work of art and knows that this hard labour pays very little. And yet he praises the hard labour for art: "Yet praise the winters gone." He now comes back to his former theme that one should be a cultivated person, an aristocrat from top to toe. He says that he makes friends with no lowly or foolish persons: "There's not a fool can call me friend." Mark again Yeats's love of aristocracy. And lastly, he says that after labouring through the works of Landor and Donne, at the end of his life — "at journey's end" — he can now understand the two great poets, both of whom were of aristocratic mentality: "And I may dine at journey's end/With Landor and with Donne." Walter Savage Landor (1775-1864) was a poet and a prose stylist. He was educated at Rugby and Trinity College from where he was expelled as the 'Mad Jacobin' and "this was the first serious appearance of the ungovernable temper and Whiggish, 'aristocratic' eccentricity which forced him to leave his country." (Daiches, 301-02). John Donne (1572-1631) was a poet and a divine. He was "appointed secretary to Sir Thomas Egerton, the Lord Keeper, in 1598, and, seemingly set for a career in the public service, entered Parliament in 1601," (Daiches, 152). Yeats compares himself with Landor and Donne in the quality of being aristocratic. A.E. Dyson writes about the concluding couplet that we "may regard the conclusion as the artist's [Yeats's] hope of enduring posthumous fame in his work." (Dyson, 18). The rhyme scheme of the poem is a a b c c b, with the third line in the second stanza rhyming with the sixth line, i.e., "may" with "Beauvarlet" (the 't' in the word "Beauvarlet" remaining silent).

24. The Hawk

When the poem was written we do not know, but we know that it was first published in *Poems* (Chicago) in February, 1916. The title of the poem derives from Yeats' s use of hawk as a symbol of the soul. The hawk is a bird that hovers high in the sky, and seldom comes down to earth. It is, as if, a dweller of the heaven like the soul. Perhaps this was the reason of Treats' s using this bird as symbol of the soul? Daniel Albright writes in his introduction to this poem: "In his autobiography, Yeats advocated 'Unity of Being'—that condition in which a man's faculties were so harmoniously arranged that (as Yeats' s fatter put it) the soul was like 'a musical instrument so strong that if we touch a string all the strings murmur faintly' (...). In the same chapter, Yeats wrote that 'the enemy of this unity was abstraction, meaning by abstraction not the distinction but the isolation of occupation, or class or faculty', and he went on to quote the first stanza of the present poem. Its theme, then, is the mind's haughty desire to isolate itself from the rest of the human sensibility, causing a general friction and cramp within the poet. (For the related theme of thinking body, see 'To a Young Beauty', 1.18). The hawk often symbolized the abstract intelligence: 'I have a ring with a hank and a butterfly upon it, to symbolize the straight road of logic, and so of mechanism, and the crooked road of intuition." (Albright, 573).

THE HAWK

'Call down the hawk from the air;
Let him be hooded or caged
Till the yellow eye has grown mild,
For larder and spit are bare,
The old cook enraged,
The scullion gone wild.'

'I will not be clapped in a hood,
Nor a cage, nor alight upon wrist,
Now I have learnt to be proud
Hovering over the wood
In the broken mist
Or tumbling cloud.'

'What tumbling cloud did you cleave,
Yellow-eyed hawk of the mind,
Last evening? that I, who had sat
Dumbfounded before a knave,
should give to my friend
A pretence of wit.'

The poem is divided into three stanzas and has the rhyme scheme a b c a b c. In the first stanza, the poet asks people to bring down the hawk that is flying high in the sky, and blindfold it or place it in a cage. The hawk which has yellow eyes is very ferocious with its pointed talions. Therefore, the poet asks them to domesticate it till it becomes mild. Otherwise, the poet is afraid, the hawk may ransack the larder, that is the place where food is kept, and the spit, that is the broach for cooking meat, are lying open. Besides, the cook and the scullion, or the menial servant, are scared by the hawk. As the hawk symbolises the soul, so the cook and the scullion, collectively, represent the common people of the earth. Likewise, the larder and the spit symbolise the things of the world for material enjoyment. In brief, the poet wants to bring down by force or otherwise the transcendental soul from its heavenly abode down to the material world of physical enjoyments and char jobs. But the hawk, in the second stanza, refuses to come down and be hooded or be caged. Neither does it like to be the play-thing of anyone, like the hawks of the middle ages that would be shown by kings and knights tied on their wrists. The hawk says that he is proud enough not to stoop so low as to enjoy the material things of the earth. Rather, he would like to fly over the high forests and over the mists and over the billowing clouds.

In the foregoing two stanzas, the meaning of the poem is not clear enough, but the meaning becomes clear only when we go through the last stanza. Here the poet says that last evening he had been engaged in a conversation with his friend, sitting near a knave. A. Norman Jeffares writes about the incident of the poet "Last evening": "the conversation is not recorded. There is a certain amount of self-analysis in Yeats's Diaries where he recorded dissatisfaction with his methods of conversing, particularly in the Arts Club. There is an example of this rethinking of past conversations or debates in *Estrangement*, II. Out of this need to develop a poised personality came the doctrine of the mask: "Style, personality—deliberately adopted and therefore a mask — is the only escape from the hot-faced bargainers and the money-changers."" (Jeffares, 153). However, in the conversation with his friend, while sitting "Dumbfounded before a knave", he said something that seemed to be witty but did not contain any wisdom: "Should give to my friend/A pretence of wit." The poet thinks that this lack of wisdom in his conversation was due to the absence of his true soul, the hawk, that cleave to the "tumbling cloud" above the earth and does not generally come down to mankind in their earthly needs. In the last stanza, the poet calls the hawk or the soul the "Yellow-eyed hawk of the mind", and this makes the meaning of the whole poem quite clear.

In this beautiful lyric, the poet is perhaps talking about the need of the vision of the mystery in man's life. But only the soul, the hawk, can have the vision. The common man may talk about the vision, but they cannot get it, for the simple reason that it needs the help of the "hawk of the mind". The common man talks with the help of the mind, but wisdom is possible only with the help of the "hawk of the mind". And so the poet wants to bring down the hawk from the heaven. Actually the poem is a dialogue between what Yeats calls the self (the hawk) and the anti-self (the Mask). Yeats had been thinking in these terms since around 1907, and he expressed his thoughts in *A Vision.* He believed that human beings suffer the tension between the soul and the anti-soul, or between the self and the anti-self.

He says that the real or ideal or the higher soul is eremitic and spiritual, and so it is averse to the material and earthly matters. On the other hand, the anti-soul or the second self (the Mask) is half-beastly, sensuous and earthly. The former is heavenly and visionary and lonely, like the hawk, but the second self is half-perceptive and gregarious, like the cooks and the scullions. The former is ethical, idealistic and unitary, while the latter is practical, racial, autochthonous and therefore theatrical or dramatic (wearing the Mask). The real self is disciplined and Apollonian while the second self is undisciplined and Dionysian. Yeats says that the undisciplined second self or the lower self can be disciplined only when the real self or the higher self-controls it. And so, in this poem, the poet asks the real or higher self (the hawk) to come down to earth and discipline his second self or the lower self, to wit, his personality.

25. The Phases of the Moon

The poem was written in 1918 and was first published in *The Wild Swans at Coole.* Yeats's note to the poem, in the section *The Wild Swans at Coole* of his *Collected Poems* (1933) reads: "Years ago I wrote three stories in which occur the names of Michael Robertes and Owen Aherne. I now consider that I used the actual names of two friends, and that one of these friends, Michael Robertes, has but lately returned from Mesopotamia, where he has partly found and partly thought out much philosophy. I consider that Aherne and Robertes, men to whose namesakes I had attributed a turbulent life or death, have quarrelled with me. They take their place in a phantasmagoria in which I endeavour to explain my philosophy of life and death. To some extent I wrote these poems as a text for exposition." (Jeffares, 173). From this we know something about the two characters in the poem, Michael Robertes and Owen Aherne, and also a little about the theme of the poem. Harold Bloom writes: "This poem, despite its eloquence, is something closer to a 'text for exposition' than *Ego Dominius Tuum* is." (Bloom, 204). Bloom is quite right, for Yeats here, in this poem, partly exposes his mysterious philosophy about the relation of human nature with the phases of the moon, details of which he wrote in *A Vision.*

Daniel Albright has written a relatively long introduction to this complex poem. He writes: "After wrestling for some months with the difficult doctrines educed from his wife's automatic script —... — Yeats wrote this summarizing poem. Whereas the point of view of *A Vision* is that of a tenacious man of no particular brilliance of mind wrestling with advanced, intractable ideas, the point of view of this poem is that of his supernatural instructors, effortlessly wise, derisive of Yeats's dim-witted misunderstandings. It pleased Yeats to suppose that the doctrines of *A Vision* could be compressed to a point of transcendental simplicity; 'The Phases of the Moon' is half a statement of these terse truths, half an apology for the cloudiness, the obscurity, of any attempt to render these truths intelligible. Yeats hinted that *A Vision* was only a stylized reconstruction of human life, and the pleasure of studying it was akin to that of cubist art (*AV*, p. 25); similarly the pleasure of reading this poem is like that of an animated cartoon in which a welter of human shapes take form from clay, whirl about in a frantic circle, and at last subside into clay again. Yeats was diffident about 'The Phases of the Moon', and even wrote to Pound (on 15th July, 1918) that it should be published only because 'Without it "The Double Vision [of Michael Robertes]" is too obscure."' (Albright, 589-90).

THE PHASES OF THE MOON

An old man cocked his ear upon a bridge;
He and his friend, their faces to the South,
Had trod the uneven road. Their boots were soiled,
Their Connemara cloth worn out of shape;
They had kept a steady pace as though their beds,
Despite a dwindling and late-risen moon.
Were distant still. An old man cocked his ear.

Aherne. What made that sound?
Robertes. A rat or water-hen
Splashed, or an otter slid into the stream.
We are on the bridge; that shadow is the tower,
And the light proves that he is reading still.
He has found, after the manner of his kind,
Mere images; chosen this place to live in
Because, it may be, of the candle-light
From the far tower where Milton's Platonist
Sat late, or Shelley's visionary prince:
The lonely light that Samuel Palmer engraved,
An image of mysterious wisdom won by toil;
And now he seeks in book or manuscript
What he shall never find.
Aherne. Why should not you
Who know it all ring at his door, and speak
Just truth enough to show that his whole life
Will scarcely find for him a broken crust

Of all those truths that are your daily bread;
And when you have spoken take the roads again?

Robertes. He wrote of me in that extravagant style
He had learnt from Pater, and to round his tale
Said I was dead; and dead 1 choose to be.

Aherne. Sing me the changes of the moon once more;
True song, though speech: 'mine author sung it me.'

Robertes. Twenty-and-eight the phases of the moon,
The full and the moon's dark and all the crescents,
Twenty-and-eight, and yet but six-and twenty
The cradles that a man must needs be rocked in:
For there's no human life at the full or the dark.
From the first crescent to the half, the dream
But summons to adventure and the man
Is always happy like a bird or a beast;
But while the moon is rounding towards the full
He follows whatever whim' s most difficult
Among whims not impossible, and though scarred,
As with the cat-o'-nine-tails of the mind,
His body moulded from within his body
Grows comelier. Eleven pass, and then
Athena takes Achilles by the hair,
Hector is in the dust, Nietzsche is born,
Because the hero's crescent is the twelfth.
And yet, twice born, twice buried, grow he must,
Before the full moon, helpless as a worm.
The thirteenth moon but sets the soul at war
In its own being, and when that war's begun
There is no muscle in the arm; and after,
Under the frenzy of the fourteenth moon,
The soul begins to tremble into stillness,
To die into the labyrinth of itself!

Aherne. Sing out the song; sing to the end, and sing
The strange reward of all that discipline.

Robertes. All thought becomes an image and the soul
Becomes a body: that body and that soul
Too perfect at the full to lie in a cradle,
Too lonely for the traffic of the world:

Body and soul cast out and cast away
Beyond the visible world.

Aherne. All dreams of the soul
End in a beautiful man's or woman's body.

Robertes. Have you not always known it?

Aherne. The song will have it
That those that we have loved got their long fingers
From death, and wounds, or on Sinai's top,
Or from some bloody whip in their own hands.
They ran from cradle to cradle till at last
Their beauty dropped out of the loneliness
Of body and soul.

Robertes. The lover's heart knows that.

Aherne. It must be that the terror in their eyes
Is memory or foreknowledge of the hour
When all is fed with light and heaven is bare.

Robertes. When the moon's full those creatures of the full
Are met on the waste hills by countrymen
Who shudder and hurry by body and soul
Estranged amid the strangeness of themselves,
Caught up in contemplation, the mind's eye
Fixed upon images that once were thought;
For separate, perfect, and immovable
Images can break the solitude
Of lovely, satisfied, indifferent eyes.
And thereupon with aged, high-pitched voice
Aherne laughed, thinking of the man within,
His sleepless candle and laborious pen

Robertes. And after that the crumbling of the moon.
The soul remembering its loneliness
Shudders in many cradles; all is changed,
It would be the world's servant, and as it serves,
Choosing whatever task's most difficult
Among tasks not impossible, it takes
Upon the body and upon the soul
The coarseness of the drudge.

Aherne. Before the full
It sought itself and afterwards the world.

Robertes. Because you are forgotten, half out of life.
And never wrote a book, your thought is clear.
Reformer, merchant, statesman, learned man,
dutiful husband, honest wife by turn,
Cradle upon cradle, and all in flight and all
Deformed because there is no deformity
But save us from a dream.
Aherne. And what of those
That the last servile crescent has set free?
Robertes. Because all dark, like those that are all light,
They are cast beyond the verge, and in a cloud,
Crying to one another like the bats;
And having no desire they cannot tell
What's good or bad, or what it is to triumph
At the perfection of one's own obedience;
And yet they speak what's blown into the mind;
Deformed beyond deformity, unformed,
Insipid as the dough before it is baked,
They change their bodies at a word.
Aherne. And then?
Robertes. When all the dough has been so kneaded up
That it can take what form cook Nature fancies,
The first thin crescent is wheeled round once more.
Aherne. But the escape; the songs not finished yet.
Robertes. Hunchback and Saint and Fool are the last crescents.
The burning bow that once could shoot an arrow
Out of the up and down, the wagon-wheel
Of beauty's cruelty and wisdom's chatter —
Out of that raving tide—is drawn betwixt
Deformity of body and of mind.
Aherne. Were not our beds far off I'd ring the bell,
Stand under the rough roof-timbers of the hall
Beside the castle door, where all is stark
Austerity, a place set out for wisdom
That he will never find; I'd play a part;
He would never know me after all these years
But take me for some drunken countryman;
I'd stand and mutter there until he caught

'Hunchback and Saint and Fool,' and that they came
Under the three crescents of the moon,
And then I'd stagger out. He'd crack his wits
Day after day, yet never find the meaning.
And then he laughed to think that what seemed hard
Should be so simple — a hat rose from the hazels
And circled round him with its squeaky cry,
The light in the tower window was put out.

This is a beautiful dialogue-poem in which two speakers, Aherne, an old man, and Robertes, speak about the phases of the moon, with which the soul's cycle of reincarnation corresponds. The poem cannot be understood without some knowledge of Yeats's concept of the Great Wheel (see p. 72). Yeats thought that each incarnation of the soul corresponds to a phase of the moon. The personae of Aherne and Robertes dominated Yeats's imagination for a long time. "... Aherne explains how Michael Robertes, despite his long enmity with Mr. Yeats, decided to share with the poet the mysterious wisdom he had brought back from Arabia, the diagrams of lunar motion he had seen traced in (he sand by the feet of dancers. Aherne is a kind of Roman Catholic, austere and ceremonious, heretical in that he believes in the reincarnation of the soul. Robertes is a kind of high priest of imagination, eager to find expression of the supernatural in rituals, designs, artifices." (Albright, 590). According to Daniel Albright, "'The Phases of the Moon', then, could have been as dialectical as 'Ego Dominus Tuus', a true dialogue between a character representing the values of the full moon (Robertes) and one representing the values of the new moon (Aherne)." (Albright, 590). Perhaps Yeats conceived of Aherne basing on the personality of Lionel Johnson, and of Robertes basing on the personality of MacGregor Mathers.

The poem begins with a prologue which explains the occasion of the dialogue between the two characters, centering on the phases of the moon. An old man (Aherne) and his friend (Robertes) were returning home. Walking on the "uneven road", they reached a bridge. "Their boots were soiled" and their clothes got creased. Over the bridge, they were walking swiftly in the moon-light for their homes were still at a considerable distance. On the bridge Aherne heard a sound very intently and asked Robertes what the sound might be. Robertes said that it was perhaps the sound of a rat or water-hen jumping into water, or the sound of an otter sliding "into the stream." Robertes showed his friend the tower in the distance that stood like a shadow, and in the tower, there was a light which indicates that somebody has been reading there. Or, perhaps, the man is viewing in the book mere images, i.e., an illustration by Samuel Palmer (1805-81) who was a water-colour landscape painter and etcher. Actually, the following description accompanied the illustration: "Here poetic loneliness has been attempted: not the loneliness of a desert, but a secluded spot in a genial pastoral country, enriched also by antique relics such as the so-called druidic stones upon the distant hill. The constellation of the 'Bear' may help to explain that the building is the tower of *II Penseroso*. Two shepherds watching their flocks speak together of the mysterious light above them... There is a waning crescent moon in the illustration which connects with the poem's title—phases of the moon ." (Jeffares, 173-74). The "Milton's Platonist" is the illustration of the tower which image was also used by Shelley (Jeffares, 174):

> Or let my lamp, at midnight hour,
> Be seen in some high lonely tower,
> Where I may oft outwatch the *Bear*,
> With thrice great *Hermes*, or unsphere
> The spirit of *Plato,* to unfold
> What worlds, or what vast regions hold
> The immortal mind that hath forsook
> Her mansion in the fleshy nook;...

The light of the tower in the illustration by Palmer is lonely, which implies that it is the "image of mysterious wisdom won by toil."

Aherne asks Robertes why he does not tell the truth and walk again. Robert essays that following Pater (1839-94), the English essayist, the artist of that illustration etched everything and showed Robertes to be dead. Aherne then asks him to explain the changes of the moon: "Sing me the changes of the moon once more."

Robertes then says that supposedly the moon has twenty-eight phases, but actually it has only twenty-six phases. Man swings in this chain of twenty-six phases: "The cradles that a man must needs be rocked in." It is twenty-six and not twenty-eight, because in the full-moon and in the complete darkness, there is no change in the human being: "For there's no human life at the full or the dark." From the first crescent moon to the thirteenth phase, man dreams of adventure and he is "happy like a bird or a beast." From Phase 2 to 8, man grows in individuality and strength. This goes on till Phase 14.

Robertes says that the Phase 12 "is that of the hero, the man who overcomes himself." (Jeffares, 176). Frederick Nietzsche (1844-1900), the

German philosopher, and Hector, the oldest son of Prium, are of the 12th Phase. But the hero has to die twice and buried twice, before he becomes a hero. In contrast to this Phase, Phase 13 "sets the out at war/In its own being." In Phase 14, man becomes weaker and the soul trembles and becomes still, and it dies within itself. Hearing all this, Aherne asks Robertes to go on explaining his ideas further, and accordingly Robertes continues explaining. He says that intense thought is transformed into an image and then the soul becomes a body. After that the union of the soul and the body occurs, and then the two live in a world which is invisible and is beyond this material world. This is Phase 14 about which Yeats wrote in *A Vision*: "The being has selected, moulded and remoulded, narrowed its circle of living, being more and more the artist, grown more and more 'distinguished' in all preference. Now contemplation and desire, united into one, inhabit a world where every beloved image has bodily form, and every bodily form is loved. This love knows nothing of desire, for desire implies effort, and though there is still separation from the beloved object, love accepts the separation as necessary to its own existence... As all efforts have ceased, all thought has become image, because no thought could exist if it were not carried towards its own extinction, amid fear or in contemplation: and every image is separate from every other, for if image were linked to image, the soul would awake from its immovable trance. All that the being has experienced as thought is visible to its eyes as a whole, and in this way it perceives, not as they are to others, but according to its own perception, all orders of existence." (Jeffures, 176-77).

Aherne requests Robertes to complete his explanation: "Sing out the song to the end, and sing/The strange reward of all I hat discipline." And Robertes goes on: thought ultimately becomes an image and the soul becomes a body. In the full-moon, both the body and the soul are perfect, but they remain in a lonely and transcendental world. Just at this point, Aherne interpolates his thought that the dreams of the soul in the end materialise in the body either of a man or that of a woman. He further says that our loved ones got their bodies from death or from wounds (Christ's wounds) or from Moses who preached on the Sinai mountain, i.e., from the eternity. With their bodies they move from birth to birth ("cradle to cradle"), and in the course of their journey, they lost their beauty — the beauty of eternity. Robertes understands this and says that a lover knows this perfectly. Aherne continues his peroration. He says that before it is "fed with light", i.e., before it gets the supreme knowledge, the soul will have a fore-knowledge or memory of this secret and supreme knowledge, and consequently will feel horrified. The soul will get the supreme knowledge only when the heaven will open itself before the soul. Robertes then says that in the full moon or in Phase 15, the body and the soul are estranged from each other, that is, the soul is liberated from the body. The soul then remains engrossed in contemplation, and the mind remains fixed in images. At this point, Aherne, the old man, laughed loudly, thinking of his soul within: "thinking of the man within,/His sleepless candle and laborious pen."

Then, after the full-moon, Phase 16 comes: "after that the crumbling of the moon." It is the phase "which finds within itself an aimless excitement, and the examples given it in *AV* [*A Vision*] are William Blake, Rabelais, Aretino, Paracelsus and some beautiful women." (Jeffares, 177). Robertes says that in this way everyone is moving from one Phase to another—reformer, merchant, statesman, learned man, all. When again the moon is completely blotted out and all is dark, the soul becomes absolutely passive. In that state, the soul does not know even what is good and what is bad. Next, the same first crescent, or Phase 1, appears. However, Robertes says that the last crescent of Phase 14 is the image of the Hunchback, the Saint and the Fool. He thus completes the description of the Phases of the moon. Aherne tells that the tower, in which somebody is passing a sleepless night by the candle-light (the soul), is still far off. If he could accost the man in the Tower, then that man would accept Aherne as a "drunken countryman" — as an ignorant and irrational man. At last Aherne again laughs loudly because what he thought to be very hard to understand (i.e. the phases of the moon) now seems to be very simple. Then the Muse of wisdom sits upon him: "A bat rose from l lie hazels/And circled around him with its squeaky cry." And then there was no more need of explanation or enlightenment: "The light in the tower window was put out."

This is a very beautiful poem — very attractive, but at the same time very difficult. The difficulty lies in the fact that Yeats here is dealing with the Gnostic philosophy and mysticism. The beauty of the poem has been enhanced by the drama in it. It begins with a prologue where Robertes and Aherne stop for a while to converse on the phases of the moon. It has also an epilogue where the poet beautifully compares the enlightenment of Aherne and the superfluity of further enlightenment with the putting out of the light in the tower. The meaning of the poem may become clearer to us if we follow the diagram of Yeats's phases of the moon.

26. The Cat and the Moon

The final poems of *The Wild Swans at Coole* all concentrate on the mystery of Yeats's Great Wheel of the phases of the moon. These "attempt to relate the abstract entities posited in 'The Phases of the Moon' to common life. It is as if Robertes and Aherne had delivered a challenge to the poet burning the midnight oil in his lower — in the following poems Yeats tried to show that the most abstruse and difficult parts of the Great Wheel exert power over the particulars of man's existence." (Albright, 595). In 1926, that is about nine years after he wrote this poem, Yeats published a play of the same name, *The Cat and the Moon,* which begins with the first eight lines and ends with the last twelve lines of this poem. Both the poem and the play are based on the same theme. According to A. E. Dyson, this poem is "Certainly one of the finest cat poems ever written, whatever we make of the moon." (Dyson, 21). Dyson takes this poem as a test poem for Yeats-lovers: "As a teacher, I tend to regard this as a test poem. Any student who isn't enchanted will probably never like Yeats."(Dyson, 22).

The poem was written in 1917 and it first appeared in *Nine Poems* (1918). In 1917, Yeats was staying with the Gonne family in Normandy. The cat Minnaloushe refers to the black Persian cat that the Gonnes kept. In a note to this poem Yeats wrote: "I wrote a little poem where a cat is disturbed by the moon, and in the changing pupils of its eyes seem to repeat the movement of the moon's changes and allow myself as I wrote to think of the cat as the normal man of the moon as the opposite he seeks perpetually, or as having any meaning I have conferred upon the moon elsewhere. Doubtless, too, when the lame man takes the saint upon his back, the normal man has become one with his opposite." (Albright, 595-96). In the play *The Cat and Moon* also the characters A Blind Beggar and A Lame Beggar form the opposites trying to unite with each other to make a complete man. But Daniel Albright writes: "The poem can also be interpreted as an exposition of the tidal pressure exercised upon unconscious human life by the moon' s changes of phase. Yeats associated his wife with a cat, as he explained in his account of how her dreams sometimes interfered with the transmission of the automatic script: 'she dreamed she was a cat lapping milk or a cat curled up asleep and therefore dumb. The cat returned night after night, and once when I tried to drive it away by making the sound one makes playing at being a dog to amuse a child, she awoke trembling' *(AV, p.* 10). Yeats also suggested at the end of 'The gift of Harun Al-Rashid' that *A Vision* was nothing more than an expression of his wife's body. The shift of the pupils of the cat's eyes, then, can be seen as an anticipation of Mrs. Yeats's trance-sensitivity to the lunar forces that dictated *A Vision*—though the cat here is male." (Albright, 596).

THE CAT AND THE MOON

The cat went here and there
And the moon spun round like a top,
And the nearest kin of the moon.
The creeping cat, looked up,
Black Minnaloushe stared at the moon,
For, wander and wail as he would,
The pure cold light in the sky
Troubled his animal blood.
Minnaloushe runs in the grass
Lifting his delicate feet.
Do you dance, Minnaloushe. do you dance?
When two close kindred meet,
What better than call a dance?
Maybe the moon may learn,
Tired of that courtly fashion.
A new dance turn.
Minnaloushe creeps through the grass
From moonlit place to place,
The sacred moon overhead
Has taken a new phase.
Does Minnaloushe know that his pupils
Will pass from change to change,
And that from round to crescent,
From crescent to round they range?
Minnaloushe creeps through the grass
Alone, important and wise,
And lifts to the changing moon
His changing eyes.

Minnaloushe, the cat, is very frivolous: he was jumping from place to place. Iseult Gonne writes about the cat and the history of the poem: "at the time when the thought of the phases of the moon was beginning to take shape in [Yeats's] mind and this cat used to dance wonderfully in the moonlight, take huge leaps. And... that gave the kind of poetic urge to the idea which otherwise would have been a little bit too coldly philosophical." (Albright, 596). The cat stared at the moon performing random motions and was growling ("wander and wail"), because the "pure cold light of the sky/Troubled his animal blood." This means that the moon's changes were influencing the cat below. The cat is now frolicking in the grass, alternately lifting and stamping its feet, in the grass. It seems to the poet that the cat is dancing. He says that when two kindred beings meet, it is very natural that they dance. The moon and the cat are kindred beings, they are being transcendental and earthly, ideal and fleshy, the self and the anti-self, the soul and the Mask,—beings opposite and complementary to each other—, and so when they meet in the moonlight, they may be dancing. The poet now thinks that as the cat is being influenced by the moon, so the moon is also, perhaps, being influenced by the cat, for the moon is perhaps tired of her transcendental existence: "May be the moon may learn,/ Tired of that courtly fashion,/A new dance turn."

Minnaloushe, who is representing all beings, is creeping from place to place in consonance with the changes in the moon. The poet means to say that every being passes through consecutive incarnations like the changing phases of the moon. The poet asks: is the cat aware of its changes in the eyes, that is, do the beings know that they are passing through kaleidoscopic changes in their beings like the moon passes from the stage of being a crescent to the stage of being a full moon and back to its former stages: "Does Minnaloushe know that his pupils/Will pass from change to change,/And that from round to crescent,/From crescent to round they range?" The poet presumes that the cat knows about this mysterious phenomenon and so says that Minnaloushe is walking alone, being a wise being: "Minnaloushe creeps through the grass/Alone, important and wise,/And lifts to the changing moon/His changing eyes."

MICHAEL ROBERTES AND THE DANCER — 1921

This collection of poems includes Yeats's mature poems which are very rich in suggestiveness and depth of thought, complex in imagery, and intricate in construction and meaning. Yeats is now a mature man having gathered all sorts of experiences, read diverse tractuses on occultism, Gnostic philosophy and symbolism. The influences of Blake and Shelley are more apparent in the poems of this collection. The poems are very rich in imagery: Yeats moves from one image to another with agility and deftness. The poems are very difficult because so many things — images, thoughts, Gnostic and other occult philosophies, etc. —are heaped up here. Further the poems are all the more complex because many words in the poems carry different meanings, sometimes all at the same time. A. Norman Jeffares wrote about this collection of poems: "Some of the poems in this volume were written in 1916 but not publicly circulated until 1920. His early mockery — 'Romantic Ireland's dead and gone' — has vanished, and he records in these poems his clear perception of what was achieved by the Rising, by the leaders who have joined the long procession of Ireland's martyrs. The magnificent poems based on *AV*'s [*A Vision*'s] thought blend imaginative experience and explanation in a manner which imparts a sense of revelation." (Jeffares, 184).

The title of this volume derives from the title poem 'Michael Robertes and the Dancer'. The concept of the Dancer is based on Iseult Gonne, and that of Michael Robertes "was originally an unworldly persona associated with the imagination's pride in its images (...), then a code name for the instructors who presented Yeats with supernatural revelation (...), and at last simply an emphatic and self-confident disguise of Yeats himself." (Albright, 604). Daniel Albright introduces this volume thus:' 'The theme of the poem that gives the title of this volume is education — the superiority of the discipline of the body, of the whole self, to the schooling of the mind alone. This theme is pursued in several more poems: the contrast between abstract mental hatred and physical grace ('On a Political Prisoner', 'A Prayer for my Daughter'); or the contrast between the aged and disengaged poet, freed at last from bodily passion, and the fauna of nature ('Demon and Beast'). In many ways Yeats attempts to sec the body as the vehicle of true wisdom; even the historical process of *A Vision* has a little meaning unless a rough beast (in 'The Second Coming') can be found to embody it. "A feature of this book is the poet's unusual candour about his relation to his wife (in poems such as 'Under Saturn'), and his unusual specificity about politics. In certain poems, such as 'To a Wealthy Man...' and 'Paudeen', Yeats discussed local politics and urban situations. But there he wrote chiefly to disparage them against the background of antiquity; in this volume Yeats attempts to write sympathetically of contemporary events, and to use the doctrines of *A Vision* to see a design in modern history, to show how political actions are governed by forces beyond the ordinary world. In 1932 Yeats, reviewing the evolution of modern Irish literature, noted with some displeasure that 'a school of satire' become dominant: 'we might... have founded a school that could have substituted, as only a literature without satirical or realistic prepossessions could, positive desires for the negative passion of a national movement'. (...). Here the satirist becomes, guardedly, a panegyrist." (Albright, 603).

27. Easter, 1916

This is an ode and an occasional poem that has a reference to the poem 'September 1913'. In 'Easter, 1916', Yeats expressed his reaction to the 1916 Easter Rising in Dublin. "The Irish Republic was proclaimed on Easter Monday, 24 April and the centre of Dublin occupied by the Republicans.

They were the Irish volunteers of the Irish Republican Brotherhood, probably about seven hundred in all. They held out until 29 April. From 3 to 12 May fifteen of the leaders were executed alter a series of courts martial." (Jeffares, 190). A few days after that, i.e. on 11 May Yeats wrote a letter to Lady Gregory, which will through light on Yeats's mood at that time and also on the mood of the poem. Yeats wrote in that letter: "I am trying to write a poem on the men executed — 'terrible beauty has been born again'. If the English Conservative party had made a declaration that they did not intend to rescind the Home Rule there would have been no Rebellion. I had no idea that any public event could so deeply move me — and I am very despondent about the future." (Jeffares, 191).

Once Yeats boasted of Ireland's hills and dales, flora and fauna, myths and mysteries; and thought that though the whole of Europe might have gone boisterously crazy for scientific and technical advancements, shattering nature's bounteous beauty, the Celtic Ireland would herself remain quiet and beauteous. He thought when in the near future the scientific credo in Europe would spawn political hatred and barbarism, under the shade of vulgar materialism, Ireland would worship only love. But now in 1916 he realised that his thoughts were but dreams. In 1916, Yeats saw the other side, the ugly side, of Ireland's face , he saw that hatred dwelt also in Ireland. But, nevertheless, he is not all despair, for after the internecine battle and the bloody battle with England, he says that a "terrible beauty" is born out of the 1916 Easter Rising.

EASTER, 1916

I have met them at close of day
Coming with vivid faces
From counter or desk among grey
Eighteenth-century houses.
I have passed with a nod of the head
Or polite meaningless words.
Or have lingered a while and said
Polite meaningless words,
And thought before I had done
Of a mocking tale or a gibe
To please a companion
Round the fire at the club,
Being certain that they and I
But lived where motley is worn:

All changed, changed utterly:
A terrible beauty is born.

That woman's days were spent
In ignorant good-will,
Her nights in argument
Until her voice grew shrill.
What voice more sweet than hers
When, young and beautiful,
She rode to harrier?
This man had kept a school
And rode our winged horse;
This other his helper and friend
Was coming into his force;
He might have won fame in the end,
So sensitive his nature seemed,
So daring and sweet his thought.
This other man I had dreamed
A drunken, vainglorious lout.
He had done most bitter wrong
To some who are near my heart,
Yet I number him in the song;
He, too, has resigned his part
In the casual comedy;
He, too, has been changed in his turn,
Transformed utterly:
A terrible beauty is born.

Hearts with one purpose alone
Through summer and winter seem
Enchanted to a stone
To trouble the living stream.
The horse that comes from the road,
The rider, the birds that range
From cloud to tumbling cloud,
Minute by minute they change;
A shadow of cloud on the stream
Changes minute by minute;
A horse-hoof slides on the brim,
And a horse plashes within it;

The long-legged moor-hens dive,
And hens to moor-cocks call;
Minute by minute they live:
The stone's in the midst of all.

Too long a sacrifice
Can make a stone of the heart.
when may it suffice?
That is Heaven's part, our part
To murmur name upon name,
As a mother names her child
When sleep at last has come
On limbs that had run wild.
Was it but nightfall?
No, no, not night but death;
Was it needless death after all?
For England may keep faith
For all that is done and said.
We know their dream; enough
To know they dreamed and are dead;
And what if excess of love
Bewildered them till they died?
I write it out in verse —
MacDonagh and MacBride
And Connolly and Pearse
Now and in time to be,
Wherever green is worn,
Are changed, changed utterly:
A terrible beauty is born.

The poet says that he would meet the executed revolutionaries ("them") when they would come with fresh countenances from counters or desks of the "grey/Eighteenth-century houses." The houses are grey because in the 18th century most of the houses would be built with granite blocks collected from hills or with lime-stones collected from plains, sometimes, when the poet would meet them, he would only nod his head or use some "polite meaningless words" in courtesy. Or he would pass a few minutes with them and talk a few "meaningless words", again only for courtesy. Again, sometimes, at some clubs, near the fire-place, he would think for a few moments and tell them some "mocking tale" or express his scoffing or gibe at something to "please a companion" (one of those executes). The poet would do all these because he thought that jester-like conversations were rare in their times. But now these companions are no more—they have been executed for their involvement in the Easter Rising. Therefore, now there is no occasion for courtesy or jests — things have changed. And yet, in spite of the greatest sacrifices of these patriots, a great hope seems to be within view: "A terrible beauty is born." This compound concept, "terrible beauty", reminds one of Shelley's notions of Medusa, one of the mythological Gorgons. Medusa had bundles of snakes for hair and could turn beholders into stones. Medusa, whose head was cut off by Perseus, was beautiful but terrible. Like Shelley, Pater also thought of "interfusion of the extremes of beauty and terror" (Albright, 610). Yeats here means to say that after the 1916 Easter Rising, the beautiful Ireland has turned terrible, too.

In the second stanza, Yeats recalls, and mourns for, those executed nationalists, one by one. He first tells of Constance Gore-Booth (Markievicz) who took part in the Easter Rising and was sentenced to death, but later on, her death sentence was commuted to penal servitude for life, and still later, she was released. Yeats met Gore-Booth for the first time in 1894 and wrote about the Gore-Booth family: "They are delightful people... All the while I was at Lissadell I was busy telling stories—old Irish stories—first to one then another and then telling them over again to the sick Miss Gore upstairs. Miss Gore-Booth shows some promise as a writer of verse." (Jeffares, 191). In this poem Yeats is referring to Constance Gore-Booth who married Count Casimir Markievicz (1847-1932). Yeats recalls that Gore-Booth was a simple woman with a good-will for everyone. She would think for the nation and its problems till late at night: "Her nights in argument/Until her voice grew shrill." When she was young, she was very beautiful, and she possessed a sweet voice. She used to ride with a hunting dog or harrier.

Next, Yeats mourns for Patrick Pearse ("This man"). About him A. Norman Jeffares writes: "Patrick Pearse (1879-1916), the founder of St. Enda's School for Boys at Rathfarnham, Co. Dublin, was Commandant-General and President of the provisional government in Easter week and surrendered in the Post Office. He was a member of the Irish Bar, an orator, and had published poetry and prose in Gaelic and English." (Jeffares, 192). Yeats, in this poem, recalls that Pearse "Kept a school/And rode our winged horse." The third person about whom the poet laments is Thomas MacDonagh who taught English literature in University College, Dublin. He was a poet, dramatist and critic. In *Estrangement,* Yeats wrote about him: "In England this man would have become remarkable in some way, here he is being crushed by the mechanical logic and common place eloquence which gives power to the most empty mind, because, being 'something other than human life', they have no use for distinguished feeling or individual thought. I mean that within his own mind this mechanical thought is crushing as with an iron roller all that is organic." (Jeffares, 192). This notion of Yeats about MacDonagh is beautifully expressed in the following five lines of the poem:

> This other his helper and friend
> Was coming into his force;
> He might have won fame in the end,
> So sensitive his nature seemed,
> So daring and sweet his thought.

Yeats, next, laments for Major John MacBride(1865-1916) who was Maud Gonne's husband. MacBride fought against England in the Boar War. Yeats thought MacBride to be a "drunken, vainglorious lout." MacBride broke his marriage with Maud in 1905 thereby causing sorrow to Maud and her two children, Iseult MacBride and Sean MacBride, both of whom were very dear to Yeats: "He had done most bitter wrong/To some who are near my heart." Yeats, therefore, hated him and yet the poet sings in praise of MacBride, for he too had taken part in the "causal comedy", i.e., in the national movement. Further, says the poet, MacBride also changed much in his character during the Irish national movements. Nay, says the poet, MacBride became very much changed: "Transformed utterly." And he too took part in the "causal comedy" that has given birth to a "terrible beauty."

All those, who were executed, always jointed their hearts together for only one determined purpose that was like a stone with which they were to trouble "the living stream" of England. During the Easter Rising of 1916, everything changed the course of Ireland — the horse, the rider, the birds in the sky that bounced over the clouds, and everything has been changing since the uprising, minute by minute. The dark shadow over the stream is changing minute by minute. A horse comes near the brim of the stream and a horse bend its head in the stream. The long-legged moor dive in the stream and the moor-hens calls moor-cocks. In short, now everything in Ireland is living, unlike before, and everything is enjoying each moment of its life. The poet recalls that those people who were executed had flints in their hearts: they had determination to free their motherland: "A stone in the midst of all." Jeffares writes: "hearts enchanted to a stone were Yeats's symbol for those who had devoted themselves to a cause without thought of life or love. The stone was a symbol of how politics had affected, in particular, Maud Gonne." (Jeffares, 192-93).

In the last stanza, Yeats probably speaks about Maud Gonne's immense sacrifice for the cause of Ireland. He says that for long she suffered, and this transformed her soft heart into a stone: "Too long a sacrifice/Can make a stone of the heart." But how much more sacrifice will be needed for the liberation of the land? The poet says that only the heaven knows that. Betimes, he says, we can only go on counting the number of Ireland's martyrs or the number of those who are sacrificing themselves for Ireland's cause: 'To murmur name after name." Ireland is like a mother who has witnessed series of the deaths of her children—children who died because they became violent: "As a mother name her child/When sleep at last has come/On limbs that had run wild." The poet compares the state of Ireland with nightfall or death. He questions: were all those deaths, those sacrifices of his compatriots, needless or were of no avail? He raises this question because the Irish people, at first, did not support the Rising. However, he hopes that after such a great blood-bath, England "may keep faith". Jeffares adds: "the Bill for Home Rule for Ireland received the Royal assent in 1914 but was suspended at the beginning of the 1914-18 war, the English government promising to enact it after the war was over." (Jeffares, 193). The poet says that we know what the dream of those who sacrificed their lives was. Their dream was to liberate Ireland at all costs. He says that they died for they loved their motherland excessively: "And what if excess of love/Bewildered them till they died?"

Lastly, the poet recounts the immeasurable contributions of MacDongh, MacBride, Connolly and Pearse. About Connolly, Jeffares writes: "James Connolly (1870-1916), a trade union organiser and author of *Labour in Irish History*, founded the *Irish Worker* and Workers' Republic, organised the Citizen Army, was military commander of all Republican forces in Dublin and Commandant in the Post Office during the rising. He was wounded and was brought to his execution on 12 May, 1916 in a wheel-chair. He is said to have remarked: 'You can shoot me if you like but I am dying for my country." (Jeffares, 193). The poet writes these verses in memory of these people and will continue to write so in the future whenever Ireland will be subdued: "Whenever green is worn." This part of speech, "Whenever green is worn", refers to the songs of the 1798 Irish revolution: 'Green on my Cape' and 'The wearing of the Green'. The poet says that whenever the "green" will be destroyed, i.e., whenever Ireland's prosperity will be hampered, a "terrible beauty" will be born.

A.E. Dyson comments on this poem: "Technically, the poem is a celebration of the dead men, and a monument meant for them; it is poetry becoming part of the war that they fought. More personally, the framework records the initiation of a diverse group of men, whom Yeats had thought of as 'ordinary', into a pantheon of the mighty, and now symbolic, dead. They are translated from the everyday world, the world of fools, of 'causal comedy' where we gossip in motely, into the unchanging world of 'the glorious dead'. The whole life they once led is transcended, in this heroic transposition, this 'terrible beauty' — yet, by the same token, it is also cancelled out for good or ill. Horsemen, thinker, beautiful women, 'drunken, vainglorious lout' — in life, that is what Yeats made of them (the last, of course, Maud Gonne's husband), but all are 'changed, changed utterly' by their final destiny: they are to be remembered as heroes, by generations who never knew them, not gradually forgotten as most of us are, as the years erode memory and history steals for oblivion all that we were." (Dyson 23). W.H. Auden wrote about the poem: "Yeats could write great poetry about the Troubles in Ireland, because most of the protagonists were known to him personally and the places where the events occurred had been familiar to him since childhood." (Albright, xviii). And lastly, Daniel Albright has this to write about this poem: "The poem turns on the mutation of comedy into tragedy. Yeats described the differences between the two genres as follows: 'tragedy must always be a drowning and breaking of the dykes that separate man from man, and... it is upon these dykes comedy keeps house'; and he quoted a phrase of Congreve's to define 'humour' itself — the foundation of comedy — as a 'singular and unavoidable way of doing anything peculiar to one man only' (...). The rebels of 'Easter, 1916' are comedians, full of idiosyncrasy, of 'character', until the rebellion begins: then, under a kind of historical pressure, coal fuses into diamond, and the rebels grow impersonal, universal, outside the flux of nature, no more individual than stones or tombstones. In his portraits of the rebels, Yeats shows how attractive youth, a somewhat lax sweetness of disposition, a comic boastfulness, can be altered by extreme tension into self-resignation, self-oblivion." (Albright, 609).

28. The Second Coming

This is one of the most famous poems of Yeats. It contains the poet's conception of historical progression and his soteriological views. The poem was written in January 1919, at a time when the poet was passing through intense apprehension of Irish Civil War that followed the First World War, along with the several continuing disturbances throughout Europe. But he was particularly apprehensive of the "Russian Revolution and its menace, particularly to aristocrats, to *antithetical* men. In a way instantly familiar to a student of Blake and Shelley, as Yeats was, the

Revolution suggests an apocalypse, and the time of troubles preceding it. But unlike his Romantic precursors, Yeats is on the side of the counterrevolutionaries, and his apocalyptic poem begins by seeing the intervention against revolution as being too late to save the ceremoniously innocent: 'The Germans are... now to Russia come/Though every day some innocent has died." (Bloom, 318). In his *Letters* (ed. Allan Wade), Yeats wrote: "What I want is that Ireland be kept from giving itself (under the influence of its lunatic faculty of going against everything which it believes England to affirm) to Marxian revolution of Marxian definition of value in any form. I consider the Marxian criterion of values as in this age the spear-head of materialism and leading to inevitable murder. From that criterion follows the well-known phrase 'Can the bourgeois be innocent?'" (Jeffares, 204).

'The Second Coming' was first published in *The Dial* in November, 1920. In the first draft of this poem, its title was 'The Second Birth'. Harold Bloom says that that title was more appropriate, because according to him, as also according to Donald Davie, the present title "is a misnomer, since Christ's advent was not for Yeats the First Coming." (Bloom, 318). Bloom further says that "the title is not only a misnomer, but a misleading and illegitimate device for conferring upon the poem a range of reference and imaginative power that it does not possess and cannot sustain." (Bloom, 318). The meaning of the poem will be clearer if we understand Yeats's philosophy of history as explained in *A Vision.* It is a prophetic or visionary poem, because it foretells the coming of a new god or saviour on the ruins of the present civilisation as per the Christian belief. "It blends Christ's prediction of this second coming in Matthew XXIV and St. John's description of the beast of the Apocalypse in Revelations. The location of the birthplace in Bethlehem, traditionally associated with the idea of the gentle innocence of infancy, and with eternal love, adds horror to the thought of the rough beast." (Jeffares, 201). Yeats himself annotated the poem following the story of the mythical Judwalis and Robertes. We can, perhaps profitably, quote Yeats's annotation, here, quoted by Daniel Albright according to whom the poem is "not only a poem about history; it is also a poem about the process of image-making. Indeed it is almost a versification of Yeats's story of an occult experiment in imagination conducted by MacGregor Mathers on Yeats and other researchers". (Albright, 619). Yeats wrote in *Autobiographies (Four Years),* by way of annotating this poem, about Mathers's experiment on him: "He gave me a cardboard symbol and I closed my eyes. Sight came slowly ... there rose before me mental images that I could not control: a desert and Mack Titan raising himself up by his two hands from the middle of a heap of ancient mins. Mathers explained that I had seen a being of the order of Salamanders because he had shown me their symbol, but it was not necessary event to show the symbol, it would have been sufficient that he imagined it... [I discovered] that for a considerable minority ... the visible world would completely vanish, and that world, summoned by the symbol, take its place." (Albright, 619-20).

Daniel Albright beautifully introduces this poem: "According to orthodox Christianity, the faithful live in expectation that, after a Second Coming, Christ will establish on earth a kingdom of sanctity and bliss. The purpose of the present poem is to subvert that happy hope: the poet predicts that, at the end of the millennium, there will arise not Christ but Christ's opposite, a savage god whose reign will establish a system of behaviour antithetical to that recommended by Christ. At the end of the previous poem ['Demon and Beast'], demon and beast — the poet's personal passions and hatreds — ran away, left the poet evacuated and content; in this poem the beast reappears, as a monster to reinvigorate not just the poet but the whole world. "In his long note to this poem, Yeats described the system of the gyres: how all the progress of the human soul and the progress of history can be analysed mathematically as the movement of two interlocking cones, the apex of one screwing into the centre of the base of the other. All movement, then, consists of a simultaneous diminishing of one cone and an expanding of the other (...). In our age the *primary* cone, the cone of the Christian era, objective and self-effacing, has expanded almost to its maximum extent. But as it has enlarged, it has weakened, lost its fervour; and at the turning point of the gyres, a new god,... will be born at the narrow point of the *antithetical* cone, and will inaugurate a subjective age, violent, arrogant, hierarchical polytheistic, aesthetic, and immoral: "All our scientific, democratic, fact-accumulating, heterogenous civilisation belongs to the outward gyre and prepares not the continuance of itself but the revelation as in a lightning flash that will not strike only in one place, and will for a time be constantly repeated, of the civilisation that must slowly take its place (...)." (Albright, 619).

THE SECOND COMING

Turning and turning in the widening gyre
The falcon cannot hear the falconer;
Things fall apart; the centre cannot hold;
Mere anarchy is loosed upon the world,
The blood-dimmed tide is loosed, and everywhere
The ceremony of innocence is drowned;

The best lack all conviction, while the worst
Are full of passionate intensity.
Surely some revelation is at hand;
Surely the Second Coming is at hand.
The Second Coming! Hardly are those words out
When a vast image out of *Spiritus Mundi*
Troubles my sight: somewhere in sands of the desert
A shape with lion body and the head of a man,
A gaze blank and pitiless as the sun,
Is moving its slow thighs, while all about it
Reel shadows of the indignant desert birds.
The darkness drops again; but not I know
That twenty centuries of stony sleep
Were vexed to nightmare by a rocking cradle,
And what rough beast, its hour come round at last,
Slouches towards Bethlehem to be born.

The poet is greatly disturbed by the contemporary uprisings, rebellions, executions, murders, etc., not only in Ireland following the Easter Rising of 1916, but also elsewhere in the whole of Europe. A.E. Dyson very perceptibly writes: "This was the period when Yeats's metaphysical gloom deepened assisted by personal, political and occult promptings." (Dyson, 27). His Gonne was gone, the First World War made him horrified, the communist movement in Russia was a nightmare to him, etc. In a letter of 1936, Yeats adumbrated to his state of mind during this period: "... as my sense of reality deepens [...], I think it does with age, my horror at the cruelty of governments grow greater, and... to hold one form of government more responsible than any other ... would betray my convictions. Communist, Fascist, nationalist, clerical, anti-clerical, are all responsible according to the number of their victims.... If you have my poems by you, look up a poem called *The Second Coming.* It was written some sixteen or seventeen years ago and foretold what is happening... I am not callous every nerve tremble with horror at what is happening in Europe, 'the ceremony of innocence is drowned.'" (Rosenthal, 42). Now, in this poem, the poet thinks that the great cone of civilisation is turning and turning "in the widening gyre." As he believed, due to the gyre, first, the circumference of the civilisation will disintegrate, and the process of disintegration will go centripetally to the point at the centre. Our civilisation is in the process of disintegration and this disintegration began at the circumference. When the process of disintegration will be completed, a new civilisation will be born. Yeats believed that each civilisation continues for two thousand years, after which it disintegrates completely giving place to a completely new civilisation. For example, he believed, the Greco-Roman civilisation continued for two thousand years and disintegrated completely about the time of the advent of Christ. Now, this Christian civilisation is about to complete its allotted life of two thousand years, and so something terrible is about to show itself, as usual. The Greco-Roman civilisation was born when the god Zeus or Jupiter mated with Leda, and from this mating Helen and Clytemnestra were born. This civilisation began about 2,000 B.C. and died at the beginning of the Christian era. Again, the Christian era is about to complete its allotted span of 2,000 years, when the wheel will come full circle in A.D. 2,000. The poet says that this is why everything ominous is showing itself — everything is "Turning and turning in the widening gyre" causing uproarious tumult. Everything is getting apart from everything else. (By the by, this idea favourably compares itself with the present state of the universe as interpreted by the physicists following the Big Bang theory). Due to this process of widening, man is gradually going away from Christ. Yeats here uses the symbol of a falcon for man, and so the falconer in the poem is a symbol of Christ. Jeffares writes: "The falcon represents man, present civilisation, becoming out of touch with Christ, whose birth was the revelation which marked the beginning of Christianity." (Jeffares, 203). Because the falcon is moving away from Christ or the falconer, the falcon cannot hear the call of Christ to turn back from sin or immorality: "The falcon cannot hear the falconer."

For the same reason, the centre of the cone cannot hold the circumference of the cone, and therefore, diversity destroys unity: "Things fall apart; the centre cannot hold." Asa result, the poet says, "Mere anarchy is loosed upon the world" — such as murders, suppressions, executions, treachery, war, etc. The poet sees bloodbaths everywhere, and the cruelty and the oppression do not spare even the innocent people: "The ceremony of innocence is drowned." The best people—those that are wise and have moral predilection—have lost faith in their wisdom and morality. On the other hand, evil ones are hill of extreme passions being unrestrained and unrestrainable by reason, religion or morality. Yeats says that this is the state of affairs in our civilisation.

But what does this state of affairs suggest? The poet expresses his conviction that this is the signal and warranty of the coming of a new and beautiful civilisation in place of the worn out and decrepit civilisation: "Surely some revelation is at hand." As suggested before, Yeats had his own conception of historical changes, which he to an extent explained in

A Vision. There he wrote about the Second Coming: "Each age unwinds the threads another age had wound, and it amuses me to remember that before Phidias, and his westward moving art, Persia fell, and that when full moon came round again, amid eastward moving thought, and brought Byzantine glory, Rome fell; and that at the outset of our westward moving Renaissance Byzantium fell; all things dying each other's life, living each other's death." (Jeffares, 204). The present moribund condition of our civilisation is a revelation of the truth that Christ is coming for the second time: "Surely the Second Coming is at hand." As soon as the poet utters the words "Second Coming", a host of images rushes into his view, out of the *Spiritus Mundi.* The *Spiritus Mundi* or the World's Soul or the *Anima Mundi* is a "general storehouse of images which have ceased to be a property of any personality or spirit." (Jeffares, 204). This *Spiritus Mundi* may be compared with C.G. Jung's collective Unconscious, from where the archetypes come out. In *Mythologies* (1959), Yeats himself wrote about the *Anima Mundi:* "I think of *Anima Mundi* as a great pool or a garden where [a series of images] moves through its allotted growth like a water- plant or fragrantly branches in the air." (Albright, 621). A. E. Dyson also found similarities between *Yeats's Anima Mundi and* C.G. Jung's Collective Unconscious, and also a "similar cast of mind" in both of them. (Dyson, 29). However, here, in the poem, the image that come out of the *Anima Mundi* is that of "A shape with lion body and the head of a man." According to Daniel Albright, the beast ("A shape with lion body and the head of a man") is the sphinx of the Oedipus legend, which is opposite to Christ. He writes: "In 'A Packet for Ezra Pound', Yeats takes Oedipus as the opposite of Christ (...); and the sphinx's bloodiness and sexiness make it also as the contrary of the pale, abstract Christ." (Albright, 621). "The image, as Peter Ure first pointed out in TM *[Towards a Mythology* (1946)], may be related to the Introduction to *The Resurrection* where Yeats wrote: 'I began to imagine, as always at my left side just out of the range of the sight, a brazen winged beast that I associated with laughing, ecstatic destruction.'" (Jeffares, 205). The poet imagines the beast "somewhere in sands of the desert.' The eyes of the beast are "blank and pitiless as the sun", because it is intent on destruction.

The horrific beast now slowly rises from its stupor by moving its thighs, and as the beast begins to move, flocks of desert birds fly away from near it in fear. These desert birds forebode evil as it is their nature to pick up dry bones in Calvary, the place where Christ was crucified: "Is moving its slow thighs, while all about it/Reel shadows of the indignant desert birds." The poet sees darkness and decadence all around—darkness and decadence that have come again after a lapse of the fixed period of two thousand years, that presages the coming into being a new civilisation. The poet compares this period of "twenty centuries" or two thousand years with a "stony sleep" in which the civilisation remains morally, artistically and spiritually as insensitive as a man in deep sleep. At the end of this "stony sleep" the civilisation is disturbed by fearful phenomena in dreams —"vexed to nightmare" — and these frightening dreams are caused by "a rocking cradle", the cradle of a newly born baby, i.e., the rocking cradle of a new civilisation. But the baby or the new civilisation is not still actually born: it will be born after this horrific beast slowly moves towards and reaches Bethlehem "to be born", after its end or destruction has "come round at last", after the "stony sleep." According to A.E. Dyson, the meaning of the phrase "stony sleep" is obscure: "The 'stony sleep' is, presumably, the slumber of the 'rough beast' during the Christian centuries, and the 'rocking cradle' the cradle of Christ's birth. Does this mean that 'vexed to nightmare' was, in these centuries, *contained*— in the uneasy sleep of the monster waiting its own moment — or does it suggest that in some sense, the night-side of the Christian age has been conscious of the terror now to come to full birth, to full daylight consciousness, in the coming millennia?" (Dyson, 30). It may be mentioned here that Yeats may have taken the image of the 'rough beast' from Shakespeare, for "Professor A.M. Gibbs has suggested parallels between the 'rough beast' of this poem and the 'rough beast' in Shakespeare's *Lucrece.* The images of the falcon and the tide of blood were also used by Shakespeare in that poem." (Jeffares, 205).

This short poem of only twenty-five lines has received wide acclaim from critics. It is a very compact poem with intense emotion. Yeats has managed very dexterously a great theme within the compass of only twenty five lines. The myth of the beast of the Judwalis has been profitably employed here. Blackmur praised its right use of words while C.M. Bowra was charmed by its measured verse, terrible images, amazing vision and concentrated moment. The influence of Shelley and Blake is evident here Shelley, principally because of its romantic tone; and Blake, primarily because of the images in the poem. In the poem, as interpreted by Jeffares and shown above, Christian theme has been invoked, but here Harold Bloom differs. Bloom says that the falcon is not man and the falconer is not Christ, rather, he says, the fact of the matter is the other way round: the falconer is man and "the falcon his mastery of nature, now in the act of falling apart. The centre is man: he cannot hold the falcon to an imposed discipline, and the widening gyre is therefore one with the loosening of anarchy upon the world." Interpreted in this wise, the advancement of the material civilisation — the industrialisation, the scientific credo, the matter-is-everything philosophy — has gone beyond the control of man, and hence the falconer (man) cannot hold his "mastery of nature" (the falcon), and hence the ensuing destruction of the civi lisation, probably for the birth of a new one.

29. A Prayer for my Daughter

According to Harold Bloom, this is a "matched poem" with 'The Second Coming', because in both the poems, the poet speaks of "the soul's solipsistic knowledge of its own autonomy, and is born only out of ritual, 'where all's accustomed, ceremonious.'" (Bloom, 322). This poem of ten stanzas, each stanza having eight lines, was written between February and June, 1919, and it first appeared in *Poetry* in November, 1919. The occasion of this poem was the first girl child of Yeats, Anne Butler Yeats, who was born on 26th February, 1919. The poem was written in the old tower or castle at Thoor Ballylee, that Yeats purchased shortly before, renovated and settled in it soon after his marriage. Yeats began to write it shortly after his daughter's birth, when he did not occupy the tower, but finished the poem after settling in the same.

Apparently, the poem celebrates the birth of the poet's daughter and rings like a prayer for her, but, as Harold Bloom suggests, the subject of this poem is not the little Anne Butler Yeats, but rather Maud Gonne: "Its actual subject is not the new born Anne Butler Yeats but Maud Gonne, and the bridegroom who ends the poem in so movingly archaic a fashion is Yeats himself, making in a phantasmagoria the marriage he was denied in life, yet ironically marrying only his own soul." (Bloom, 326). Bloom further says: "In its eighty lines we are given a complete map of Yeats's social mind, at least of that mind in the act of idealization." (Bloom, 325). Bloom is, perhaps, perceptive here because in this poem Yeats demonstrates his "daemonic hatred of the contemporary world", as he did in 'The Second Coming'. He is indignant at the evils of the contemporary society—at the extreme materialism, corruption and faithlessness. His hatred is daemonic because it does not show itself from his conscious mind but from his unconscious mind. The ancient Greeks believed in daemons (or daimons) or guardian spirits. A daemon is something like the "voice of conscience." The hatred shown in this poem towards the society came out of Yeats's conscience and so it is daemonic.

Daniel Albright introduces the poem thus: "'The Second Coming' foresees a future that, for all the horror of its approach, will offer a civilization superior to that in which the poet lives; 'A Prayer for my Daughter' laments the loss of some attractive features of past ages. 'The Second Coming' ends with the birth of a monster that embodies the energies of a new age; 'A Prayer for my Daughter' begins with the birth of an untremendous baby who will shatter no worlds (although Yeats may have entertained some notion of becoming the father of a god—when his wife was pregnant, in 1918, he wrote in a notebook, 'For the first time a [n automatic] script suggesting that our child would be in some way *an avatar*' (...). Here the poet hopes that she will not become troublingly beautiful (...), that she will possess such moderate and civil virtues as courtesy "The wish for a well-mannered, human daughter instead of a harrowingly attractive one suggests that Yeats was himself somewhat disillusioned by the over-intense, the too-shivery. Such visions as that recorded in 'The Second Coming' would give good reason for a desire to find a lower tension-level of existence; and the behaviour of amazing women, such as Maud Gonne — estranged from mankind and liable to craziness — did not provide a model for a girl to follow." (Albright, 622- 23).

In the early drafts, the poem consisted of three more stanzas at the end. There the poet imagined Anne Yeats, at the age of twenty-five, at Coole Park. The three concluding stanzas of the draft poem were the following:

Daughter if you be happy & yet grown —
Say when you are five & twenty — walk alone
Through Cole Domain & visit for my sake
The stony edges of the lake,
Where every year I have counted swans, & cry
That all is well till all that's there
Spring sounding on to the hill air
And all is sound between the lake & sky

Then where what light beach foliage can let through
Falls green on ground the ivy has made blue
Cry out that all is well but cry it not
Too loud for that is a still spot
And after to the garden on that side
Where the Katalpa's grow & call
Until an echo in the wall
Above Maecenas' image has replied.

What matters it if you be overheard
By gardener, labourer or herd
They must that have strong eye-sight meet my shade
When the evening light's begun to fade
Amid the scenery it has held most dear
Till many a winter has gone by
No common man will mock the cry
Nor think that being dead I cannot hear.

Why these three stanzas were later on deleted, we do not know. But, perhaps, the stanzas did not contain any very new ideas, and so the poet dropped these stanzas.

A PRAYER FOR MY DAUGHTER

Once more the storm is howling, and half hid
Under this cradle-hood and coverlid
My child sleeps on. There is no obstacle
But Gregory's wood and one bare hill
Whereby the haystack—and roof-levelling wind,
Bred on the Atlantic, can be stayed;
And for an hour I have walked and prayed
Because of the great gloom that is in my mind.

I have walked and prayed for this young child an hour
And heard the sea-wind scream upon the tower,
And under the arches of the bridge, and scream
In the elms above the flooded stream;
Imagining in excited reverie
That the future years had come,
Dancing to a frenzied drum,
Out of the murderous innocence of the sea.

May she be granted beauty and yet not
Beauty to make a stranger's eye distraught,
Or hers before a looking-glass, for such,
Being made beautiful overmuch,
Consider beauty a sufficient end,
Lose natural kindness and may be
The heart-revealing intimacy
That chooses right, and never find a friend.

Helen being chosen found life flat and dull
And later had much trouble from a fool,
While that great Queen, that rose out of the spray,
Being fatherless could have her way
Yet chose a bandy-legged smith for a man.
It's certain that fine women eat
A crazy salad with their meat
Whereby the Horn of Plenty is undone.

In courtesy I'd have her chiefly learned;
Hearts are not had as a gift but hearts are earned
By those that are not entirely beautiful;
Yet many, that have played the fool
For beauty's very self, has charm made wise,
And many a poor man that has roved,
Loved and thought himself beloved,
From a glad kindness cannot take his eyes.

May she become a flourishing hidden tree
That all her thoughts may like the linnet be.
And have no business but dispensing round
Their magnanimities of sound,
Nor but in merriment begin a chase,
Nor but in merriment a quarrel.
O may she live like some green laurel
Rooted in one dear perpetual place.

My mind, because the minds that I have loved,
The sort of beauty that I have approved,
Prosper but little, has dried up of late,
Yet knows that to be choked with hate
May well be of all evil chances chief.
If there's no hatred in a mind
Assault and battery of the wind
Can never tear the linnet from the leaf.

An intellectual hatred is the worst,
So let her think opinions are accursed.
Have I not seen the loveliest woman born
Out of the mouth of Plenty's horn,

Because of her opinionated mind
Better that horn and every good
By quiet natures understood
For an old bellows full of angry wind?
Consider that, all hatred driven hence,
The soul recovers radical innocence
And learns at last that it is self-delighting,
Self-appeasing, self-affrighting,
And that its own sweet will is Heaven's will;
She can, though every face should scowl
And every windy quarter howl
Or every bellows burst, be happy still.

And may her bridegroom bring her to a house
Where all's accustomed, ceremonious;
For arrogance and hatred are the wares
Peddled in the thoroughfares.
How but in custom and in ceremony
Are innocence and beauty born?
Ceremony's a name for the rich horn,
And custom for the spreading laurel tree.

In the first stanza, the poet says that a strong storm is blowing over the tower in which his family is keeping, but his infant child, Anne Yeats is protected from the howling storm because she is sleeping under 'cradle hood and coverlid." As there is real storm outside, so there is a mental 'storm' within the mind of the poet, for he is disturbed by the social anomie and societal restlessness and uncertainties. Stallworthy says that the "early drafts show that Yeats conceived a metaphysical storm ('a popular tempest') before the real one." (Albright, 623). However, the poet is in a gloomy mood whose objective correlative is the real storm outside. The storm that is littering the haystack and levelling the roofs of houses is coming from the Atlantic Ocean. There is nothing to stop the raging assault of the storm but only the thickly grown trees and one treeless hillock of lady Gregory's estate. "But Gregory's wood and one bare hill / Whereby the haystack —and roof-levelling wind;/ Bred on the Atlantic, can be stayed." To diffuse his anxiety and restlessness, the poet has walked for an hour, and has prayed for his child, in apprehension of her future, owing to the social turmoil outside. At the beginning of the second stanza, the poet again says that he has walked and prayed for his child for an hour. Here he is elaborating the ferocity and the all-pervading destructiveness of the storm. He has heard the sea-wind, or the storm coming from the Atlantic Ocean, upon the tower and "under the arches of the bridge." He has heard the screaming of the storm among the elm-trees standing by the side of the rushing stream. The fierce storm outside arouses in the mind of the poet an apprehension about the shape of things in the proximate future. He foresees that the future will be anomic and mad like the rhythmless dancer gone amuck trying to keep time with the frenzied beatings of the drum. The poet knows that all these are the imagination of his excited brain — excited by the war-torn, blood-bathing tumult of the world: "Imagining in excited reverie/That the future years had come,/Dancing to a frenzied drum,/Out of the murderous innocence of the sea." The word 'murderous' here does not mean anything harmful, but it is used in the sense in which we often speak of a woman's extremely charming beauty as 'murderous beauty'. A. Norman Jeffares says that the last three lines of this stanza may be compared with the following two lines of 'The Second Coming': "The blood-dimmed tide is loosed, and everywhere /The ceremony of innocence is drowned." In both the places, the poet is apprehensive of the oncoming ominous future. Daniel Albright says that the phrase "the murderous innocence of the sea" may refer to the sea: "perhaps the sea—the force of historical process — is innocent because it is impersonal, not petty, spiteful, or divided against itself." (Albright, 623).

In the third stanza, the poet prays for his daughter's beauty, but he will not like exquisite beauty for her—such beauty as "make a stranger's eye distraught" or make herself proud for her beauty (like Maud Gonne) when she may look at herself in the looking-glass. He is averse to exquisite beauty because if a woman has it then she takes beauty as an end in itself. Such a woman (like Gonne) forgets the "natural kindness" of women, and also forgets the need of a fast friend to whom that woman may reveal her mind in absolute intimacy. Further, such a woman (again like Maud Gonne) is concerned only with what is right and what is wrong (as Gonne was in politics) and so can hardly make a true friend (like Yeats). In the fourth stanza, the poet cites the instances of such women—women who, being too proud of their intoxicating beauty, ultimately did something abjectly foolish. Helen, the great beauty of Greece, and daughter of Jupiter and Leda, married the 'fool' Menelaus and caused the Trojan war. Another such woman was "that great Queen" Aphrodite. She was born, as the Greek mythology tells us, out of foam ('Aphros' in Greek means 'foam'): "that rose out of the spray." She was the goddess of beauty, love and fertility, but foolishly and out of extreme pride she ultimately married Haphaestus, the lame god of fire—"the armour-maker of the gods" ("smith") and cuckolded husband of Aphrodite—"chose a bandy-legged smith for a man." Citing these two examples from mythology, the poet comes to the conclusion that beautiful women (like Maud Gonne) choose either foolish or deformed men as their life-partners: "fine women eat/A crazy salad with their meat." And thus such women block the way of peace and happiness and plenty of love that they could get otherwise: "Whereby the Horn of Plenty is undone." The Horn of Plenty refers to the mythical goat that sucked Zeus and whose horns "flowed with nectar and ambrosia", therefore, the Horn of Plenty is a magical object which can deliver anything one may want. The poet means to say that due to their foolishness, the paragons of beauty reject men who might prove Horns of Plenty to them.

In the fifth stanza, the poet wishes her daughter to be courteous. He says that one is not born a hearty or generous being, but one has to acquire courtesy and generosity. Not the extremely beautiful but only the moderately beautiful can acquire the art of being courteous and generous. Yeats always emphasised the necessity of being courteous and generous. "Yeats regarded courtesy and self-possession and style in the arts as the result of 'a deliberate shaping of all things'. There is an interesting passage on the role of aristocrats, countrymen and artists in this connection in 'Poetry and Tradition', which is echoed in 'The Municipal Gallery Revisited'." (Jeffares, 206). Yeats wishes that his daughter may be courteous and generous and artistic, but not immoderately beautiful. Because many have become fools being drawn to such extreme beauty. They have foolishly thought that beauty and wisdom are the same thing. Again, "many a poor man" (like the poet himself), being attracted to paragons of beauty (like Maud Gonne), loved than and roved or toiled for them, and thought that they woe loved by those beautiful women, in turn. Such men have not been able to turn their eyes away from the beautiful women, but ultimately, they proved themselves fools. On the other hand, some women with simple charms have proved to be possessing "glad kindness" (like the poet's wife Mrs. Georgie Hyde-Lees), and such women have proved to be fountains of peace and happiness.

In the sixth stanza, Yeats prays so that his daughter may grow up like a tree, that is, she may flourish in all respects of the tradition, without being ostentatious. The tree here may symbolise constancy, tradition and generosity; for a tree is rooted in the soil (tradition), is constant, and offers generosity to men. The tree, further, does not sport itself, but keeps itself "hidden". The poet wishes that his child daughter, when grown up, may have enough of idealism in her mind, and may be like the happy finches or linnets and sing, like them, magnanimous songs ("magnanimities of sound"). Again, may she not, inhere agility and ostentatiousness ("merriment"), hunt for someone peremptorily ("begin a chase"); nor may she pick up a quarrel with anybody. This may also mean that she should not quarrel with the tradition and hunt for another style of life or culture or tradition. The poet wishes that his daughter may be prosperous ("green laurel") in her peaceful home and may follow the dear ancient tradition: "O may she live like some/green laurel / Rooted in one dear perpetual place" A.E. Dyson summarises the four stanzas, from the third stanza to the sixth stanza, thus (Dyson, 33-34): "Stanzas iii — v might be thought of as straight forward whatever we personally make of them, and to contain a sequence of undeniable, if unexciting truths. 'Courtesy' is a key word, foreshadowing the climax, and signalling the internal balance this poem will achieve. For Yeats, 'courtesy' is always a good word. It belongs with aristocracy, tradition, friendship, artistry — though always, naturally, in tension with other qualities, various in kind. ... 'Yeats's choice — for moderate beauty, 'natural kindness', 'heart-revealing intimacy', the charm that earns friendship — translates, in stanza vi, to organic growth. There is no play of wit here—nothing in the least to remind us of Marvell's 'The Garden', despite the metamorphosis of possible passion to amorous green. We are more likely to think of Wordsworth's Lucy: 'A violet by a mossy stone,/Half-hidden from the eye...' For a moment, there is a real, even simple, craving for bliss without stress, harmony without competition, 'business' without society. The girl is to be 'a flourishing hidden tree', 'a linnet'. She is to dispense 'magnanimities of sound' (...). She is to assimilate all, quarrel and love alike, to 'merriment'. Stanza vi seems to swell with blessing, as if detaching itself momently from the poem, attaching itself entirely to the simple, deep core of love for a baby who is still nothing — still all to become: 'O may she live like some green laurel / Rooted in one dear perpetual place.' 'Rooted' is, of course, another great word for Yeats — little though we think of him as a 'nature' poet. Consider the force of the word in 'The Municipal Gallery Revisited'.:

> And here's John Synge himself, that rooted man,
> 'Forgetting human words', a deep grave face."

In the seventh stanza, the poet looks into his own mind. He recalls that once he loved beautiful women (like Maud Gonne) but they have not prospered. A. Norman Jeffares thinks that this has obvious reference to Maud Gonne and says that "Maud Gonne returned to Ireland in December 1918. Both she and Con Markievicz were in prison afterwards." Thus Maud had to face adversity, in the end. The poet says that such women now know that extreme hatred (hatred may here mean Gonne's extreme nationalism and/or her rejection of Yeats's love) is the chief evil: "Yet knows that to be choked with hate/May well be of all evil chances chief." A mind that is not foil of hatred will not be assaulted and torn into pieces by "battery of the wind." Here Yeats shows his extreme hatred of hatred itself, and he repeats this in the following two lines of the last stanza of the poem: "For arrogance and hatred are the wares/Paddled in the thoroughfares." He says that a mind without any hatred is like a linnet, and no assault and no "battery of the wind" can dislodge the linnet from its place of peace. In the eighth stanza, the poet elaborates on hatred; but this time, it is not ordinary hatred, but it is intellectual hatred. He says that the most heinous hatred is the intellectual hatred — hatred that grows out of an idolised opinion that women do generally possess. Yeats wrote in his Diary in 1910: "Women because the main event of their lives has been a giving of themselves give themselves to an opinion as if it were a stone doll.... women should have their play with dolls finished in childhood for, if they play with ideas again it is amid hatred and malice." (Jeffares, 207). This has also a reference to Maud Gonne, and so Harold Bloom is quite right when he says that not Anne Butler Yeats but Maud Gonne occupies the centre-stage of this poem. However, keeping in view the harmful effects of hatred, Yeats wishes that his child daughter may take opinions, or *idees fixe*, as "accursed." He says that he has seen "loveliest women" (like Maud Gonne) who possessed everything admirable ("born/Out of the mouth of Plenty's horn"). But due to their "opinionated mind" exchanged their wealth of beauty and "everything good" for some worthless men who are extremely arrogant: "For an old bellows full of angry wind?" The poet says that why these women did so nobody knows but their own nature.

Therefore, the poet wishes his daughter free from all sorts of opinionated thoughts, so that her soul may find its inborn innocence which the poet calls "radical innocence" in contrast to "murderous innocence" explained above. When she will see her own soul's innocence, she will find that this innocence is the most self-delighting and pleasant. She may even be frightened at the sight of that innocence, because innocence has its own immeasurable strength and might. She will also learn to understand that, cleansed of all the aforesaid evils, the will in soul is the sweetest, because it is actually the will of God who resides within the soul. When she will be able to attain to this state, she will be happy, in spite of people hating her or being jealous of her, and in spite of people heaping acrimony and hatred and vituperations upon her: "She can, though every face should scowl/And every windy quarter howl /Or every bellows burst, be happy still." And lastly, in the last stanza, the poet wishes that she be married, alter attaining age, to a husband from a traditional and cultural house: "may her bridegroom bring her to a house/Where all's accustomed, ceremonious." He says that in the traditional and cultured house, there is no arrogance and no hatred—things that belong to the lowly folk: "For arrogance and hatred are the wares/Peddled in the thoroughfares." The poet says that only in an aristocratic house of tradition and culture, there are innocence and beauty. Ceremony, or the spiritual values, and custom, or tradition, belong only to an affluent and aristocratic house ("rich horn"), where there is dignity and lofty ideals("laurel tree"): "Ceremony's a name for the rich horn,/And custom for the spreading laurel tree."

This beautiful poem abounds in mythology, images and emotional intensities. Its rhyme-scheme is a a b b c d d c. It is one of the most memorable poems of Yeats. Daniel Albright writes about the purpose of writing this poem: "Much of the purpose of 'A Prayer for my Daughter' is to embed the child in a richly articulated social world, to make no prayers for unusual glory of self." (Albright, 625-26).

THE TOWER — 1928

Yeats's poetic maturity did not come to him overnight, but gradually, and it reached its apex in the poems of this collection, which were earlier published in *Seven Poems and A Fragment* (1922). When these poems were rearranged and published in *The Tower,* Yeats was a poetically mature, philosophically serene and worldly happy man, accustomed with the affairs of the world. He is now acclaimed one of the greatest poets of the 20th century, this acclamation being authenticated by the Nobel Prize of literature, conferred on him in 1923. He is also a responsible public man, being appointed a Senator of the Republic of Ireland. But all these accolades did not dwindle his poetic genius; contrary, he began to pour in poems of new themes and new techniques. Yeats once described the old Wordsworth — laurel-burdened Wordsworth — as the 'honoured and empty-witted' Venerable Old Poet. Yeats did not like to lose his hold on the poetic genius like old Wordsworth, rather he wanted to drink life to its dregs and tell the world about his idea of the quality of life. The old Yeats — unwilling to accept his old age — now was writing poems about self-analysis and about eschatological and soteriological themes, wearing altogether new personae. Daniel Albright writes about the Yeats of this period: "But the persona of the public man [Yeats], visiting schools (in 'Among School Children'), talking with soldiers ('The Road at my Door') and versifying his senate speeches ('The Tower' III 6-13), is not the only persona found in this volume. The sage is equally common, and equally ironical. Many of these poems are written by the author of *A Vision,* the Platonist labouring in his Tower to construe difficult texts dictated from beyond the grave, 'the half-read wisdom of daemonic images' (...). In *A Vision* (1925), this persona is usually quite serious — he is the medium through whom ecstatic wisdom is transmitted to mankind. But in Yeats's poetry, starting as early as 'The Phases of the Moon' (1918), the Platonist is often derided for his pretension and futility, as if he were less a conductor of wisdom than a resistor to it. Ezra Pound wrote much of his greatest poetry on the theme of his inadequacy as a poet, from 'Near Perigord' to Canto 81 and beyond. Yeats was not quite so dependent for inspiration on his anxiety about lack of inspiration, but self-mockery, both of the senator and of the sage, provides much of the tension of this great volume. The poet contemplates his defective wisdom, his aging, impotent body, and his aging, impotent historical era, and grows potent from the sad spectacle." (Albright, 628).

A. Norman Jeffares writes about this volume and its author: "Yeats's change of style and his maturity were probably not generally recognised until the publication of *The Tower* in 1928. This volume was a collection of poems which reflect the richness of his life: marriage, a family, senatorship of the Irish Free State, the Nobel Prize for poetry, *AV*[*A Vision*] published, the discovery of his Anglo-Irish ancestry in politics and literature. There was also the sharpened apprehension, brought by Ireland's civil war, of approaching conflagration in the world and, by approaching age, of ruin and decay. Yeats had become 'a smiling sixty-year old public man', but with ironic memories of lost youth and love, with the tower to remind him that the glory of a family or house can vanish, and an ideal ised Byzantium to set against the realities of living in a country of the young. His verse took on new eloquence, itdealtfreelywith many of his moods and interests: politics, philosophy, friendship, and love. He wrote of them as they affected his own imaginative life: and his imagination grew stronger as his body decayed: an idea he had seized upon in Blake when he himself was only thirty-four. He looked back on the poetry of *The Tower* in surprise at its bitterness and power, yet it also carried antithetical view:

> When such as I cast out remorse
> So great a sweetness flows into the breast
> We must laugh and we must sing,
> We are blest by everything,
> Everything we look upon is blest."

(Jeffares, 211).

Daniel Albright comments on the theme and technique of the poems of this volume: "The structure of *The Tower* is congruent to the structure of *A Vision* (1925). The first book of *A Vision* describes the Great Wheel, the progress of the soul through the twenty-eight incarnations of the lunar month: similarly the opening poems in *The Tower* trace the progress of Yeats's soul, from Ireland to Byzantium, from rural simplicity to the brink of the grave, from his comfortable home to a landscape desolated by war. The third book of *A Vision* describes the historical gyre, offers a map of the events of the last 4000 years arranged in great cyclical heaves, each initiated by the birth of a god; and in the middle of *The Tower* there appear poems on historical themes; the chaos of the first world war in 'Nineteen Hundred and Nineteen', a summary incantation of the gyres in 'Two Songs from a Play; and the spasmodic birth-processes of a new age in 'Leda and the Swan'. The fourth and final book of *A Vision* describes the journey of the soul after death, its passage from reenactments of its past life to blessed oblivion; and the last poem in *The Tower*, 'All Souls' Night', presents the ghosts of Yeats's friends and prepares the poet for his own assimilation to their company. Indeed 'All Souls' Night' is also printed on the final pages of *A Vision*—thus it is the common epilogue to *A Vision* and *The Tower*." (Albright, 628-29).

30. Sailing to Byzantium

This poem was written in the autumn (August-September) of1926, and it was first published in *October Blast* (1927). The first draft of the poem was edited by the poet several times before i t was given the fi nal shape. The title of the poem derives from the name of the city of Byzantium, an ancient city that was built by the Roman Emperor Constantine (?287-337). From A.D. 395 to 1453, it was the headquarters of the Eastern or Greek empire and also for the Eastern Christianity. The city was believed to be the place where God existed. The name of the city was changed first to Constantinople and then to Istanbul. A. Norman Jeffares writes: "Yeats's knowledge of the city was largely derived from reading W.G. Holme's *The Age of Justinian and Theodora* (1905), Mrs A. Strong. *Apotheosis and After Life: Three Lectures on Certain Phases of Art and Religion in the Roman Empire* (1915) and O.M. Dalton, *Byzantine Art and Archaeology* (1911). He also read Gibbon' s *Decline and Fall of the Roman Empire*, *The Cambridge Medieval History*, the *Encyclopaedia Britannica* and other general reference works. R. Ellmann has suggested that J. B. Bury, the historian, who was Latin master for a time at the High School, Dublin [where Yeats read], may first have interested Yeats in Byzantium." (Jeffares, 211-12). Yeats expressed his fascination in *A Vision:* "I think if I could be given a month of Antiquity and leave to spend it where I chose, I would spend it in Byzantium, a little before Justinian opened St. Sophia and closed the Academy of Plato." (Jeffares, 212). "In November 1924 Yeats had been ill, out of breath, with high blood pressure, and Mrs. Yeats brought him to Sicily where he saw the Byzantine mosaics of Monreale and the Capella Palatina at Palermo.... On 5th September, 1926 Yeats wrote to Mrs. Shakespeare: 'There have been constant interruptions — the last time I wrote a poem about Byzantium to recover my spirits." (Jeffares, 213). A Norman Jeffares further writes to introduce the poem: "The best comment on the poem, however, is contained in a paragraph Yeats wrote for a broadcast of his poems (BBC Belfast, 8th Sept. 1931) which was not included in the final version of the script: 'Now I am trying to write about the state of my soul, for it is right for an old man to make his soul, and some of my thoughts upon that subject I have put into a poem called 'Sailing to Byzantium'. When Irishmen were illuminating the Books of Kells [in the eighth century] and making the jewelled croziers in the National Museum, Byzantium was the centre of European civilisation and the source of its spiritual philosophy, so I symbolise the search for the spiritual life by a journey to that city." (Jeffares, 213).

To Yeats, Byzantium was a sort of paradise, a *Tir na nóg,* for which the mythical character Oisin had been searching all his life. And search was the subject of many of Yeats's early poems. There in the poems, he hoped for, but yet unattained, paradise which was full of promises: beauty, peace, happiness—all. But the paradise, now represented by Byzantium, holds no promise to the poet, and he is therefore frustrated. However, Daniel Albright recounts the features of the Byzantium of this poem: "The characteristics of Byzantium, then, are: (1) an almost complete dematerialization, as if the city were the pleasure dome in Coleridge's 'Kubla Khan' (1797), manufactured out of air and shadowed on water— in fact a draft of 'Sailing to Byzantium' mentioned 'St. Sophia's sacred dome... Mirrored in water' (...); (2) a deliberate destruction of the boundary between life and art—men are translated into mosaic, while symbols have the presence of 'a perfect human body'; (3) anonymity — art is the cooperative effect of a community of workers and thinkers; the oblivion and beatitude of dead souls were realized there on earth. Byzantium is an abstraction from life, and Byzantine art is notable for its abstract character." (Albright, 629).

SAILING TO BYZANTIUM

I

That is no country for old men, The young
In one another's arms, birds in the trees,
— Those dying generations — at their song,
The salmon-falls, the mackerel-crowded seas,
Fish, flesh, or fowl, commend all summer long
Whatever is begotten, born, and dies.
Caught in that sensual music all neglect
Monuments of unageing intellect.

II

An aged man is but a paltry thing,
A tattered coat upon a stick, unless
Soul claps its hands and sing, and louder sing
For every tatter in its mortal dress,
Nor is there singing school but studying
Monuments of its own magni ficence;
And therefore I have sailed the seas and come
To the holy city of Byzantium.

III

O sages standing in God's holy fire
As in the gold mosaic of a wall,
Come from the holy fire, perne in gyre,
And be the singing-master of my soul.
Consume my heart away; sick with desire
And fastened to a dying animal
It knows not what it is; and gather me
Into the artifice of eternity.

IV

Once out of nature I shall never take
My bodily form from any natural thing,
But such a form as Grecian goldsmith make
Of hammered gold and gold enamelling
To keep a drowsy Emperor awake;
Or set upon a golden bough to sing

To lords and ladies of Byzantium
Of what is past or passing or to come.

This poem of thirty-two lines is divided into four stanzas, each stanza consisting of eight lines rhyming a b a b e d e e. In the first stanza, the poet says that old as he is, he does not like the country in which he is now living: "That is no country for old men." A. Norman Jeffares and Daniel Albright suggest that the country referred to here may be Ireland. Albright writes: "the following details suggest that the country is Ireland, famous for salmon-streams; but the line also contains a pun on *Tir na nóg*, literally the *Country of the Young*, the Celtic name for paradise. Yeats at one time thought that this first line should read: 'Old men should quit a country where the young' —... In the early drafts Yeats intended further to contrast the old and the young by juxtaposing the 'old gods' of pagan Ireland with the infant Christ, 'a smiling child upon his mother's knees' (...)." (Albright, 630). But A. E. Dyson disagrees with them: "I disagree with Jeffares in his comment that is intended (the use of 'This' instead of 'That' in the manuscript version is irrelevant, since clearly all changes were made toward the effect of the work as finally printed.) I have never doubted that the 'country' is a symbolic island or continent of 'the young', allegorised in the first stanza, and akin to the island which 'The Wanderings of Oisin' (1889) pioneered. It is an emphatic start, even if the first reading, as I have said, might/Seek to achieve neutrality. In other words, the statement will be made to sound in essence a commonplace, a truism, requiring matter-of-fact recognition, without special emotion." (Dyson, 49). However, the poet is indignant of his country because here everyone, particularly the young folk, are given to sensuality. Here the young boys and girls are in one another' s arms, the birds are singing on the trees, the salmons are jumping, and the mackerels are swimming in the seas—all these me romantic scenes implying the sensuousness of his country, i.e., of this earth. About the phrase 'In one another's arms', Jeffares writes: "Stallworthy quotes a first and illegible draft in which the poet writes that the time has come to speak of his loves 'in my first youth' and contains these lines 'For many loves have I taken off my clothes'... 'but now I will take off my body/That they might be enfolded in that for which they (had longed). In 'that', as Stallworthy points out, is probably the poet's soul." (Jeffares, 213). Therefore, according to Daniel Albright, 'The young/In one another's arms' refers to sensuality, rather sexuality, for this, again, refers to 'For many loves have I taken off my clothes." The falling of the salmons refers to the memory of the poet of his showing his wife the falling of salmons at Galway. Hence, falling of salmons may mean worldly love, consisting of physical and mental union of the opposite sexes. The poet also remembers the "memories of the mackerel 'coming in' to harbours and shores in the west of Ireland." (Jeffares, 214). The poet also remembers "Fish, flesh and fowl" —all that are engrossed only in births, sensuousness and deaths. The poet means to say in the first stanza that in such a country (in this world), everybody is engrossed in sensuousness, and consequently, everybody is forgetful of art and philosophy—the two "Monuments of unageing intellect." Art and philosophy are unageing because men will eternally aspire after these and because these two have a sort of eternal ontological existence.

In the second stanza, the poet tells us that in this country, an aged man is neglected like a "paltry thing". He says that an old man is like a "tattered coat upon a stick" — a caricature of a man — unless the old man aspires after the heavenly bliss: "unless/Soul clap its hands and sing." The clause "Soul clap its hands and sing" "recalls Blake's vision of his brother's soul clapping its hands, as it flew up to heaven." (Jeffares, 214). Daniel Albright here adds: "according to *A Vision, p.* 168, impersonal and impartial artists, such as Rembrandt and Synge, 'look on and clap their hands' at the spectacle of the objective world." (Albright, 630). The poet means to say that unless an old man elevates himself above his tottering body and engages himself in the pursuits of art and philosophy, he is a contemptible thing. Therefore he wants to leave this country to reach Byzantium where there is no school of music (sensuality), but where he can study art and philosophy: art and philosophy that are but "Monuments of its own magnificence." With this end in view, *i.e.*, with a view to studying art and philosophy, the poet has set sail and has reached the city of Byzantium: "And therefore I have sailed the seas and come/To the holy city of Byzantium."

In the third stanza, the poet invokes the sages and the wise men who are "standing in God's holy fire" as "in the gold mosaic of a wall." The phrase "sages standing in God's holy fire" refers to the statues of "martyrs in the frieze at S. Apollinare Nuovo at Ravenna" in Italy, (Jeffares, 214), and the phrase "gold mosaic of a wall" symbolises art. The poet invokes the saints to come out of the "holy fire" and move in a circle ("perne in a gyre") so that his sensuousness and passions may be disentangled from his soul. He also asks them to teach him how to sing the songs of the soul. The poet urges the sages and wise men to lift him up from the dross of his animal passions and desires that, even though he is now an old man, entail to him: "Consume my heart away; sick with desire/And fastened to a dying animal." The poet says that his soul does not know its true nature, and therefore, he urges them to take his soul upwards and emplace it in

Byzantium, which is the symbol of eternity, for the city of Byzantium is the centre of art and philosophy—disciplines that are eternal, disciplines that have eternal appeal: "and gather me/Into the artifice of eternity." This means that the poet wants their help to enjoy the eternal bliss in the disciplines of art and philosophy: "Monuments of unageing intellect." Here one may be reminded of Boethius's *Consolations of Philosophy.*

In the fourth or the last stanza, the poet declares that once he has been lifted up from this sensuous natural world, he will never come back to put on flesh: "Once out of nature I shall never take/My bodily form from any natural thing." Rather, he will take such a shape as "Grecian goldsmiths make", that is, he will take the form of art itself. Then he will put on a dress which is made of "hammered gold and gold enamelling" — a dress that will be too astonishing even to an Emperor: "To keep a drowsy Emperor awake." Or, says the poet, he would like to be a golden bird and be sitting on a "golden bough" and sing celestial songs to infatuate the lords and ladies of Byzantium. And in his songs, he will sing about the past, the present and the future, i.e., he will sing about eternity. Daniel Albright comments on the concluding line: "the poet, fastened to the temporal world, dreams of eternity; the bird, twittering in eternity, sings of time, history. This ending seems to foreshadow a return to nature, perhaps a rebirth of the poet's soul." (Albright, 632).

Yeats wrote another poem the title of which is almost synonymous with the title of this poem: 'Byzantium'. He wrote 'Byzantium' about four years after 'Sailing to Byzantium'. Perhaps Yeats wrote the second poem in order to explicate the meaning contained in 'Sailing to Byzantium'. But actually the second poem has become even more difficult. Further, according to F.L. Gwynn, the two poems contain two similar but not the same themes. Harold Bloom writes: "F.L. Gwynn was the first, I believe, to indicate a crucial difference between the historical vision of the two poems." (Bloom, 344). In 'Sailing to Byzantium' the poet simply wants to escape from this sensuous world whereas in 'Byzantium' he says that the soul cannot reach Byzantium unless it is purified through suffering. 'Sailing to Byzantium', one of the memorable poems of Yeats, is very rich in imagery and allegories. It is so complex and compact that the paraphrasing of a single line may require pages of prose. But the theme is pointed and clear: the poet has grown old, his body is decaying, and he looks like, as he ironically tells us, a "tattered coat upon a stick."(cf. T.S. Eliot: I have grown old, l have grown old/I shall wear my trousers rolled.') But he does not despair for that because he thinks that the decaying of the body is rather essential for the spirit's union with the Supreme Spirits — with art and philosophy, in

Byzantium. In this sense, the poem bears an optimistic note. But, as Daniel Albright has shown, "for all its seductiveness, Byzantium is finally forced to confess its inadequacy. There is a covert allusion in the poem's first line to *Tir na nóg,* the paradise for which Oisin searches in *The Wandering of Oisin*, and in that early poem, as in so many later ones, paradise at last famishes the appetites that promises to glut. All representations of the supernatural must contain some grotesquerie, a straining for effect, a juxtaposition of incompatible elements, as Yeats himself noted *(AV,* p. 292); but the poet's metamorphosis into a golden bird, at the end of this poem, may suggest a certain laborious triviality as well as an eerie splendour, as if life in Byzantium were at last shown as a super sort of folly." (Albright, 630).

31. The Tower

This is the title poem of the volume of poems *The Tower.* To Harold Bloom, this long poem is "more impressive than *Sailing to Byzantium,* though it has less reputation at this time." (Bloom, 349). The poem was written in October, 1926, and was first published in *The New Republic* on 29th June, 1927. Therefore it was written about one year after 'Sailing to Byzantium'. But for reasons best known to himself, the poet put it after 'Sail ing to Byzantium' in *'The Tower-1928.* During the period of *The Tower,* Yeats was undoubtedly an old man, in the wrong side of sixty, with fast decaying body and sensuality. But, contrarily, he became intellectually even more alert. Harold Bloom and Whitaker suggest that artists want to be their own contraries. Whether this is true or not, Yeats's case well fits into their theory: the more Yeats became physically weak, the more he became intellectually and spiritually alert. Of course, "Whitaker subtly presents the analogue of Tennyson's Ulysses, another old man who lusts after action, seeking a death that will be his own creation. Other Victorian dramatic monologues suggest themselves also, including perhaps the greatest, Browning's visionary Pope brooding on the abyss of history, and on the necessity for accepting human responsibility, lest all action be wasted, and human death lose all significance." (Bloom, 349-50). In this volume, the poet is in a tension between spiritual upward motion and the bodily downward motion: "The poet is growing old, but his vision refuses to darken, and his ear and eye continue to expect an impossible sublimity. With Blake he continues to know that less than all cannot satisfy man, yet his decrepit age threatens to make his desire merely grotesque." (Bloom, 350). Shelley's conviction was that "the most prophetic images are necessarily those of unfulfilled and unfulfillable desire." (Bloom, 350). In

'The Tower', Yeats seeks for such an unfulfilled and unfulfillable desire. His desire is like that of a lame man to sit on the top of a mountain or roll up a huge stone to the top of a hill like Sisyphus. Yeats showed his spirit of contrariety as early as in *The Wanderings of Oisin* where Oisin rose in rage against old age and decrepitude. The desire in Yeats in his old age is the desire for enjoying the spiritual beauty that is there at the vantage point of the tower or on the apex comer of the cone-shape in which the manifold of the world are arranged hierarchically, according to the philosophy of Aristotle, or, it may be, for the beauty that is transcendental and eternal beyond the flux of the manifold. Looking through the corridor of history, the poet finds that he is not alone or unique in his peculiar and obdurate desire, but there were others, like him, who broke their knees because of "the horrible splendor of desire." But for all that, he is conscious about failures, including the failure of his love for Maud Gonne. And therefore, at the end of the poem, he composes his mind into serenity, and concludes that peace resides not in the impossible made possible, but in the contemplation on the elements of the highest spheres: art, philosophy and love. And here Daniel Albright very perceptively comments: "As in 'Sailing to Byzantium', the poet here struggles to translate himself into a being immune from the ravages of old age. But instead of mutating into an unnatural artifice—a golden bird—the poet finds that his natural self, battered and feeble as it is, can be so transfigured by the imagination that no ascent out of common life is needed. The face and the mask almost coincide—here Yeats bequeaths himself to posterity as a kind of cultural artifact." (Albright, 632).

THE TOWER

I

What shall I do with this absurdity —
O heart, O troubled heart—this caricature,
Decrepit age that has been tied to me
As to a dog's tail ?
Never had I more
Excited, passionate, fantastical
Imagination, nor an ear and eye
That more expected the impossible —
No, not in boyhood when with rod and fly,
Or the humbler worm, I climbed Ben Bulben's back
And had the livelong summer day to spend.

It seems that I must bid the Muse go pack,
Choose Plato and Plotinus for a friend
Until imagination, ear and eye,
Can be content with argument and deal
In abstract things; or be derided by
A sort of battered kettle at the heel.

II

I pace upon the battlements and stare
On the foundation of a house, or where
Tree like a sooty finger, starts from the earth;
And send imagination forth
Under the day's declining beam, and call
Images and memories
From ruin or from ancient trees,
For I would ask a question of them all.

Beyond that ridge lived Mrs. French, and once
When every silver candlestick or sconce
Lit up the dark mahogany and the wine,
A serving-man, that could divine
That most respected lady's every wish,
Ran and with the garden shears
Clipped an insolent farmer's ears
And brought them in a little covered dish.

Some few remembered still when I was young
A peasant girl commended by a song,
Who'd lived somewhere upon that rocky place,
And praised the colour of her face,
And had the greater joy in praising her,
Remembering that, if walked she there,
Farmers jostled at the fair
So great a glory did the song confer.

And certain men, being maddened by those rhymes,
Or else by toasting her a score of times,
Rose from the table and declared it right
To test their fancy by their sight;
But they mistook the brightness of the moon

For the prosaic light of day —
Music had driven their wits astray —
And one was drowned in the great bog of Cloone.

Strange, but the man who made the song was blind;
Yet, now I have considered it, I find
That nothing strange; the tragedy began
With Homer that was a blind man,
And Helen has all living hearts betrayed.
O may the moon and sunlight seem
One inextricable beam,
For if I triumph I must make men mad.

And I myself created Hanrahan
And drove him drunk or sober through the dawn
From somewhere in the neighbouring cottages.
Caught by an old man's juggleries
He stumbled, tumbled, fumbled to and fro
And had but broken knees for hire
And horrible splendor or desire;
I thought it all out twenty years ago:

Good fellows shuffled cards in an old bawn;
And when that ancient ruffian's turn was on
He so bewitched the cards under his thumb
That all but the one card became
A pack of hounds and not a pack of cards,
And that he changed into a hare.
Hanrahan rose in frenzy there
And followed up those baying creatures towards —

O towards I have forgotten what — enough!
I must recall a man that neither love
Nor music nor an enemy's clipped ear
Could, he was so harried, cheer,
A figure that has grown so fabulous
There's not a neighbour left to say
When he finished his dog's day:
An ancient bankrupt master of this house.

Before that ruin came, for centuries,
Rough men-at-arms, cross-gartered to the knees
Or shod in iron, climbed the narrow stairs,
And certain men-at-arms there were
Whose images, in the Great Memory stored,
Come with loud cry and panting breast
To break upon a sleeper's rest
While their great wooden dice beat on the board.

As I would question all, come all who can;
Come old, necessitous, half-mounted man;
And bring beauty's blind rambling celebrant;
The red man the juggler sent
Through God-forsaken meadows; Mrs. French,
Gifted with so fine an ear,
The man drowned in a bog's mire,
When mocking Muses chose the country wench.

Did all old men and women, rich and poor,
Who trod upon these rocks or passed this door,
Where in public or in secret rage
As I do now against old age?
But I have found an answer in those eyes
That are impatient to be gone;
Go therefore; but leave Hanrahan,
For I need all his mighty memories.

Old lecher with a love on every wind,
Bring up out of that deep considering mind
All that you have discovered in the grave,
For it is certain that you have
Reckoned up every unforeknown, unseeing
Plunge, lured by a softening eye,
Or by a touch or a sigh,
Into the labyrinth of another's being;

Does the imagination dwell the most
Upon a woman won or woman lost?
If on the lost, admit you turned aside
From a great labyrinth out of pride,

Cowardice, some silly over-subtle thought
Or anything called conscience once;
And that if memory recur, the sun's
Under eclipse and the day blotted out.

III

It is time that I wrote my will;
I choose upstanding men
That climb the streams until
The fountain leap, and at dawn
Drop their cast at the side
Of dripping stone; I declare
They shall inherit my pride,
The pride of people that were
Bound neither to Cause nor to State,
Neither to slaves that were spat on,
Nor to the tyrants that spat,
The people of Burke and of Grattan
That gave, though free to refuse —
Pride, like that of the mom,
When the headlong light is loose,
Or that of the fabulous horn,
Or that of the sudden shower
When all streams are dry,
Or that of the hour
When the swan must fix his eye
Upon a fading gleam,
Float out upon a long
Last reach of glittering stream
And there sing his last song.
And I declare my faith:
I mock Plotinus thought
And cry in Plato's teeth,
Death and life were not
Till man made up the whole,
Made lock, stock and barrel
Out of his bitter soul,
Aye, sun and moon and star, all,
And further add to that
That, being dead, we rise,

Dream and so create
Translunar Paradise.
I have prepared my peace
With learned Italian things
And the proud stones of Greece,
Poet's imaginings
And memories of love,
Memories of the words of women,
All those things whereof
Man makes a superman
Mirror-resembling dream.

As at the loophole there
The daws chatter and scream,
And drop twigs layer upon layer.
When they have mounted up,
The mother bird will rest
On their hollow top,
And so warm her wild nest.

I leave both faith and pride
To young upstanding men
Climbing the mountain-side,
That under bursting dawn
They may drop a fly;
Being of that metal made
Till it was broken by
This sedentary trade.

Now shall I make my soul,
Compelling it to study
In a learned school
Till the wreck of body,
Stow decay of blood,
Testy delirium
Or dull decrepitude,
Or what worse evil come —
The death of friends, or death
Of every brilliant eye
That made a catch in the breath —

Seem but the clouds of the sky
When the horizon fades,
Or a bird's sleepy cry
Among the deepening shades.

This poem of 195 lines is divided into three sections—the first section containing 16 lines, the second 104 lines, and the third section 75 lines. The first and the third section rhyme a b a b, while the second section rhymes a a b b e d d e. The title of the poem derives from the tower-house of the poet at Thoor Ballylee. Yeats was very fond of the tower and wrote: "I like to think of that building [the Tower] as a permanent symbol of my work plainly visible to the passer-by." (Albright, 63 3). I n the first section, the poet expresses his disgust at his decrepitude that seems to him absurd or irrational, in the sense that there is no reason, almost in the sense of the existentialist philosophy, for his being old and decrepit. He is old with a decrepit body, and so he seems to himself to be a caricature of himself, and this pains him the most: "What shall I do with this absurdity —/O heart, O troubled heart—this caricature." Against his will, this decrepitude has been, as if, tied to him, as a rattling play-thing is sometimes tied to a dog's tail: "Decrepit age that has been tied to me/As to a dog's tail?" But, none the less, his spirit—his passion and imagination — has rather grown stronger. Never before did he desire to do the impossible as he now does. He feels, like Blake, a contradiction between the decaying body and the upsurging spirit, and this he expressed in a letter to the *Boston Pilot* in 1889: "I have been very near the gates of Death, and have returned very weak, and an old man feeble and tottering, but not in spirits and life, not in the real man, the imagination which liveth ever. That I am stronger as this foolish body decays." (Jeffares, 216). The poet says that even in his younger days he was not so strong, spiritually. In his boyhood, he would climb up the Ben Bulben hill, north of Sligo, carrying with him a rod and a fly or a worm, and spend long summer days catching fishes, or sporting with the creatures. While recalling these romantic moments, the poet suddenly turns his back to romanticism and poetry and thinks that he should now rather devote himself entirely to the transcendental I philosophies of Plato and Plotinus: "It seems that I must bid the Muse go pack,/Choose Plato and Plotinus for a friend." Yeats read Plato (7427-348) in the 1890s, being persuaded by Lionel Johnson. He perhaps used the five-volume *Plato* by Thomas Taylor. He also read Plotinus (7203-62), extensively. His interest in Plotinus can be gauzed in a letter from MacKenna to E.R. Debenham, written in October, 1926: "Another little encouragement: Yeats, a friend tells me, came to London, glided into a bookshop and dreamily asked for the new Plotinus, began to read there and then, and read on and on till he'd finished (he has really a colossal brain, you know), and now is preaching Plotinus to all his train of attendant duchesses: he told my friend he intended to give the winter in Dublin to Plotinus." (Jeffares, 217). Both Plato and Plotinus believed in a transcendental world, that was, to them, more real than this one. The poet intends to barter his poetry for the abstract philosophy of Plato, till he is satisfied with his philosophical arguments, or till he becomes skilled in thinking abstractly, or till the hard reality brings him down to earth from his philosophical flight: "Until imagination, ear and eye,/Can be content with argument and deal/ In abstract things; or be derided by / A sort of battered kettle at the heel."

The second section of the poem is divided into thirteen stanzas. In the first stanza, the poet says that he is pacing on the roof of the tower which was once a battlement and now is his house, and that he is surveying the surrounding. He is staring at the fountains of a house nearby and at the tree standing thither. The tree seems to him to be a hand with spread-out fingers that grew out of the earth. The poet thinks that perhaps the tree, whose roots are fixed in the soil, is spreading imagination upwards. This sight, or rather this illusion, recalls in the mind of the poet half-forgotten images and memories. The poet would like to ask the images and memories how do they arise upwards out of the dross of the earth. This question of the poet has a reference to another question of the poet in the first and the second lines of the last stanza of the second section of the poem: "Does the imagination dwell the most/Upon a woman won or woman lost?"

In the second stanza of the second section, the poet says that he sees beyond the ridge or crest of earth the house where the aristocratic lady, Mrs. French, once lived, in the eighteenth century: "every silver candlestick or sconce/Lit up the dark mahogany and the wine." Yeats here relates a story about the lady to draw a pen-picture of her aristocratic culture and bearing. The story runs like this. Once at night-fall, the silver candlesticks and sconces, or lanterns with handles, lighted up the upholstery of the lady's house, made up of dark mahogany. The servant poured wine in a glass for her consumption. Being inebriated by the spirit, the dignified lady somewhat lost her temper, and desired that the ears of an insolent farmer be immediately cut off and brought to her. The ever-obliging servant could intuitively ken the wish of the lady, and forthwith obeyed: he cut off the farmer's ears with a pair of garden-shears and brought the cars in a covered dish to the lady. Yeats wrote about the Mrs. French and other persons of this poem: "The persons mentioned are associated by legend, story and tradition with the neighbourhood of Thoor Ballylee or Ballylee Castle, where the poem was written. Mrs. French lived at Peterswell in the eighteenth century and was related to Sir Jonah Barrington who described the incident of the ears and the trouble that came of it." (Jeffares, 217). In the third stanza the poet relates the story of a peasant girl (Mary Hynes, a famous local beauty) that the poet heard when he was young. The peasant girl was as beautiful as her song was sweet. She lived somewhere upon a rocky place. The farmers would jostle against one another in the fair or market-place when she would sing a song: "Farmers jostled at the fair/So great a glory did the song confer." In the fourth stanza, the poet says that being attracted by her song some men would toast to her "a score of times" and leaving their drinking would go out to see her with their own eyes, in order to compare their imagination about her with her person. After thus comparing the two — their imagination and their perception— they could understand I hat their imagination was less than reality: she was actually like the sun, but they thought in their imagination that she was like the moon: "But they mistook the brightness of the moon/For the prosaic light of day —". So much were they maddened by her song ("Music") that one of them was even drowned "in the great bog of Cloone." In the fifth stanza, the poet says that it is strange to learn that the girl's song was composed by a blind man —the Irish or Gaelic poet Anthony Raftery (1784-1834). But the very next moment, He thinks that there was nothing strange or tragic in the poet's being blind, because Homer, who sung about Helen, the paragon of beauty, was also blind (Helen, here, perhaps, refers to Maud Gonne). The blind Homer sang of Helen who betrayed "all living hearts." This thought immediately refers the Poet to his own life — to the 'betrayal' of Maud Gonne, and he vows that if he survive his decrepitude, if he live longer, he will make men mad with his songs in which imagination will take a body, in which imagination and reality would be inextricably woven: "O may the moon and sunlight seem/One inextricable beam,/For if I triumph I must make men mad." Daniel Albright here adds: "the poet prays for Raftery's sort of poetic power, prehistoric or Druidical in intensity, capable of direct imaginative influence: 'Instead of learning their craft with paper and a pen they [early poets] may have sat for hours imagining themselves to be stocks and stones and beasts of the wood, till the images were so vivid that the passers-by became but a part of the imagination of the dreamer, and wept or laughed or ran away as he would have them." (Albright, 636). A.E. Dyson has found a skein run through the stanzas from the third to the fifth: "The next stanzas (iii-v) start from a peasant (to balance the aristocrat?), along with her victim (if someone unknown to her can be called her victim —a delicate point). We know that the incident concerning Mrs. French was being read aloud to Yeats at about this time by his wife, in a version written by Sir Jonah Barrington, and that the legend of Mary Hynes and 'blind Raftery' (to give them the names not put into this poem) has been recorded by Yeats himself in *Celtic Twilight.* These episodes have therefore the force of historical events, known chiefly through legend—and known of course locally(...). The 'peasant girl' is, however, the stuff of more general legend, and no doubt Yeats relied on the archetype to have its effect. In essence, we have a peasant girl whose real (or fabled) beauty has powers of destruction — a local Helen, or Maud Gonne." (Dyson, 40).

In the sixth stanza, we hear the poet say that it was he who created the romantic character of Hanrahan who appeared in *Stories of Red Hanrahan* (1904). Hanrahan, being made for the beauty of her sweetheart Mary Lavelle, went one morning to the neighbouring village in search of her. The poet thought about this story of Hanrahan "twenty years ago." Actually, *Stories of Red Hanrahan* was written in 1904 and this poem in 1925, and therefore, historically, the poet is quite correct. In this story, Yeats says that once Hanrahan was the owner of the house (the Tower) where the poet is now putting up. The poet says that when Hanrahan passed through the neighbouring village in search of his sweetheart, he was caught by an old wizard or juggler who threw a spell round him, so that Hanrahan "stumbled, tumbled, fumbled to and fro. Then, for years together, he had to toil hard ("broken knees") for hire (wages). Nevertheless Hanrahan had a great desire for life, for his sweetheart: "And had but broken knees for hire/And horrible splendour of desire." The autobiographical element of these two lines can easily be seen if we take Yeats for Hanrahan and Maud Gonne for Hanrahan's sweetheart. In the seventh stanza, the poet continues the story of Hanrahan. He says that in a bawn, or enclosure for cattle, some good fellows were playing at cards, and that Hanrahan was taking part in the playing. When he was about to deal his card, Hanrahan found that the wizard or juggler, with the help of his jugglery, converted all his cards, but one, into a "pack of hounds", and the remaining card into a hare. At this, Hanrahan flew into a rage and pursued the hounds. A. Norman Jeffares writes: "a similar trick is described in Lady Gregory, *God and Fighting Men*, 109 (sic), where several animals and men are created consecutively, who follow each other up into the sky." (Jeffares, 221). In the eighth stanza, the poet pretends to continue the story of Hanrahan, but abruptly stops and then calls up a man in his memory who lived about a hundred years ago —a man who does love "Nor music nor an enemy's clipped ear." This man, who was lowly and a bankrupt, lived in the tower—the house of Yeats — before the poet occupied it. Daniel Albright here adds a very illuminating note on the unnamed "man": "a former owner of Thoor Ballylee during the early nineteenth century—Yeats's note to the poem adds, 'According to one legend he could only leave the Castle upon a Sunday because of his creditors, and according to another he hid in the secret passage' (...). The four anecdotes of 'The Tower' II progress from Mrs. French, whose whims were so easily gratified that she needed no imagination or art, to this bankrupt tower-dweller, whose needs were so extreme that no imagination or art could suffice to satisfy them. Artists like Raftery and Hanrahan built great edifices of dreams because poverty compelled them; but there exists a level of poverty where dreams themselves fail." (Albright, 637).

But even before these occupants of the tower, Yeats says in the ninth stanza, armed soldiers, or mercenaries, lived in the house (tower). The tower house then was not in ruins. The armed men, or men-at-arms were cross- gartered and clad in coat of arms: "Rough men-at-arms, cross-gartered to the knees/Or shod in iron, climbed the narrow stairs." Some of them, whose memory will never be erased — because these people are but archetypal images — would come to the house, howling loudly and panting highly. Their noise over the chess-board would awaken a sleeping man: "And certain men-at-arms there were/Whose images, in the Great Memory stored,/Come with loud cry and panting breast/To break upon a sleeper's rest/While their great wooden dice beat on the board." Actually, the "men-at-arms" are the ghosts that Yeats had seen. Yeats himself wrote: "The ghosts have been seen at their game of dice in what is now my bedroom." (Albright, 037). Daniel Albright comments on this stanza: "The tower, like all symbols, is somewhat animate; and in this stanza the tower's own soul or *genius loci* seems to embody itself in these fierce, coarse revenants of soldiers once quartered there. Yeats's imagination, as it works up its rage against old age, is best satisfied by such ugly, turbulent images as these." (Albright, 637). And the "Great Memory" of this stanza is the storehouse of archetypal images, and therefore it is the *Amina Mundi.*

In the tenth and the eleventh stanza, the poet calls the roll of those characters described before: the necessitous or bankrupt old man, the spell-bound Red Hanrahan, Mrs. French, and the man who followed a "country wench" being attracted by her exquisite beauty and "drowned in bog's mire." The poet recalls all these because he will now ask a question to them—the question the poet told of earlier. The poet's question is simple enough: Were these people outrageous against, and indignant at, their old age, as he now is against his own old age? The poet says that their answer is not necessary, for he has known the answer to the question in their eyes:

"But I have found an answer in those eyes." He therefore likes to forget all of them, but Hanrahan, for the moment: "Go therefore; but leave Hanrahan/For I need all his mighty memories." Daniel Albright comments on this stanza: "Go *therefore; but leave Hanrahan*: of the conviction of phantoms summoned to provide wisdom about old age, all but Hanrahan can be dismissed. The cultural unanimity that guided Mrs. French is impossible in the troubled modern age; the magical art of Raftery is difficult except among pre-literate peoples. But Yeats was neither a squirearch nor an antique bard, and so he had to look to some intimate, harassed, and diminished model. In part I Yeats asked whether he must 'Choose Plato and Plotinus for a friend' (I 12); but instead he chose Hanrahan, the body's squalor and not the mind's abstraction. It is typical of Yeats (as in the case of Michael Robertes) to choose his mentors from the cast of his own creations." (Albright, 638).

In the twelfth stanza, the poet calls Hanrahan a lecher. (But actually the lecher is Yeats himself, as will be clear in the next stanza.) He says that Hanrahan was very romantic in his avocation of love, and that his images bring into memory all the deeply buried passions that are no more existent, because Hanrahan (like Yeats) once had been "lured by a softening eye,/ Or by a touch or a sigh", whereby he lost his being into the being of his beloved. And in the thirteenth or the last stanza, the poet asks the central question even more clearly: "Does the imagination dwell the most/Upon a woman won or woman lost?" The implied answer of the poet to his own question is that imagination pursues a lost woman the most. Clearly, Yeats here is referring to Maud Gonne whom he has lost, but, nevertheless, it is she on whom his imagination dwell the most. He recalls that he was turned out by Maud Gonne because of her pride, or cowardice, or "some silly over- subtle thought", or because of her so-called conscience. But when memory comes to him, it seems to him that the sun is eclipsed and the day is blotted out, that is, the poet feels that he is blind, but he knows that "imagination both begins in blindness [like in Homer, for example] and ends in it." (Albright, 639).

The last section of the poem is divided into four stanzas. In the first stanza, the poet says that he will leave behind his testament that he will choose "upstanding men"—those young men that can climb a mountain and jump from its top. He will leave behind him his pride for them who are "Bound neither to Cause nor to State,/Neither to slaves that were spat on,/Nor to the tyrants that spat"—people that are like the two great Irish men: Burke and Grattan. Edmund Burke (1729-97) was a great orator and a politician, and Henry Grattan was a great Protestant leader who supported Catholic emancipation. But it is not the ordinary pride that the poet will leave behind, but a pride that looks like the morning glow; or he will leave behind the pride of plenitude, or the pride that is like the song of a swan floating on the stream. A.E. Dyson writes: "The main gift, then, is pride—which is associated equally with his country (may be the roll-call of Irish patriots from earlier days determined this metre), and with natural beauty [symbolised by the swan]." (Dyson, 46). But the very next moment the poet shifts from pride to faith, and says that he will leave behind him his faith as a testamentary gift for the younger generation. The poet says that he hates Plato's and Plotinus's abstract philosophy: "I mock Plotinus's thought/And cry in Plato's teeth." He says that the concrete world (and not the abstract world of Plato and Plotinus) was made by man out of his bitter soul (reference to Maud Gonne) and so this concrete world cannot be neglected. But, says the poet, we can "create/Translunar Paradise" after our sufferings and death in this concrete world: "That being dead, we arise,/ Dream and so create/Translunar Paradise." And the next moment he says that he has also found peace in arts and imaginations (of the Italian masters of yore, i.e., in the ancient art and architecture of Greece and Italy)—peace that is the essence of paradise: "I have prepared my peace/With learned Italian things/And the proud stones of Greece." The poet says that man can make the superhuman being out of our dreams or out of the imagination of the poet, or out of the memories of love: "Poet's imaginings/And memories of love,/Memories of the words of women,/ All those things whereof/Man makes a superhuman/Mirror-resembling dream."

In the second and the third stanzas, the poet says that as he is old and is suffering, he will leave behind a testament. In the second stanza, he paints an image of decrepitude: daws are chattering and screaming on the hollow top of the tower that has loopholes here and there. All these symbolises his old age and senility. So he says, in the third stanza, that he is leaving for the young generation of "upstanding men" two testamentary gifts: pride and faith: "I leave both faith and pride/To young upstanding men." He remembers that once he was also as strong as these young men, but now his strength is no more with him for his old age and consequent decrepitude. Now he can only sit and sit and while away the time: "Being of that metal made/Till it was broken by/This sedentary trade."

In the final stanza, the poet prepares his soul for the last journey. He says that he will henceforth study art and philosophy in "a learned school" in spite of "the wreck of body", "Slow decay of blood", the "death of friends", or death of "every brilliant eye" (like those of Maud Gonne). He will then leave his 'mortal coil' and "Seem but the clouds of the sky"; and then darkness will be descending on the earth and the birds, feeling sleepy after day's toil, will be fading into the forest with a faint cry. It is tempting to add here an excerpt from Dyson about this poem: "It is extraordinarily moving to look at John Stallworthy's reproduction of, and commentary upon, this poem written on his [Yeats's] death bed. The infinite labour and revision of composition [of this poem] are still to be seen, in eleven loose-leaf sheets of manuscript, worked upon by a dying man, and in the single corrected typescript bearing that date [21st January, 1939]. On 28th January, 1939, seven days later, the poet died." (Dyson, 47).

32. Nineteen Hundred and Nineteen

This poem was written in 1919, when the First World War just concluded, and was first published in *The Dial* in September, 1921, with the present title. But when, after two months, it was published in *London Mercury*, in November, 1921, it bore the title Thoughts upon the Present State of the World'. But, Daniel Albright does not agree with Jeffares regarding this dating and says that the "poem was first published as Thoughts upon the Present State of the World' (and dated 'May, 1921')." (Albright, 651). However, A. Norman Jeffares writes about the occasion of the poem: "The poem arose out of 'some horrors of Gort', Co. Galway during the period when fighting between the Irish Republican Army (the IRA) and the English army and Royal Irish Constabulary (the RIC) increased." (Jeffares, 229). At that time the members of the Auxiliaries and the Blacks and the Tans—the mercenary soldiers of the British—committed much atrocities in Ireland. It is one of the most beautiful and powerful poems of Yeats. Harold Bloom writes: 'This is one of Yeats's masterpieces, and in some ways a triumphant return to *The Wind Among the Reeds*, twenty years after." (Bloom, 356). This poem can be compared with the poems in *Meditations in Time of Civil War*. According to Bloom, whereas the poems in *Meditations are* full of Yeats's personal prejudices, his theories of history and obscure vision, 'Nineteen Hundred and Nineteen' is remarkably free from all these, though it expresses his most bitter emotion.

Daniel Albright has discovered that the first four poems of *The Tower* deal with the relation between life and art, and show that the relation can be of four-fold nature: "Each of the first four poems in this volume offers a definition of the relation between art and life. In 'Sailing to Byzantium', art and life are antithetical, as distant from one another as Byzantium from Ireland. In The Tower', art is seen not as a refuge from life but as an expression of it. In 'Meditations in Time of Civil War', art is still expressive of life's violence and bitterness, but that violence, that bitterness, threaten to overwhelm any attempt at order or stability. In 'Nineteen Hundred and

Nineteen', art fails—it can offer neither refuge nor insight nor adornment. It should be noted that this remarkable sequence of four poems at the beginning of *The Tower* was written in reverse order: 'Sailing to Byzantium', with its fervour, its numbness, its slightly eccentric composure, was the last written; yet its placement, in the book makes the reader feel that all its mosaic saints and golden birds are being sucked into the whirlpool of 'Nineteen Hundred and Nineteen.' In this poem of iconoclasm, art is shattered, and the artist mocked. There is a kind of appetite for chaos — 'A bunch of martyrs (1916) were the bomb and we are living in the explosion.' (Albright, 651).

The poem is divided into six parts, which, apparently, may seem to be disjointed, but a thread of unity runs through them all. In the first section, the poet is embittered at the atrocities committed upon the Irish by the British soldiers; and in the second section, he generalises the experience of Ireland over the whole history of civilisation. Human beings, he says, create machines for their own destruction. In the third section, Yeats says that the human soul has the power to rise above the worldly afflictions. The fourth section is the briefest of all, where Yeats shows how fast human conviction changes. Only seven years ago, the Irish people talked "of honour and of truth", and now they find pleasure in internecine war. Again, in the fifth section, he speaks of the changing world, as he spoke before about the changing mind. He says that nothing that wise men thought to be permanent and imperishable are now in existence. And in the last section, he repeats his indignation at the violence all around.

NINETEEN HUNDRED AND NINETEEN

I

Many ingenious lovely things are gone
That seemed sheer miracle to the multitude,
Protected from the circle of the moon
That pitches common things about. There stood
Amid the ornamental bronze and stone
An ancient image made of olive wood—
And gone are Phidias' famous ivories
And all the golden grasshoppers and bees.

We too had many pretty toys when young:
A law indifferent to blame or praise,

To bribe or threat; habits that made old wrong
Melt down, as it were wax in the sun's rays;
Public opinion ripening for so long
We thought it would outlive all future days.
O what fine thought we had because we thought
That the worst rogues and rascals had died out.

All teeth were drawn, all ancient tricks unlearned,
And a great army but a showy thing,
What matter that no cannon had been turned
Into a ploughshare? Parliament and king
Thought that unless a little powder burned
The trumpeters might burst with trumping
And yet it lack all glory ; and perchance
The guardsmen's drowsy chargers would not prance.

Now days are dragon-ridden, the nightmare
Rides upon sleep: a drunken soldiery
Can leave the mother, murdered at her door,
To crawl in her won blood, and go scot-free;
The night can sweat with terror as before
We pierced our thoughts into philosophy,
And planned to bring the world under a rule,
Who are but weasels fighting in a hole.

He who can read the signs nor sink unmanned
Into the half-deceit of some intoxicant
From shallow wits, who knows no work can stand,
Whether health, wealth or peace of mind were spent
On master-work of intellect or hand,
No honour leaves its mighty monument,
Has but one comfort left: all triumph would
But break upon his ghostly solitude.

But is there any comfort to be found?
Man is in love and loves what vanishes,
What more is there to say? That country round
None dared admit, if such a thought were his,
Incendiary or bigot could be found
To burn that stump on the Acropolis,

Or break in bits the famous ivories
Or traffic in the grasshoppers or bees.

II

When Loie Fuller's Chinese dancers enwound
A shining web, a floating ribbon of cloth,
It seemed that a dragon of air
Had fallen among dancers, had whirled them round
Or hurried them off on its own furious path;
So the Platonic year
Whirls out new right and wrong,
Whirls in the old instead;
All men are dancers and their tread
Goes to the barbarous clangour of a gong.

III

Some moralist or mythological poet
Compares the solitary soul to a swan;
I am satisfied with that,
Satisfied if a troubled mirror show it,
Before that brief gleam of its life be gone,
An image of its state;
The wings half spread for flight,
The breast thrust out in pride
Whether to play, or to ride
Those winds that clamour of approaching night.

A man in his own secret meditation
Is lost amid the labyrinth that he has made
In art or politics;
Some Platonist affirms that in the station
Where we should cast off body and trade
The ancient habits sticks,
And that if our works could
But vanish with our breath
That were a lucky death,
For triumph can but mar our solitude.

The swan has leaped into the desolate heaven:
That image can bring wilderness, bring a rage

To end all things, to end
What my laborious life imagined even
The half-imagined, the half-written page;
O but we dreamed to mend
Whatever mischief seemed
To afflict mankind, but now
That winds of winter blow
Learn that we were crack-pated when we dreamed.

IV

We, who seven years ago
Talked of honour and of truth,
Shriek with pleasure if we show
The weasel's twist, the weasel's tooth.

V

Come let us mock at the great
That had such burdens on the mind
And toiled so hard and late
To leave some monument behind,
Nor thought of the levelling wind.

Come let us mock at the wise;
With all those calendars whereon
They fixed old aching eyes,
They never saw how seasons run,
And how but gape at the sun,

Come let us mock at the good
That fancied goodness might be gay,
And sick of solitude
Might proclaim a holiday;
Wind shrieked — and where are they?

Mock mockers after that
That would not lift a hand may be
To help good, wise or great
To bar that foul storm out, for we
Traffic in mockery.

VI

Violence upon the roads: violence of horses;
Some few have handsome riders, are garlanded
On delicate sensitive ear or tossing mane,
But wearied running round and round in their courses
All break and vanish, and evil gathers head:
Herodias' daughters have returned again,
A sudden blast of dusty wind and after
Thunder of feet, tumult of images,
Their purpose in the labyrinth of the wind;
And should some crazy hand dare touch a daughter
All turn with amorous cries, or angry cries.
According to the wind, for all are blind.
But now wind drops, dust settles; thereupon
There lurches past, his great eyes without thought
Under the shadow of stupid straw-pale locks,
That insolent fiend Robert Artisson
To whom the love-lorn Lady Kyteler brought
Bronzed peacock feathers, red combs of her cocks.

The first section of the poem consists of six stanzas. In the first stanza, the poet is very much disturbed by the atrocities and hooliganism of 1919 in Ireland, created by the Blacks and Tans — the mercenary soldiers of England — and by the consequent lawlessness. He says that due to the lawlessness, many of the artistic things, that people thought to be simply miraculous and imperishable, have been destroyed. Those things were believed to be permanent and protected from the ravages of time: "Protected from the circle of the moon." The symbolism of the "seems closer to the medieval symbolism of 'sublunary' — the sphere of change, as opposed to the immortal world beyond." (Dyson, 60). The poet says that there were "ornamental bronze and stone" suggesting the glorious Greek art of yore, and an "ancient image made of olive wood", and even all these things have been destroyed. Daniel Albright writes about the line 'An ancient image made of olive wood—' that it refers to 'an image of Athena carved of olive wood (was) kept in the Erechtheum, on the Acropolis of Athens. The olive tree was sacred in Athens, when Poseidon and Athena competed for the patronage of Attica, Poseidon created a salt spring on the Acropolis, while Athena caused an olive tree to grow." (Albright, 652). Not only the olive wood image, but even "Phidias' famous ivories" and the "golden grasshoppers and bees" have been mutilated by the mercenary and barbarous hordes of England. Jeffares writes about Phidias that he was "the famous Athenian sculptor (c. 490-417 B.C.); primarily a bronze worker, he also acquired his fame from chryselephantine statues, of gold and ivory, of which his Athena Parthenos survives in copies, though his Zeus of Olympia is only a memory. Pericles commissioned him to design the marble sculptures of the Parthenon and he made the models for the sculptors who worked under him." (Jeffares, 230). The symbols of grasshoppers and bees refer to the golden broaches in the shapes of grasshoppers and bees, worn by the ancient women of Greece, to hold up their hair. The poet says that all these mementoes of Greek art and culture have been mutilated by the Blacks and the Tans, or the army of England: "Many ingenious lovely things are gone."

In the second stanza of the first section, the poet innuendoes to his theory of history, detailed in *A Vision*. He says that historical events are moving in a cyclic order, in a gyre, in which nothing remains permanent. He says that once Ireland had her own immutable laws that were impartial, and that would be dispensed without fear or favour: laws that were "indifferent to blame or praise,/To bribe or threat." With such laws by them, the people of Ireland once thought that they had become civilised, and that their ancient barbarous habits and customs were now driven into the limbo, as if those ancient barbarous laws melted down like wax, under the white heat of the sun of the new legal system: "habits that made old wrong/Melt down, as if it were wax in the sun's rays." People thought that the new civilisation, created by the new laws ("Public opinion"), was eternal and immutable: "We thought it would outlive all future days." They thought that as they were now a civilised people, there would be no more barbarous men amongst them. All the people, including the poet in his young days, thought that barbarous people were all dead then: "That the worst rogues and rascals had died out." But after the utter lawlessness unleashed in Ireland in 1919, to the poet's great amazement, all the new laws, new habits, and new thoughts, that went into making the new civilisation, now seem to be no better than little boys' brittle toys: "We too had many pretty toys when young."

In the third and the fourth stanzas, the poet is elaborating his contention put forward in the first and the second stanzas: he is describing the barbarity in Ireland in details. In the third stanza, he says that the people thought the old barbarism and cozenages were forgotten: "All teeth were drawn, all ancient tricks unlearned." The people thought that now the army was not for destruction but for decoration, for the decoration of the state. Therefore they desired that the cannons be changed into ploughshares. Yeats here alludes to the Biblical prophecy in Isaiah ii, 4: "And they shall beat their swords into ploughshares and their spears into pruning hooks: nation shall not lift up sword against nation, neither shall they learn war anymore." (Jeffares, 230-31). People thought that there would never be any war in the future. Actually, Yeats himself also believed in this and in a speech on 2nd August, 1924, he said: "'There will never be war', that was our opium dream." (Jeffares, 231). But all these are not to happen now. Both the parliament and the King want that the war should continue. But the poet says that this war is not a glorious thing for the nation: "And yet it lacks all glory." In the fourth stanza, the poet says that the continuance of the barbarism is nightmarish and dragon-inspired, the people are passing nights sleeplessly, and now a soldier, being inebriated, can murder a mother and leave her at her doorstep, without any threat of being punished: "a drunken soldier/Can leave the mother, murdered at her door,/To crawl in her own blood, and go scot-free." In this horrible condition, people are sweating in terror at night. It is to be noted that the poet here is not concerned only with the condition prevailing in Ireland, but with the condition prevailing throughout the whole of Europe. He says that we have killed our rationality for a radical philosophy that wants the world to be brought under one single rule (the poet here may refer to communism then raging in Russia) and pooh-poohs at the idea. He says what we are doing now can be compared with the fighting of some weasels in a hole. The people of Ireland are blind like the fighting weasels, and are as narrow-minded as they, because like the weasels in a hole, they are fighting amongst themselves — they are fighting an internecine war.

In the fifth stanza, the poet says that there are people with "shallow wits", people who cannot "read the signs", and they think that "health, wealth or peace of mind" are everlasting. But there are also people "who can read the signs", who are not deceived or intoxicated, and they think and knows that "no work can stand" — not even great works of art of unforgettable masters can stand the test of time. Such wise men know that nothing, not even honour, is imperishable: "No honour leave its mighty monument." But in spite of the perishability of things, they have at least one comfort and that is that they can get peace in their "ghostly solitude", i.e., in the inner regards of their hearts or souls where the tumult of the earth cannot reach: "Has but one comfort left: all triumph would/But break upon his ghostly solitude." But in the very next stanza (in the sixth or the last stanza), the poet questions even this possibility of peace or comfort: "But is there any comfort to be found?" In answering his own question, he philosophises on the prevailing age of destruction. He says that it is the eternal law that things and events will whirl or move in the appointed gyre: destruction will follow creation and creation destruction. And so, "is there any comfort to be found?" He says that men must love loveable things, but even the loveable things are perishable. He goes even further and says that men love only those things that are perishable: "Man is in love and loves what vanishes." This may have a reference to Yeats's love of Maud Gonne — Gonne who also vanished from him. And so he answers his question in the negative: there can be no comfort when man loves only those things that vanish (like Maud Gonne). At the end of the first section, the poet once again comes to the case of Ireland and says that once Ireland ("That country round") was invincible to incendiary armies and hordes of bigots. Then no one dared to "burn that stump on the Acropolis,/Or break in bits the famous ivories", or none could dare to be indecent to the women: "traffic in the grasshoppers or bees."

In the second section, Yeats dwells on the philosophy of history that presents before us the ontology of change. He remembers the dance performance of the famous American dancer Loie Ful ler (1862-1928) who "used sticks to whirl glittering lengths of cloth" and whose "dancing represented a 'kind of spatial equivalent of music'" (Albright, 653). When her dancing troupe would unfurl and whirl a "shining web, a floating ribbon of cloth", then it would seem to be "a dragon of air." In the same way, says the poet, the things and events of the world are being whirled round and round (as if in a gyre). The things and events of the world are being whirled by the "Plantonic Year" Daniel Albright says that the "Platonic Year" is "the most inclusive of all cycles, the period during which the constellations make a full circuit of the zodiac — Yeats quoted Taylor's speculation that it lasted 36,000 years." (Albright, 653). In *A Vision,* Yeats wrote that there are seventeen theories about the duration of the Platonic Year, one such theory being that its duration is our 36,000 years, each year consisting of 360 days. However, Yeats says that this long cycle of time moves everything, of necessity, and thus ultimately leads everything to the spiritual destination (suggested by the "gong" which appears in 'Byzantium' also with the same meaning). The poet says that men are but marionette-dancers, their strings being in the hand of the changing time — time that pushes everything, through gyres, to spirituality: "All men are dancers and their tread/Goes to the barbarous clangour of a gong." In the second section, the poet means to say that the Irish people are now frenziedly dancing to the measure of the barbarous time of the Platonic Year. He knows that at the end of each Platonic Year, there will be an announcement of the ushering in of a new year: "Barbarous clangour of a gong." In the present chaos of Ireland, the poet is hearing that "barbarous clangour of a gong" announcing the coming into being of a new era.

The third section of the poem is divided into three stanzas. Of all the six sections of the poem this is the most difficult. In the first stanza of this section, Yeats says that some 'moralist' or 'mythological poet' believe that the soul is like a swan, and the poet agrees with them. By 'moralist' the poet may mean some philosophers and by 'mythological poet' he may mean P.B. Shelley who also compared the soul with a swan, for, in his *Prometheus Unbound* (II, V, 72-77), Shelley sings *(Asia sings):*

> My soul is an enchanted boat,
> Which like a sleeping swan, doth float?
> Upon the silver waves of thy sweet singing;
> And thine doth like an angel sit
> Beside the helm conducting it,
> Whilst all the winds with melody are ringing.

Daniel Albright adds: "In Browning's Shelleyan poem *Pauline* (1833), II, 102-11, the poet compares his soul, choking in solitude, to a swan trapped in a dark cave. Yeats associated swans with absence in 'The Wild Swans at Coole'; and in the present poem too he uses the swan as an emblem of departure, absence, willed vanishing. In 'Coole and Ballylee, 1931', I.19, Yeats would extend the metaphor of soul as swan." (Albright, 654). Yeats, in this stanza, says that he would be happy to imagine the soul as a swan, if the soul could fly from this trouble-torn world up into the heaven, before his natural death: "I am satisfied with that,/Satisfied if a troubled mirror shows it,/Before that brief gleam of its life be gone." Daniel Albright writes about the metaphor 'troubled mirror' that it is "the swan, studying its image on the rippling surface of historical change, is another of the many jejune or poorly constituted images in this poem. In 1937 Yeats wrote to Dorothy Wellesley: "I begin to see things double—double in history, world history, personal history... Perhaps there is a theme for poetry in this "double swan and shadow"."" (Albright, 654). Yeats says he would really be happy if the swan (the soul) could beat its wings in upward flight and rise high up, with pride, and leave behind the "clamour of approaching night."

But in the second stanza, the poet doubts the teachings of the moralist and the mythological poet (Shelley), because he thinks that man's soul is enmeshed in the labyrinth of man's own creations "In arts and politics." His contention is supported by the theory of some Plalonist who believes that the soul of man takes with it its former experiences and attachments of this world. Jeffares writes about the Plalonist that he is "possibly Thomas

Taylor, *De Antro Nympharum,* where after the dead pass the Styx they are ignorant of their former lives on earth, but recognise material forms 'and recollect their pristine condition on earth.'" (Jeffares, 233). Here the philosophy of *De Antro Nympharum* may be compared with the concept the *sukshma sharira* (the light and invisible elements of the human beings) of the Indian philosophies, that sometimes accompany the soul after the death of the body. Yeats also believes in such ideas: "Some Platonist affirm that in the station/Where we should cast off body and trade/The ancient habit sticks." The poet says that if, on the other hand, even the "ancient habit" and the memories of our achievements would not accompany our souls but would be destroyed with the death of our bodies, that would be the best. Because, then our souls would remain lonely in silence and would not be disturbed by the memories of our previous lives: "And that if our works could/But vanish with our breath/That were a lucky death,/ For triumph can but mar our solitude."

In the third stanza of the third section, the poet says that whatever man has dreamed of and whatever man has created has now vanished, after the brutal and wholesale destruction by the barbarous army of England: law, morality, art, culture — everything. Therefore, the soul (the swan) "has leaped into the desolate heaven." Plotinus taught that if one wishes to forget the grim reality and find the peace of mind, then one has to destroy all his creations. The Blacks and the Tans have now destroyed the creations of mankind (to be precise, of Ireland). Therefore, humankind can now perhaps enjoy absolute peace in the inner regard of their hearts. The poet here finds some sort of happiness of the ascetics in the wilderness and ruin of the world. He now welcomes destruction so much so that he even wants to destroy his own creations: "To end all things, to and/What my laborious life imagined, even/The half-imagined, the half-written page." Daniel Albright writes that "the poet is sick of his own vision — his imagination can terminate in no fixed or satisfying image. The poet seems ready to destroy the text of this very poem." (Albright, 654). A.E. Dyson's comment on the third section of the poem may help understand this section better: "The poem's third, and pivotal, section strikes me as beautiful but elusive, even though its concluding quatrain brings it back sharply enough to present disgust. The image of the swan recurs, symbolic less of art's beauty (it now seems) than of those who have falsely trusted to such symbolism in a darkening season. The words 'I am satisfied with that' are both brooding and tentative: the reading voice can, and I think should, linger, as if on a final statement, then allow 'Satisfied if to pick up the thoughts still to come. Swan and poet are closely identified, but through a curious paradox. The 'troubled mirror' is no doubt the poet' s art reflecting back truths to the poet. The promise contained in 'An image of its state' now includes transience ('Before that brief gleam of its life be gone') but with little irony. In 'The Tower', the poet's 'pride' was one of his two legacies 'two young upstanding men'. Here, may be, the swan's 'pride' is very similar, *except* that the threat of death now extends beyond personal destiny and rage gives way to stoic celebration (as in the 'swan' passage in 'The Tower' itself):

> The wings half spread for flight,
> The breast thrust out in pride
> Whether to play, or to ride
> Those winds that clamour of approaching night."
>
> (A.E. Dyson, 64).

The fourth section of the poem consists of only four lines, where the poet compares the state of affairs of the world (at least that of Ireland) before the present lawlessness or wilderness, with the state of affairs of the world after the War ensued. He says that only seven years ago, people talked of the pride of and felt proud of their honour and of their pursuit of truth. But now they find pleasure rather in their spree of destruction: "Shriek with pleasure if we show/The weasel's twist, the weasel's tooth." Daniel Albright says that "Here the poet, staring at his own image in the 'troubled mirror' (III4) of society, sees not a swan but a puny, vicious animal." (Albright, 655). Again, A.E. Dyson says that the fourth section or Part IV "is an entrance designed, I take it, to confirm the return to the main theme and to prepare us for the poem's closing movements." (Dyson, 66).

The fifth section is divided into four stanzas, each stanza consisting of five lines. In the first stanza, the poet urges us to mock at the great men of art, philosophy and culture, who guilefully thought that their great works were immutable and permanent: "Come let us mock at the great." These people did not know that the wind of lawlessness and destruction can level anything great or small. At the beginning of the second stanza, the poet now urges us to mock at the wise men, as in the previous stanza, he urged us to mock at the great men. Yeats says that these wise men, astonishingly, did not know that things change with the changes of time. He says that now these wise men, in their moment of truth, are seeing what they did never think to see—those things change with changes of time—and so they are looking helplessly at the heaven with their mouths azar: "They never saw how seasons run,/And now but gape at the sun." In the third stanza, the poet urges us to mock at the good people: "Come let us mock at the good." Yeats says that once the good people thought that goodness would never go away from the land, and that they would remain good and gay. But at the turn of the season, their dreams have all vanished: "Wind shrieked—and where are they?" The bitterness of the poet reaches its climax in the last stanza. Here the poet urges us to mock even at the mockers themselves — mockers who mock at the great, the wise and the good; mockers who do not lend a helping hand to restore that that has been lost; or the mockers who do not come out to oppose the wave of destruction, but only mock at the topsy-turvy, when there remains nothing else to mock at. Daniel Albright here adds that "the poem's fury recoils on the poet himself — the desire for annihilation easily turns into a desire for self-annihilation." (Albright, 655).

The sixth or the final section of the poem is a continuous passage that summarises the whole poem. The poet says that at present violence is everywhere: "Violence upon the roads: violence of horses." Yeats explained the phrase "violence of horses" thus: "The country people see at times certain apparitions whom they name now "fallen angels", now "ancient inhabitants of the country", and describe as riding at whiles "with flowers upon the heads of the horses." I have assumed in the sixth poem [the sixth section of the poem] that these horsemen, now that the times worsen, give , way to worse... Are not those who travel in the whirling dust in the Platonic Year (...)?" (Albright, 655). Some people have welcomed the violence with garlands and so violence was mounted on violence. The "cyclical course of the horsemen is reminiscent of the historical gyre." (Albright, 655). Witnessing all these the poet thinks that perhaps Herodias's daughters have become furious. In the mythology of the Middle Ages, Herodias is the wife of Herod with whom she entered into an incestuous wedlock. Herodias' daughters represent sexual perversion. In the Middle Ages, people thought that wind blew due to the dance of the daughters of Herodias. Therefore, the dance of the daughters of Herodias symbolises both sexual perversion and lawlessness. The poet says that the wind, due to the dancing of the daughters of Herodias, has thrown up a cloud of dust, and with the wind, hordes of devastators are marching. He says that should anyone dare to oppose the dance of the daughters, they shriek in amorousness and anger, and that this is so because the people have become blind:[1] 'And should some crazy hand dare touch a daughter/All turn with amorous cries, or angry cries./According to the wind, for all are blind." However, says the poet, the storm has now stopped and the dust has settled. And then the "insolent fiend", Robert Artisson, marches past with his hordes. Yeats wrote about Robert Artisson: "My last symbol, Robert Artisson, was an evil spirit much run after in Kilkenny at the start of the fourteenth century." (Jeffares, 235). "According to Holinshed's *The Historie of Ireland* (1577) the sacrifice to the evil spirit is said to have consisted of nine red cocks, and nine peacocks' eyes." (Jeffares, 236). To assuage the evil spirit Robert Artisson, Lady Kyteler brought, "Bronzed peacock feathers, red combs of her cocks." Daniel Albright writes: "Dame Alice Kyteler, a fourteenth-century witch said to have poisoned three husbands and to have summoned an incubus, Robin son of Art, who came to her in the shape of a Negro, a cat, and a hairy black dog (...). Yeats seems to suggest that historical depravity and chaos are explicitly willed by mankind in order to gratify an appetite for the loathsome. W.H. Auden would later speak of the imagination's "'promiscuous fornication with her own images'(...)—a good description ...) of what is happening in this poem." However, the poet here means to say that as evil has taken control of the whole world, people have somehow accepted it with all sorts of rituals, and without any urge to oppose it.

33. A Prayer for my Son

This is a rather simple poem, and it is a sort of invocation to some unknown god, or, may be to the absolute God. It was written in December, 1921, and was first published in *Seven Poems and a Fragment* (1922). The occasion of the poem was a premonition that Yeats received through the 'medium' of his wife in a stance. The premonition was that the poet's son, Michael Butler Yeats, who was born on 22nd August, 1921, would soon fall ill. Being very superstitious, Yeats believed in the evil omen that somehow soon proved true. To protect his child from the evil, the poet, in this poem, invokes the unknown god for protecting the child. Yeats wrote at some length about such parapsychological phenomena in *A Vision.* At some place in it he wrote, "Sometimes if 1 had been ill some astringent smell like that of resinous wood filled the room, and sometimes, though rare, a bad smell. These were often warnings: a smell of a cat's excrement announced some being that had to be expelled, the smell of an extinguished candle that the communicators were 'starved'. A little after my son's birth I came home to confront my wife with the statement 'Michael is ill'. A smell of burnt feathers had announced what she and the doctor had hidden. When regular communication was near its end and my work of study and arrangement begun, I was told that henceforth the Frustators would attack my health and that of my children, and one afternoon, knowing from the smell of burnt feathers that one of my children would be ill within three hours, I felt before

I could recover self-control the medieval helpless harrow at witchcraft." (Jeffares, 237-38). Yeats further wrote in the same book; "Sometimes my wife saw apparitions: before the birth of our son a great black bird, persons in clothes of the late sixteenth century and of the late seventeenth. There were still stranger phenomena that I prefer to remain silent about for the present because they seemed so incredible that they need a long story and much discussion." (Jeffares, 238).

A PRAYER FOR MY SON

Bid a strong ghost stand at the head
That my Michael may sleep sound,
Nor cry, nor turn in the bed
Till his morning meal come round;
And may departing twilight keep
All dread afar till morning's back,
That his mother may not lack
Her fill of sleep.

Bid the ghost have sword in fist:
Some there are, for I avow
Such devilish things exist,
Who have planned his murder, for they know
Of some most haughty deed or thought
That waits upon his future days,
And would through hatred of the bays
Bring that to naught.

Though You can fashion everything
From nothing every day, and teach
The morning stars to sing,
You have lacked articulate speech
To tell Your simplest want, and known,
Wailing upon a woman's knee,
All of that worst ignominy
Of flesh and bone;

And when through all the town there ran
The servants of Your enemy,
A woman and a man,
Unless the Holy Writings lie,

Hurried through the smooth and rough
And through the fertile and waste,
Protecting, till the danger past,
With human love.

The poem is divided into four stanzas, each stanza consisting of eight lines rhyming a b a b c d d c. In the first stanza, the poet prays to some unknown god or spirit to send some ghost who will stand guard beside the head of his sleeping child, Michael, so that he can sleep well. If the child is thus protected, it will neither cry nor toss in the bed till next morning, or till its morning meal is served: "Bid a strong ghost stand at the head/That my Michael may sleep sound,/Nor cry, nor turn in the bed/Till his morning meal come round." The poet also prays so that the mother of the child (Hyde-Lees) may sleep well till next morning, while the twilight of the evening may drive away all dreadful things away from her: "And departing twilight keep/All dread afar till morning's back." In the second stanza, Yeats supplicates to the god to bid the ghost to stand guard with a sword in hand, because the poet is afraid that some vicious spirit may have some design to kill his child. He says that if the child grows up into manhood, he will do some great deed with extreme violence, or maybe he will possess some great revolutionary thought in his mind. The poet says that because such a deed or thought will go against the evil spirits, they are planning to kill the child. Yeats believed that there were two categories of spirits — the friendly spirits and the hostile spirits whom he called the Frustrators. He believed that "when spirits narrated the truths of/1 *Vision* through his wife's trances, a hostile class of spirits (called Frustrators) would sometimes confuse the transmission." (Albright, 658).

The third stanza is apocalyptic, because here the poet discloses the real identity of the child. He now says that the child is actually the Supreme Being or God (according to Daniel Albright, Christ himself), in human form—in diminished form. We have seen that Yeats believed in some sort of Upanishadic philosophy: '*Tat tam asi*' or 'that thou art'. Here, therefore, he conceives of his child as the incarnation of the Supreme Being. That is why he says that the child, Michael, can give shape to anything, can make anything from mere nothingness, and can bid the morning stars to sing: "You can fashion everything/From nothing every day, and teach/ The morning stars to sing." But only one thing the child (or the Supreme Being) lacks in, and that is that it cannot speak out its thoughts and it cannot express its wants. Nevertheless, the child knows the evils and sins resident in the human body of flesh and blood. The line "Wailing upon a woman's knee" doubly assures us that the child is but Christ himself — Christ who laid on the knees of Maty. The poet says that as the child is actually Christ, it knows "All of that worst ignominy/Of flesh and bone." In the last stanza, the poet resorts to a Hebrew mythology which tells about the persecution of the Jews at the hands of the Egyptians. The Egyptians determined to kill all the Jewish children in order to extirpate Judaism from the earth. But God, the Almighty, protected the Jewish children from the scourge of the Egyptians by sending a male and a female angels: "A woman and a man." The man and the woman, here, means Joseph and Mary who took the child Jesus to Egypt in order to escape the wrath of Herod. They stayed in Egypt till the death of Herod. Joseph and Mary protected the Jews in Egypt with their "human love." The poet prays to the unknown god, now known as the Child god, to send ghosts or spirits who will protect his child, Michael, from supposed imminent danger, like the angels — Joseph and Mary.

This is very simple and beautiful. It is packed with allusions, mythology and occult philosophy. The theme is simple, but touching, because it deals with parental affection for a child, very picturesquely. The Upanishadic philosophy of one universal spiritual being and the concept of Child God, here in this poem, are very attractive.

34. Leda and the Swan

This is a sonnet, and it is one of the finest poems of Yeats. The poem was written on 18September, 1923, and after doctoring for several times, appeared for the first time in *The Dial*, in June, 1924. It was written at the request of George Russell (A.E.), the editor of *The Dial.* Yeats wrote about the origin of the poem that he wanted to write some political poem, "but as I wrote, bird and lady took such possession of the scene that all politics went out of it." (Jeffares, 247). The character of Leda in (he title of the poem derives from the Greek mythology of Leda, the wife (according to A.N. Jeffares, daughter, vide Jeffares, 247) of Tyndareus or Tyndarus, King of Laconia (according to Jeffares, king of Sparta, *ibid).* Leda was visited by Jupiter or Zeus in the shape of a swan, was impregnated by him and gave birth to Pollux and Helen. She also gave birth to Castor and Clytemnestra, being impregnated by her husband Tyndareus. The draft poem was entitled 'Annunciation[9]. It may be mentioned here that Yeats had a copy of Michelangelo's painting of Leda and the Swan on his writing desk. Perhaps this painting influenced the poet to think about politics in terms of the bird and the woman.

A.E. Dyson writes about the poem: "Though it [the poem] apparently originated in the request for a political poem for the *Irish Statesman*, it mutated by way of a typically Yeatsian reflection that 'the individualist, demagogic movement, founded by Hobbes and popularised by the Encyclopaedists and the French Revolution' had exhausted 'the soil', leaving nothing 'now possible but some movement or birth from above, preceded by some violent annunciation." (Dyson, 86). This poem is a counterpart to the poem 'Two Songs from a Play'. This poem also appears in *A Vision* in the section *Dove or Swan* in which Yeats wrote: "I imagine the annunciation that founded Greece as made to Leda, remembering that they showed in a Spartan temple, strung up to the roof as a holy relic, an unhatched egg of hers: and that from one of her eggs came Love and from the other War." (Jeffares, 248). Daniel Albright writes about the poem: "Fragments showed the exhausted soil of which Yeats's note speaks, the impoverished and impoverishing idea-world of empiricist philosophy and democratic politics; 'Leda and the Swan' offers a vivid metaphor for the terror of the *antithetical* age soon to be born. According *to A Vision,* 2000 BC (the year at which the swan came to Leda to inaugurate the heroic age) and AD 2000 rhyme with each other; and so it is to be expected that this poem bears many similarities to 'The Second Coming'. Indeed there is a sense in which both poems depict beast-rapes of Yeats's imagination by a vehement overwhelming image. The sexual frenzy, the emphatic jagged diction of the sonnet's opening, were unprecedented in Yeats's poetry." (Albright, 664).

LEDA AND THE SWAN

A sudden blow: the great wings beating still
Above the staggering girl, her thighs caressed
By the dark webs, her nape caught in his bill.
He holds her helpless breast upon his breast.
How can those terrified vague fingers push?
The feathered glory from her loosening thighs?
And how can body, laid in that white rush.
But feel the strange heart beating where it lies?

A shudder in the loins engenders there
The broken wall, the burning roof and lower
And Agamemnon dead
Being so caught up,
So mastered by the brute blood of the air,
Did she put on his knowledge with his power
Before the indifferent beak could let her drop ?

Leda, the girl, was standing in a pool of water, when a swan suddenly flew towards her and she was frightened. It was a sort of blow to her: "A sudden blow." The wings of the bird was still beating in the air and the bird was caressing the girl's thighs with its "dark webs" of feet. The bird had caught the back of the girl's nape or neck with its bill. And the bird (swan) was holding the breast of the girl upon its breast. It may be mentioned here that "in the first printing these lines read, 'A rush, a sudden wheel, and hovering still/The bird descends, and her frail thighs, are pressed/ By the webbed toes, and that all-powerful bill/Has laid her helpless face upon his breast." (Albright, 665). Though there is no change in the meaning in the two versions, the final version is certainly an improvement, in diction and style. According to A.E. Dyson, the opening words 'A sudden blow' add dramatic quality to the poem. In the next quatrain, the poet says that Leda was unable to tear her thighs from the clutch of the bird ("feathered glory"), with her weak fingers: "How can those terrified vague fingers push/The feathered glory from her loosening thighs?" As she could not push the bird away—bird with heaps of snow-white feathers ("white rush") —, she lay on the bird and felt the heart-beats of the strange bird: "But feel the strange heart beating where it lies?"

Now she feels a stimulation in the loin — in the genital organs: "A shudder in the loins." Yeats writes: "*Shudder* is [a symbol] of the sexual act, the moment of orgasm, as all husband-men know: but it is also anticipation in fear." (Jeffares, 249). This symbolism brings in the mythology of the Trojan war, in the next one and a half line: "The broken wall, the burning roof and tower/And Agamemnon dead." The cohabitation of Leda and the swan was the union of a human being with a godhead, that produced both birth and war—birth of Helen and Clytemnestra, and the war of Troy — the one, of course, leading to the other. The birth of Helen was the distant or primordial cause of the Trojan war. The great wall of the walled city of Troy was broken in the Trojan war. The roofs of houses and the tower of Troy were burnt down in the same war. And, also, Agamemnon, brother of Meneleus, was killed by Aegisthus, the lover of Agamemnon's wife Clytemnestra, while the great warrior was returning home from the Trojan war. Therefore, one can say that Leda, being impregnated by the divine swan, gave rise to both birth and war: "The broken wall, the burning of roof and tower/ And Agamemnon dead." In the last three and a half lines, the poet says that Leda was caught tightly by the swan or by the "blood of the air." The poet asks: while thus remaining subdued in the iron embrace of the swan, did Leda 'sucked' the knowledge and power of the bird, or, was the human Leda thus infused with divine knowledge and power, before the satiated bird released Leda from its embrace? A.E. Dyson paraphrases the question of the poet, here, thus: "The question remains calculatedly suspended: *is* a mortal half-divinised by the god's descent, however strange and terrifying; or are men pawns in a greater, and perhaps not even well-thought-out game, a mere moment's sport?" (Dyson, 87).

Henn's interpretation of this poem is very interesting: "Two Annunciations form a pattern in history: Leda and the Virgin. The Virgin is linked, mistakenly, to St. Anne, via Pater's Essay. Both events concern the union of godhead and woman. Both produce momentous births. The eggs of Leda give rise to the fall of Troy: from them emerge the legend of two destined women Helen and Clytemnestra. Helen has long been a personal symbol for Maud Gonne. The swans are archetypal, everywhere; in Spenser, emblems, paintings, Celtic myth, and concretely on the Lakes at Coole. The swan stands for power, phallic strength, purity, spirit and spirits (as all white birds), fidelity: fire and air(as the dove): the infallible Godhead. In the act of Congress the *loosening thighs* and the *white rush* are antithetical aspects. Into the softness and whiteness is concentrated all the sensuality of touch. The outcome of the union is further history or myth, pagan or Christian, Love and War. But what of the woman? Yeats speculates continually on the emotion of woman in such a crisis. Did Leda or Mary by that act become half or wholly divine? Did a god share with beast the lassitude that overcomes all animals, save only the lion and the cock? *Shudder* is the sexual act, the moment of orgasm, as all husbandmen know: but it is also anticipation in fear." (Jeffares, 248-49). Balachandra Rajan is all praise for this sonnet of Yeats. He writes: *Leda and the Swan,* one of the most unimprovable poems ever written, is the final fusion of history, myth and vision. Using the sonnet form, which is employed traditionally for love and public issues, Yeats writes a poem which is about both and neither. Except for the daringly judged break in the eleventh line, the formal requirements are rigorously observed and the great power of compression, which can force such massive themes into so brief and tightly controlled a compass, finds its reward in the power and richness of the poem. Yeats did not come to this perfection easily. Ellmann shows that at least six stages of revision were needed and that it was not until the second published version that Yeats achieved the onslaught of the first line, the 'sudden blow', the impact of which is the poem." (Rajan, 132-33).

35. Among School Children

Yeats wrote 'Among School Children' on 14th June, 1926, and the poem first appeared in *The Dial* in August, 1927. About three months before writing this poem, Yeats made a draft for the poem on 14th March, 1926: "Topic for poem — School children and the thought that live [life] will waste them perhaps that no possible life can fulfil our dreams or even their teacher's hope. Bring in the old thought that life prepares for what never happens." (Jeffares, 251). The occasion of the poem was Yeats's visit to St. Otteran's School, Waterford, in February, 1926. It was a school that followed the Montessori system of teaching. Yeats was very much impressed by the school and praised the school even in the Senate house. The poet was then a famous and popular public figure: "the sixty-year old smiling public man." The theme of the poem is education, but Yeats's conception of education was different from the common concept of education. Therefore, though he was impressed by the method of teaching in St. Otteran's School, yet "he regards St. Otteran's School with cooler eyes: as in an earlier poem about education, 'Michael Robertes and the Dancer'. Yeats here concludes that education should be a dance, not ciphering or reading or sewing or another sort of labour. The poet rejects any sort of education (such as that associated with Plato's academy) that excludes any part of existence; instead he finds that life gains purpose, gains meaning, only by moving towards ever-greater wholeness and largeness." (Albright, 668). Balachandra Rajan sees a contrariety between this poem and the poem 'Leda and the Swan': *Among School Children* moves in a different element to Leda though it does deal ironically with the 'daughters of the swan'.... it begins naturalistically enough with the standardised pattern of the guided tour. But the fading into symbol is soon under way and a 'Ledaean body' bent over a sinking fire recalls a moment of childish communion when two natures blended into a sphere, or into the yolk and white of the same shell. The alteration of Plato's parable in the *Symposium* serves to remind us that the sphere and the egg, which can turn perpetually inside out without breaking, are Yeatsian symbols of ultimate reality. It also reminds us that Yeats regards the restoration of innocence as the highest achievement of the intellect." (Rajan, 134).

AMONG SCHOOL CHILDREN

I

I walk through the long school room questioning;
A kind old nun in a white hood replies;
The children learn to cipher and to sing,
To study reading-books and history,
To cut and sew. be neat in everything

In the best modern way — the children's eyes
In momentary wonder stare upon
A sixty-year-old smiling public man.

II

I dream of a Ledaean body, bent
Above a sinking fire, a tale that she
Told of a harsh refroof, or trivial event
That changed some childish day to tragedy —
Told, and it seemed that our two natures blent
Into a sphere from youthful sympathy,
Or else, to alter Plato's parable,
Into the yolk and white of the one shell.

III

And thinking of that fit of grief or rage
I look upon one child or t'other there
And wonder if she stood so at that age —
For even daughters of the swan can share
Something of every paddler's heritage —
And had that colour upon cheek or hair,
And thereupon my heart is driven wild:
She stands before me as a living child.

IV

Her present image floats into the mind —
Did Quattrocento finger fashion it
Hollow of cheek as though it drank the wind
And took a mess of shadows for its meat?
And I though never of Ledaean kind
Had pretty plumage once — enough of that.
Better to smile on all that smile, and show
There is a comfortable kind of old scarecrow.

V

What youthful mother, a shape upon her lap
Honey of generation had betrayed,
And that must sleep, shriek, struggle to escape
As recollection or the drug decide,

Would think her son, did she but see that shape
With sixty or more winters on its head,
A compensation for the pang of his birth.
Or the uncertainty of his setting forth ?

VI

Plato thought nature but a spume that plays
Upon a ghostly paradigm of things;
Soldier Aristotle played the taws
Upon the bottom of a king of kings;
World-famous golden-thighed Pythagoras
Fingered upon a fiddle-stick or strings
What a star sang, and careless Muses heard:
Old clothes upon old sticks to scare a bird.

VII

Both nuns and mothers worship images.
But those the candles light are not as those
That animate a mother's reveries,
But keep a marble or a bronze repose.
And yet they loo break hearts — O Presences
That passion piety or affection knows.
And that all heavenly glory symbolise —
O self-born mockers of man's enterprise.

VIII

Labour is blossoming or dancing where
The body is not bruised to pleasure soul.
Nor beauty born out of its own despair,
Nor blear-eyed wisdom out of midnight oil.
O chestnut tree, great rooted blossoms,
Are you the leaf, the blossom or the bole?
O body swayed to music, O brightening glance.
How can we know the dancer from the dance?

The poem is divided into eight stanzas, each stanza consisting of eight lines rhyming ababcdee, with variations. In stanza I, the poet speaks in the first person, and says that he is walking "through the long schoolroom" with a "kind old nun in a white hood." In reality this nun was Rev. Mother Philomena. The poet is questioning about different matters of the school and the nun is answering his questions. From her answers. Yeats can learn that the children of the school are taught arithmetic's ("cipher") and to sing. They also learn how to study reading-books and history and also how to cut and sew clothes. Yeats learns that the children are taught to be "neat in everything / In the best modern way." This means that the children are taught according to the principles of Dr. Maria Montessori (1870-1952) who "aimed at creating neatness and spontaneity in children." (Jeffares, 251). As Yeats stood in a class-room, the children looked inquisitively at the poet who was then a sexagenarian political figure by virtue of being a member of the Senate. The last line of this stanza — "A sixty-year old smiling public man." — is ironical and self-pitying: compare with the last line of the fourth stanza: "There is a comfortable kind of old scarecrow." Daniel Albright writes about this line: "the self-conscious poet is aware of the disengaged, arbitrary roles he plays, the appearances he presents (...) — he has lost the integrity of being that is celebrated..." (Albright, 668).

The second stanza is introspective and it deals with the remembrances of the poet. He says that the faces of the little girl children revive in the mind of the poet the memory of Maud Gonne ("I dream of a Ledaean body") who was as beautiful as the mythical Leda, wife to Tyndarus and mother to Helen. The poet recalls that one day Maud Gonne told him, near an about-to-be-extinguished fire of the fireplace, about petty incidents in her school days. She said that she would sometimes be reproved by the teachers and then she would fly into a rage and thereby her days would become spoilt: "Told of a harsh reproof, or trivial event/ That changed some childish day to tragedy—". As the poet would hear her story, he would feel, as if, their two youthful souls were getting merged into one another in mutual sympathy. He would feel that for the moment they were inseparable, both physically and mentally, from one another, like the white and the yolk of an egg. Plato spoke of bodiless spiritual love ("Plato's parable") But the poet then felt that in true love the love-partners are united spiritually as well as physically, as against ("alter") Plato's doctrine: "it seemed that our two natures blend/Into a sphere from youthful sympathy,/Or else, to alter Plato's parable,/Into the yolk and white of the one shell." In stanza III, the image of Maud thickens and almost assumes a concrete shape. In his grief ("or rage"), the poet looks at the faces of the children in the class and imagines that in her school days Maud also would stand in sonic place in the class. Maud, the poet says, is the daughter of the divine swan and is the inhabitant of the celestial sphere. But such daughters of the celestial sphere also can share something with the daughter of the common folk, like sitting in a class-room meant for common children: "For even daughter of the swan can share/something of every paddler's heritage —So the poet can imagine Maud in the class-room of common children. But the poet imagines, when Maud had been in such a class, she certainly wore that bright and distinctive colours in her cheek and hair. As the poet deeply recalls the memory of Maud, he becomes romantically inspired, and now, as if, can see with his physical eyes the flesh-and-blood young Maud Gonne in the class-room where he now stands: "She stands before me as a living child."

In stanza IV, the poet compares the Maud of the bygone days with the present Maud: "The present image floats into the mind—". She is now gaunt in her look with caved-in cheeks, as though she lives on wind and shadows. Yeats asks: has the "Quattrocento finger" painted this image of Maud? The Italian word 'quattrocento' means 'four hundred'. The word refers to the 15th century Italian art, particularly the works of the great painter Leonardo da Vinci (1452-1519). Yeats says that though Maud is now gaunt, yet she is still as beautiful as the works of Leonardo da Vinci — gaunt and pale, yet attractive. Therefore, he wants to know if the present Maud Gonne is shaped or painted by da Vinci: "Did Quattrocento finger fashion it/Hollow of checks as though it drank the wind/And took a mess of shadows for its meat?" A chain of images now passes kaleidoscopically before the poet's mind. He recalls that though he was never attractively beautiful, yet once he had "raven-coloured hair" ("Pretty plumage"). But he stops short of further dwelling on these images and recollections — perhaps because these are too painful to him. Rather, he says that it is now better to smile ironically at those bright days and think that even one in decrepitude, like him, has some sort of comfort. He says that he is now no better than a scarecrow in looks, and yet it is better to smile at everything smiling, attractive: "Better to smile on all that smile, and show/There is a comfortable kind of old scarecrow."

The meaning of stanza V will be dear to us if we read a passage that Torchiana finds in Gentile's book *The Reform of Education* and which Yeats read in translation: "'The mother who tenderly nurses her sick child is indeed anxious for the health of the body over which she worries, and she would like to see it vigorous and strong. But that body is so endeared to her, because by means of it the child is enabled to live happily with her; through it his fond soul can require maternal love by filial devotion; or in it he may develop a powerful and beautiful personality worthy to be adored as the ideal creature of maternal affection. If in the bloom of physical health he were to reveal himself stupid and insensate, endowed with mere instinctive sensuality and bestial appetite, this son would cease to be the object of his mother's fondness, nay, he would arouse in her a feeling of loathing and revulsion. It is this sense of loathing... that we... feel for the human corpse from which life has departed; for life is the basis of every psychological relation, and therefore of every possible sympathy.(Jeffares, 252). However, the poet wonders what a youthful mother would think of her son ("a shape") if she would see the son grow old: "With sixty or more winters on its head?" The poet calls the son "Honey of generation." Here honey signifies "pleasure arising from generation" or pleasure that a mother derives from nursing her child. Yeats look the phrase "honey of generation" from Porphyry's essay 'The Cave of the Nymphs'. "Porphyry was a Neoplatonic philosopher; he wrote a famous essay on Homer's Cave of the Nymphs, showing it as an allegory of the unborn soul's descent — the sexual pleasure of the parents acted as a kind of honey, luring the child's soul into incarnation (...)" (Albright, 670). The poet says that the mother expects her child grows healthy physically and mentally. But if it grows, instead, old and develops decrepitude, then the mother's hope is betrayed: "Honey of generation had betrayed." It may be mentioned here that the same idea is to be found in Yeats's *At the Hawk's Well:*

> What were his life soon done!
> Would he loose by that or win?
> A mother that saw her son
> Doubled over a speckled shin,
> Cross-grained with ninety years,
> Would cry, 'How little worth
> Were all my hopes and fears
> And the hard pain of his birth.'

The poet says that if the child does not grow up to the expectation of the mother, then the labour of the mother will not be compensated; The pain of a mother and the dreadful work of uncertainly is beautifully depicted by Balke: (Dyson, 92):

> My mother groaned, my father wept;
> Into the dangerous world I leapt.
> Hapless, naked, piping loud,
> Like a fiend hid in a cloud.

The poet says that the "Honey of generation" will bet rayed if the child grows only in sensuality and in forgetfulness of his previous spiritual life ("sleeps"): "And that must sleep, shriek, struggle to escape/As recollection, or the drug decide." Here 'drug' means 'honey' and 'recollection' means the recollection of the prenatal state of the soul. But A.E. Dyson questions: who is the sufferer here—the child or its mother? To Dyson this is not clear here. (Dyson, 92).

In stanza VI, the poet decries the philosophies of Plato, Aristotle and Pythagoras by saying that abstract speculations are of no avail. The world is too hard, and time is too unsparing, and so their skills could not save them from becoming like scare-crows in appearance at the end of their lives: "Old clothes upon old sticks to scare a bird." Plato thought the world to be a shadow or foam ("spume") of something else. To him, this phenomenal world was but an instance of another real world—the noumenal world. Plato "taught that the physical world, mutable and corruptible, was only a humble shadow, an undignified copy of a world of ideal Forms." (Albright, 670). Aristotle, pupil of Plato and master of the great soldier Alexander the Great, was not so other-worldly as Plato had been. "Plato's pupil Aristotle (384- 322 BC) gave a little more dignify to the physical world, by teaching that reality was form ingredient in matter. An early draft of this stanza stressed Aristotle's talent for category: 'Aristotle was/The first who had a place for everything.'" (Albright, 670). Yeats fancies that Alexander the Great, in his childhood, would be beaten up by Aristotle, his teacher. That is Aristotle would sometimes use branches of the birch tree ("taw") to beat Alexander with: "Soldier Aristotle played the taws/Upon the bottom of a king of kings." But Aristotle, the great philosopher, like Plato, also had to become old and wasted. In a letter, written about the time when the poem was written, to wit, on 24th September, 1926, Yeats wrote that he had then been reading Croce and composing verses: "Here is a fragment of my last curse on old age. It seems that even the greatest of men are owls, scarecrows, by the time their fame has come. Aristotle, remember, was Alexander's tutor, hence the taws (form of birch)." (Jeffares, 253). Pythagoras was yet another philosopher like Plato and Aristotle, and he was world-famous and "golden-thighed". Pythagoras (6th century BC) believed in the other worldly existences and in immortality of the soul, and said that everything, including even musical notes, originated only in numbers. That is, according to him, the ultimate reality was only numbers that are immaterial and so other worldly. However, the poet says that even all these great philosophers had to become old and to look like scarecrows: "Old clothes upon old sticks to scare a bird." Balachandra Rajan's comment on this sixth stanza deserves our attention: "The fluent singing moment of the sixth stanza signalises the shift into philosophy, but the consolations of wisdom are ironic. Plato suggests to us that we live among phantoms. Aristotle's more substantial knowledge is gently mocked and one is reminded that Alexander learned little from his mentor. Golden-thighed Pythagoras (Tindall quotes Plutarch for the detail and Wain, Diogenes Laertius) represents the philosophy of art in contrast to that of nature, or ideas; but even the music of the spheres is, in the last analysis, the song of a scarecrow." (Rajan, 135). The epithet "golden-thighed" was applied to Pythagoras in the ancient times.

In stanza VII, the poet says that not only intellect and wisdom, like those of the great philosophers, are ephemeral, but passion also is ephemeral and illusory. He says that nuns enlighten the images of divine beings, but what they actually worship are not the images. Likewise, mothers nurse their children of flesh and blood, but their children of fancy are quite different. The objects of worship of the nuns are made of marble or bronze, and the objects of mothers' passions are not the fleshy bodies. The nuns and the mothers know this well, and yet they passionately attach themselves to the images that symbolise the heavenly glories (the gods and the souls of the sons). And so the symbols of heavenly glories mock at the foolishness of human beings (for instances, the nuns and the mothers) for they try to find eternal heavenly glories in ephemeral objects made by man to symbolise those heavenly glories: "And that all heavenly glory symbolise —/O self-born mockers of man's enterprise." To express his sense of the ephemerality of earthly things, the poet addresses the "Presences." "Parkinson comments that these [the "Presences" Jean only be taken to mean the statues and children that are knowable by passion, piety, or affection." (Jeffares, 255). We may add here Ba lachandra Rajan's comment on this stanza for more clarification of this stanza. Rajan says: "The three selves of child, lover and the scarecrow and the three philosophers, give way to another triad: the 'Presences' worshipped by the passion of lovers, the piety of nuns and the affection of mothers. These are mockeries of the heart but the poem has already suggested that there are also mockeries of the mind. Nevertheless it is man who creates the ideals which he is ironically unable to attain; heavenly glory only exists as the intellect and the imagination shapes it. This is the familiar and central Yeatsian movement—out of absurdity into an affirmation of man's creative power, validated by the irony through which it has been made to live." (Rajan, 135).

In a sense, the poet summarises the whole poem in the last stanza. He says that perfection is attained when both body and mind develop equally, and not the one at the expense of the other. If the soul or the spirit blossoms without bruising the body—only that is perfection: "Labour is blossoming or dancing where/The body is not bruised to pleasure soul." That is, perfection is not possible if the beauty or the hill growth of the soul is achieved by sacrificing the growth of the body ("despair"). Therefore, the poet does not desire to be a wise man with blear eyes or watery eyes of the old man, by studying till late at night. He says that both the body and the mind must grow in unison, and equally. Yeats believed that life is the unity of body and mind, and that life is thus the unity of the two opposing phenomena — body and mind. To illustrate this philosophy, the poet resorts to the imagery of the chest-nut tree. Is the chest-nut tree only its leaves, or only its flowers, or simply its trunk? No, says the poet; it is rather the unity of the three parts: the leaves, the flowers and the bole. In the same way, man is the unity of body and spirits: "O chestnut tree, great rooted blossomer,/Are you the leaf, the blossom or the bole?" To illustrate the same philosophy of unity, Yeats takes yet another example. When the body is swayed by music, there is the unity of the body and the mind; or when we are stimulated by an attractive glance (this may have a reference to Maud Gonne), our body is moved by passion (mind)—there is the unity of body and mind. Therefore, the dancer, while she is dancing, is but a unity of body and mind. The unity is so fast that while in dancing, the body of the dancer cannot be separated from her attention or mind, or the other way round: "O body swayed to music, O brightening glance./ How can we know the dancer from the dance?"

36. All Souls' Night

(*Epilogue to 'A Vision'*)

As we know, Yeats believed in ghosts and magic and in other parapsychological phenomena. This poem bears witness to his belief in these things. He also believed in the truth of some of the Upanishadic teachings, such as in the transmigration of the soul which is also clear from this poem. The poem was written in November, 1920, at Oxford, as an 'epilogue' to *A Vision*. Yeats wrote this poem in a moment of spiritual exaltation. He wrote is *A Vision*: "I have moments of exaltation like that in which I wrote 'All Souls' Night.'" (Jeffares, 263). The title of the poem is derived from the (day of) All Souls' Night, that generally falls on 2 November, each year. In that night, the Christians pray for the soteriological emancipation of all souls that are still suffering in Purgatory. On All Souls' Night in 1920, Yeats was in Oxford near the Christ Church College. As the liturgy of the All Souls' Night began with the ringing of the Church bell at Christ College at midnight, Yeats was instantaneously transported to an exalted state in which he passionately remembered some of his dead friends. The poem was first published The New Republic on 9 March, 1921, and later on it was published as an epilogue to the 1937 version of *A Vision*. Daniel Albright introduces this poem thus. "The strongest theme of The Tower is the poet's labour to engage himself with an image, to construct adequate symbols of life—even the title of the volume suggests this sort of edification. But the volume ends with a counter-theme, present earlier in such poems as 'Nineteen Hundred and Nineteen' III (also similar in metre to "All Souls' Night'): The soul's effort to discern body itself, to free itself from every image and symbol. This poem offers some points of comparison with an earlier elegy, 'In Memory of Major Robert Gregory': at the centre of each poem is a trio of ghosts, who while living experimented with various strategies for escape from the natural world, as if in anticipation of their ghostly selves. But whereas the earlier poem moved on to a fourth ghost, that of Robert Gregory, 'All Souls' Night' returns immediately to the poet, who seems to be spiritualizing before the reader's eyes — as if the poem were a funeral elegy for the elegist himself." (Albright. 689). Balachandra Rajan's brief commentary on this poem may also seive as an introduction to this poem: "All Souls' Night which ends The Tower is a poem written well on the way to Byzantium. The ghosts Yeats calls up are not ordinary ghosts but the ghosts of occultists — William Thomas Horton, MacGregor Mathers of the Golden Dawn and Florence Farr, who taught in Ceylon and died of cancer, but not before providing Yeats, via a 'learned Indian', with corroborative evidence of the fifteenth phase. The truths Yeats has to tell are 'Mummy' truths—a willy word suggesting the wisdom of the dead and wisdom that is unageing — and the living who mock those truths remain governed-by them. Over the muscatel we are informed that the 'gross palates' of the living can drink of the whole wine, while ghosts must satisfy themselves with the 'wine-breath'. By the end of the poem the mummy-cloth has been wound around sufficiently to permit a reversal of this statement. 'No living man can drink from the whole wine'. It is the fume of the eternal which is the quintessence of things." (Rajan, 136).

ALL SOULS' NIGHT

(*Epilogue to 'A Vision'*)

Midnight has come, and the great Christ Church Bell
And many a lesser bell sound through the room;
And it is All Souls' Night,
And two long glasses brimmed with muscatel
Bubble upon the table. A ghost may conic;

For it is a ghost's right,
His element is so fine
Being sharpened by his death,
To drink from the wine-breath
While our gross palates drink from the whole wine.

I need some mind that, if the cannon sound
From every quarter of the world, can stay
Wound in mind's pondering
As mummies in the mummy-cloth are wound;
Because I have a marvellous thing to say,
A certain marvellous thing
None but the living mock,
Though not for sober ear;
It may be all that hear
Should laugh and weep an hour upon the clock.

Horton's the first I call. He loved strange thought
And knew that sweet extremity of pride
That's called platonic love,
And that to such a pitch of passion wrought
Nothing could bring him, when his lady died.
Anodyne for his love.
Words were but wasted breath;
One dear hope had he:
The inclemency
Of that or the next winter would be death.

Two thoughts were so mixed up I could not tell
Whether of her or God he thought the most.
But think that his mind's eye,
When upward turned, on one sole image fell;
And that a slight companionable ghost,
Wild with divinity,
Had so lit up the whole
Immense miraculous house
The Bible promised us,
It seemed a gold-fish swimming in a bowl.

On Florence Emery I call the next,
Who finding the first wrinkles on a face?
Admired and beautiful,
And knowing that the future would be vexed
With 'minished beauty, multiplied commonplace.
Preferred to teach a school
Away from neighbour or friend,
Among dark skins and there
Permit foul years to wear
Hidden from eyesight to the unnoticed end.

Before that end much had she ravelled out
From a discourse in figurative speech
By some learned Indian
On the soul's journey. How it is whirled about.
Wherever the orbit of the moon can reach.
Until it plunges into the sun;
And there, free and yet fast,
Being both Chance and Choice,
Forget its broken toys
And sink into its own delight at last.

And I call up MacGregor from the grave.
For in my first hard spring lime we were friends.
Although of late estranged.
I thought him half a lunatic, half knave.
And told him so, but friendship never ends;
And what if mind seem changed.
And it seems changed with the mind.
When thoughts rise up unbid
On generous things that he did
And I grow half contented to be blind!

He had much industry at setting out.
Much boisterous courage, before loneliness
Had driven him crazed;
For meditations upon unknown thought
Make human intercourse grow less and less;
They are neither paid nor praised.
But he'd object to the host.

The glass because my glass;
A ghost-lover he was
And may have grown more arrogant being a ghost.

But names are nothing. What matter who it be.
So that his elements have grown so fine
The fume of muscatel
Can give his sharpened palate ecstasy.
No living man can drink from the whole wine
I have mummy truths to tell
Where at the living mock,
Though not for sober ear,
For maybe all that hear
Should laugh and weep an hour upon the clock.

Such thought — such thought have I that hold it tight
Till meditation master all its parts.
Nothing can stay my glance
Until that glance run in the world's despite
To where the damned have howled away their hearts.
And where the blessed dance;
Such thought, that in it bound
I need no other thing,
Wound in mind's wandering
As mummies in the mummy-cloth are wound.

The poem is divided into ten stanzas, each stanza consisting of ten lines rhyming a b c a b c d e e d. In the first stanza, the Poet says that it is midnight, and the great Christ Church Bell and other small bells of lesser Churches are ringing, because it is the All Souls' Night. The Christ Church at Oxford is a college which was founded by Cardinal Wolsey (c. 1475-1530). Two glasses, on the table before the poet, are filled up with muscatel or rich spicy wine. The wine was just poured in, and so there are bubbles still on the wine. The poet thinks that as it is the All Souls' Night, ghosts may come out of their graves. The ghosts are made up of elements finer than the elements with which mortals are made, for the ghosts leave behind the grosser elements at the time of their departing from the mortal bodies. Therefore while mortals drink the "whole wine", the gliosis drink only the "wine breath." The poet thinks that the ghosts, just come out of the graves, have drunk the "wine breath" from the two glasses of wine on the table before him. In the second stanza, the poet wants his mind to be absolutely calm and concentrated, so that even the sound of a cannon cannot disturb him. He wants his mind to be wrapped up in some thought, as the mummies of the Egyptian pyramids are wrapped up in clothes: "As mummies in the mummy-cloth are wound." He wants this to occur because he has something very important to say: "Because I have a marvellous thing to say." What this marvellous thing is we do not know, and, perhaps, the poet himself has not divulged this secret and marvellous thing to us i n the whole poem. He only says that those who are living will laugh at I hat edification and that this tiding is not meant for the common folk. He says that those who will hear it will "laugh and weep an hour." Perhaps (he "marvellous thing" is that the ghosts of his dead friends have now come to him from out of their respective graves. However, now the poet recalls the ghosts of his friends one by one.

Firstly, in the third stanza, he calls the ghost of William Thomas Horton (1864-1919) who, being influenced by Blake and Beardsley, wrote *The Way of the Soul* (1910). He was a mystic, a member of the mystical Order of the Golden Dawn, and a painter. Many of the paintings of Horton still exist. Daniel Albright writes about Horton: "A scrap of paper that Horton once sent to Yeats contained a mysterious warning (alluding to the figure from Plato's *Phaedrus* of the white and black horses that pull the Soul's chariot) that helped Yeats to formulate the idea of the anti-self (...). In *A Vision's* lunar scheme, Horton was placed at the extremely *primary* Phase 25 (...). In 1917 Horton became angry with Yeats for republishing his Introduction to Horton's *A Book of Images* while deleting references to Horton (...)." (Albright, 689). The poet says that William Horton loved "strange thought", that is, mystical thoughts or concepts. He was also very fond of his wife, but his love for his wife was purely platonic: "And knew that extremity of pride/That's called platonic love." Daniel Albright writes: "in the Dedication to *A Vision* (1925), p.x, Yeats alluded to Horton as one who 'lived through that... strangest of all adventures — Platonic love... he gave himself up to all kinds of amorous adventures, until at last, in 1 think his fiftieth year but when he had still all his physical vigour, he thought "I do not need women but God." Then he and a very good, charming, young fellow-student fell in love with one another and though he could only keep down his passion with the most bitter struggle, they lived together platonically, and this they did ... from a clear sense of something to be attained by what seemed a most needless trampling of the grapes of life. She died, and he survived her but a little time during which he saw her in apparition and attained through her certain of the traditional experiences of the saint'. Yeats also believed that Jonathan Swift, with his fakir-like contempt for all human desire' (...), pursued a relation with Stella of 'platonic love' (...)" (Albright, 690).

Yeats recalls that when Horton's wife, Audrey Locke (1881-1916), died, nobody could stop his grief and console him: "Nothing could bring him, when his lady died,/Anodyne for his love." All consolation was futile, ineffective: "Words were but wasted breath." Only one hope remained with Horton after the death of his wife and that was that he thought that he would die of the shock (inclemency) of his wife's death either very soon or by the next winter. In stanza IV, the poet says that he cannot say for sure if Horton loved God more than his wife, but this he certainly knew that when Horton looked above in prayer, God and his wife's soul seemed to be mixed up: "Two thoughts were so mixed up I could not tell/Whether of her or God he thought the most." Horton later made n portraiture of his wife ("companionable ghost") which was like a companion to Horton. Yeats says that the portraiture, as if, radiated divinity, lighted up the whole "Immense miraculous house" of Horton—a peaceful house that we hear of in the Bible. The portraiture was so vivid and lively that it seemed to move about within the whole house of Horton, like a gold-fish moves in the aquarium: "It seemed a gold-fish swimming in a bowl." A. Norman Jeffares writes that actually "a bowl of goldfish was kept on one of the windows of Yeats's house in Broad Street, Oxford, to amuse Anne Yeats, Yeats's daughter." (Jeffares, 264).

In stanza V, Yeats, next, calls the ghost of Florence Farr Emery (1869- 1917), an actress and a believer in occultism. She "first met Yeats in 1890 when she was acting in *A Sicilian Idyll* by John Todhunter (1839-1916); she produced Yeats's *The Land of Heart's Desire* as a curtain raiser at the Avenue Theatre on 29th March, 1894, acted the part of Aleel in *The Countess Cathleen* in Dublin 1899, and gave a performance of his *The Shadowy Waters* for a Theosophical convention at the Court Theatre, London on 8th July, 1905. She was a member of the group of students of the occult which centred on MacGregor Mathers, her initials in the Order of the Golden Dawn being SSDD (Sapientia Sapienti Dono Data). She recited Yeats's poems to the Psaltery and wrote *The Music of Speech* (1909). Ellmann says Yeats had an affair with her after 1903. "(Jeffares, 264). Bernard Shaw described her as "a young independent professional woman, who enjoyed, as such, an exceptional freedom of social intercourse in artistic circles in London. As she was clever, good natured, and very good-looking, all her men friends fell in love with her. This had occurred so often that she had lost all patience with the hesitating preliminaries of her less practised adorers. Accordingly, when they clearly longed to kiss her, and she did not dislike them sufficiently to make their gratification too great a strain on her excessive good nature, she would seize the stammering suitor firmly by the wrists, bring him into her arms by a smart pull and saying, 'Let's get it over' allowed the startled gentleman to have his kiss, and then proceed to converse with him at her ease on subjects of more general interest." (Jeffares, 264-65). Yeats himself described her as possessing "three great gifts, a tranquil beauty like that of Demeter's image near the British Museum Reading Room door, and an incomparable sense of rhythm and a beautiful voice, the seeming natural expression of the image. ... Her sitting-room at the Brook Green lodging-house was soon a reflection of her mind, the walls covered with musical instruments, pieces of Oriental drapery, and Egyptian gods and goddesses painted by herself in the British Museum." (Jeffares, 265). However, in the poem, the poet says that Emery was very beautiful in her youth, but in her late years she developed wrinkles in her face. She knew that in her old age, with her diminished beauty and expressed signs of senility, she would no longer enjoy the flattery that she used to enjoy earlier, and so she gracefully chose the career of a school teacher (leaving behind her previous attractive career of an actress):"And knowing that the future would be vexed/With, minished beauty, multiplied commonplace,/Preferred to teach a school/Away from neighbour or friend." Jeffares writes: "In 1912 Mrs. Emery went to teach in a Buddhist Institution, Ramanathan College, in Ceylone, where she died on 29th April, 1917." (Jeffares, 265). To join the school, she had to go away from her neighbours and friends. There in Ceylone, she taught the Ceylonese dark-skinned boys and girls, and thus passed her years of decrepitude: "Permit foul years to wear/Hidden from eyesight to the unnoticed end." Emery suffered "foul years" because she suffered from cancer from which she died.

In stanza VI, the poet says that before she died, Florence Emery disclosed the meanings of many intricate religious concepts that she heard about from some "learned Indian." F.F. Farag suggests that this "learned Indian" may be Mohini Chatterjee, but Jeffares suggests that in the poem, by "learned Indian" Yeats probably meant Ponnambalam Ramanathan, the founder of the school where Emery served. Florence Farr Emery met Ponnambalam Ramanathan (1851-1930) in England in 1902 when Ramanathan exercised a great influence on her. However, Emery learned the secret knowledge about the soul's journey from the "learned Indian". We may also guess that Emery learned the *(Upanishadic* theory of the transmigration of the soul, after the death of the body. The poet says that Emery learned how the soul, leaving the body behind, hovers over the earth and takes a flight to the orbit of the moon; and thence travels to the sphere of the sun: 'How it is whirled about,/Wherever the orbit of the moon can reach,/ Until it plunges into the sun." While in the sphere of the sun, the soul becomes disentangled from the entailments of the earthly life, and so becomes light and then lighter and acquires the capacity of moving fast. The soul also forgets the memories of its earthly existence and then is guided either by fate ("Chance") or by Karma or the eternal chain of cause and effect ("Choice"): "Being both Chance and Choice,/Forget its broken toys." And at last, the soul merges itself with the Supreme Being which is nothing but absolute delight: "And sink into its own delight at last."

In stanza VII, the poet calls up the ghost of MacGregor Mathers (1854-1918) as the last candidate. Jeffares writes that Mathers was "originally Samuel Liddle Mathers, studied occultism in London from 1885. He was appointed Curator of the Horniman Museum at Forest Hill in 1890, lost his post through a quarrel and lived in Paris from (probably) 1894. Interested in Rosicrucianism and Free masonry, he translated the *Kabalah Denudata.*" (Jeffares, 265). Both Rosicrucianism and Freemasonry are sorts of occultist disciplines. Yeats probably met Mathers in 1887 and wrote about him: "At the British Museum Reading-Room I often saw a man of thirty-six, or thirty-seven, in a brown velveteen coat, with a gaunt resolute face, and an athletic body, who seemed, before I heard his name, or knew the nature of his studies, a figure of romance. Presently I was introduced, where or by what man or woman I do not remember. He was called Liddell Mathers, but would soon, under the touch of the Celtic Movement', become MacGregor Mathers, and then plain MacGregor. He was the author of *The Kabbala Unveiled,* and his studies were two only — magic and theory of war, for he believed himself a born commander and all but equal in wisdom and power to that old Jew." (Jeffares, 265). However, the poet says that in his early youth, MacGregor was his friend, but soon they somehow became strangers to each other: "For in my first hard springtime we were friends,/Although of late estranged." Yeats thought MacGregor to be a mad man, or a simpleton ("half knave"). Yeats even told this to him without causing any injury to their friendship. Though their relationship has become cold, yet the poet recalls some acts of generosity by MacGregor, and this delight him very much: "And what if mind seem changed,/And it seems changed with the mind,/When thoughts rise up unbid/On generous things that he did/And I grow half contended to be blind!"

In stanza VIII, Yeats recalls that MacGregor was an industrious man with "boisterous courage." MacGregor became crazy from a sense of being lonely while practicing meditation keeping himself aloof from society: "For meditations upon unknown thought/Make human intercourse grow less and less." The poet feels sorry because people like MacGregor are "neither paid nor praised." MacGregor would not like the company of friends, and he would also not like to drink wine. He was a ghost-lover. MacGregor was a haughty person, and the poet thinks that perhaps being turned into a ghost he has become more haughtier: "But he'd object to the host/The glass because my glassy; A ghost-lover he was/And may have grown more arrogant being a ghost"

In stanza IX, the poet says that he does not like to call up any more ghosts by their names: "But names are nothing." He says that all ghosts are of the same ilk because all of them are "elements have grown so fine." He says that MacGregor's elements have also, for the same reason, must have grown fine, and that therefore he can taste only the finer elements of the fume of wine and enter into an ecstasy. The poet says that men who are living, can drink the gross elements of wine, and not only the finer elements comprised in it. After this, the poet takes a sharp turn and returns to his former statement that he has a "marvellous thing to say": "I have mummy truths to tell." That is, he has some prophetic words to say, at which living men would mock and laugh and weep for an hour: "For may be all that hear/Should laugh and weep an hour upon the clock." And, in the last stanza, the poet says that one can get such truths only in deep meditation, and only if one can disentangle oneself from the world: "Nothing can stay my glance/Until that glance run in the world's despite/ To where the damned have howled away their hearts." He says he possesses such a truth or such a thought To get such a truth or thought, one will have to fix one's attention within one's self or consciousness "where the blessed dance". The poet, when he fixes his mind or attention on such a truth, needs nothing else. He will then remain, as if, wound with the vagaries of the mind: only in the surface of the mind, then there will be fleeting sensations, but the centre of the mind will remain all fixed, like mummies bound in plies of clothes: "Such thought, that in it bound/I need no other thing,/ Wound in mind's wandering/As mummies in the mummy-cloth are wound."

A.E. Dyson has found at least two flaws in this poem of Yeats. Firstly, he says that the mood in which the poem was composed is not consistent with the meaning of the poem: "Yeats said in A Vision, 'I have moments of exaltation like that in which I wrote "All Souls' Night". But is the poem consistent with this?" (Dyson, 102). Secondly, Dyson writes: "I do not see how the poet moves from the thought in the first stanza that 'our gross palates drink from the whole wine' (where 'our' clearly distinguishes living people from ghosts) to the thought in the penultimate stanza 'No living man can drink from the whole wine'. On the other hand, this problem may be closer to optical illusion than to real contradiction." (Dyson, 102).

THE WINDING STAIR AND OTHER POEMS — 1933

This collection of poems contains those of *A Woman Young and Old* and five other poems. *The Winding Stair* was first published by the Foundation Press in 1929. In 1933, it was again published by Macmillan when it comprised the poems of *Words for Music Perhaps*, also. One peculiarity of the collection of poems entitled *The Winding Stair and Other Poems* is that there is no poem in which bears the title 'The Winding Stair'. *The Winding Stair* includes two very important poems: 'A Dialogue of Self and Soul' and 'Blood and the Moon'. About the stair referred to in the title of this collection, A.E. Dyson writes: "It is the single steep stair which winds up, in spiral, round the inside of Thoor Ballylee, with the large room which makes each floor opening from it; if you start at the bottom and proceed to the top of the stair, you emerge on the roof of Yeats's Tower. This stair became mingled with the gyres (or Yin and Yang, if you want to avoid the mathematics), and is a symbol of the soul's upward but spiral progress." (Dyson, 104). Daniel Albright very beautifully compares between *The Tower* and *The Winding Stair*: "*The Tower* and *The Winding Stair and Other Poems* are, to an extent, companion volumes. Some poems in *The Tower* have a kind of twin in the present book *[The Winding Stair]*: 'Sailing to Byzantium' and 'Byzantium'; 'The tower' and 'Blood and the Moon'; 'My Table' and 'A dialogue of Self and Soul'; and the publication *of The Winding Stair* ended withal *Woman Young and Old*, a sequence parallel to 'A Man Young and Old' at the end of *The Tower.*" (Albright, 692). Further, Albright introduces this volume (*The Winding Stair)* very beautifully, too: "The poems in the previous volume, *The Tower*, were written at the zenith of Yeat's public career, the period when he served as a senator, won the Nobel Prize, and wrote much of his autobiography; the poems of the present volume *[The Winding Stair]* represent a turning inward, a concentration. Yeat's health was deteriorating. In 1928 he needed to recuperate from lung congestion in Spain, late in 1929 he suffered first a dangerous lung haemorrhage, then, in Italy, a bout of Malta fever so severe that he made an emergency will, witnessed by Ezra Pound; and the shadow of death lies over many of these poems. In *The Tower*, the time of day was, so to speak, a sunny evening in which the moon was visible; but here the time of day is midnight—a dark field intermitted by a few dazzles that only intensify the darkness." (Albright, 692). While Albright finds in these poems Yeats's turning inward, W.W. Robson goes further and says that in these poems

Yeats shows the fundamental contradiction in the inner regard of his soul, for, for instance, while some of the poems are extremely sensuous, some others are equally stoic: "In *The Winding Stair* (1933) the contrasting moods and themes of *The Tower* are more marked. But instead of tension or ambivalence within a single poem, the poems now each tend to explore a single attitude. Some strike a note of stoic acceptance; others, a note of frank sensuality. Some convey the poignant sense of life's passing; others record intuitions of the things that transcend time and mortality." (Robson, 56). This collection of poems was dedicated to Yeats's friend Edmund Dulac who was a painter, a designer and a musician.

37. A Dialogue of Self and Soul

Mrs. Yeats said that Yeats wrote this poem between My and December, 1927, but Yeats himself wrote in his Notes that it was written "in the spring of 1928 during an illness, indeed finished the day before a Cannes doctor told me to stop writing." (Jeffares, 271). Here, either Mrs. Yeats or Yeats himself could not exactly remember the time of the composition of this poem. This is a mystical poem, in the sense that the theme of it is the soul and the self. What Yeats actually meant by soul and self, we do not know; but, perhaps, by soul he meant the this-worldly, practical and experimental element of a man (which in Indian philosophical terminology is called *aham*)\and by self he perhaps meant the permanent, eternal, transcendental and other worldly element of a man (which in Indian philosophical terminology is called *atman).* When Yeats wrote this poem, he was around sixty-two and, so, it was almost natural that the thoughts about the self and the soul came to his head. As he was feeling the pull of Atropo, the Greek goddess of death, he was naturally concerned about eschatology. On the other hand, the backward pull of the earthly life was not diminishing. In the tension between the two pulls, Yeats felt ambivalent, but ultimately decided in favour of the pull of the earthly life, whatever might be the consequence of neglecting the opposite pull of the other. Balachandra Rajan writes that the "emblem of the self [in this poem] is the five-hundred- and-fifty-year-old sword given to Yeats by Junzo in Portland, Oregon, during his 1920 American tour. Sheathed in its scabbard, still razor-keen and unspotted by the centuries, the combination represents the looking glass and the embroidery of art, the energies that survive time, love and war, and the masculine and the feminine." (Rajan, 138). A.E. Dyson writes that in this poem, the self "symbolises the joy of incarnate life, variety, the world of transience."(Dyson, 108).

Daniel Albright introduces the poem thus: "This poem is based on a traditional theme in English poetry, the most famous example of which is Andrew Marvell's 'A Dialogue between the Soul and the Body'; but the strenuous tone of Yeats's poem is far removed from the urbane 'metaphysical' wit of Marvell. Yeats personifies, instead of body and soul, the competing stresses towards subjectivity (the Self) and objectivity (the Soul). In such earlier poems as 'The Tower', Yeats treated the poet's conflicting desires for imaginative engagement with natural life, and for philosophical detachment from it; but here these desires build themselves into subpersonalities, voices in everyman's head. Although Yeats could not have known it, in 1910-11, T.S. Eliot wrote, but did not publish, two poems on similar themes, a 'First Debate between the Body and Soul' and a second debate... "The structure of this poem shows how successfully Yeats had internalized the system of *A Vision* (...): this is a gyreshaped poem, in which the Soul is at its point of maximum intensity at the beginning, incantatory and compelling, while the Self is at its weakest; as the poem progresses the Soul loses confidence and energy and, at last, the power of speech (140), while the Self-steadily gains until it reaches its climax at the poem's end." (Albright, 696).

A. N. Jeffares guesses that the poem might be inspired by Andrew Marvell's poem 'A Dialogue between the Soul and the Body' which Yeats probably read in Grierson's anthology of metaphysical poems. The original title of this poem was 'Sword and Tower'. Yeats wrote about this poem: "I am writing a new tower poem 'Sword and Tower', which is a choice of rebirth rather than deliverance from birth. I make my Japanese sword and its silk covering my symbol of life." (Albright, 697).

A DIALOGUE OF SELF AND SOUL

I

My Soul. I summon to the winding ancient stair;
Set all your mind upon the steep ascent,
Upon the broken, crumbling battlement,
Upon the breathless starlit air,
Upon the star that marks the hidden pole;
Fix every wandering thought upon
That quarter where all thought is done:
Who can distinguish darkness from the soul?

My Self. The consecrated blade upon my knees
Is Sato's ancient blade, still as it was,
Still razor-keen, still like a looking-glass
Unspotted by the centuries;
That flowing, silken, old embroidery, torn
From some court-lady's dress and round
The wooden scabbard bound and wound,
Can, tattered, still protect, faded adorn.

My Soul. Why should the imagination of a man
Long past his prime remember things that are
Emblematical of love and war?
Think of ancestral night that can,
If but imagination scorn the earth
And intellect its wandering
To this and that and tother thing,
Deliver from the crime of death and birth.

My Self. Montashigi, third of his family, fashioned it
Five hundred years ago, about it lie
Flowers from I know not what embroidery—
Heart's purple — and all these I set
For emblems of the day against the tower
Emblematical of the night,
And claim as by a soldier's right
A charter to commit the crime once more.

My Soul. Such fullness in that quarter overflows
And falls into the basin of the mind
That man is stricken deaf and dumb and blind,
For intellect no longer knows
Is from the *Ought,* or *knower* from the *known* —
That is to say, ascends to Heaven;
Only the dead can be forgiven;
But when I think of that my tongue's a stone.

II

My Self. A living man is blind and drinks his drop.
What matter if the ditches are impure?

What matter if I live it all once more?
Endure that toil of growing up;
The ignominy of boyhood; the distress
Of boyhood changing into man;
The unfinished man and his pain
Brought face to face with his own clumsiness;

The finished man among his enemies? —
How in the name of Heaven can he escape
That defiling and disfigured shape
The mirror of malicious eyes
Casts upon his eyes until at last
He thinks that shape must be his shape?
And what's the good of an escape
If honour find him in the wintry blast?

I am content to live it again
And yet again, if it be life to pitch
Into the frog-spawn of a blind man's ditch,
A blind man battering blind men;
Or into that most fecund ditch of all,
The folly that man does
Or must suffer, if he woos
A proud woman not kindred of his soul.

I am content to follow to its source
Every event in action or in thought;
Measure the lot; forgive myself the lot!
When such as I cast out remorse
So great a sweetness flows into the breast
We must laugh and we must sing,
We are blest by everything,
Everything we look upon is blest.

The poem is divided into two parts; Part I comprises five stanzas, and Part II consists of four stanzas. Each stanza consists of eight lines rhyming a b b a c d d c. In stanza i, the poet's (objective) Soul persuades his (subjective) Self to climb up the winding stair of the Tower (renamed Thoor Ballylee by Yeats after he bought it). The Soul asks the Self to concentrate all its attention "upon the steep ascent" and upon "the breathless starlit air." It persuades the Self to look above and at the star where there is something hidden, something prophetic, something mysterious: "Upon the star that marks the hidden pole." There in the "hidden pole" all thoughts of the Self will vanish, or merge in the mysterious wisdom there. The Soul says that the "hidden pole" is absolutely dark, and that it (the Soul) is nothing other than this absolute darkness. In this stanza, the poet means to say that the desire of the Soul of man is to rise from the dross of life up to the total darkness above which symbolises the Absolute Soul or the Greater Soul, and that the Soul of man wants to merge itself in the Absolute Soul or the Greater Soul—the "steep ascent": "Upon the broken, crumbling battlement,/Upon the breathless starlit air,/Upon the star that marks the hidden pole." That is, the "hidden pole" is beyond the battlement, the "breathless starlit air" and even the distant stars. There in the "hidden pole", there in that "quarter", there is no thought, no discourse, no debate, no doubt—nothing; and there is therefore only darkness. It is here that the Soul abides, and actually it is nothing else than this darkness. In stanza ii, the Self replies to the call of the Soul. It says that it does not want to part with its identity and merge itself with the Absolute, rather it wants to live in this world of action and love. Action, here, is symbolised by Sato's sword. Life is a struggle, a battlefield, where the sword of action is essential, and one is attracted to action because action is tied to love. Here love is symbolised by the embroidery on the hilt of the sword. In a letter to Mrs. Olivia Shakespeare, written on 2nd or 4th October, 1927, Yeats said: "I make my Japanese sword and its silk covering my symbol of life." (Jeffares, 271). The Self says that it is still craving action, that it has been craving action ever since time immemorial: "The consecrated blade upon my knees/ Is Sato's ancient blade, still as it was,/Still razor-keen; still like a looking-glass/Unspotted by the centuries." The Self is also attracted by the love offered by life which is symbolised by the embroidery of the cloth round the hilt of the sword. The poet says that perhaps the piece of cloth is culled from the garment of some court-lady. The piece of cloth, therefore, symbolises sensuous love by which the Self of the poet is attracted. Here the poet contends that the earthly life of sensuous love and action is more desirable than the ascetic life of the Soul's darkness, above.

In stanza iii, the Soul parries the Self's charge that the life of the Soul is ascetic. The Soul tells the Self that it is the life of beatitude that is more to be desired than the life of sensuality. The Soul says that the life of sensuality is not the true life but the life of emblems only. It says that particularly when one has attained old age and lost his youthful conviviality, one should only seek the life of actuality or the life of beatitude, and renounce the life of emblems or symbols, to wit, the earthly life: "Why should the imagination of a man/Long past his prime remember things that are/Emblematical of love and war?" The poet means to say that man should or may enjoy the earthly world—the world of love and war—but when he has attained old age, he should turn his mind towards beatitude. The Soul says that when one is no more capable of actual action ("war"), love in old age, one can only recreate his previous actions and love-affairs in his imagination and thus can get some satisfaction. But if one does so, then he only engrosses himself in remembrances and emblems, and not in actual things and actions. The Soul, therefore, urges the Self to abjure the life of sensuality. It says that the Self should, instead, fix its focus of attention on the Supreme Soul or beatitude or the "ancestral night." In its old age, the imagination of the Self should renounce the sensuous life and its intellect should stop its incoherent ponderings over the manifold of the earthly world ("wandering"): "If but imagination scorn the earth/ And intellect its wandering/To this and that and t'other thing." But if the Self does otherwise, that is the Self still then engrosses itself in sensuality, then it will not be able to release itself from the chain of (or "crime" of) births and deaths. Therefore the Soul urges the Self to renounce the life of sensuality and to engross itself in the beatific ultimate reality, so that it can disengage itself from the eternal chain of births and deaths: "Deliver from the crime of death and birth." The Soul's philosophy here reminds one of the philosophies of the Upanishads and that of Lord Buddha, which say that the chain of births and deaths is due to ignorance, and so when the soul acquires the wisdom of the ultimate reality, it gets released from the chain of births and deaths. The soul then becomes merged in the Absolute.

The "fourth stanza is undoubtedly difficult." (Dyson, 110). Here we find that the Self would not budge even an inch from its earlier stand: it would not abide by the call of the Soul to relinquish the sensuous earthly life of love and action. Rather it says that it is so much attracted to these that it would like to dive once more into the stream of births and deaths, or, rather, it will entangle itself once more in the chain of births and deaths. The Self of the poet tells his Soul that the sword (of life) was made by the famous sword-maker Montashigi or Bishu Osafumé Motoshigé who lived in Osafume in the era of Oei (1394-1428). This means that Montashigi made this sword about five hundred years ago. Flowers are etched in purple colour in the hilt of the sword: "about it lie/Flowers from I know not what embroidery—". These flowers are the symbol of the daily life of this earth as against the eternal night of the Absolute Soul (the Tower). The Self will not relinquish the daily life of the earth; contrarily, it wishes to commit the 'crime' (or sin)of taking birth and consequently suffer death, again and again, just as a soldier battles with a sword and never parts company with his sword: "And claim as by a soldier's right/A charter to commit the crime once more." Though Dyson said that the fourth stanza is "undoubtedly difficult", actually the fifth stanza is the most difficult among the five stanzas of Part I of the poem. However, in stanza v, to the obdurate stand of the Self, the Soul takes a more persuasive stand. The Soul says that the Absolute Soul is over-flowing with every desirable thing and when these things are poured on the mind of a man, he gets so much awe-struck and transported that he becomes "deaf and dumb and blind" to the things of the earth: "Such fullness in that quarter overflows/And falls into the basin of the mind/That man is stricken deaf and dumb and blind." The soul says that one cannot comprehend the Absolute Soul with intellect or cannot distinguish between what is happening in this world (*Is*) and what should actually happen in this world (*Ought*) with that intellect. Further, the Soul says that intellect cannot distinguish between the small soul ("knower") and the greater Soul ("Known"): For intellect no longer knows/Is from the *Ought, or Knower* from the *Known*—". The knower or the smaller soul has to die and thus has to renounce its earthly engagements in order to ascend to the Absolute Soul: "That is to say, ascends to Heaven;/Only the dead can be forgiven." But the smaller soul cannot perfectly describe the mystic state of its being when it is merged in the Absolute Soul, and therefore, the poet says that when the smaller soul tries to speak about that state, it becomes befuddled and dumb: "But when I think of that my tongue's a stone." The meaning of this stanza is not much clear, and even A.E. Dyson writes: "I find that I can do nothing but doodle mentally around this. Is Soul suggesting that the way of Self, which leads to a darkening of the senses (though darkness has been associated with Soul), leads also, by a paradox, to enlightenment? May be in Heaven, as in sensuous and sensual awareness of spirit, the distinctions between 'Is' and 'Ought', 'Knower' and 'Known' cancel out." (Dyson, 110).

The polemics between the Soul and the Self of the poet is dropped in Part II of the poem, where the Self of the poet speaks out its mind. It declares (or the poet declares) that it is not going to opt for the life of an ascetic for the "fullness" that it can derive by merging itself in the Absolute, rather, the Self is content with the "sweetness" that the life on earth has to offer, along with the "buffets" and the "slings and arrows of outrageous fortune." In stanza i of Part II, the Self of the poet says that an earth-bound being (man) may be blind to the mystic Absolute, but, yet, it enjoys the honey of life: "A living man is blind and drinks his drop." It knows that the affairs of the earth are as impure as the things of a ditch, and yet it likes to live on this earth, enduring the "toil of growing up;/The ignominy of boyhood; the distress/Of boyhood changing into man." It knows that man has to bear with all his own infirmities ("clumsiness"), and yet it will prefer the earthly life. In stanza ii of Part II, the Self further says that even when a boy continues to grow up as a full man, he is not free, because he has so many enemies. It says that man has to be defiled, disfigured, has to become malicious in the unwholesome environment of the earthly world. Man cannot escape this *fiat*, this design, of the world: "How in the name of Heaven can he escape/That defiling and disfigured shape/ The mirror of malicious eyes/Casts upon his eyes until at last/He thinks that shape must be his shape?" And, yet, the Self will not escape from this world, because it does not see any good in such escape, and because it will be satisfied with the "honour" even if that "honour" if to be had in this pernicious world: "And what's the good of an escape/If honour find him in the wintry blast?"

In stanza iii, the Self-expresses more emphatically its desire not to part company with the life of the earth. It will be content to live here over and over again, even if it has to live blindly in a ditch where frogs spawn. Even if one ignorant man batters another ignorant man, as it happens in this world, the Self will not leave this earth. The Self (or the poet) says that the most foul ditch is that in which a man has to suffer for loving a "proud woman" (reference to Maud Gonne). But, even if it has to suffer that kind of sufferance, yet it will not leave this earth but will to come here again and again. And, in the last stanza, the Self says that it will follow every action and every thought of this world and suffer its appointed fate with contentment, and will forgive itself its lot: "I am content to follow to its source/Every event in action or in thought;/Measure the lot; forgive myself the lot!" The Self says that when it will be able to cast away the pain and remorse arising out of its actions and thoughts of this world or of this life, it will be able to enjoy a great sweetness: "When such as I cast out remorse/ So great a sweetness flows into the breast." Then the Self will laugh and sing and enjoy everything as then everything will seem to be beautiful, enjoyable, happy and blessed: "We must laugh and we must sing,/We are blest by everything,/Everything we look upon is blest." The last line may remind one of the following lines in Alexander Pope's *Essay on Man*: "Whatever is, is good." The dialogue between the Soul and the Self recalls in our mind the Dialogues of Plato and the dialogues in some of the Upanishads, However, in this poem, the poet shows that he is now absolutely no more a poet of escape, as he once had been in his early years, but that he is now very much a down-to-earth poet.

38. Byzantium

This is one of the few very difficult poems of Yeats—difficult because of its compact imageries and meanings and scant suggestions for elaborate references. It was composed in September, 1930, and was first published in *Words for Music Perhaps and Other Poems* (1932). Yeats wrote a prose draft of this poem in his *Diary* (in 1930), which runs thus: "Subject for a poem. Death of a friend... Describe Byzantium as it is in the system towards the end of the first Christian millennium. A walking mummy. Flames at the street comers where the soul is purified, birds of hammered gold singing in the golden trees, in the harbour [dolphins] offering their backs to the wailing dead that they may carry them to Paradise." (Jeffares, 293). This note or draft and the following view of Yeats about this poem will go a long way in disentangling the knots of meanings of the poem. Yeats wrote: "In my late poems I have called it ['it' was an example of magnificence: and style, whether in literature or life, comes, I think, from excess, from that something over and above utility, which rings the heart'], that city where the Saints showed their wasted forms upon a background of gold mosaic, and an artificial bird sang upon a tree of gold in the presence of the Emperor; and in one poem ['Byzantium'] I have pictured the ghosts swimming, mounted upon dolphins, through the sensual sea, that they may dance upon its pavements." (Jeffares, 294). Yeats wrote that subjects like that in 'Byzantium' had been haunting him for a long time. He wrote about his view of 'Byzantium' also in *Vision:* "I think that in early Byzantium, and may be never before or since in recorded history, religious, aesthetic and practical life were one, that architect and artificers—though not, it may be, poets, for language had been the instrument of controversy and must have grown abstract—spoke to the multitude and the few alike. The painter, the mosaic worker, the worker in gold and silver, the illuminator of sacred books, were almost impersonal, almost perhaps without the consciousness of individual design, absorbed in their subject-matter and that the vision of a whole people. They could copy out of old Gospel books those pictures that seemed as sacred as the text, and yet weave all into a vast design, the work of many that seemed the work of one, that made building, picture, pattern, metal-work of rail and lamp, seem but a single image; and this vision, this proclamation of their invisible master, had the Greek nobility, Satan always the still half-divine Serpent, never the homed scarecrow of the didactic Middle Ages." (Jeffares, 294).

'Byzantium' has some affinity with 'Sailing to Byzantium' which Yeats wrote about four years ago (in August or September, 1926). "On 4 October [1930] Yeats wrote to Sturge Moor to tell him that 'Byzantium' originated from his criticism of 'Sailing to Byzantium' which had showed Yeats 'that the idea needed exposition'" (Jeffares, 294). But actually 'Byzantium' could not clarify the idea of 'Sailing to Byzantium', rather it became a new poem and more complicated at that. However, Daniel Albright introduces the poem thus: "This poem was partly inspired by Sturge Moore's letter on the inadequacy of 'Sailing to Byzantium': Moor was 'sceptical as to whether mere liberation from existence has any value or probability as a consummation. I prefer with Wittgenstein, whom I don't understand, to think that nothing at all can be said about ultimates, or reality in an ultimate sense.... Your *Sailing to Byzantium,* magnificent as the first three stanzas are, lets me down in the fourth, as such a goldsmith's bird isas much nature as a man's body, especially if it only sings like Homer and Shakespeare of what is past or passing or to come to Lords and Ladies' (...). Yeats replied that this objection 'showed me that the idea needed exposition' (...). Moore was alluding to the final proposition of Wittgenstein's *Tractatus* (1921). 'Whereof one cannot speak, thereof one must be silent'; and Yeats's 'Byzantium' pushes speech to its limit in order to point at the unspeakable. Such constructions as 'image, man or shade,/Shade more than man, more image than a shade'(..) hover among vagueness and frustrate the referentiality of language.

"This poem's treatment of pictures is as daring as its treatment of words. 'Sailing to Byzantium' proposed two models to describe the soul's condition after death — a glittering mosaic image of a saint and a golden bird; the mosaic saints are the agents of the poet's transformation, the golden bird is an eidolon of the transformed poet. 'Byzantium' offers a more elaborate guided tour of the afterlife—a mummy, a bird made metal, a self-sustaining flame, a statue—in the hope that a congeries of unnaturalness will somehow constitute the genuinely unearthly. Each of these entities seems at once a guide initiating the poet into further mysteries, and an experiment in defining the poet's own eerie shape after he is transfigured by death. Each thing defines, scorns, consumes, or assaults the natural, organic, physical world; amidst these violent assertions of the metaphysical, no image can constitute itself with any durability of precision. The poem presents a succession of fringe-images on the verge of indefiniteness." (Albright, 717-18).

BYZANTIUM

The unpurged images of day recede;
The Emperor's drunken soldiery are abed;
Night resonance recedes, night-walkers's song
After great cathedral gong;
A starlit or a moonlit dome disdains
All that man is,
All mere complexities,
The fury and the mire of human veins.

Before me floats an image, man or shade,
Shade more than man, more image than a shade;
For Hades' bobbin bound in mummy-cloth
May unwind the winding path;
A mouth that has no moisture and no breath
Breathless mouths may summon;
I hail the superman;
I call it death-in-life and life-in-death.

Miracle, bird or golden handiwork,
More miracle than bird or handiwork,
Planted on the star-lit golden bough,
Can like the cocks of Hades crow,
Or, by the moon embittered, scorn aloud
In glory of changeless metal
Common bird or petal
And all complexities of mire or blood.

At midnight on the Emperor's pavement flit
Flames that no faggot feeds, nor steel has lit,
Nor storm disturbs, flames begotten of flame,
Where blood-begotten spirits come
And all complexities of fury leave,
Dying into a dance,
An agony of trance,
An agony of flame that cannot singe a sleeve.

Astrade on the dolphin's mire and blood,
Spirit after spirit! The smithies break the flood,
The golden smithies of the Emperor!
Marbles of the dancing floor
Break bitter furies of complexity,

Those images that yet
Fresh images beget,
That dolphin-torn, that gong-tormented sea.

The poem is divided into five stanzas, each stanza consisting of eight lines. The rhyme scheme of the poem is a a b b c d d c. In stanza i, the poet describes the present state of Byzantium, the capital of the Eastern Section of the Holy Roman empire. He says that it is now nighttime in Byzantium, and so the "unpurged images" of the daytime are not to be found there. The images of the day time are filthy and evil, and therefore these are unpurged or unpurified. And now as it night, all the images are purified: "The unpurged images of day recede." The soldiers of the Emperor are now tired of keeping vigilance all day long, and so they have gone to bed. The dins and bustles of the daytime that continued till dusk are also no more to be heard. And even the casual song of a night-walker or prostitute and the sound of the cathedral gong are not to be heard. Therefore, the night is absolutely silent and peaceful: "The Emperor's drunken soldiery are abed;/Night resonance recedes, night walkers' song/After great cathedral gong". F.A.C. Wilson in his *W.B. Yeats and Tradition* (1958), "regards the gong as being a warning sign, an intimation of the nearness of death." (Jeffares, 295). Therefore, we may construe that the poet here wants to say that now at night all the mortals are asleep, and soon their souls will depart their "mortal coil". At this hour of the night, the poet looks at the high-rise and therefore proud dome of a Church. According to Jeffares, this is "the dome of Santa Sophia or Hagia Sophia, the Church that the Emperor Justinian I (483-565; ruled 527-565) had constructed (532-7) in Byzantium." (Jeffares, 295). The dome is dimly visible in the light of the moon or of the stars, and it seems to the poet that the dome is despising all the human beings that are sleeping under its canopy: "A starlit or a moonlit dome disdains/ All that man is." It seems to the poet that the dome is looking down upon the complex human condition of the earth, that is full of "fury" and "mire". The word "mire" here may mean the impurity of the body of a man, that is subject to births and deaths. The word "fury" may mean the bickering and wrangles amongst human beings. The fury and the mire constitute the complexities of the earthly life. The word "complexities" may also mean the fact that man is not only the body but also the spirit, and hence the poet may mean that man is a complex being. According to Jeffares, the poet compares the human body with mire because, according to the Christian belief, the body is composed of clay. Again, the "fury" may mean the passions of human beings, that reside in the blood. Further, the human being is ever in tension between his spiritual nature and his earthly nature, and this gives rise to the complexity within him: "All mere complexities./The fury and the mire of human veins." Stallworthy has found suggestion of this complexity of the human condition also in Blake's poem 'London' which, he says, was, perhaps, in Yeats's mind when he composed these lines (Jeffares, 295):

> The hapless soldier's sigh
> Runs in blood down palace walls.
>
> But most through midnight streets I hear
> How the youthful harlot's curse
> Blasts the newborn infant's tear.

Edward Engelberg further suggests that in the first and in the second stanzas of 'Byzantium', there is an echo of Dante's Purgatorio, viii. (Jeffares, 295).

In stanza ii, the poet says that he is now seeing an image which is, as if, floating in the air and seeming to be either a man or a shade: "Before me floats an image, man or shade,/Shade more than man, more image than a shade." The "shade" or "image" refers to the half-incarnation of the soul after it disentangles itself from the gross body. Yeats wrote about this in his note on his play *The Dreaming of the Bones*: "the worldwide belief that the dead dream back for a certain time, through the more personal thoughts and deeds of life.... The Shade is said to fade out at last, but the Spiritual Being does not fade, passing on to other states of existence after it has attained a spiritual state, of which the surroundings and aptitudes of early life are a correspondence." (Jeffares, 295). The "shade" in the poem, therefore, perhaps, means the dead man's memories of his past life. Yeats believed that the spiritual element of a human being may assume, after the death of the body, a new body, attracting to itself by its inherent force the minutest elements of the gross things of the earth, and thus can take the similitude of an incarnate personality. In *Mythologies* (1959) Yeats wrote: "The vehicle of the human soul is what used to be called the animal spirits, and Henry More quotes from Hyppocrates this sentence: 'The mind of man is... not nourished from meats and drinks from the belly, but by a clear luminous substance that redounds by separation from the blood.' These animal spirits fill up all parts of the body and makes up the body of air, as certain writers of the seventeenth century have called it. The soul has a plastic power, and can after death, or during life, should the vehicle leave the body for a while, mould it to any shape it will by an act of imagination, though the more unlike to the habitual that shape is, the greater the effort. To living and dead alike, the purity and abundance of the animal spirits are a chief power. The soul can mould from these an apparition clothed as if in life, and make it visible by showing it to our mind's eye, or by building into its substance certain principles drawn from the body of a medium till it is as visible and tangible as any other object. ... Our animal spirits or vehicles are but, as it were, a condensation of the vehicle of *Anima Mundi*, and give substance to its images in the faint materialisation of our common thought, or more grossly when a ghost is our visitor." (Jeffares, 296).

The poet compares this "image" or "shade" with "Hades' bobbin." Bobbin is a spool around which thread is wound, and, in the same way, thinks the poet, the temporal elements are wound round the soul. Yeats believed that "The soul has a plastic power, and can after death.... mould it[s vehicle] to any shape it will by an act of imagination'(...), and the mummy was often a convenient image. In his account of the dead soul's self- purgation, Yeats wrote that at one point 'the whole cloth is unwound.'" (Albright, 718-19). The image or shade has a reference to Plato's mythology of Er in his *Republics.* G.R.S. Mead in *Echoes from the Gnosis* compared the soul with a bobbin. It may be that Yeats followed the account of the soul made by Mead. Hades or Pluto is the lord of the underworld where the spirits, after the death of the body, stay for some time. In the third and fourth lines of the second stanza, the poet presumes that the visible shade has come out of the underworld, being covered with clothes, like mummies. The poet presumes that the apparition will disclose the history of its former life ("unwind the winding path"). According to mythologies, the spirit of a man, after death, enlivens the memories of the former life and thus suffers the pains of the former life's sinful acts, and thus gets purified. So the poet presumes that the particular ghost or image or shade will recall the memories of its former life: "For Hades' bobbin bound in mummy-cloth/ May unwind the winding path." The ghost seems to have a dry mouth, as all ghosts do have; and it does not respirate, dead as its body is. But the poet says that even such a breathless ghost can summon its memories. He says that if a man with both a body and a spirit be called a human being, then this ghost without the body may be called a super human being. The poet says that this superhuman ghost is recalling its former life's sinful misdeeds and thus undergoing pains, and so it must have a sort of life; but as it is experiencing the excruciating pains while recalling its former misdeeds, it must also experience a sort of death, while in its recreated life: "I hail the superhuman;/ call it death-in-life and life-in-death." Stallworthy and Daniel Albright believe that while writing the foregoing two lines, Yeats had the Coleridgean image of the following two lines:

> The Nightmare Life-in-Death was she,
> Who thicks man's blood with cold.

Yeats further says that life and death are not two separate phenomena, but are two aspects of the same thing. He had always kept in mind the saying of Heraclitus: 'God and man die each other's life, live each other's death.' So, if we believe in Heraclitus's saying, we must say that Yeats very appropriately equated 'death-in-life' with 'life-in-death'.

In stanza iii, the vision of the ghost or "shade" immediately transports the poet to the imagery of the ancient Byzantium. The poet sees a mircale: he sees that an actual bird or a bird made of hammered gold is sitting on a golden bough under a starry sky. "The bird may have [more] symbolic meaning: it might be related to the 'one white fowl wearing a crown' on the highest bough of the Tree of life which was seen by a young Irish woman in trance." (Jeffares, 297-98). Yeats uses the image of the golden bird, a handiwork, as a symbol of the ancient artistic glory of Byzantium: "Miracle, bird or golden handiwork,/More miracle than bird or handiwork,/Planted on the starlit golden bough." According to mythology, ghosts produce sounds like the crowing of cocks. The poet remembers that the cocks of Hades wake up the spirits of the underworld by crowing. He thinks that tonight, when darkness and silence pervades everywhere, the cocks of Hades have summoned up the ghosts or spirits of the underworld to come on the plains of Byzantium. But the poet is not certain about this. He says that the cocks, rather, may be scorning the eternal glory of the golden bird. The golden bird, here, represents the permanence of art which is above the "complexities of mire or blood." The codes of Hades are suffering as impermanent beings, and so they are jealous of the golden bird which represents permanence (or the permanence of art). In the moon light the golden bird seems to be boasting for its glory and this, as if, is intensifying the jealousy of the cocks of Hades, and so they are suffering bitterness in them, and scorning the golden bird loudly: "Or, by the moon embittered, scorn aloud/In glory of changeless metal/Common bird or petal/And all complexities of mire or blood."

In stanza iv, the poet resorts to an image in Homer's *The Odyssey* where Odysseus visits Hades. As soon as Odysseus reaches Hades, he is surrounded by the spirits of the underworld who live on the blood of sacrificed animals ("blood-begotten spirits"). Gwendolen Murphy described these "blood-begotten spirits" as human ghosts. Ellmann agrees with him and further says that these human ghosts, according to mythology, have to be purified by fire before their release from the confinement in Hades. Yeats wrote, in a note for *A Vision*, about these phenomena, two years before writing 'Byzantium': "At first we are subject to Destiny... but the point in the Zodaic where the whirl becomes a sphere once reached, we may escape from the constraint of our nature and from that of the external things, entering upon a state where all fuel has become flame, where there is nothing but the state itself, nothing to constrain it or end it. We attain it always in the creation or enjoyment of a work of art, but that moment though eternal in the Daimon passes from us because it is not an attainment of our whole being..." (Jeffares, 298). In this stanza, the poet says that in the dead of night, the spirits of the underworld gather on the Emperor's mosaic pavement in Byzantium. On the pavement, there is a mysterious fire which is neither produced by striking steel nor is supplied with any fuel, nor can the fire be put out by any storm. This fire, therefore, resembles that of the Purgatory: "At midnight on the Emperor' s pavement flit/Flames that no faggot feeds, nor steel has lit,/Nor storm disturbs, flames begotten of flame." As this fire is lighted, the "blood-begotten spirits" rush to it to singe themselves in order to burn out their "complexities" of births and deaths, and their passions: "Where blood-begotten spirits come/ And all complexities of fury leave." The spirits dance in the fire, and thus get themselves purified through the sufferance of agony in the fire. This is a mysterious fire because though it burns all impurities, it does not burn anything else, not even singe anything else — not even a sleeve: "Dying into a dance,/An agony of trance,/An agony of flame that cannot singe a sleeve."

In the last stanza, the poet refers us to the mythology according to which spirits, after their purification through the "flames begotten of flames", sail towards Byzantium across the sea of time, sitting on the back of a dolphin and keeping a leg against each side of the dolphin ("Astradle"). Mrs. Strong, in *her Apotheosis and the After life*, says that "the dolphin is an 'emblem of the soul or its transit', and states 'The dead man — or his soul — might be conveyed thither [after life] by boat, or on the back of a sea monster, a dolphin, sea-horse or triton. The dolphins form 'a mystic escort of the dead' to the island of the Blest." (Jeffares, 298). We may recall here that in Hindu mythology also there is a belief that the soul, after leaving this world, has to cross the river *Vaitarani*, holding the tail of an ox, so as to reach the paradise. However, the poet is seeing that spirit after spirit is coming to the shore of Byzantium, on dolphins' backs. The sea across which the dolphins are swimming is tumultuous with high waves.

But the smiths—the gold-smiths of the Emperor, —are breaking the flood or the sea. Even the marbles of the Emperor's pavement are being broken by the smiths. To explain the word 'break', as used here, Harold Bloom writes: "To break is to divide, but to divide is to make, whether the divisions be of human fury, images, or waves, so that *Byzantium* 'break' seems to mean both 'mar' and 'create'. (Bloom, 392). The smiths of the Emperor break the furies of complexities to prepare the spirits for reaching *Byzantium*: "The smithies break the flood,/The golden smithies of the Emperor! /Marbles of the dancing floor/Break bitter furies of complexity". After the breaking up of the images or recollections of the spirits of their previous lives, the spirits or ghosts get new images, and after this the dolphins are no more necessary for crossing the fearful sea: "Those images that yet/Fresh images beget,/That dolphin-torn, that gong-tormented sea." According to Daniel Albright, 'That dolphin-torn, that gong-tormented sea' means "natural life, tortured by the conflicting impulses of sexuality (suggested by the dolphins) and spirituality (suggested by the gong...) — in other words, of Self and of Soul." (Albright, 721).

Harold Bloom compares this poem with *Kubla Khan* of Coleridge and *Ode on a Grecian Urn* of Keats. According to him, the difficulty and ambiguity of this poem is due to Yeats himself. He writes: "Yeats is responsible for the poem's ambiguity, since the central image, the dome, is starlit or moonlit. The poem's phase therefore is 1 or 15, Phase 1 being the death before life, and Phase 15 the full perfection of images." (Bloom, 384). How, then, can there be purgatorial travail? However, Bloom beautifully exposes the meaning of the theme of this poem: "*Byzantium* is, among much else, an elegy for the poetic self, and appears to have at least partly elegiac in its genesis. As Shelley's *Adonais* is more Shelley's elegy for himself than one for Keats, so *Byzantium* is *A Vision* granted to Yeats to help warm his back into life after a loss of being, but consciously for a little time only. Like *Adonais*, *Byzantium* is a high song of poetic self-recognition in the shadow of mortality, and is deliberately purgatorial and Dantesque in its situation and imagery." (Bloom, 384). It is purgatorial, because it emphasises the need for suffering (remember T.S. Eliot) to get purified so as to be able to realise the pure self or soul. In the span of only forty lines, Yeats, in this poem, has succeeded in presenting a vast philosophy with the help of a lot of beautiful images. The poem, therefore, justly stands out as one of the most beautiful poems of Yeats: Balachandra Rajan complements this poem with these words: "The magnificent last line which guides the poem into its stormy peace suggests through the embattled force of 'torn' and 'tormented' how man's life is split asunder by forces which he cannot evade but to which he cannot surrender without denying his nature. Man remains suspended between flesh and spirit, and cannot choose either without ceasing to be man. The conflict which rends him is the sign that he is human." (Rajan, 145).

39. Crazy Jane Talks with the Bishop

This is one among several poems that were first published under the general title *Words for Music Perhaps and Other Poems* (1932), but afterwards were published in *The Winding Stair and Other Poems* (1933). It was written in November, 1931. Yeats thought of writing a series of poems on the theme of the relation between the spirit (or mind) and the body, and to give these poems the group name *Words for Music Perhaps.* In the spring of 1929, while he was convalescing, he wrote: "life returned to me as an impression of the uncontrollable energy and daring of the great creator; it seemed to me that for journalist and criticism, all that evasion and explanation, the world would be torn in pieces. I wrote... almost all that group of poems, called in memory of those exultant weeks Words for Music Perhaps." (Albright, 730). Daniel Albright writes that these "poems, then, try to eliminate every prosaic component, 'evasion and explanation'; by becoming expressions of sheer force, unimpeded emotion, they approach the condition of music." (Albright, 730). And on 2nd March, 1929, Yeats wrote to Mrs. Shakespeare that he was "writing *Twelve poems for music*—have done three of them (and two other poems)—no[t] so much that they may be sung as that I may define their kind of emotion to myself. I want them to be all emotion and all impersonal." (Jeffares, 307). On 13th September, 1929, Yeats again wrote to her that he wanted to finish "the book of thirty poems for music I am more than half through. 'For Music' is only a name, nobody will sing them." (Jeffares, 307). Still again, and before this, on 17th August, 1929, he wrote to Mrs. Shakespear "that the 'Crazy Jane' poems and the little group of love poems that follow are, I think, exciting and strange. Sexual abstinence fed their fire—I was ill and yet full of desire. They sometimes came out of the greatest mental excitement I am capable of." *(ibid).*

Crazy Jane was not the real name of the woman Yeats here refers to. However, she was known as 'Cracked Mary' and was "'the local satirist and really a terrible one' (Yeats wrote). Therefore the title of the collection of these poems when first printed was 'Cracked Mary'.... [She] lives in a cottage near Gort. She loves her flower garden — She has just sent Lady Gregory some flowers in spite of the season and [has] an amazing power of audacious speech. One of her great performance is a description of how the meanness of a Gort shopkeeper's wife over the price of a glass of porter made her so despair of the human race that she got drunk. The incidents of the drunkenness are of an epic significance." (Jeffares, 307). Daniel Albright writes to introduce the poems of *Words for Music Perhaps:* "This is the first of two sequences appended to *The Winding Stair and Other Poems.* The title suggests that Yeats intended these poems as texts for songs; but few composers have so far risen to this challenge, and in fact Yeats himself explained that he gave this title 'no[t] so much that they may be sung as that 1 may define their kind of emotion to myself. I want them to be all emotion and all impersonal' (...); "'For Music' is only a name, nobody will sing them" (...). Many of these poems do have song-like features—refrains, short lines, stanzaic construction, easy vocabulary—but their 'musical' character lies principally in their emotional directness and their impersonality. Large, free floating emotions (such as lust, anxiety, self-confidence, loneliness, protectiveness, madness) build around themselves extremely simple masks. These emotions are Moods, in Yeats's technical sense (...) — disembodied intensities that, instead of embedding themselves in Yeats's particular life, remain disembodied, little connected to individuals. Here we have no tower, no Japanese sword, no Maud Gonne, nothing from Yeats's private cache of symbols; instead we have vagrants and crackpots, people with little steadiness of character, little history, people who are nothing except vehicles of songs." (Albright, 729-30).

CRAZY JANE TALKS WITH THE BISHOP

I met the Bishop on the road
And much said he and I.
'Those breasts are flat and fallen now,
Those veins must soon be dry;
Live in a heavenly mansion,
Not in some foul sty.

'Fair and foul are nearofkin,
And fair needs foul,' I cried.
'My friends are gone, but that's a truth
Nor grave nor bed denied,
Learned in bodily lowliness
And in the heart's pride.

'A woman can be proud and stiff
When on love intent;

But Love has pitched his mansion in
The place of excrement;
For nothing can be sole or whole
That has not been rent.'

The poem is divided into three stanzas, each stanza comprising of six lines. In the poem Crazy Jane talks in the first person and says that she met the bishop on the road and talked with him. The bishop advised her to part with her abject life of physical love. He told her that she had grown old and lost her physical attraction: her bosom now was not pyramidal, and it seemed that she would soon become decrepit: "Those breasts are flat and fallen now,/Those veins must soon be dry." Therefore, the bishop advised her to take recourse to the spiritual pursuits, and to reject the despicable life of a lout: "Live in a heavenly mansion,/Not in some foul sty." But Crazy Jane would not take the advice of the bishop. She told him that what she was doing might be foul, and what he advised her to do might be fair, but fair and foul are complementary; rather, even fair needs foul. By 'fair' is to be meant the spiritual path, and 'foul' the satisfaction of bodily desires.

In the second stanza, Crazy Jane tells the bishop that man's perfection lies in the satisfaction of both the spiritual and the bodily desires—the two complementary desires: "Fair and foul are near of kin,/And fair needs foul', I cried." Crazy Jane told the bishop that her young friends, for whom she bore physical love, are no more available now, but then she could still find bodily enjoyments, and she would still find her grave: "My friends are gone, but that's truth/Nor grave nor bed denied." She still desires to be learned in the lowly and bodily appetites and their satisfactions and also in the exultations of her spiritual elevation: "Learned in bodily lowliness/ And in the heart's pride."

In the third stanza, the poet expresses his own opinion about the necessity of both physical love and spiritual love or enlightenment. Love, he says, is divine, but the divinity of love abides when the spiritual love finds its consummation in the bodily love. He says that a woman can boast of pure love and abhor the carnal love: "A woman can be proud and stiff/When on love intent." But the poet says that perfect love, or love in its entirety is not possible without the accompaniment of the body (reference to the pudenda). To warrant his view, the poet says that love resides at the place from where the body releases its wastage (reference to pudenda): "But love has pitched his mansion in/ The place of excrement." Lastly the poet says that love in its entirety can be had only when the body is torn asunder. Here, he, perhaps, insinuates to the act of cohabitation: "For nothing can be sole or whole/That has not been rent." Thus the poet concludes by saying that the physical chapter of love-making is not to be despised, rather it should be understood that it fulfils the whole project of love-making — of making both physical and spiritual love.

LAST POEMS (1939)

New Poems was published in 1938 and *Last Poems* in 1939. *New Poems* was, actually, the last volume of poems arranged by the poet himself, which the poet saw as published before his death. But before his death, Yeats made a list of poems that were not till then published. Curtis Bradford published these poems under the convenient title *Last Poems*. In *New Poems*, the poet presented tragic joy, but in *Last Poems* he shows not the proper tragic joy, but an approach-way to it. Here the poet shows "truth so profoundly incarnated itself that it became ragged, excrementitious, sexy." (Albright, 808). Daniel Albright writes about *Last Poems*: "An important feature of this volume is its recapitulatory character: many of Yeats's favourite characters come out for a final bow. However, they are often strangely humbled: Cuchulain has become a seamstress (in 'Cuchulain Comforted'); Oisin has gone to a celestial old-folks' home, where the goddess Niamh appears to be little more than a barmaid (in 'News for the Delphic Oracle'); Maud Gonne has withered into a bronze head. (...) This is another aspect of the same tendency to embodiment: even the noblest, the most unearthly of beings must show itself in an unmistakably human body; and even the feeblest body, even the body of a seventy-three-year-old poet whose health had never been good, must show itself to have a transcendental referent." (Albright, 808).

40. The Circus Animals' Desertion

If we like, we may divide poetry into two categories: poetry of self-expression or personal poetry, and selfless poetry or impersonal poetry. In his early years, Yeats wrote mostly personal poetry, but as he advanced in years, the stint of personality gradually faded away from his poetry. In his last phase, he was in favour of deconstructing the self in his poetry, and urged other poets to follow his example. Daniel Albright writes: "In his old age Yeats often urged the artist to express himself, not as he actually is, but in some simplified and intensified form: the poet 'is never the bundle of accident and incoherence that sits down to breakfast; he has been reborn as an idea, something intended, complete... he is more type than man'; 'all that is personal soon rots; it must be packed in ice or salt... If I wrote of personal love or sorrow in free verse, or in any rhythm that left it unchanged, amid all its accidence, I would be full of self-contempt because of my egotism and indiscretion (....). This is the final development of the doctrine of the Mask: the poet presents less an anti-self than a stylized self, made shapely in conformity to old principles of verbal form." (Albright, 840).

But, strangely, in some of the poems of his last years, Yeats himself wrote contrary to his vow. 'The Circus Animals' Desertion' is one such poem. Here he "wished not only to construct such a self but to deconstruct it, to reduce it to the 'bundle of accident and incoherence' from which it sprang... In this poem Yeats's myth of his identity, so carefully formulated through his career, breaks down into naked self-expression." (Albright, 840). We do not know the exact date of the composition of this poem, but we know this only that it was written, probably, between November, 1937, and September, 1938. The idea of the circus, A. Norman Jeffares says, may have come to the poet from the drawings and paintings that his brother Jack Yeats made for the Cuala Press.

THE CIRCUS ANIMALS' DESERTION

I

I sought a theme and sought for it in vain,
I sought it daily for six weeks or so.
May be at last being but a broken man
I must be satisfied with my heart, although
Winter and summer till old age began
My circus animal were all on show,
Those stilted boys, that burnished chariot,
Lion and woman and the Lord knows what.

II

What can I but enumerate old themes,
First that sea-rider Oisin led by the nose
Through three enchanted islands, allegorical dreams,
Vain gaiety, vain battle, vain repose,
Themes of the embittered heart, or so it seems,
That might adorn old songs or courtly shows;
But what cared I that set him on to ride,
I, starved for the bosom of his fairy bride.

And then a counter-truth filled out its play,
The Countess Cathleen was the name I gave it.

She, pity-crazed, had given her soul away
But masterful Heaven had intervened to save it.
I thought my dear must her own soul destroy
So did fanaticism and hate enslave it,
And this brought forth a dream and soon enough
This dream itself had all my thought and love.

And when the Fool and Blind Man stole the bread
Cuchulain fought the ungovernable sea;
Heart mysteries there, and yet when all is said
It was dream itself enchanted me:
Character isolated by a deed
To engross the present and dominate memory.
Players and painted stage took all my love
And not those things that they were emblems of.

III

Those masterful images because complete
Grew in pure mind but out of what began?
A mound of refuse or the sweepings of a street,
Old kettles, old bottles, and a broken can.
Old iron, old bones, old rags, that raving slut
Who keeps the till. Now that my ladder's gone
I must lie down where all the ladders start
In the foul rag and bone shop of the heart.

The poem is divided into three Parts. In the first Part, the poet says that he was seeking after some theme to write poetry daily for as long as six weeks, but could not find one. This was really a fact, for Yeats himself wrote about the origin of this poem in a letter to Dorothy Wellesley: "For five weeks I could not write a line, and then the poem came and a new mass of themes." (Albright, 840). From this Yeats could realise that "We cannot discover our subject-matter by deliberate intellect." *(ibid).* After six weeks' hibernation, the poet, on a sudden, when he was despairing for lack of a theme, decided to concentrate on his own heart: "l sought a theme and sought for it in vain,/I sought it daily for six weeks orso./May be at last being but a broken man/I must be satisfied with my heart." The poet saw within his heart multifarious jejune poetic symbols and techniques, which he calls "circus animals." According to Daniel Albright, the "circus animals" are "poetic themes and devices that reliably please an audience, somewhat overfamiliar to the elderly poet who has long employed them." (Albright,

841). The poet compares these hackneyed images and techniques with the stilted boys, burnished chariots, lions and women of a circus party — all those that contribute to the enjoyment of witnessing a circus show. The "burnished chariot" may mean Cuchulain's chariot of war, and "Lion and woman" may refer to Maud Gonne, for Yeats called her 'Halflion, half child'.

Part II of the poem comprises three stanzas. In the first stanza, the poet is recalling his old themes of poetry, one by one. Firstly, he recalls the sea- rider Oisin, who, being lured by the goddess Niamh, did "gallop over the sea to three false paradises, each an attempt to extrapolate partial pleasure into total bliss." (Albright, 841). Niamh fell in love with Oisin and kidnapped him and rode across the sea on a horse, holding Oisin by herself: "that sea-rider Oisin led by the nose." Oisin, the hero is here reduced to the ponies of the circus. However, Niamh thus led Oisin through three enchanted or charmed islands that were raising their heads out of the sea. In a letter of 6th February, 1889, Yeats wrote to Katharine Tynan: "There are three incompatible things which man is always seeking—infinite feeling, infinite battle, infinite repose—hence the three islands." (Jeffares, 425). These islands are the allegorical dreams of man: "Through three enchanted islands, allegorical dreams,/Vain gaily, vain battle, vain repose." These three are the themes of the frustrated heart—themes which are appropriate for old songs or courtly melodrama. But the poet desired not the melodramatic poetry, but carnal satisfaction: "But what cared I that set him onto ride, I, starved for the bosom of his fairy bride." Daniel Albright writes: "the poet regards the poem as a gaudy sublimation of his wayward sexual desire." (Albright, 841).

In the second stanza of Part II, the poet recalls the "counter-truth" of his play *The Countess Cathleen.* This "counter-truth" or dream is the dream of Maud Gonne who, in her real life, resembled the legendary Countess Cathleen. Countess Cathleen sold her soul to the Devil, like the German legendary hero Faust, not to know the unknown and the unknowable, but "to feed the populace of Gonegal during a famine (...)." (Albright, 841- 42). Maud Gonne is "pity-crazed" because she was all sympathy for all. Due to her extreme concern for her countrymen, she was about to be destroyed but for the help of the heaven: "And then a counter-truth filled out its play,/The Countess Cathleen was the name I gave it,/She, pity-crazed, had given her soul away/But masterful Heaven had intervened to save it." A. Norman Jeffares here writes: "the Countess was like Yeats's early interpretation of Maud Gonne's character. He told her the after they had met in London in 1891 (the year he first proposed marriage to her) he had come to understand the tale of a woman selling her soul to buy bread for her starving people as symbol of all souls who lose their peace or fineness of soul or beauty of spirit in political service, but chiefly as a symbol of her soul that seemed to him incapable of rest. In the play two agents of the Devil come to Ireland in a time of famine (Maud Gonne had become ill through overstrain aiding in relief work among the peasants in Donegal who were threatened with famine) and take advantage of the starvation of the peasants to offer to buy their souls for gold. The Countess Cathleen sacrifices her goods to get money for food for her people. She is about to sell her soul when the poet Kevin (Aleel) tries to stop her, but in vain." (Jaffares, 425).

The poet thought that due to her extreme political fanaticism and her extreme hatred for the enemies of Ireland — the two things that enslaved her soul—Maud Gonne ("my dear") might be destroyed: "I thought my dear must her own soul destroy/So did fanaticism and hate enslave it." The poet was so much engrossed in the thought about Maud's danger and her possible means of safety that this thought itself, as if, became an object of love: "And this brought forth a dream and soon enough/This dream itself had all my thought and love."

In the third stanza of Part II, the poet recalls the memory of Cuchulain ("the Fool") and King Conchubar ("Blind Man"). Daniel Albright writes about the Fool and Blind Man that these are "characters in *On Baile's Strand* (1904), respectively representing strength and wisdom (or body and soul); they feed themselves by collaborating on minor thefts. The Fool is a parody of the hero Cuchulain, and the Blind Man a parody of the crafty High King, Conchubar, who binds Cuchulain to his service. Yeats may mention these shadow-relations here because they hint at the farce latent in high tragedy. In the mythology *of A Vision,* the Fool came to represent the *antithetical* gyre and the Blind Man the *primary* — 'Li fe drifts between a fool and a blind man/To the end, and nobody can know his end.'" (Albright, 842). Yeats recalls the exploits of Cuchulain who, being enraged on account of killing his own son *incognito*, fought endlessly, charmed as he was, against the high-rise waves of the "ungovernable sea." Bradford speculates that the correct terms here would be "invulnerable tide." However, these exploits of Cuchulain are a mystery to the poet: "Heart mysteries there." Daniel Albright here writes: "Yeats might have found the legend of Cuchulain relevant to his personal life in a number of ways; for example, Yeats struggled for years against his own father's rationalism and scepticism — they once quarrelled so violently that John Butler Yeats 'broke the glass in a picture with the back of my head.'" (Albright, 843).

The poet stops recalling his memories on a sudden and realises that all these recollections are but dreams, and so looks the reality in the face: "Heart mysteries there, and yet when all is said/It was dream itself enchanted me." A. Norman Jeffares says that here there "may be a reference to Yeats's personal life after John MacBride married Maud Gonne in 1903. He took up the management of the Abbey Theatre from 1902 to 1910." (Jeffares, 426). The poet now understands that all those characters [of Oisin, Countess Cathleen, Cuchulain, Conchubar and such others] concentrated in their deeds only, and they were isolated from the reality, were all abstractions. Such abstract characters enchanted us only momentarily and then remained in the nook of our memories. The poet wants to tell us that "such concentration, such abstraction from mundane life, are slightly sinister, famishing." (Albright, 843). The poet recalls that he had been engrossed till now in the outer show and not in the inner spirit; not in the real thing, but only in the symbols thereof: "Players and painted stage took all my love/And not those things that they were emblem of." Daniel Albright comments on these two lines: "the sensuous charms of the spectacle seduce the poet away from its inner meaning, its psychological truth—the vehicle overwhelms the tenor.... In his last essay on the drama, Yeats repeated Matthew Arnold's complaint in his 1853 Preface against psychological dramas, dramas of passive suffering: "I had begun to get rid of everything that is not, whether in lyric or dramatic poetry, in some sense character in action... I delight in action men... I would have poetry turn its back upon all that modish curiosity, psychology' (...). But Yeats here suggests that the psychology of the playwright is the truest theme of his plays." (Albright, 843).

In Part III of the poem, the poet says that his "masterful images" (of Oisin, Cuchulain, etc. and other beautiful images) originated and grew complete, rounded, in his pure mind, feeding on his blood, i.e., on the "most grotesque matter." The poet, perhaps, means to say that his "masterful images" were created with the gross realities of his own life: "Old kettles, old bottles, and a broken can,/Old iron, old bones, old rags." And the poet used to use the common and passionate speech, like that of the "raving slut", in his poetry, to make it more passionate and enjoyable. The poet is now old and decrepit, and feels frustrated. Once he climbed upwards from the dry-as-dust reality with the ladder of his romantic imagination. But now all his romanticism is gone, and so he determines to remain fastened tightly to reality: "Now that my ladder's gone/I must lie down where all the ladders start/In the foul rag and bone of the heart." Daniel Albright writes that the "rag and bone stop" is "Yeats's most abject term for the *Anima Mundi*, the imagination's storehouse of images, now located in a private slum. Yeats once thought that his symbols—the matter of his art — were taken from some celestial public domain; but now he has come to agree with Carlyle, who argued in *Sartor Resartus* (1831) that symbols were earthly, indeed subject to decay: 'are not the tatters and rags of superannuated worn-out symbols (in this Rag-fair of a World) dropping off everywhere...? But Yeats here speaks less of the rot of used-up symbols than of their messy origins." (Albright, 844). However, Balachandra Rajan summarises the theme of the poem thus: "*The Circus Animals' Desertion* uses the trappings of *High Talk but* this time the stilts and the ladders which might have replaced the stilts are gone. The circus animals, the trained performers of poetic language, had all been 'on show' till 'old age began'; now that they have departed, we are driven back from the dream to the dream's origins. The themes of the poet are themes of the 'embittered heart' or, in a more telling phrase, 'heart mysteries'; but it is the dream itself, the shape and the life of the art work, the deed which isolates and breaks open character, to which the artist gives his 'thought and love'. The circus animals, the 'players and painted stage', are more attractive than the truths of which they are emblems." (Rajan, 181-82).

41. Politics

The poem was written on 23rd May, 1938, and was first published in *Atlantic Monthly*. It was written as a reply to an article, 'Public Speech and Private Speech in Poetry' by the American poet Archibald MacLeish, published in *yale Review* in the spring of 1938. In a letter of 24th May, 1938, Yeats wrote to Dorothy Wellesley: "There has been an article upon my work in the *Yale Review*, which is the only article on the subject which has not bored me for years. It commends me above other modern poets because my language is "public". That word which I had not thought of myself is a word I want. Your language in 'Fire' is public, so is that of every good ballad. (...). It goes on to say that, owing to my age and my relation to Ireland, I was unable to use this "public" language on what it evidently considered the right public material, politics. The enclosed little poem is my reply." (Jeffares, 426). Further, Daniel Albright writes about this poem: "Its placement at the end of Yeats's last volume of poems makes it a kind of valediction: and it fulfils this role, first by dismissing every topical theme in favour of the most universal, and second by its deliberate appeal to one of the oldest and most famous lyrics in modern English, the anonymous 'Westron Wind': 'Westron winde, when wilt thou blow,/The smalle raine downe can raine?/Christ if my love were in my arms,/And I in my bed againe.'" (Albright, 844-45).

POLITICS

'In our time the destiny of man presents its meanings in Political terms.' — *Thomas Mann*

How can I that girl standing there,
My attention fix
On Roman or on Russian
Or on Spanish politics,
Yet here's travelled man that knows
What he talks about,
And there's a politician
That has both read and thought,
And maybe what they say is true
Of war and war's alarms,
But O that I were young again
And held her in my arms.

The poet is in a dilemma whether he should fix his attention on fleeting and particular events or things, such as Roman. Russian or Spanish politics, or on the universal theme of love. He is in a dilemma whether to follow the appeals of the instincts, or to follow the persuasions of intellect. He says that there are wise men who, perhaps, know everything of everything, and there are politicians who can tell about approaching wars and their consequences. But the poet is not at all interested in these particular events, rather he is enamoured of the fascinating beauty of the young girl standing there. The poet means to say that particular worldly things may draw our attention only temporarily, but universal, eternal and transcendental things, like love, will ever attract mankind.

Chapter 7

A General Evaluation of Yeats's Poetry

It is not easy to measure the greatness of Yeats as a poet. He wrote for so long and wrote so much in so many ways that one often finds oneself in a labyrinth after pursuing Yeats for some time. Yet, if one wants to estimate the greatness of the poet, perhaps, one should better keep in mind what his contemporary and a great poet, Ezra Pound, wrote about him in his *Pavannes and Divagations:*

> Neath Ben Bulben's buttock lies
> Bill Yeats, a poet twoice the soize
> Of William Shakespeare, as they say
> Down Bally Killywuchlin way.

Pound held Yeats in high estimation as a poet and so once he went to Yeats to learn how to write modern poetry. Pound wrote about Yeats: "... I can only say that Mr. Yeats's vitality is quite unimpaired and that I dare say he'll do a good deal; and that up to date no one has shown any disposition to supersede him as the best poet in England, or any likelihood of doing so for some time..." Yeats is undoubtedly the greatest poet of Ireland, and one of the greatest poets of the world. Daniel Albright writes in the Introduction to his edition of Yeats's collected poems: "Yeats's size is difficult to measure. Pound's mean parody of 'Under Ben Bulben' suggests that Yeats appears to be twice the size of Shakespeare only because Ireland is a quarter the size of England. Today Ireland is not a small country — such modern Irishmen as James Joyce, Samuel Beckett, Bernard Shaw and Yeats himself have so powerfully shaped European literature that Ireland looms as large as France or Germany on the cultural map." (Albright, xvii). Yeats's achievement must be admitted to be even greater because he was not born in a country where there was a certain poetic tradition. Daniel Albright again writes: "When William Butler Yeats was born, in 1865, Ireland had little tradition of imaginative literature written in English — to an ambitious poet unacquainted with Gaelic, Ireland might have seemed a cramped, remote, ingrown island. To some extent Yeats suffered from this insularity:

> Great hatred, little room,
> Maimed us from the start.
>
> ('Remorse from Intemperate Speech')."
> (Albright, xvii).

Whether Yeats's poetry can be divided into early poetry and later poetry or no is a debatable issue—and, in fact, Balachandra Rajan *et al* see no sense in such a division—but, for the sake of convenience, we may agree to such a division, and, further, agree that his early poetry suffered from certain flaws; but, we must, at the same time, admit that his later poetry or mature poetry is a treasure-trove for any poetry-lover in any language. That some of his early poems are below average in quality is certain, and so Daniel Albright is not squamish when he writes: "Many of Yeats' early poems deserve oblivion." (Albright lii). Yeats's later poetry, on the other hand, deserves a permanent place of prominence. While his early poetry is romantic and mythopoeic, his later poetry is realistic and philosophic. Again, while his early poetry is simple, his later poetry is complex and difficult to understand. This is so because his later poetry is a complex potpourri of Irish mythology, magic, automatic writing, painting, history, politics, philosophy, French symbolism, etc. There is also the influence of the French *fin-de-siécle* in his later poetry. The early poetry originated in a desire for escapade, but, as Yeats matured, he began to grimly face the concrete reality on the "bestial floor." His poems, particularly those since *Responsibilities,* gradually began to bear a sense of morality also. Yeats's mature poetry is distinguished by directness, lack of ornamentation, and compactness—qualities that his early poetry wanted. In his old age, Yeats tried to redact some of his early poems and the poems of his middle period, keeping in view his conception of poetry of his old age. Unlike the poems of his early period, his mature poems concentrate on one single image, instead of a multiplicity of images. In his later period he abhorred ornamentation in poetry so much so that Ire could not bear with the presence of even flowers in poetry. Harold Bloom writes: "Dorothy Wellesley remembered the old Yeats as crying aloud: 'Why cant you English poets keep flowers out of your poetry?" (Bloom, 434) His early poetry is ornate and elaborate; it draws the complete picture. For instance: "Where dips the rocky highland/ Of Sleuth Wood in tire lake/There lies a leafy island/Where flapping herons wake/The drowsy water-rats." But this later poetry shows us only the bare outline; it paints with only a few bold strokes, and leaves the reader free to imagine to fill up the gaps; but thereby the emotion to be evoked is nowise minimised. For instance: "What shall I do with this absurdity —/O heart, O troubled heart, —this caricature,/Decrepit age that has been tied to me/As to a dog's tail?"

In the last decade of the 20th century, Yeats began to use symbols increasingly in his poetry. Nevertheless, there are critics who do not like to take Yeats for a *symboliste* poet. Edward Engelberg writes about the controversy over whether Yeats was a *symboliste* poet or not: "Whether in practice Yeats was a Symbolist poet (in the Blakean sense) or a *symboliste* poet has been in dispute ever since Edmund Wilson confidently placed Yeats among the latter *in Axel's Castle.* The question is not likely to be decided to everyone's satisfaction. It has often been argued that Yeats was not a *symboliste* poet because he got his doctrine second hand from Arthur Symons and could read French only slowly and with great difficulty. This is a pretty thin argument; apply it more generally, and you deprive Yeats of an understanding of all foreign literatures, since he was a poor reader of any language except his own. All the evidence indicates that Yeats's understanding of *symbolisme* was neither shallow nor haphazard; if he departed from these doctrines he did not do so out of ignorance of what he was departing from and his own goals were very clearly set. A tentative distinction between Yeats's conception of symbol and that *of the symbolistes* is possible, though I would be careful to point out that the distinction does not hold either for all of Yeats's poetry or for all of the poetry of *symbolisme* — luckily, I would add, since no great poets fit intellectual distinctions rigidly. Yet I do think it is possible to say that for the *symboliste* poet, let us say Baudlaire, the symbol is the end product, not the starting point. So Baudlaire's Paris (like Eliot's London) is his starting point, and oflena very realistically rendered one; it is only gradually that the city itself becomes the City, and the City in turn something else — a hospital full of sick people, a hell, a house of prostitution. Baudlaire is interested in his symbol, not that which goes into its making; the world is used to evoke the symbol. Yeats, I think, came to work in the opposite direction: he would use the symbol to evoke the world, and his interest, ultimately, was less in the symbol than in the things evoked. Hence, of course, his great desire to achieve 'multitude'. For Yeats the symbol became a true metaphor which evoked the world in terms of itself..." (Cowell, 95).

Yeats believed that like symbols, words, representing sounds, colours, etc., also have great power of expressing the poet's feeling and emotion. In his essay 'The Symbolism of Poetry' (1900), Yeats wrote: "All sounds, all colours, all forms, either because of their pre-ordained energies or because of long association, evoke indefinable and yet precise emotions, or, as I prefer to think, call down among us certain disembodied powers, whose footsteps over our hearts we call emotions." (Wimsatt, 598). Yeats was always fascinated by the power of words and the power of arts that is created with words. But he would never waft himself above the ground for a flight on the wings of art, but would, rather, have a dialogue between art and reality — a constant conversation between the two. Laurence Lerner writes: "Yeats wrote poem after poem in praise of art, and some of them are his finest. The very first poem in his first volume says 'words alone are certain good'; and though he learned to understand more and more fully what this meant, and what difficulties it implied, he never forsook the theme, or ceased to believe in words. In old age he praised art as the one form of abstraction that did not involve rejection of the salmon-falls, the young men fishing, the pride like that of the mom. And all through his life he praised it for another reason that widens beyond a theory of art, and becomes a philosophy of living." (Cowell, 107). Y eats' s art and philosophy, technique and theme, so much attracted Arnold Bennett(1867-1931)that he was all praise for Yeats: "It dawns upon me that he is one of the men of the century, so aloof, so intensely spiritual, and with a style which is the last word of simplicity and natural refinement." (Cowell, 2). Like Arnold Bennett, Arthur Symons (1865-1945) also highly praised Yeats's simplicity and unmusicality (pace T.S. Eliot) of Yeats's style: "But after all, though Mr. Yeats will probably regret it, almost everything in his book can be perfectly understood by any poetically sensitive reader who has never heard of a single Irish legend, and who does not even glance at his notes. For he has made for himself a poetical style which is much more simple, as it is much more concise, than any prose style; and, in the final perfecting of his form, he has made for himself a rhythm which is more natural, more precise in its slow and wandering cadence, than any prose rhythm. It is a common mistake to suppose that poetry should be ornate and prose simple. It is prose that may often allow itself the relief of ornament; poetry, if it is to be of the finest quality, is bound to be simple, a mere breathing, in which individual words almost disappear into music. Probably, to many people accustomed to the artificiality which they mistake for poetic style, and to the sing-song which they mistake for poetical rhythm, Mr. Yeats' style, at its best, will seem a little bare, and his rhythm, at its best, a little uncertain. They will be astonished, perhaps not altogether pleased, at finding a poet who uses no inversions, who says in one line, as straightforward as prose, what most poets would dilute into a stanza, and who, in his music, replaces the aria by the recitative. How few, it annoys me to think, as I read over this simple and learned poetry, will realize the extraordinary art which has worked these tiny poems, which seems as free as waves, into a form at once so monumental and so alive! Here, at least, is poetry which has found for itself a new form, a form really modern, in its rejection of every artifice, its return to the natural chant out of which verse was evolved; and it expresses, with a passionate quietude, the elemental desire of humanity, the desire of love, the desire of wisdom, the desire of beauty." (Cowell, 5-6).

On the other hand, Horatio Sheafe Krans was enamoured of the lyricism and spiritual overtones of Yeats' poetry. In 1905, Krans wrote:

"Nothing could serve better to bring into relief Mr. Yeats's point of view and peculiar lyrical gifts than a comparison of his poetry with that of Mr. Kipling. Mr. Kipling, too often hard, flashy and materialistic, is the celebrator of imperialism. He loves the tumult of war and the din of labour, and sings of them with a rough and gusty energy, and in a language so plain that he who runs may read its whole meaning. He is too often an indifferent artist, speaking in the slang of the camp, and in accordance with the standards of the music-hall. Mr. Yeats is the reverse of all this. He, and with him the men of the revival, stand opposed to the encroachments of a uniform civilization that is destructive of national and provincial variations of every kind. He shuns the distractions of the workaday world and courts the solitary delights of the spirit. His poems are full of thought, spirituality and lyrical phantasy, and have a music that is subtle, sweet and beguiling. They are the product of an exacting artistic conscience, and everywhere wrought with the utmost care. If Mr. Kipling seeks too eagerly to catch the ear of the crowd, Mr. Yeats tends, on the contrary, to address himself to a cult, that understands the content of his art and speaks its language." (Cowell, 6). So we can say that Yeats had the special gift of being a poet, appropos of Aristotle's notion of an ideal poet, who could 'think like a wise man, yet express himself like the common people'

A vital question is sometimes raised regarding Yeats's total collection of poems: is there any consistency or coherence among his poems? Laurence Lerner writes the following to answer this question: "When you read Yeats's poetry, purely as poetry, what is it about? Is it about anything coherent? Did he write a lot of individual poems merely, or did he create a poetic world? 'Tam sure he did: as coherent and valuable a world as any modern poet. It's true that his poems occasionally contradict one another: total consistency is an appalling virtue. In particular, he varies between the joyous view that 'everything we look upon is blest', and the bleak view that love is a consolation in a world.

[Where] the crime of being born
Blackens all our lot.

But a lot of what may look like inconsistency is simply the evidence of the ceaseless dialogue that he held with himself. More than once he held the dialogue out loud and explicitly, most notably in his 'Dialogue of Self and Soul'. I believe that this poem lies in the very centre of Yeats's work. If I was forced to name his best single poem I'd be tempted to choose it; if I had to name the most typical of his best poems, the one with most repercussions in his other work, I'd choose it without hesitation." (Cowell, 102). Lerner is quite right in saying that "total consistency is an appalling virtue." How can a man, let alone poets, be totally consistent in a world of flux? And so, if we ignore the demand for total consistency, we must say that Yeats' s poems are certainly coherent, and that Yeats had a great theme for all his poetry that bounced between the heaven and the earth, between the demands of the Self and those of the Soul. Whoever misses this point, misses the deeper meaning of Yeats's poetry.

Further, the altercation between the Soul and the Self within the poet reflects very much the psychic predicament of the modern world. Denis Donoghue very appropriately writes: "Reading Yeats, we would posit a poet who suffered from a psychosis characteristic of our time and familiar to other times: namely, an intense and painful preoccupation with the seemingly irreconcilable claims of Soul and Body. Intense and painful, because being a poet he was driven, as by an entelechial motive typical of the artist, toward image of wholeness, unity, and perfection." (Cowell, 69). But though he strove intensely and painfully to achieve the wholeness and the total consistency or total coherence, he certainly failed, as all human beings will.

However, there are critics who find Yeats's lack of skill in writing narrative poems. But Daniel Albright thinks that this is wrong, for, he says, Yeats's 'The Wandering of Oisin' (1889), for instance, is a beautiful narrative poem. Albright writes that "Oscar Wilde, one of its earliest reviewers, praised its 'nobility of treatment and nobility of subject matter, delicacy of poetic instinct, and richness of imaginative resource." (Albright, 397). But it is time that Yeats was not a fine narrative poet. Daniel Albright explains why he was not: "Yeats was not to become a distinguished narrative poet—he tended to rely on an abundance of cunningly contrived tropes and pictures, all present at about the same speed, where a more economical poet, like Chaucher or William Morris, would offer swift summary gestures and a better control of pace. Kinesthetic precision, fascination with weapons, tools, and other action-helpers, sympathy for muscular strain, were all missing from Yeats's armamentarium." (Albright, 397).

Yeats had no dearth of critics of his poems. William Archer (1856-1924) took cudgel for Yeat's "fossilized symbolism" and "hieroglyphs" "One other word and I have done. It appears from the notes to *The Wind among the Reeds,* rather than from the poems themselves, that Mr. Yeats is becoming more and more addicted to a petrified, fossilized symbolism, a system of hieroglyphs which may have had some inherent significance for their inventors, but which have now become matters of research, of speculation, of convention. I cannot but regard this tendency as ominous. His art cannot gain and may very easily lose by it. A conventional symbol may be of the greatest interest to the anthropologist or the antiquary; for the poet it can have no value. If a symbol does not spring spontaneously from his own imagination and express an analogy borne in upon his own spiritual perception, he may treasure it in his mental museum, but he ought not to let such a piece of inert matter cumber the seed-plot of his poetry." (Cowell, 2). T.S. Eliot has found lack of appropriate quantity of emotion in Yeats's poetry, from which reason he calls Yeats a "poet of middle age". Eliot writes: "The intensity of Yeats's own emotional experience hardly appears. We have sufficient evidence of the intensity of experience of his youth, but it is from the retrospections in some of his later work that we have our evidence." (Eliot, 255). In support of this contention of Eliot, we can say that Yeats often first made prose drafts for poems and then wrote them, as if he was only to find appropriate words that could express his *intended* feeling which was actually not his own.

W.W. Robson innuendoes to the supposed dishonesty in Yeats. He says that what Yeats expressed in his poetry, Yeats himself did not believe in that: "[Yeats] himself confessed that much of his work was make-believe, covering the personal uncertainty of a deeply divided man. Yeats attracts cranks. But we cannot be sure whether he himself believed in all his eccentric ideas." (Robson, 58). By the by, Robson also denies to admit Yeats as an English poet, inspite of the feet that Yeats wrote only in English. Robson writes: "Yeats, though a great master of the English language, is an un-English poet. His early poetry has affinities with the vague sad Gaelic poetry of western Ireland or the Hebrides, or with Galician folksong; it is poetry of the Atlantic seaboard. His later poetry also has little common with English tradition." (Robson, 58). But, inspite of all his criticisms, Robson admits that Yeats's greatness as a poet cannot be gainsaid' "But in the end Yeats stands or falls by the power of his writing, and his contribution to the art of poetry. Here his achievement was astonishing. Alone among the poets of his time, he succeeded in renewing himself as an artist and surviving triumphantly into a new literary period. He created a new kind of lyric verse in the reverie-poems of his later work, more formal and varied in diction, looser in rhythm, than lyric poetry had ever been; yet capable of great dignity, beauty and majesty. It can still haunt the minds of those who do not agree with Yeats that poetry has only flourished in ages of aristocracy, and who do not share his disillusion with the practical effects of modern civilization, or his doubts whether the concepts of the Scientific Age are ultimate." (Robson, 58-59). But F.R. Higgins has some reservations in admitting that Yeats was a lyric poet, though Higgins remembers that Yeats at times even sang his own poems: "Indeed, when we were together, he [Yeats] sang in his own uncertain, shy way, some of these poems. Whenever these poems were again repeated, at later dates, he always sang them to the same halting lilt." (Cowell, 16). Higgins says that "Yeats had no melodic ear; he could not measure words to musical stresses — he realized their significance, sought hard to employ them; but they were not at his ready command."(*ibid*).

However, Yeats's poetry should be evaluated against Yeats' own conception of poetry. What was Yeats's conception of poetry? Richard Ellamnn, in an imaginary conversation between Yeats and W.H. Auden, exposes Yeats's conception of poetry:

"YEATS: I believe in the poet's evocation of disembodied powers which, assuming form through the mind, effect changes in the world. The proper metaphor for poetry is magic.

AUDEN: Poetry is not magic. Insofar as it has an ulterior purpose, this is, by telling the truth, to disenchant and disintoxicate.

YEATS: Truth is the dramatic expression of the highest man, of the poet as hero.

AUDEN: The poet no longer fancies himself a hero; he is an explorer of possibility.

YEATS: Say impossibility rather.

AUDEN: All that is passé with the romantic movement, thank God. Crying has gone out and the cold bath has come in.

YEATS: The whale is extinct and the little fish lie gasping on the strand.

AUDEN. The artist no longer wanders about in exile, he builds irrigation ditches like Faust in his old age, he votes in elections.

YEATS: The artist has much more in common with the flood than with irrigation. He breaks out of every social dam or political enclosure.

AUDEN: You belong to the school of Mallarmd; you think of yourself as a god who creates the subjective universe out of nothing.

YEATS: You belong to the school of Locke; you split the world into fragments and then worship the cutting edge.

AUDEN: Your world isa chimera.

YEATS: Yours is an urban renewal project," (Cowell, 98-99).

However much Yeats may have used magic, data of automatic writing, personal equations, etc. in his poetry, he was basically interested in the man and in his situation. Balachandra Rajan beautifully expresses this when he writes: "With Yeats the centre is man, and if his place in the tradition is more central than Eliot's it is because his primary concern is with man rather than meaning. The quest for belief and the hunger for significance are the very substance of Eliot's poetry, defining both its intense integrity and its specific narrowness. For Eliot, the vision revealed or the hints and guesses permitted constitute the end of the search. For Yeats, belief is merely the platform from which he advances into poetry or, to use a more decorative phrase employed by his father, the leafy wood out of which the nightingale sings. Yeats' interest is less in knowledge than in how man lives his knowledge. 'Man can embody truth but he cannot know it' is his closing conviction stated in the last of his letters. His poetry is the record of that embodiment." (Rajan, 190-91). Yeats was particularly interested in the condition of the modern man in all his dimensions. "Toward the end of his long career, William Butler Yeats wrote: 'I seek an image of the modern mind's discovery of itself.' He never described his own work more truly or more succinctly. Yeats spoke to the modern mind in every way. The rise of nationalism and the political problems that were to create two world wars, the shattering and challenging effects of new science on old beliefs, the reopening of every question of truth and value — all these elements entered his imagination and were there absorbed and transmuted into the symbolic structure of his poetry." (Rosenthal, 28). And, lastly, let us conclude this chapter with J.M. Cohen's summary comment on Yeats's poetry: "Yeats's poetry is on the whole less simple than that of his great European contemporaries, and this because he was seldom capable of unifying his vision. Contradictions run through his work from beginning to end. The Romantic ego appears, disappears and returns in a new shape; myths are adopted, broken, recombined and again melted down in the fire of feeling. Yeats wore many masks, but was never satisfied with any one of them. Like Baudlaire, he was by turns clairvoyant, prophet, fool and dreamer, and it was perhaps his constant unrest that made out of the minor poet of 1908, the greatest figure in English poetry since the death of Tennyson." (Cohen, 79).

Chapter 8

Yeats as a Dramatist

[THE PLAYS]

W.B. Yeats's genius was singularly one dimensional: it was only for poetry, his dramatic accompaniment being diversional. A.C. Ward is correct when he writes: "But it still seems impossible that Yeats can be established as a play-wright for the living stage." (Ward, 13). Nevertheless, of recent years, some critics are of the opinion that Yeats's plays were not properly judged by his contemporary critics, dramatists and historionists, and that therefore these should be re-evaluated afresh. For instance, Russell Taylor writes: "In recent years Yeats's drama has been widely studied and revalued, and it is possible that some at least of it will find its way back into a theatre which was not ready for it at the time." (Talyor, 292). In this connection, we should remember that no English, since Dryden, was so much intimately acquainted with the theatre as Yeats had been. It was he who, along with Lady Greogry, founded the great Abbey Theatre; and moreover, for a considerable time he was the director of the same. From these we must admit that Yeats was sincerely interested in the theatre.

Yeats's dramatic skill was not a serendipity, but it was acquired by him through hard labour and wide experience. This is evident from the constant revisions of some of his plays by himself. He was always intent upon perfection and he was always ready to barter hard labour for it. Yeats deserves to be considered as an influence on the Irish drama, for he, along with Lady Gregory, touched off a new dramatic movement in Ireland. He introduced the poetic drama and inducted a semblance of the Japanese Noh drama in the Irish theatre. The new dramatic movement found its fructification in the dramas of such stalwarts as J.M. Synge (1871-1909), Oscar Wilde (1854-1900), Bernard Shaw (1856-1950) and Sean O' Casey (1880-1964). Yeats's influence on these dramatists may not be direct, but certainly, there was some indirect influence of Yeats on these play-wrights. All this speaks for a permanent place for Yeats in the history of Irish drama.

Yeats is a modern dramatist. But what distinguishes a modern drama from the earlier dramas, and in what characteristics of the modern drama Yeats excells in? James McFarlane says that modern drama stands unique for two of its chief characteristics: "The first was the desire to liberate the contemporary theatre from its continuing naturalistic constraints—physical (the 'missing fourth wall)—by the introduction of new methods of staging and the encouragement of freer intercourse with other art forms. The second was the emergence of a deeply and destructively *ironic* attitude to naturalistic reality, a determination to replace the illusionistic counterfeiting of reality by the recognition of the profound reality of illusion. Of the first of these developments, Yeats (following Apollinaire) is the supreme representative; of the second, Pirandello. They find common ground in their obsessive preoccupation with *masks*." (Bradbury and Farlane, 561). Yeats's most important contribution to theatre was the introduction of the technique of Japanese Noh plays. Along with the Noh technique, Yeats used the blank verse for the theatre, introduced dance, pantomime, etc. to bring in almost a revolution in dramaturgy. H.H. Anniah Gowda summarises Yeats's innovations in the theatre and comments on his plays, thus: "[Yeats's plays] are in the conventional forms of blank verse or lyric poetry, yet in their theatrical style they are for the most part non-European. Emphasis falls heavily on the dancing and stage symbolism. They are, perhaps, better poetry than the Japanese Noh plays, on which they are to a great extent based, for the Japanese give their drama a low place in their literature, but Yeats's plays depend on very different media of expression than the more nearly naturalistic drama of his contemporaries Dance, opera and pantomime mean relatively more. Their art belongs mote to ritual than to an imitation of the surface of life. In other words they are by so much the more explicitly poetic. The words remain important; indeed as dramatic poems the best of Yeats's drama stands in quality unsurpassed among modern English plays. But his works are brief, with more than half the pitying time devoted to gesture and dance.... Also the drama draws further away from the spirit of epic, history, narrative, biography and comes much closer to that of pure poetry..." (Gowda, 286). In some of his comedies Yeats used prose also, but his prose could never reach the brilliance of his verse. Gowda further writes: "In a few cases Yeats wrote prose comedies using the racy Irish vernacular, much as in the work of his associates, J.M. Synge, Lord Dunsany and Lady Gregory. The last-mentioned, his close friend, collaborated with him in several pieces, notably those in dialect and prose written in the earlier part of his career. Also, he occasionally condescended to his actors by translating a verse play of his own into prose His style in drama evolves along the general lines of his style in poetry, that is, away from a lush romantic prolixity and toward a greater firmness, compression and difficulty of allusion. But the density of his dramatic verse never quite equals the degree reached in his pure poetry... The play changes from narratory to symbolic and from declamatory to ritualistic." (Gowda, 287-88).

Yeats was interested in drama since his boyhood. His first published dramatic work in verse is *Mosada* (1886) when he was about 21. Not only *Mosada,* but most of his earliest poetic works are dramatic in form. T.S. Eliot insisted that poetry should be dramatic and drama poetic; and one can find this poetic and dramatic demand of Eliot met with in Yeats. Yeats's dramatic production is considerable in quantity, for he wrote no less than thirty plays "in a variety of styles, ranging from pate Celtic-Twilight romanticism in his early works to the stark severity of his last plays." (Taylor, 292). Some of his early plays, such as the *Land of Heart's Desire* (1894), *The Countess Cathleen* (1889-99), *The Shadowy Waters*(1885-1906), are thin plays with high poetic elements, symbolism and legends; and these have some sort of affinity with the plays of Maurice Maeterlinck (1862-1949), the Belgian dramatist writing in French. Yeats's early plays are mostly romantic, but in the last decade of the 19th century, he changed his romanticism for realism in his plays, as he did in his poetry. In 1901, he wrote the realistic peasant drama *Cathleen ni Houlihan* and in the next year another peasant plays *The Pot of Broth,* the latter in collaboration with Lady Gregory. Lady Gregory collaborated with him also in his *The King's Threshold* (1903) and *The Unicorn from the Stars* (1907). As we have seen, Yeats translated some of his verse plays into prose, so also did he transform some of his prose dramas into vase (harms. For instance, he transformed his prose drama *The Hour Glass,* written in 1902, into vase drama in 1903. Since 1901, Yeats began to produce plays on purely Irish themes, and turned such dramas out one after another as; *On Baile's Strand* (1901-4), *Deirdre* (1905-6), *The Green Helmet* (1908-10), *At the Hawk's Well* (1915-16), *The Only Jealousy of Enter* (1916) and *The Death of Cuchulain* (1938).

Just before the First World War, being influenced by the Eastern dramas, particularly by the Japanese *No* or *Noh* drama, Yeats introduced in some of his play's elements or techniques of the *Noh* drama, and called these dramas 'plays for players'. These Plays are: *At the Hawk's Well, The Only Jealousy of Emer, The Dreaming of the Bones* and *Calvary.* The Japanese *Noh* is a lyrical drama that evolved in the fifteenth century. It is played principally by two actors: the first actor or the *shite* and the second actor or the *waki.* The play is shown on a square stage slightly raised from the ground. The audience are not separated from the actors, but they occupy a portion of the same stage on which the drama takes place. The stage is almost bare: no decoration and no scenery are necessary. Masks and dances are frequently used. The themes are generally based on mythology. Perhaps the most striking feature of the *Noh* drama is its simplicity, and this simplicity and the woven mythology of the *Noh* drama attracted Yeats so much that he himself produced at least four dramas keeping the *Noh* drama as his model. Yeats continued to produce plays, side by side poetry, till the very end of his life. In 1926, he wrote *Oedipus at Colonus.* His *The Words upon the Window-pane,* which he wrote in 1930, is a sort of autobiographical play on the life of Jonathan Swift(1667-1745). In 1938, just one year before his death, he produced *The Herne's Egg,* and in the year in which he died, i.e. in 1939, he wrote *Purgatory* and *The Death of Cuchulain.*

In the twentieth century, we find a revival of the spirit of drama—the spirit that was absent in the nineteenth century. Sir Ifor Evans very succinctly describes the state of affairs of the drama in the nineteenth century: "The drama of the early nineteenth century was on the whole deplorable. While poetry and fiction were drawing upon the genius of the romantics, the theatre was the home mainly of irregular spectacle, melodrama, and farce ... Most of the romantic poets attempted drama, but with little success. A number of reasons have been assigned to this decay of the drama. A simple external reason can be found in the monopoly held by two of the houses, Convent Garden and Druary Lane, for the performance of serious drama The Act of 1843 for regulating the theatre removed the monopoly and allowed the smaller theatres to produce drama equally with the two patent houses." (Evans, 132). The revival of the English drama in the twentieth century was to some extent due to the Irish dramatists, among whom Yeats appears prominently. A.C. Ward writes: "From the middle of the eighteenth century down to the beginning of the twentieth the chief additions to English drama were the works of Irishmen. Until the end of the nineteenth century, however, there was no genuinely Irish drama. Sheridan, Goldsmith, Wilde and Shaw, were not engaged with the Irish themes. Bernard Shaw's *John Bull's Other Island*, an Irish play, is an isolated example. Shaw, like his predecessors, was an English *dramatist* though he was an Irish *man.*" (Ward, 110).

However Yeats's major plays may be divided into five groups:

I. The Early Plays (... upto 1900):

i. *The Countess Cathleen* (1892)

ii. *The Land of Heart's Desire* (1894).

II. The Middle Plays (1900-1914):

i. *Cathleen Ni Houlihan* (1902)

ii. *The Pot of Broth* (1904)

iii. *The King's Threshold* (1904)

iv. *Deirdre* (1901)

v. *The Green Helmet* (1910)

vi. *The Unicorn from the Stars* (1908)

vii. *On Baile's Strand* (1904)

viii. *The Shadowy Waters* (1911)

ix. *The Hour-Glass* (1914)

III. The Four Plays for Dancers (1917-1920):

i. *At the Hawk's Well* (1911)

ii. *The Only Jealousy of Emer* (1919)

iii. *The Dreaming of the Bones* (1919)

iv. *Calvary* (1920)

IV. The Later Plays (1922-35):

i. *The Player Queen* (1922)

ii. *The Resurrection* (1931)

iii. *The King of the Great Clock Tower* (1935)

iv. *A Full Moon in March* (1935)

v. *The Words Upon the Window-Pane* (1934)

vi. *Sophocles Oedipus at Colonus* (1934)

vii. *Sophocles' King Oedipus* (1928)

viii. *The Cat and the Moon* (1926)

V. The Last Plays (1938-39)

i. *The Heme's Egg* (1938)

ii. *Purgatory* (1939)

iii. *The Death of Cuchulain* (1939)

These divisions are never absolute, for in some cases the plays cut across the assigned periods, as they were either translated from verse to prose or the other way round. Again, the periods are not water-tight. For instance, according to some critics, Yeats's early dramatic period does not end in 1900, but in 1911 when he snapped his relations with the Abbey Theatre. Yeats did not write all the plays for the stage, but some of them he wrote for reading aloud or for hearing. In the Preface to the first edition of his collected Plays, published by Macmillan and Co. in 1934, Yeats wrote about the above-mentioned 26 plays included in the volume: "The plays in this book are intended for hearers and for readers". However, to understand a little of Yeats as a dramatist, let us discuss the five dramatic periods of the dramatist at some length, and follow at least one play of each period in some detail.

THE EARLY PLAYS (1894-1900)

Yeats's early poetic creations were the result of his internal conflict between desire and necessity—between what his heart would like to have and what he had to obey in the world. The unsatisfied and despairing poet sought after an escapade. This is true regarding both the poetry and the play of Yeats's early period. The poet wanted to be away from this hard world and roam in some 'Forest of Arden', like the thicket near Howth which the poet sometimes frequented. Actually, *Mosada,* his earliest verse play, was written in the Howth thicket. The argument of *Mosada* can be understood from a letter of the poet, written in 1899, to Katherine Tynan: "That thicket gave me my first thought of what a long poem should be; I thought of it as a region into which one should wander from the cares of life.Thecharacters were to be no more real than the shadows that people the Howth thicket. Their mission was to lessen the solitude without destroying its peace." (Rajan, 19). *Mosada* was never staged; the first play of the early period that was staged is *The Countess Cathleen* that Yeats wrote for and dedicated to Maud Gonne, in 1899. It underwent nine or ten revisions, and in the last revision it was finally entitled *The Countess Cathleen.*

1. The Countess Cathleen

The play was published in 1892. Like all other plays of Yeats, excepting *The Unicorn from the Stars* which is divided into three Acts, this play is not divided into Acts, but in five scenes. The main characters are: Shemus Rua, a peasant; Mary, his wife; Teigue, his son; Aleel, a poet; the Countess Cathleen; and Oona, her foster-mother. The first scene is laid in a wood in Ireland and the time is ancient. Scene I opens on a cottage near a wood. The whole region is groaning under the distress of famine. The Countess, Aleel and Oona wander through the wood, meet the poor and hungry family of Shemus. Cathleen offers Shemus some money when

Aleel plays on a string-instrument. Cathleen is roaming there because she has read of some sorrow in a book and that sorrow has become hers:

> Sorrows that she's but read in a book
> Weigh upon her mind as if they had been her own.

After Cathleen's departure, a man, dressed like an Eastern merchant, comes near the cottage of Shemus, unrolls his carpet, sits on it, takes out his purse and begins to count the money on the carpet. Next comes another merchant like the first. The first merchant says that he has travelled long and needs food and rest, and Shemus agrees to offer both of them food and shelter in return of money. But Mary, his wife, would not cook for them, because she thinks that the merchants are not human beings. She thinks that if they are really human beings with so much money, they would have spent some money for the starving poor. First Merchant tells Shemus that the poor people may sell their souls for their much needed money. At this, Teigue and Shemus offer their souls to the merchants for money. But before taking their souls, First Merchant tells Shemus and Teigue that they are

> to cry aloud at every cross-road,
> At every house door, that we buy men's souls
> And give so good a price that all may live
> In mirth and comfort till the famine's done
> Because we are Christian men.

Scene II also opens in a wood where Oona and Aleel nurse the despairing Cathleen. Shemus and Teigue happen to meet Cathleen there, and Teigue discloses to Cathleen the secret that "There are two gentlemen who buy men's souls." Cathleen also learns that Shemus and Teigue have already sold their souls to those two men (the merchants), and tells them

> Give twice and thrice and twenty times their money,
> And get your souls again. I will pay all.

But they would not take back their souls, because, they say, souls "But keep the flesh out of its merriment." The Countess Cathleen is determined to change the heartless land into a land full of sympathy — into a land where "all weak of heart,/May escape from beak and claw"— into a land where there will be no heartless torturous impostors.

In scene III, we find Cathleen praying before an altar. Aleel requests her to leave the place for peace, but she would not:

> I have sworn,
> By her whose heart the seven sorrows have pierced,
> To pray before this altars until my heart

Has grown to Heaven like a tree, and there
Rustled its leaves, till heaven has saved my people.

Cathleen had so long been despairing for lack of love, and now she feels an attraction towards Aleel who is a poet and a poor man. Cathleen tells him:

If the old tales are true,
Queens have wed shepherds and kings beggar-maids;
God's procreant waters flowing about your mind
Have made you more than kings and queens; and not you
But I am the empty pitcher.

Then Aleel kisses Cathleen's hand and she kisses his forehead and bids Aleel to go away never to turn back and look upon her, and Aleel obeys. Just at that moment, the two merchants appear before Cathleen after thieving her treasury. Cathleen asks First Merchant, ignorant of the plundering of her treasury by the merchants, when the famine will be done and the latter answers: "And there's no sign of change, nor can it change,/ With the wheat withered and the cattle dead." Cathleen learns that the merchants buy souls, which news sends a shudder through the length and breadth of her body and then the merchants steals away. Immediately after, Oona discovers that the treasury was stolen away.

Scene IV is the briefest, where Aleel mourns that he is forbidden to express his love for Cathleen:

Impetuous heart be still, be still,
Your sorrowful love can never be told,
Cover it up with a lonely tune.
He who could bend all things to His will
Has covered the door of the infinite fold
With the pale stars and the wandering moon.

The last scene opens on the house of Shemus Rua, where the merchants are on bargain with peasants who have come to sell their souls. The merchants buy the soul of a middle-aged man and that of a woman. Then Aleel enters and offers his soul to the merchants freely (without taking any money):

The trouble that has come on Countess Cathleen,
The sorrow that is in her wasted face,
The burden in her eyes, have broken my wits,
And yet I know I'd have you take my soul.

But First Merchant would not because he says that Aleel's soul belongs to Cathleen: "We cannot take your soul, for it is hers."

Meantime, the souls of Middle-aged Man and Woman go out and in intense pain they demand the return of their souls. Now Cathleen enters and asks the merchants to take her soul for "live hundred thousand crowns" and the returning of the souls of Middle-aged Man and Woman. They agree and Cathleen signs the contract after Aleel attempted in vain to stop signing the contract. Cathleen collects the money promised by the merchants and goes out to spend the money buying succour for the famine stricken peasants. Cathleen understands that she is nearing her death and tells Oona and Aleel:

> Bend down your faces, Oona and Aleel;
> I gaze upon them as the swallow gazes
> Upon the nest under the cave, before
> She wander the loud waters.

Cathleen dies and The Angel announces that though she sold her soul to the merchants, her soul would not go to the Hell as stipulated but would, instead, fly to the Heaven, for the Heaven always pronounces its judgement on the motive and not on the deed:

> The light beats down; the gates of pearl are wide;
> And she is passing to the floor of peace,
> And Mary of the seven times wounded heart
> Has kissed her lips, and the long blessed hair
> Has fallen on her face; The Light of Lights
> Looks always on the motive, not the deed,
> The Shadow of Shadows on the deed alone.

Even after a superficial reading of the play, one will be able to recognise the easy analogies between Cathleen and Maud Gonne, and between Aleel and the poet himself. Really, Maud was as reckless and generous a woman as Cathleen is; and Yeats was as helpless for love as Aleel is. But, nevertheless, we cannot say that this is an autobiographical play, because the analogies can never be stressed further: Cathleen is not as fanatic and full of hate as Maud had been, and Aleel is not as ambitious as Yeats had been. Rajan writes about the probable personal elements in the play: "The four stages of revision which the play underwent may show the increasing intrusion of the personal element, but even in its final form *The Countess Cathleen* is clearly a statement of responsibility, with Aleel representing the temptation of the dream. It is in this direct sense that it *[The Countess Cathleen]* is a counter-truth to Oisin." (Rajan, 25). This is more clearly shown in the poem *The Circus Animals 'Desertion* where *The Countess Cathleen* is "explicitly presented as a counter-truth to Oisin":

> And then a counter-truth filled out its play,
> *The Countess Cathleen* was the name I gave it;
> She, pity-crazed, had given her soul away,
> But masterful Heaven had intervened to save it.
> I thought my dear must her own soul destroy,
> So did fanaticism and hate enslave it.

Yeats said that *The Countess Cathleen* is based on the moral question: can one sacrifice oneself for some good end? But Rajan says that "*The Countess Cathleen* does not have this effect, and is unsuccessful in defining the crisis of choice either in terms of character or values." (Rajan, 25). Yeats himself, *in his Dramatis Personae* admitted that the play is 'ill- constructed'. At the end of the play, we suppose that Cathleen's soul is redeemed, but there is no reference beforehand of such redemption in the play. This is certainly a flaw in the play. According to Rajan the plot-construction and character-drawing are also not up to the mark.

It may be mentioned here that *The Countess Cathleen* was one of the few plays that touched off the new movement in the theatre of Ireland. Yeats's idea of the theatre, in the early years of the Abbey Theatre, can be understood from a document entitled 'Advice to Playwrights who are Sending Plays to the Abbey, Dublin': "The Abbey Theatre is a subsidized theatre with an educational object. It will, therefore, be useless as a rule to send it plays intended as popular entertainments and that alone, or originally written for performance by some popular actor at the popular theatres. A play to be suitable for performance at the Abbey should contain some criticism of life, founded on the experience or personal observation of the writer, or some vision of life, of Irish life by preference, important from its beauty or from some excellence of style; and this intellectual quality is not more necessary to tragedy than to the gayest comedy. "We do not desire propagandist plays, nor plays written mainly to serve some obvious moral purpose; for art seldom concerns itself with those interests or opinions that can be defended by argument, but with realities of emotion and character that become self-evident when made vivid to the imagination.... A work of art, through it must have the effect of nature, is art because it is not nature, as Goethe said: and it must possess a unity unlike the accidental profusion of nature." (Styan, vol. 1, 95-96).

The Land of Heart's Desire is also a verse drama like *The Countess Cathleen*, and it was first performed in London i n 1894. *The Land of Heart's*

Desire is a thin play dedicated to Florenc Farr. It is divided neither into Acts nor into scenes. It may be mentioned here that only one play of Yeats, *The Unicorn from the Stars*, is divided into three Acts, no act being subdivided into scenes. J.L. Styan writes: "Yeats's early verse plays like *The Countess Cathleen* (1892) and *The Land of Heart's Desire* (1894) had been lyrical, romantic and nationalistic. They had been as mystical and moody as Maeterlinck, mixing a little symbolism of the broadest kind with their Irish myth." (Styan, vol. 2,63). The story of *The Land of Heart's Desire* is simply this: a child is brought into a house on a May Night. Gradually the child grows in power and finally occupies the whole house. It takes possession even of a newly married bride. The house is a symbol of love that dwells far from the elemental forces or from the worldly forces that madden and bewilder human beings:

By love alone
God binds us to Himself and to the hearth,
That shuts us from the waste beyond His peace,
From maddening freedom and bewildering light.

The Land of Heart's Desire is a maudlin play full of uncontrollable sentiment, for which reason Yeats himself repudiated this play later on. In a letter, he wrote about this play: "In my *Land of Heart \s Desire* and in some of my lyric verse of that time, there is an exaggeration of sentiment and sentimental beauty which I have come to think unmanly. The popularity of *The Land of Heart's Desire* seems to me to come not from its merit but because of this weakness. I have been fighting the prevailing decadence for years and have just got it under foot in my own heart.... it is sentiment and sentimental sadness, a womanish introspection .... this region of shadows is full of false images of the spirit and of the body .... I cannot probably be quite just to any poetry that speaks to me in the sweet insinuating feminine voice of the dwellers in that country of shadows and hollow images. I have dwelt there too long not to dread all that comes out of it."(Rajan,34).

THE MIDDLE PLAYS (1900-1914)

Critics do not agree as to when Yeats's early dramatic period ceased to be. According to some critics, Yeats's early dramatic period ran up to 1911, the year in which he snapped his relations with the Abbey Theatre. However, as we have said earlier, the periodisation is not absolute; and so we may, perhaps, take the period from 1900 to 1914 as the middle period. This period, particularly from 1900 to 1910, was very painful to Yeats. In the earlier period, his poems were better than his plays, but during this period his plays were superior to his verses. In 1902, Yeats wrote *Where There Is Nothing.* The same year, he wrote the 'inconsequential' play *The Pot of Broth.* "*Where There Is Nothing* was written hurriedly .... to anticipate Moore who was threatening to write a novel on the same theme and to obtain an injunction if Yeats used the plot in a play." (Rajan, 50-51). Harold Bloom writes about this play: "*Where There Is Nothing* (1902- 3) is an attempt to work out the implication of a Blakean-Nietzschean world-view in the context of an Ibsenite social drama. The result is very bad, but very important for an understanding of Yeats's creative mind, particularly in relation to Blake and Romantic tradition. Yeats rejected *Where There Is Nothing,* replacing it by *The Unicorn from the Stars,* where most of the writing is Lady Gregory's. In the original version of *Where There Is Nothing,* some of the writing is by Lady Gregory and Douglas Hyde, but the revised text seems altogether Yeats's. I agree with Ure that *The Unicorn from the Stars* has more coherent symbolism and better developed minor character than *Where There Is Nothing* but imaginatively it is a much less interesting, and hardly Yeats's own." (Bloom, 144-45).

Like his many other plays, *The King's Threshold* was also revised several times, but not always for the better. It was first published in 1904 and again in 1906, and after that, before publishing it in 1922, even its character was changed: earlier it was a tragi-comedy, and now it was transformed into a tragedy. In the earlier versions of the play, Seanchan the poet ends his hunger strike when the king grants his prayer of restoring poetry in its ancient rights at court. But in the 1922 version of the play, Seanchan starves himself to death. Seanchan believes like Shelley and Blake that only poetry can make this world of necessity and confusion liveable and loveable. The beauty of the play is enhanced by the bitterness of Seanchan. *On Baile's Strand* is a tragi-comedy, perhaps Yeats's best tragi-comedy. Brenda S. Webster summarises the story of this play thus: "The play begins with low farce. A Fool and a Blind Man are partners in theft. The Fool steals a chicken and the Blind Man prepares to cook it so that they can eat it together. The Blind Man says he has heard that the warrior queen Aoife has sent her son to kill Cuchulain. The action shifts to the throne room. Cuchulain, whose father is Mannanan, god of the sea, is pressured by the High King Conchubar to give up his wild ways and take an oath of allegiance. At length, Cuchulain submits and takes the oath; immediately afterward a strange Young man (Cuchulain's son by Aoife, unknown to his father) arrives, and refusing to identify himself challenges

Cuchulain. Cuchulain, reminded by the Young Man's features of his beloved Aoife, pledges friendship, but persuaded by the High King that he has been bewitched—that the Young Man is an enemy—he fights with him and kills him. On finding out from the Fool that he has killed his son, he goes mad and rushes off with his sword to fight the waves. The play ends as the Fool, who has been tricked of his chicken by the Blind Man, nonetheless admits his dependence on him and, still directed by him, takes advantage of the distinction to steal bread from the ovens." (Webster, 164-165).

Cathleen ni Houlihan was written about two years before *On Baile's Strand* Rajan writes about this play: "*Cathleen ni Houlihan*, though one of the most popular plays in the theatre's repertoire, is too slight to illustrate these theories. Cathleen, an old woman who symbolises Ireland, visits a cottage where a young man is about to marry security. She offers him nothing but blood, sweat and tears, but when she leaves the cottage he is committed to her. The younger son runs in, shouting that the French are landing at Killala. The elder son follows the old woman. When asked if he had met an old woman outside the cottage, the younger son replies:

> I did not, but I saw a young girl, and she had the
> walk of queen....

The play is full of political overtones and perhaps consists of nothing but the overtones." (Rajan, 52). *The Pot of Broth* is of little importance, except that it entertains. In 1904, Yeats wrote about this play: "I hardly know how much of the play is my work, for Lady Gregory helped me as she helped in every play of mine where there is a dialect.... I had no mastery of speech that purported to be of real life." (Webster, 99). Brenda S. Webster comments: "In a way, then, Lady Gregory taught Yeats to talk." *(ibid). The Unicom from the Stars* is nothing more than the revised version of *Where There Is Nothing.*

2. The Shadowy Waters (Acting Version 1911)

The acting version of the play appeared in 1911. The play is not divided into Acts or scenes. The persons in the play are: Forgael, Aibric, Sailors and Dectora. The sailors are sea-robbers who are for days on end on high sea waiting upon plundering ships, but till now no ship has come within view. Forgael is love-sick. First Sailor suddenly discovers a ship of spice on board of which there are a king and a queen (Dectora). The sailors plunder the ship and return to their ship along with Dectora, after killing the king. Dectora mourns the death of her husband and her own plight:

> Would that the storm that overthrew my ships,

And drowned the treasures of nine conquered nations,
And blew me hither to my lasting sorrow,
Had drowned me also. But, being yet alive,
I ask a fitting punishment for all
That raised their hands against him.

Dectora tells Forgael that he is mad in showing love to her, which Forgael denies. He tells her that though she is now his captive, yet he will not demand her love by force: "Until your lips/Have called me their beloved, I'll not kiss them." Dectora, unbending and fearless, rejects Forgael's love; but Forgael tells her:

Do what you will,
For neither I nor you can break a mesh
Of the great golden net that is about us.

Dectora vows prizes for anyone who will kill Forgael and all the sailors vow to kill him. Dectora stands before Forgael with a sword in hand as if to kill him. She laments for her former lover or husband Iollan. She feels that she is in a magic spell as Forgael plays on the harp. As Dectora is lamenting for Iollan, Forgael tells her:

Do you not know me, lady? I am he
That you are weeping for.

But Dectora replies:

No, for he is dead.
O!O!O!O! for golden-armed Iollan.

However, after some time, Dectora condescends, but wonders because now Forgael turns his face from her. Forgael tells her that he has deceived her, and further he wants to tell her the story of this deception. But Dectora is not repulsed by this confession of Forgael, rather she says that her love for her deceased husband is now over and that she is now burning for Forgael's love:

What do I care,
Now that my body has begun to dream,
And you have grown to be a burning coal
In the imagination and intellect?
If something that's most fabulous were true —
If you had taken me by magic spells,
And killed a lover or husband at my feet —
I would not let you speak, for I would know
That it was yesterday and not to-day

I loved him; 1 would cover up my ears,
As I am doing now.

Now Forgael weeps because their mutual love seems without decorations, and Dectora consoles him:

Forgael. I weep because I've nothing for your eyes
But desolate waters and a battered ship.
Dectora. O' why do you not lift your eyes to mine?
Forgael. I weep — I weep because bare night's above,
And not a roof of ivory and gold.
Dectora. I looked upon the moon,
Longing to knead and pull it into shape
That I might lay it on your head as a crown.

Dectora leaves behind her ship, which drifts away, and she goes to the ship of Forgael with him. Dectora says: "The world drifts away,/And I am left alone with my beloved." She prays to Forgael: "Bend lower, that I may cover you with my hair,/For we will gaze upon this world no longer."

Brenda S. Webster's comment on the play *The Shadowy Waters* is very illuminating. She writes: "In *The Shadowy Waters,* the destructive possibilit ies of poetry are symbolically represented by the effects of the harp. It belongs to the god Aengus and, played by his messenger the Fool, casts a spell on all who hear it. Once having heard it, Forgael becomes discontented with all life and isolated from the world about him. But though poetry here is in the service of death, Yeats suggests that it can have other functions. In a draft of 1899 Dectora taunts Forgael because of his ugly and misshapen body (...), but the power of the harp enables him to make her love him. This wish that poetry might bright him love did not work out in the way Yeats hoped, but through his conception of the great value of the poetic harp he came to have a kinder vision of himself as its master." (Webster, 61).

3. Deirdre

Deirdre, though a relatively long play, is also not divided into Acts or scenes. The principal dramatis personae are: Fergus, an old man; Naoise [pronounced Neesh-e], a young king; Deirdre, his queen; and Conchubar [pronounced Conohar], the old king of Uladh, who is still strong and vigorous. The play opens on a guest-house in wood where musicians, mostly women, have gathered round Fergus. First Musician says that this guest-house was built by Conchubar and that Deirdre grew up in the hills near the guest-house. Conchubar, the old king of Uladh, decided to marry the beautiful Deirdre, but a "month or so before the marriage day" Naoise eloped with Deirdre. Conchubar, though jealous, says that he will forgive both of them who have been wandering for half a dozen years, should they return to his kingdom. Being persuaded by Fergus, Naoise wants to return home with Fergus.

Deirdre understands that "this king/Will murder Naoise, and keep me alive." She now feigns to feel love for Conchubar, for which Naoise tells:

> What woman is there that a man can trust
> But at the moment when he kisses her
> At the first midnight?

At this, Naoise despairs, but Fergus soothes Naoise by saying that she is only arousing jealousy in him: "Fool, she but seeks to rouse your jealousy/With crafty words." Before this, Conchubar also despaired for the flight of Deirdre. Therefore, Deirdre now feels sorry for all these—for the sorrow of both Conchubar and Naoise, and so she says:

> ....
> I'll spoil this beauty that brought misery
> And houseless wandering on the man I loved.
> These wanderers will show me how to do it;
> To clip this hair to baldness, blacken my skin
> With walnut juice, and tear my face with briars.
> O that the creatures of the woods had torn
> My body with their claws!

A dark-faced Messenger arrives and announces: "Supper is on the table. Conchubar/Is waiting for his guests." The messenger further announces that Deirdre and Fergus are summoned by Conchubar and "not the traitor that bore off the Queen", meaning Naoise. Naoise understands the treachery of Conchubar but Fergus still doubts it. Deirdre realises that she is at her end and so kneeling at Naoise's feet says.

> Do you remember that first night in the woods
> We lay all night on leaves, and looking up,
> When the first grey of the dawn awoke the birds,
> Saw leaves above us? You thought that I still slept,
> And bending down to kiss me on the eyes,
> Found they were open. Bend and kiss me now,
> For it may be the last before our death.
> And when that's over, we'll be different;
> Imperishable things, a cloud or a fire.

And I know nothing but this body, nothing
But that old vehement, bewildering kiss.

Now Conchubar himself arrives and says:

One woman and two men; that is the quarrel
That knows no mending. Bring in the man she chose
Because of his beauty and the strength of his youth.

And then the dark-faced man drag in Naoise is a net. Deirdre asks Conchubar if he has forgiven Naoise, and Conchubar replies in the negative. He tells Naoise that he may go free if Deirdre goes with him (Conchubar): "You may go free/If Deirdre will but walk into my house." Deirdre objects:

O no! Not that, not that!
Ask any other thing but that one thing.
Leave me with Naoise. We will go away
Into some country at the end of the earth.

But Conchubar will not let her go, and being in a double-bind, Deirdre tells Naoise:

It's better to go with him.
Why should you die when one can bear it all?
My life is over; it's better to obey.

Then Deirdre falls to the knees of Conchubar and prays: "and you will pardon us,/Although I cannot go into your house." Unnoticed by Deirdre, Naoise is gagged and taken away. Deirdre continues: "The very moment these eyes fell on him,/I told him; I held out my hands to him;/ How could he refuse?" Away from the stage, Naoise is killed and the executioner returns with blood-stained sword. Conchubar points to the sword for Deirdre who ejaculates: "O, do not touch me. Let me go with him." But after a pause she says that she is ready to go to Conchubar: "I' ll to King Conchubar's house." Conchubar advances towards Deirdre, but she tells him: "In good time,/You'll stir me to more passion than he could." And addressing the gathering women she tells them:

I will have you tell him
How changeable all women are; how soon
Even the best lover is forgot
When his day's finished.

Conchubar goes inside with Deirdre and there she stabs herself. Immediately after, Conchubar is slain by Naoise's men. In his excruciating pain Conchubar groans:

....

There's not a traitor that dare stop my way.
Howl, if you will; but I, being King, did right
In choosing her most fitting to be Queen,
And letting no boy lover take the sway.

Some critics are of the opinion that regarding action, Deirdre is analogous to *At the Hawk's Well* or *The Only Jealousy of Enter* or even to *The Dreaming of the Bones*: "In *Deirdre*, the action opens with songs by two musicians. A subsidiary character then enters and with occasional asides to and from the musicians makes an exposition of prior relevant action. The two main characters then enter to take up the action from the point that the expositor has reached, the expositor remaining on the stage as commentator on the action of the principals. Their dialogue moves towards a solution of their problem, and, at the moment of climax, the supernatural emerges upon the scene. With the action brought to completion, the singers conclude with choral comment ..... the action of *Deirdre is clearly analogous to that of* At the Hawk's Well *or* The Only Jealousy of Emer *or* The Dreaming of the Bones*—or Nishikigi*." *(Bogard*, 388).

THE FOUR PLAYS FOR DANCERS (1917-1920)

The four plays, *At the Hawk's Well* (1917), *The Only Jealousy of Emer* (1919), *The Dreaming of the Bones* (1919), and *Calvary* (1920), were published in a volume entitled *Four Plays Chiefly for Dancers.* All these four plays were very much influenced by the Japanese *No* or *Noh* drama. In the 1910's Yeats was attracted by the *Noh* drama of Japan. He was espicially attracted by its 'aristocratic form' as well as by "its simplicity, its traditional, almost ritualistic manner, and its passionate and symbolic subject matter."(Daiches, 569). *The Noh* drama is a relatively short drama. "This relatively short Japanese dramatic form, employing poetry, prose, patterned movement, dance, and music, was performed in the 14th c. Adapting with some variations, the traditional syllabic fives and sevens, the poetry is highly allusive and elevated. Such elevated richness, the religious subjects, and the slow tempo of most *No* create a drama akin to the Gr. [Greek], which it further resembles in its use of traditional materials, masks, male performers, and a chorus (that take no part in the action). *No* has broadly and rapidly influenced Western drama, non-dramatic poetry, and literary criticism since Ezra Pound first received (1914), studied, revised, and published (1916) Ernest Fenollosa's notes and rude translations." (Preminger. 571).

Yeats believed that he invented a new form of drama in his *Plays for Dancers*, though he thought that "this newness was in a sense age-old." Actually this newness he got from the Japanese *Noh* plays. Yeats was drawn to *Noh* by the influence of Ezra Pound, and Yeats, in turn, attracted T. Sturge Moore, Gordon Bottomley, Laurence Benyon and others. Yeats's first *Noh* play is *At the Hawk's Well.* Though both Pound and Yeats were drawn to Noh, yet they differed in their view of the *Noh* play. In Yeats's view, *Noh* is a cultivated "accomplishment", both childlike and noble. He very much praised its "intensity of movement, of body and spirit". Yeats, unlike Pound, viewed *Noh* through the prism of romanticism. *At the Hawk's Well* and *The Only Jealousy of Emer* are Yeats's two best *Noh* plays. Harold Bloom writes about *At the Hawk's Well:* "The hero, like the poet, is not born, but is re-born, incarnated, in a consciousness prepared to receive him. What Yeats gives us is a remarkable displacement of Romantic tradition, a hymn to intellectual courage rather than Intellectual Beauty, while maintaining Shelley's notion of'intellectual' as meaning 'beyond the senses'. Cuchulain is the lucky quester, 'such a one as all women love', but he too is intended as one of the deceived, by the Sidhe. His triumph is that he is not cheated, because he has no consciousness of deception. He moves towards fulfilment by self-recognition, and goes out to battle and to shoulder the eventual curse of the Sidhe—to defeat Aoife, beget a son upon her, unknowingly slay that son, and die at last an exhausted and indifferent death. But, as this play leaves him, he moves towards the heights, in the exultation of receiving his life's role, of incarnating the hero. "This is the climax of the play, but for all its strength it is not the play's dominant element or value. More memorable still is the play's context, the waste lands against which Cuchulain flares. The hero goes to the triumph of his equivocal victory and necessary *daimonic* defeat, but the reader's consciousness lingers with 'a well long choked up and dry' and the Old Man has watched the well vainly for fifty years. It is not possible to forget that Yeats lived fifty years when he started to write the play, however wary we are of biographical interpretations." (Bloom, 297).

4. At the Hawk's Well

This is a thin symbolic play of about 13 pages. All the dramatis personae are either wearing masks or their faces are painted like masks: three musicians, the Guardians of the Well, an Old Man, and a Young Man. The stage directions are very elaborate. The play is placed in the Heroic Age of Ireland. "*The stage is any bare space before a well against which stands a patterned screen. A drum and a gong and a zither have been laid close to the screen before the play begins.... The First Musician carries with him a folded black cloth and goes to the centre of the stage towards the front and stands motionless, the folded cloth hanging from between his hands. The two other Musicians enter and, after standing a moment at Either side of the stage, go towards him and slowly unfold the cloth, singing as they do so:*

I call to the eye of the mind
A well long choked up and dry
And boughs long stripped by the wind,..."

The place seems to be a waste land where the well has been dry and trees without leaves, for long. The next stage direction runs thus: "As they unfold their cloth, they go backward a little so that the stretched cloth and the wall make a triangle with the First Musician at the apex supporting the centre of the cloth. On the black cloth is a gold pattern suggesting a hawk. The Second and Third Musicians now slowly fold up the cloth again, pacing with a rhythmic movement of the arms towards the First musician and singing:

What were his life soon done!
Would he lose by that or win?
A mother that saw her son
Doubled over a speckled shin,
Cross-grained with ninety years,
Would cry, 'How little worth
Were all my hopes and fears
And hard pain of his birth!'

The next stage direction: "......*While the cloth has been spread out, the Guardian of the Well has entered and is now crouching upon the ground. She is entirely covered by a black cloak; beside her lies a square blue cloth to represent a well. The three Musicians have taken their places against the wall beside their instruments of music; they will accompany the movements of the players with gong or drum or zither.*" The First Musician and the Second Musician talk about the desolate condition of the place. *Then "An Old Man enters through the audience."* This technique is certainly an innovation in the history of dramaturgy. The First Musician says:

That old man climbs up hither,
Who has been watching by his well
These fifty years.

After some time, a Young Man climbs up the stage, also through the audience. When the Old Man asks who the Young Man is, the Young Man says that his name is Cuchulain and that he is the son of Sualtin, and also that he has a house "beyond the sea." The Old Man asks him:

> What mischief brings you hither? — you are like those
> Who are crazy for the shedding of men's blood,
> And for love of women.

The Young Man tells him that he has come to drink the miraculous water of the well here. But the Old Man says that to drink the water, the Young Man has to toil much more than sailing across the sea and that the well is filled up with water only for a while, and then the well again gets dry. The Young Man hopefully waits for that water.

The Old Man advises him to leave the place without waiting for water, because he says, he has also waited for long but has only been deceived. The Old Man says that he slept thrice when the well was full of water, but as he waked it soon became dry again, and thus he was deceived thrice. Nevertheless, the Young Man is hopeful of the water and would not leave the place. Then the "*Guardian of the Well gives the cry of the hawk.*" The Young Man wishes he could bring down the hawk and could blind-fold it. The Old Man advises him to be wary of that female hawk because 'There falls a curse/On all who have gazed in her unmoistened eyes." The Old Man further says that he has been waiting since long for drinking a cupful of water. The Young Man will not leave the place but will share the water when it comes out again in the well:

> We shall both drink,
> And even if there are but a few' drops,
> Share them.

The Old Man says that if both of them are to drink the water, it will be he who will drink first, because young men are greedy and so if he drinks first then no water will be left for him. The Old Man now looks at the hawk and gets afraid as "*The Guardian of the Well throws off her cloak and rises. Her dress under the cloak suggests a hawk.*"

But the Young Man is not afraid of the hawk: "I am not afraid of you, bird, woman, or witch." He tells the bird: "Do what you will, I shall not leave this place/Till I have grown immortal like yourself." Now the stage direction: "'*He has sat down; the Guardian of the Well has begun to dance, moving like a hawk. The Old Man sleeps. The dance goes on for some time.*" After some time, water is seen, and First Musician says, referring to the Young

Man: "I have heard water plash; it comes; it comes." Stage direction: "*The Guardian of the Well has gone out. The Young Man drops his spear as if in a dream and goes out.*" The Old Man inches to the Well creepingly, but finds no water. The water flowed only when he was asleep, but when he woke up the Well again became empty. Therefore the Old Man moans:

> You have deluded me my whole life through.
> Accursed dancers, you have stolen my life.
> That there should be such evil in a shadow!

The Young Man says that the hawk has fled to the rocks. The musicians cry 'Aoife!' 'Aoife!' The Old Man tells the Young Man:

> She has roused up the fierce woman of the hills,
> Aoife, and all her troops, to take your life,
> And never till you are lying in the earth
> Can you know rest.

The Old man requests the Young Man to stay with him, and assures the Young Man of not deceiving him. But the Young Man goes out with his spear. Stage direction: "*The Musicians stand up; one goes to centre with folded cloth. The others unfold it. While they do so they sing. During the singing, and while hidden by the cloth, Old Man goes out .....*" The musicians sing while unfolding and folding the cloth:

> Come to me, human faces,
> Familiar memories,
> I have found hateful eyes Among the desolate places,
> Unfaltering, unmoistened eyes.
>
> Folly alone I cherish,
> I choose it for my share;
> Being but a mouthful of air,
> I am content to perish;
> I am but a mouthful of sweet air.
>
> O lamentable shadows,
> Obscurity of strife!
> I choose a pleasant life
> Among indolent meadows;
> Wisdom must live a bitter life.

The musicians then fold the cloth while singing:

The man that I praise',
Cries out the empty well,
'Lives all his days
Where a hand on the bell
Can call the milch cows
To the comfortable door of his house.
Who but an idiot would praise
Dry stones in a well?

The man that I praise',
Cries out the leafless tree,
'Has married and stays
By an old hearth, and he
On naught has set store
But children and dogs on the floor.
Who but an idiot would praise
A withered tree?'

Then all the musicians go out, and the play comes to a close.

Balachandra Rajan summarises the story of the play thus: "*At the Hawk's Well*, Yeats's first experiment in the new form, is a taut, brief study of the anantomy of failure written in a verse as bleakly evocative as the landscape it brings to the mind's eye. The world in which it moves is akin to that of the waste land. The well, into which three withered hazels drop their nuts, choked with leaves which the wind swirls and diminishes, has three times in fifty years filled with a mere cupful of water that disappeared almost as soon as it splashed. An old man, bent double like the thorn trees, has sat by the well's edge, waiting for the 'miraculous flood', snaring the birds and eating grass for food. He has never moved too far away to hear the faint and fleeting sound of the water, but three times, awakening from a sudden sleep, he has found the stones wet and the water gone. Cuchulain who, unlike the old man, is 'not of those who hate the living world', arrives confident in his good fortune ('for never/Have I had long to wait for anything'). The guardian of the well, a girl, enters into the state of possession, 'a horrible deathless body sliding through the veins of a sudden', that accompanies the brief filling of the well. She assumes the form of a hawk and dances. The old man, unable to look at her 'unfaltering, unmoistened eyes', falls into his sleep. Cuchulain, who does not look into the dancer's gaze, is led by her away from the well, as the water fills and empties. He returns to find himself cheated of his objective and to find the women of the hills arming against him. Henceforward he can never know tranquillity. Shouldering his spear and no longer as if in a dream', he goes back into the battle of life." (Rajan, 97).

The play is quite symbolical, and therefore, it is a bit difficult to interpret the play, for the symbols are not very clear here. However, Rajan interprets the play thus: "Interpretations of the symbolism are not lacking but it is best to keep the pattern generalised so that the quest can be anybody's quest, the water, fulfilment as each man wishes to find it, and the failure, defeat, tasted by each in his own way. The point of the pattern is that failure is inevitable. The old man is defeated through his prudence, Cuchulain through his courage. Whether one looks into the hawk's eyes or not, those who seek wisdom must learn to live with frustration. The closing song ends by recommending a married life by the fireside, with children and dogs on the floor, where a hand on the bell can call the milch cows to the entrance. Wilson takes the lyric at its face value, seeing in it a resignation akin to the 'Teach us to care and not to care' of *Ash Wednesday*. But it is at least possible that Yeats's irony is sufficiently alert to leave the conclusion open. The hero finds his mask in defeat but that does not mean that he should insulate himself from the actions that lead to defeat. Only an idiot would praise 'a withered tree' and 'dry stones in a well', but perhaps this conclusion really means that those who seek fulfilment will always seem fools by certain standards. Much of the effect of the play certainly resides in the bleak, clean, almost dispassionate honesty with which the rewards that await the quester are stated; the poem is weighted towards security so that those who choose something else do so in a place that the salt sea-wind has stripped bare of illusions. "(Rajan, 97-98).

Another important *Noh* play of Yeats is *The Only Jealousy of Emer*. Unlike *At the Hawk's Well*, this play is very difficult to follow. However, Rajan summarises the story of the play thus: "The body of Cuchulain, washed ashore after his combat with the waves, is tended in a fisherman's house by Emer, his wife, and Eithnelnguba, his mistress. Bricriu, maker of discord, possesses Cuchulain's body. He demands as the price of Cuchulain' s ransom from the Sidhe the renunciation of the most precious thing that Emer possesses, namely her love for Cuchulain. Emer protests and hesitates; then as Fand, the Woman of the Sidhe, seems on the verge of claiming Cuchulain's soul she makes her renunciation and Cuchulain returns to the world in words that are pregnant both with terror and irony:

> Your arms, your arms! O Eithne Inguba,
> I have been in some strange place and am afraid." (Rajan, 98).

In this play Yeats is at Phase 15 and so he is riding high on romantic imagination. "The immense imaginative strength of *The Only Jealousy of Enter* results from its coherence and insight in handling Yeats's most difficult theme, the genesis of love and beauty in Phase 14 and 15. In his notes on the play, Yeats emphasizes this thematic concern, his 'conviction about the nature and history of a woman's beauty', centering on Castiglione's formula, 'that the physical beauty of woman is the spoil or monument of the victory of the soul.' This victory, Yeats insists, is itself occult, for it is 'the result of emotional toil in past lives." (Bloom, 303).

The Dreaming of the Bones was based on the Japanese *Noh* play *Nishikigi.* This is not very interesting either as a play or as a poem. Harold Bloom writes: "On the surface, *The Dreaming of the Bones* seems remote from Yeats' s deepest concerns, and it is a cold work, merely formulaic in its occasional intensities." Again, *Calvary* is also not a very interesting play. Bloom writes: "As a play, *Calvary* does not exist, for nothing happens in it; even in *The Dreaming of the Bones* there is one event, when the soldier refuses to forgive the lovers, but there is nothing comparable in *Calvary.*" (Bloom, 308). H.H. Anniah Gowda writes that there is a subtle sex symbolism in *At the Hawk's Well;* ironies of passion and jealousy in *The Only Jealousy of Emer,* and heroism in *The Dreaming of the Bones.* (Gowda, 291).

THE LATER PLAYS (1922-1935)

The Middle and the Later periods of Yeats are the most productive periods, regarding both poetry and plays; in each of these periods, he wrote at least eight plays. From the beginning of the 20th century, Yeats began to use symbols increasingly both in poetry and in plays, and, therefore, both in the plays for dancers and in the plays of the later period, symbolism plays a dominant part. We also find in these plays increasing induction of masks, myths and fantasies. *The Player Queen* was written in 1922. Brenda S. Webster summarises the story of *The Player Queen* thus. "A group of players have been invited to the Queen's palace to present 'The Tragical History of Noah's Deluge'. The impious chief player, Decima, has run away to avoid playing the degraded part of Noah's wife and has locked out Septimus, her poet husband. Lying drunk in the street, Septimus hears a mob threaten to kill the Queen because she is reputedly a witch who couples nightly with a Unicorn. Septimus, roused by mention of the Unicorn, defends him, and comes to feel that he shares the Unicorn's divinity and purity. An old beggar enters who is known to go into a trance and bray like a donkey when the crown is about to change hands. He feels a trance approaching. Recognizing the beggar as inspired like himself, Septimus goes off with him as the first act ends. In the second act, the Real Queen appears, nun-like and drab, hoping for martyrdom. Decima is discovered by Nona, another actress in the troupe, hiding under the Queen's throne. In the ensuing argument between Nona and Decima, Decima learns that Nona has become Septimus's mistress. Septimus enters to announce that a New Dispensation is come, and that the Unicorn is the new Adam, whom Septimus will arouse with sensual music so that he may beget a new race. Decima asks Septimus to return to her. When he refuses she changes places with the Real Queen, who flees to a convent. Decima regally confronts the submissive mob and announces she will many the Prime Minister. The play ends as she banishes the players." (Webster, 115).

Yeats wrote two plays on the theme of the death of Christ: *The Resurrection* and *Calvary.* In *The Resurrection, Yeats* "speaks of Christ's disciples as dogs without a master, contrasting them with the water birds (subjective men) who need neither Christ's love nor his sacrifice." (Webster, 183). In *The King of the Great Clock Tower,* Yeats exposes the rich ancestry of Ireland. It was first written in prose and then in poetry because, he wrote, "prose dialogue is as unpopular among my studious friends as dialogue in verse among actors and play-goers." (Rajan, 158). Ezra Pound could not accept it as good play, though Yeats could not agree with him. The three plays, *Sophocles' Oedipus at Colonus, Sophocles' King Oedipus,* and *The Cat and the Moon,* are of lesser account.

5. The Words Upon the Window-pane (1934)

The play was written in the house of, and dedicated to the memory of, Lady Gregory. The persons in the play are: Dr. Trench, Miss Mackenna, John Corbett, Cornelius Patterson, Abraham Johnson, Mrs. Mallet and Mrs. Henderson. This is also a One Act play, having no subdivisions into scenes. Dr. Trench, President of the Dublin Spiritualists' Association, introduces John Corbet, a student of Cambridge doing researches in spiritology for a Doctorate, to Miss Mackenna who is actively engaged in the said Association, alongwith Mrs. Henderson, in a private house. Corbet is sceptic about the stances that are practiced by the spiritualists. Cornelius Patterson arrives. Dr. Trench says that somebody cut some lines of a poem, written by Stella for Jonathan Swift's fifty-fourth birth, on the window- pane of the private house. Abraham Johnson, a minister of the Gospel, arrives from Belfast from the stances. Mrs. Henderson acts as the medium for séance, a phenomenon in which Johnson, like Corbet, does not believe.

Corbet wonders how Swift, a celibate, could make two women, Stella and Vanessa, fall in love with him. Johnson is intent upon getting the blessing of the spirit of Evangelist Moody through seance. Mrs. Mallet says that she receives advices from her dead husband through seances, regarding day to day affairs. Dr. Trench says that the spirits are "people like ourselves" and that he does not believe that "there are evil spirits." He says that "Sometimes a spirit relives not the pain of death but some passionate or tragic moment of life." However, Mrs. Henderson now prepares for a séance. and Corbet, the sceptic, waits to see what the stance really is. In the séance, Lulu, a female spirit, supposedly comes and Corbet apparently talks with him. Mrs. Henderson, in her stance, converses in both male and female voices, between Jonathan Swift and Vanessa. Vanessa says that she loved Swift and also believed that, in turn, Swift loved her. The spirit of Swift says that it is feeling dizzy. Vanessa asks Swift if he is satisfied with only his intellectual pursuits, or if he is suffering from pangs of love.

Next, in the séance, Vanessa departs and Stella takes her place. Mrs. Henderson, in Swift's voice, while in the stance, recites:

> 'You taught me how I might youth prolong
> By knowing what is right and wrong;
> How from my heart to bring supplies
> Of lustre to my fading eyes;
> How soon a beautious mind repairs
> The loss of chang'd or falling hairs;
> How wit and virtue from within
> Can spread a smoothness o'er the skin.'

Corbet understands that these are the lines that are cut in the window-pane of the house. He is now "deeply moved" by the seance, but not convinced about the efficacy of the seance. Though he is satisfied with the stance, he tells Mrs. Henderson: "When I say I am satisfied I do not mean that I am convinced it was the works of spirits. I prefer to think that you created it all, that you are an accomplished actress and scholar." Corbet asks her: "Was Swift mad? Or was it the intellect itself that was mad?" Mrs. Henderson says that she does not know that dirty and old man called Swift.

John Corbet. He was neither old nor dirty when Stella and Vanessa loved him.

Mrs. Henderson. I saw him very clearly just as I woke up. His clothes were dirty, his face covered with boils. Some disease has made one of his eyes swell up, it stood out from his face like a hen's egg.

John Corbet. He looked like that in his old age. Stella had been dead along time. His brain had gone, his friends had deserted him. The man appointed to take care of him beat him quiet.

Mrs. Henderson. Now they are old, now they are young. They change all in a moment as their thought changes. It is sometimes a terrible thing to be out of the body, God help us.

6. A Full Moon in March (1935)

This play is actually a revised version of *The King of the Great Clock Tower* (1935). There are only four persons in the play: First Attendant, Second Attendant, the Queen, and the Swineherd. This is also a very thin play of about nine pages. In it only the Swineherd wears a mask. The play begins with two Attendants—an elderly woman and a young man—on the stage, who sing:

Every loutish lad in love
Thinks his wisdom great enough,
What cares love for this and that?
To make all his parish stare,
As though Pythagoras wandered there.
Crown of gold or dung of swine.
....

The Swineherd is called inside the room by the Queen. The Queen will give him all her possession and be his wife who will sing best, and the Queen herself will be the connoisseur of the song. She says: "We say that song is best that moves us most. /No song has moved us yet." It is said that the Queen will be won at a full moon in March. And it is that frill Moon night. But the Queen cautions the Swineherd:

Remember through what perils you have come;
That I am crueller that solitude,
Forest or beast. Some I have killed or maimed
Because their singing put me in a rage,
And some because they came at all. Men hold
That woman's beauty is a kindly thing,
But they that call me cruel speak the truth,
Cruel as the winter of virginity.

The Swineherd is confident that he will be able to win the Queen and many her, though she is cruel enough. He tells the Queen that he has not come to her for her beauty. And the Queen does not take this confession of the Swineherd easy.

The Queen calls the headsman, Captain of the Guard, and tells the Swineherd that his head will be severed soon, but, nevertheless, the Swineherd is not afraid; rather he says:

> There is a story in my country of a woman
> That stood all bathed in blood — a drop of blood
> Entered her womb and there beget a child.

The Queen gets the head of the Swineherd cut off and she holds the head above her head, her hands being blood-stained. Now First Attendant sings as the Queen (as if the Queen herself is singing), the Queen Herself remaining motionless:

> Child and darling, hear my song,
> Never cry I did you wrong;
> Cry that wrong came not from me
> But my virgin cruelty.
> Great my love before you came,
> Greater when I loved in shame,
> Greatest when there broke from me
> Storm of virgin cruelty.

The Queen now dances to drum-taps, and is waiting for the song of the Swineherd, forgetful of the fact that the Swineherd is dead.

However, Second Attendant sings as the Swineherd, or as the severed Head of the Swineherd:

> I sing a song of Jack and Jill.
> Jill had murdered Jack;
> *The moon shone brightly;*
> Ran up the hill, and round the hill,
> Round the hill and back.
> *A full moon in March.*
>
> Jack had a hollow heart, for Jill
> Had hung his heart on high;
> *The moon shone brightly;*
> Had hung his heart beyond the hill,
> A-twinkle in the sky.
> *A full moon in March.*

The Queen becomes crazy and laughs in her craze. She now dances before the Head in adoration. Here Yeats's stage direction: "*Queen takes up the head and lays it upon the ground. She dances before it—a dance of adoration. She takes the head up and dances with it to drum-taps, which grow quicker and quicker. As the drum-taps approach their climax, she presses her lips to the lips of the head. Her body shivers to very rapid drum-taps. The drum-taps cease. She sinks slowly down, holding the head to her breast. The Attendants close inner curtain, singing, and then stand one on either side while the stage curtain descends.*

Second Attendant. Why must those holy, haughty feet descend
From emblematic niches, and what hand Ran
that delicate raddle through their white?
My heart is broken, yet must understand.
What do they seek for ? Why must they descend?

First Attendant. For desecration and the lover's night.

Second Attendant. I cannot face that emblem of the moon
Nor eyelids that the unmixed heavens dart,
Nor stand upon my feet, so great a fright
Descends upon my savage, sunlit heart.
What can she lack whose emblem is the moon ?

First Attendant. But desecration and the lover's night.

Second Attendant. Delight my heart with sound; speak yet again.
But look and look with understanding eyes
Upon the pitchers that they carry; tight Therein
all time's completed treasure is:
What do they lack? O cry it again.

First Attendant. Their desecration and the lover's night.

Apart from the dramatic significance of these two plays, Brenda S. Webster finds in these plays Yeats's problems with sexuality. In her *Yeats: A Psychoanalytic Study*, Webster says that the underlying theme of these two plays are sexual problems. For at least one clue to the psychology of sex in *The Words Upon the Window-Pane*, we may say that in this play we hear that Stella wrote the lines, to be found in the window-pane, "for Swift's fifty-fourth birthday", and that when Yeats wrote the play he was about that age, and also that during this time he had been experiencing some sort of sexual debility, to get rid of which he later on underwent the Steinach operation. However, to understand the psychoanalytic interpretation of these two plays, *The Words Upon the Window-Pane* and *A Full Moon in*

March, let us follow Webster at some lengths. About *Words Upon the Window-Pane*, Webster writes:" An important tenet of Yeats's new position was that heterosexual intercourse was necessary not only for one's art, but for one's sanity. The full extent of Yeats's fears about celibacy and (as the first draft of his autobiography shows) masturbation is revealed in *The Words Upon the Window-Pane*, a play about Jonathan Swift that Yeats wrote in 1930. Yeats had long been preoccupied with Swift's life. He wrote in the introduction to the play, 'Swift haunts me; he is always just round the next comer.' In the play, Vanessa pleads with Swift to marry her, to gratify his 'strong passions.' Her blood, she says, will overcome his heredity taint and make their children healthy. He refuses because he is afraid of passing madness on. Swift's eventual end as a 'dirty old man' his 'brain gone', his face covered with boils, serves as a terrible warning to those who abuse the body. Yeats seems to have viewed Swift's madness and certain scatological aspects of his writing as an eruption in unclean form of sexual thoughts, a frighteningly possible alternative to Yeats's new acceptance of sexuality. In a letter written in 1933 he says, 'The man who ignores the poetry of sex, let us say, finds the bare facts written upon the walls of a privy, or is himself compelled to write them there." (Webster, 100-101). In the same way, *A Full Moon in March* also presents an underlying preoccupation with sexuality. Webster writes about 'The Cap and Bells' and *A Full Moon in March*. Both embody Yeats's fantasies of submitting to a cruel mother who cuts him up and then lavishes her love on a dismembered part. In[4] Cap and Bells' the beautiful imagery fails to disguise a fantasy of self-castration, though with the recent exception of Bloom, critics have tended to ignore the poem's destructiveness and the irony with which Yeats presented it as 'the way to win woman'. The implication is that the only way a woman wants him is dismembered. This fantasy of 'the way to win woman' becomes more explicit in Yeats's late dance play *A Full Moon in March*, where Yeats makes it clear in his stage direction that the dismembered part, the head, represents not only the poet's talent but his phallus." (Webster, 215).

THE LAST PLAYS (1938-39)

In his last dramatic phase, Yeats could write only three plays: *The Herne's Egg* (1938), *Purgatory* (1939) and *Death of Cuchulain* (1939). Among these three plays, the first one is the most difficult, strange and wild. Yeats himself said that as a play *The Herne's Egg* is "the strangest, wildest thing I have ever written." (Rajan, 162). *Purgatory*, though the title of the play may suggest, has no reference to the Biblical myth of purgatory or a place where souls are cleansed after death, though one may find a distant reference in the play to the same. Again, *The Death of Cuchulain* may be compared with Shakespeare's *The Tempest,* for in both the plays the authors innuendoes to their cessation of creative activity or death.

7. The Herne's Egg (1938)

About the story and philosophy of this play, Yeats admitted that he got these from his spiritual guide or mentor Shri Purohit Swami: "'Shri Purohit Swami is with me', Yeats wrote to Dorothy Wellesley, 'and the play is his philosophy in a fable, or mine confirmed by him.'" (Rajan, 163). This verse play is divided into six scenes. The main characters are: Congal, king of Connacht; Aedh, king of Tara; Attracta, a priestess; and a Fool. Scene I opens on a battle-field where Congal and Aedh are fighting against one another with their respective numbers of soldiers. In the battle — their fiftieth battle — both the kings have sustained minor wounds. Then a temporary truce follows, and Congal and Aedh sit on a rock and converse.

> *Aedh.* A story is running round
> Concerning two rich fleas.
> *Congal.* We hop like fleas, but war
> Has taken all our riches.
> *Aedh.* Rich, and rich, so rich that they
> Retired and bought a dog.
> *Congal.* Finish the tale and say
> What kind of dog they bought.
> ....
> *Aedh.* A fat, square, lazy dog,
> No sort of scratching dog.

Scene II opens at the same place. Comey, servant to Attracta, draws "*a donkey on wheels like a child's toy, but life-size.*" Congal says he has heard that there is a hernery, on the top of a mountain, owned by priestess Attracta, and asks Mike to bring a creel-full of herne's eggs. Mike tells him that it will be unmannerly and that he should rather ask Attracta for the eggs. How to call her? Comey plays on a flute made of a herne's thigh and Attracta arrives. Attracta speaks to Congal: "What would you ask?" Congal says that he and Aedh have fought fifty battles, and will be preparing for the next; but before that they will sit for a grand dinner chiefly of herne's eggs. Attracta replies:

Custom forbids:
Only the women of these rocks,
Betrothed or married to the Herne,
The god or ancestor of hernes,
Can eat, handle, or look upon these eggs.

Congal is enraged at this reply and procures the eggs by force, and consequently, a curse of the Great Herne falls upon him:

'He that a herne's egg dare steal
Shall be changed into a fool',
Said the old, old herne that had but one leg.

'And to the end this fool breath
At a fool's hand meet his death,'
Said the old, old herne that had but one leg.

Scene III is the shortest. Here we see that the Great Herne hovers over Congal and his men, as a measure of punishment for stealing the eggs, to the great fear of them all. They try to kill the bird but in vain, and thereby get their rage exacerbated. In Scene IV, Congal becomes infuriated because, instead of the Herne's eggs, he is served with common eggs off owls, in the dinner hall. Aedh, who took part in the dinner, tells him that, perhaps, it was Congal himself who ordered for the common eggs, instead of heme's eggs for the dinner, in his drunkenness. At this, Congal becomes enraged, and in his fury kills Aedh, but afterwards becomes repentant, for he thinks that all this happened due to the Great Herne's curse. Now Attracta enters with a Herne' egg, in her sleep-walking. Infuriated, Congal orders the seven men —Patrick, Malachi, Mike, Joh, James, Mathies (and himself)—to violate the chastity of Attracta. But Attracta is unmoved. She says:

When I take a beast to my joyful breast,
Though beak and claw I must endure,
Sang the bride of the Herne, and the Great Herne's bride,
No lesser life, man, bird or beast
Can make unblessed what a beast made blessed,
Can make impure what a beast made pure,

In Scene V, Attracta wants to go back to her abode, but before that Congal tells her that she has been molested by seven men and for that he wishes her good luck. But Attracta denies being violated and says that only the Great Herne, her husband or lover, came to her last night:

What do you say?
My husband came to me in the night.

But the seven men insist that they have violated the chastity of Attracta. It then thunders and Attracta says that she shares her husband's knowledge and foreknowledge and so she prophesies that they will be punished after their death, by being created as lesser beings than those that they are now, by the Great Herne. She says that the Great Herne will

> Push you down a step or two
> Into cat or rat or bat,
> Into dog or wolf or goose.

Congal tells her that he is under the curse that he will die at the hand of a fool, and asks her when he will die. Attracta replies that he will die when the moon is full and that he will die at the top of the holy mountain Slieve Fuadh.

The last scene, Scene VI, opens on the mountain Slieve Fuadh where a fool is waiting to kill Congal who has also arrived there. Congal mourns and tells Tom, the Fool:

> I never thought of such an end.
> Never be a soldier, Tom;
> Though it begins well, is this a life?
> If this is man's life, is there any life But a dog's life?

Congal would not like to die at the hand of a fool, and so commits suicide by falling upon the sharp end of a spit that the Fool took with him here to kill Congal. Before his death, he expresses his fear that the Great Herne may "put me/Into the shape of a brute beast." After Congal dies, Attracta invites Corney:

> *Attracta.* Come lie with me upon the ground,
> Come quickly into my arms, come quickly, come
> Before this body has had time to cool.
>
> *Corney.* What? Lie with you ?
>
> *Attracta.* Lie and beget,
> If you are afraid of the Great Herne,
> Put that away, for if I do his will,
> You are his instrument or himself.
>
> *Corney.* The thunder has me terrified.
>
> *Attracta.* I lay with the Great Herne, and he,
> Being all a spirit, but begot
> His image in the mirror of my spirit,

Being all sufficient to himself
Begot himself; but there's a work
That should be done, and that work needs
No bird's beak nor claw, but a man,
The imperfection of a man.

While they are conversing, the braying of a donkey is heard. The conversation goes on.

Corney. The donkey is braying.
He has some wickedness in his mind.

Attracta. Too late, too late, he broke that knot,
And there, down there among the rocks
He couples with another donkey.
The donkey has conceived. I thought that I
Could give a human form to Congal,
But now he must be born a donkey.

Corney. King Congal must be born a donkey!

Attracta. Because we were not quick enough.

Corney. I have heard that a donkey carries its young
Longer than any other beast,
Thirteen months it must carry it, *[He laughs]*
All that trouble and nothing to show for it,
Nothing but just another donkey.

Balachandra Rajan's comments on this play is very perceptive. He writes: "Wilson, in his full examination of the play's sources, has duly and strenuously stressed the Indian influence, but it is difficult to find a play less like Indian philosophy in its tone and impact. What Yeats calls the 'wilderness' of the play and its grim tragi-comedy are characteristically Yeatsian. As for the marriage of the Herne and the priestess its source is surely the myth of the Swan and Leda (which the play specifically mentions), whatever may be its analogues in other mythologies. The state which Attracta enters is not the trance of *Samadhi*, because progress towards *Samadhi* depends, not on identifying Being with any shape, but on disengaging it from every possible shape. Congal's fall may demonstrate the fate of limited selfhood when it sets itself against unlimited reality, but it is easier to regard it as a progress in *hubris* began possibly in ignorance, but persists in with a full knowledge of what it entails. The liberal use of table-legs, candlesticks and kitchen utensils may show the progressive degeneration of man when he begins to substitute his own for a higher judgement, and the trial of Attracta is of course a pointed case of judgement usurped; but what is also represented is a further evolution in Yeats' always sharp sense of the absurd. Man is not only defeated but defeated without dignity; the holy mountain lies under the 'moon of comic tradition'. In these circumstances it is hardly answer enough to reply that man's arrogance brings on his defeat. His humiliations, moreover, are now such that he can no longer respond to absurdity by nobility. All he can do is to refuse to surrender and even in fighting for himself he can no longer be sure that he is not really doing the Herne's will." (Rajan, 163). Brenda S. Webster, on the other hand, analyses the play from the plane of psychoanalysis and compares it with the classical Oedipal situation. She writes: "*The Herne's Egg* (1935) is a grotesque farce that seems to ring a minor variation on the classical Oedipal situation of King, Queen, and Swineherd. Congal is the presumptuous son who denies his father the Heme, steals his father's bride Attracta, and after punishment is reconciled with the woman who now represents the loving mother. But on closer inspection the theme of an inverted Oedipal triangle, i.e., of rivalry with the mother, proves equally plausible as an organizing principle. Congeal envies and depreciates Attracta, steals the Herne's eggs that are in her care, and dies. The dominant fantasy here, as in *The King's Threshold*, is of outdoing the mother, arrogating her feminine privileges with the father, and putting her down." (Webster, 144).

The Death of Cuchulain is not a very interesting play. This is the last play that Yeats wrote before his death in 1939. The play is written in verse mixed with prose. Writing to Ethel Mannin, Yeats introduces *The Death of Cuchulain* with the familiar quotation from Goethe: 'A poet needs all philosophy but must keep it out of his work." (Rajan, 168). In this play, Yeats is more concerned with theatrical skill than either with the theme or with symbolism.

8. Purgatory (1939)

Brenda S. Webster, in her *Yeats: A Psychoanalytic Study*, says that in *Purgatory* Yeats is returning to the theme of one of his early plays, *On Baile's Strand.* She writes: Yeats is returning, in *Purgatory,* to the theme of one of his early plays, *On Baile's Strand*—the murder of a son by his father. The two plays can profitably be compared. *On Baile's Strand* is one of Yeats's finest plays, written during the hopeful period when he was trying to create a heroic mask and come to terms with himself and his body. Purgatory is a play from a bitter period in Yeats's old age, a period when he seems to feel the futility of any mask. The murder of a son has correspondingly different meanings in the two plays." (Webster, 157). *Purgatory* is also a thin play of about nine pages, without being divided into Acts or scenes. The dramatis personae are only two: a Boy and an Old Man: The scene is almost bare: a ruined house and a leafless tree in the background. The boy, putting down his pack, stands in the doorway and muses on the dilapidation in and around the house.

> The floor is gone, the windows gone,
> And where there should be roof there's sky,
> And here's a bit of an egg-shell thrown
> Out of jackdaw's nest.

The Old Man does not agree with the Boy and says that the house is not a condemned house, inspite of all that:

> But there are some
> They do not care what's gone, what's left:
> The souls in Purgatory that come back
> To habitations and familiar spots.

The Old Man says that he was born in this house which was later on burnt down. His father married the daughter of a wealthy man, and she died after giving birth to him (the Old Man). The house was a famous house where magistrates, colonels, members of Parliament, etc. lived, but the father of Old Man squandered away everything of the house on wine, card and woman. The Old Man takes his father's squandering away of the house to be a criminal act:

> to kill a house
> Where great men grow up, married, died,
> I here declare a capital offence.

The Old Man says that he is an illegitimate son of a game-keeper's wife by his own father, and that his father did not care to send him to school, but it was that game-keeper's wife that taught him to read. The Boy asks his father, the Old Man: "What education have you given me?" The Old Man says that he gave him that much of education that befits a bastard. He means to say the Boy was also an illegitimate son being born of a tinker' s daughter by him, like he himself is a bastard. The Old Man further says that he himself killed his father when his father, in his drunkenness, burnt the house down.

The Old Man says that it was the night of his mother's wedding anniversary. He recollects that he was conceived by his mother just on the wedding night of his mother, when his father was in drunken state. At this moment *"A window is lit showing a young girl."* The Old Man sees the apparition of his young mother and hears the trot ting of his father's horse, and sees them couple. But the Boy sees nothing and so he says that the Old Man must be mad. The Boy peremptorily tells the Old Man that he has not given him his share of money. A scuffle follows between them for the *bag* of money the Boy took back there. After that, the Boy asks the Old Man point-blank:

> What if I killed you? You killed my grand-dad,
> Because you were young and he was old.
> Now I am young and you are old.

The Old Man again sees in the lighted window that his father, the "tired beast" has come in a drunken state and that he is coupling with his dead mother. And in his frenzy he stabs the Boy to death, and justifies his action thus:

> I killed that lad because had he grown up
> He would have struck a woman's fancy,
> Begot, and passed pollution on.

But what he intended was not to occur: the apparition of his father he sees returning soon. The pollution is not to be washed away; he hears the hoof-beats of his father's horse, and ejaculates: "Hoof-beats! Dear God,/ How quickly it returns — bets — beat —!"

Brenda S. Webster's psychoanalytical interpretation of play is perhaps very correct. She writes that in this play,[44] Yeats portrays the themes of love-hate for the mother and rivalry with the father in unequivocal, not to say sordid terms. There is no ambiguity about the central character or his actions; he is a despairing, dirty old man. There is no hint at future gratification of the protagonist's passion for his mother or even a reconciliation between them as there was in *The Herne's Egg.* Instead, the Old Man is forced to watch the traumatic primal scene and must concede his own impotence to stop it. Finally, in grief and rage, he killed his son." (Webster, 157).

As we have said, Yeats is not a very accomplished dramatist. At least one point to prove this is that he revised most of his plays several times, sometimes with another playwright's help (for instance, with that of Lady Gregory). Again, he himself admitted that he was weak in devising dialogues —dialogues that form a major element of a drama. He also could not weave good scenes or situate good actions; in fact, there is hardly any action in his plays which are, in this regard, like the plays of T.S. Eliot. His characters also almost do not develop. Further, there are no lighter veins in his plays.

Against all these charges, he defended himself by saying that he never wrote plays for the common folk but for the few select ones — the "sensitive minority." Some of his plays, particularly the Plays for Dancers are very difficult to stage. He also defended himself here by saying that he wrote the plays only to be read aloud and not to be staged. But, at least the Plays for Dancers will lose most of their worth if these are only read, because these cannot be enjoyed without elaborate stage performances. And lastly, Yeats's handling of the blank verse that form the bulk of his plays is not appreciable. "Mr. Eliot has noted with satisfaction that in *Purgatory* Yeats moved toward the repudiation of the blank verse in which he had trusted for so many years." (Donoghue, 59). All these are serious limitations, for which reason Denis Donoghue is right when he writes that "None of Yeats's verse plays is a complete success."

But even these limitations will not deny a secure place for Yeats in the history of English drama. It will be wrong to evaluate Yeats's plays by keeping them beside those of Shakespeare or Shaw, because Yeats's technique was quite different from theirs. Yeats's plays are not realistic but ritualistic and symbolical. He made a dichotomy between the natural and the transcendental, and only the latter was his concern. He wanted to move his audience not in its conscious level of mind, but in its unconscious level. It was for this reason that he resorted to myths, symbols, mimes and masks. With these paraphernalia, he wished to liberate his audience from the trammels of the conscious mind. Denis Donoghue writes: In *The Symbolism of Poetry* (1900) Yeats had expressed the idea that the purpose of rhythm is 'to keep us in that state of perhaps real trance, in which the mind liberated from the pressure of the will is unfolded in symbols.' When this liberation has been achieved, the action and the words of the play can make their effect. Dance, music, masks, and costume, in addition to their parts 'within the play', prepare the audience to receive the frill impact of the drama. In this respect they illumine the theatre-form by preparing the audience to experience it in the most sensitive, will-less spirit." (Donoghue, 52-53). Donoghue further writes: "In terms of Time, the tension between Yeats's two worlds is that between the transience of the natural world and the idea of permanence; in terms of space, between Aibric's 'habitable world' and Forgael's country at the end of the world 'where no child's born but to outlive the moon'; in natural terms, between the body and that 'mysterious transformation of the flesh' which Yeats rather gnomically invoked. Each of these aspirations is part of a larger movement toward an ideal existence envisaged symbolically as the fusion of lily and rose, of Forgael and Dectora." (Donoghue, 36-37). Thus Yeats, in his. plays, creates a transcendental atmosphere to give his audience his intended emotional stimuli.

Yeats is never a realistic dramatist: he rejects realism altogether. In his *Plays and Controversies* (1923), he boldly banished realism from drama: 'Realism came in,' remarked W.B. Yeats several decades ago, 'and every change towards realism coincided with a decline in dramatic energy." (Nocoll, 68). In the same book, Yeats further wrote that we have been in error "in demanding from our playwrights personages who do not transcend our common actions any more than our common speech? If we are in the right, all antiquity has been in error." (Nicoll, 72). Yeats rejected realism because he believed that the *metier* of the playwright is not to present on the stage a few characters and to show how they act, or how their characters grow or change, but to arouse in the audience one or two primary feeling by showing on the stage certain human conditions. He believed that to arouse these emotions, it is not necessary that the playwright will present a chunk of the real life on the stage; rather he said that a symbolic situation on the stage will be of a better service for the purpose, and for the same reason, he said "My play is *the world*,; my play is *my* world." It was also for the same reason that Yeats turned to the *Noh* plays and wrote plays like Maeterlinck: "Yeats also had recourse to the term marionette to suggest something of what he wanted in the *Plays for Dancers*. Under the same symbolist influences as Maeterlinck he aims at something not dissimilar, the expression of those 'profound emotions that exist only in solitude and in silence.' His symbolism and play technique are more elaborate than Maeterlinck's but his persons are equally stripped of detail and tuned to a single chord of feeling." (Peacock, 205)

Yeats must always be remembered for his induction of the relatively obscure Japanese *Noh* plays on the English stage. The *Noh* play has more universal appeal and cognisability as it transcends the barriers of language and culture. Modern English playwrights, such as Eliot, Pound, Auden, Cummings, Fry and Stevens have realised this truth, and so have been profitably influenced by the *Noh* drama; but it was Yeats who first showed them the beacon. Yeats was also one of the first poets to bring back from the limbo the poetic drama. In an age, such as ours, it required much skill and courage on the part of Yeats to undertake such an enterprise. He gathered courage from his belief that civilisation may change, but the self remains the same — the surface changes, not the centre. However much scientific and prosaic our age may have become, the unadulterated self is still poetic. If we like the drama even to day, we must like it in the verse form. And here Yeats and Eliot agreed; and why should we not? Yeats, again, was one of the pioneers of the One-Act plays and most of his plays are One-Act plays. In our age of whistle-stop hurry, long plays like Kyd's *The Spanish Tragedy* will always discourage us; we can only go for intense enjoyments for short whiles, for which the One-Act plays are the most suitable.

When a literary-critical storm was blowing over the 'art's for art's sake or art's for people's sake' controversy, Yeats was bold and honest enough to say that he wrote his plays not for the multitude but for the "sensitive minority." That even an 'unstageable drama may have some intrinsic worth, Yeats taught us once more: he said that he wrote plays not so much for staging them as for reading them aloud. Again, as Buffon said, the style is the man, and Yeats was very genuinely concerned about the style both in his poetry and in his plays: "Yeats was much concerned with the problem of stylization in art, and some of his verse dramas are stylized almost to the point of ritual." (Daiches 1993, 234).

For all these and for many more things, Yeats will always be counted as a dramatist of great consequence. And, to conclude, whatever may be his draw-backs as a poet and as a dramatist, we may, perhaps, agree with what Una Ellis-Fermor has written about Yeats in *The Oxford Companion to the Theatre*: "Yeats's work, whether in prose *or* verse, was essentially poetic, and he was unexcelled in his own time by any other poetic dramatist writing in English."(Hartnoll, 1020).

Select Bibliography

(*Only the Titles Referred to in this Book*)

Albright, Daniel, *W.B. Yeats: The Poems*, London, J.M. Dent, 1991.

Beaty, Jerome and Matchett, William H., *Poetry: From Statement to Meaning*, London, Oxford University Press, 1965.

Bloom, Harold, *Yeats*, London, Oxford University Press, 1972.

Bogard, Travis and Oliver, William I. (Eds.), *Modern Drama: Essays in Criticism*, Oxford University Press, 1968.

Bradbury, Malcolm and McFarlane, James (Eds.), *Modernism: 1890-1930*, Penguin Books, 1976.

Brooks, Cleanth, *Modern Poetry and the Tradition*, London, Oxford University Press, 1965.

Brown, Calvin S. (General Editor), *The Reader's Companion to World Literature*, USA, A Mentor Book, 1964.

Cowell, Raymond (Ed.), *Critics on Yeats*, New Delhi, University Book Stall, 1994.

Cuddon, J. A., *A Dictionary of Literary Terms*, Penguin Books, 1982.

Daiches, David, *Critical Approaches to Literature*, Calcutta, (Indian reprint), 1993 (Longman Group, USA, 1956).

Daiches, David (Ed.), *The Penguin Companion to English Literature*, Vol. I, Penguin Books, 1971.

Donoghue, Devis, *The Third Voice*, USA, Princeton University Press, 1966.

Dyson, A.E., Yeats, Eliot and R.S. Thomas: Riding the Echo, Macmillan, 1981.

Eliot, T.S., *On Poetry and Poets*, Faber and Faber, London, 1957.

Evans, Sir Ifor, *A Short History of English Literature,* Penguin Books, 1966.

Ford, Boris (Ed.), *The Penguin Guide to English Literature: The Modern Age,* Penguin Books, 1964.

Gowda, HH. Anniah, Dramatic Poetry, *Macmillan, 1972.*

Great Writers Student Library, *20th Century Poetry,* London, Macmillan Press, 1983.

Hamlyn, London, *New Larousse Encyclopaedia of Mythology, 1994.*

Hartnoll, Phyllis (Ed.), *The Oxford Companion to the Theatre,* London, Oxford University Press, 1972.

Hollander, John (Ed.), *Modern Poetry: Essays in Criticism,* London, Oxford University Press, 1968.

Hough, Graham, *The Last Romantics,* London, Duckworth, 1983.

Jeffares, Norman A., *A New Commentary on the Poems of W.B. Yeats,* London, Macmillan 1984.

Jones, Ernest, *The Life and Works of Sigmund Freud,* Penguin, 1961.

Leavis, F.R. *New Bearings in English Poetry,* Penguin/Peregrine Books, 1963.

MacLeish, Archibald, *Poetry and Experience,* Peregrine Books, 1965.

Macmillan and Co., London, *The Collected Plays of W.B. Yeats,* 1960.

Marriott, J. W. (selected by), *One-Act Plays of To-Day,* London, George G. Harrap and Co., 1961.

Preminger, Alex, *Princeton Encyclopedia of Poetry and Poetics,* Macmillan, 1974.

Rajan, Balachandra, *W. B. Yeats: A Critical Introduction,* London, Hutchison University Library, 1969.

Robson, W .W., *Modern English Literature,* Oxford University Press, 1984.

Rosenthal, M.L., *The Modern Poets: A Critical Introduction,* New York, Oxford University Press, 1969.

Rudd, Margaret, *Divided Image: A Study of William Blake and W.B. Yeats,* London, Routledge and Kegan Paul, 1953.

Sampson, George, *The Concise Cambridge History of English Literature,* Cambridge University Press, 1970.

Styan, J.L., *Modern Drama in Theory and Practice* (3 Vols.) Cambridge University Press, 1983.

Sutherland, James (Ed.) *The Oxford Book of Literary Anecdotes,* New York, A Kangaroo Book (Pocket Book), 1976.

Taylor, John Russell, *The Penguin Dictionary of the Theatre*, Penguin Books, 1966.

Trevelyan, G.M., *English Social History,* Penguin Books, 1982.

Ward, A.C., *20th Century English Literature 1901-60,* Bombay, B.I. Publications, 1974.

Watson, Donald, *A Dictionary of Mind and Spirit,* Calcutta, Rupa & Co., 1991.

Webster, Brenda S., *Yeats: A Psychoanalytic Study,* Macmillan, 1974.

Wimsatt, William K. Jr. and Brooks, Cleanth, *Literary Criticism: A Short History,* London, Routledge & Kegan Paul, 1959.

Wordswoth Poetry Library, London, *The Works of W.B. Yeats,* 1994.

Wright, Austin (Ed.), *Victorian Literature: Modern Essays in Criticism,* A Galaxy Book, Oxford University Press, 1961.

INDEX